Breaking the Bonds

Dorothy Rowe, born in Australia in 1930, worked as a teacher and as a child psychologist before coming to England, where she obtained her PhD at Sheffield University. From 1972 until 1986 she was head of the North Lincolnshire Department of Clinical Psychology. She is now engaged in writing, lecturing and private practice. Her research and therapy are concerned with the questions of how we create meaning and how we communicate.

DOROTHY ROWE

Breaking the Bonds

Understanding Depression,
Finding Freedom

Fontana
An Imprint of HarperCollinsPublishers

First published in 1991 by Collins as
The Depression Handbook

This edition first issued in 1991 by Fontana,
an imprint of HarperCollins Publishers,
77–85 Fulham Palace Road,
Hammersmith, London W6 8JB

9   8   7   6   5   4   3   2   1

Printed and bound in Great Britain by
HarperCollins Book Manufacturing, Glasgow

To Diana, Ron and Ed

Contents

Acknowledgements

The author and publishers would like to thank the following for their permission to reproduce copyright material:

Penguin Books for *The Penguin Dictionary of Psychology*, Arthur S. Reber.

The British Broadcasting Corporation and Joe La Fatch for *Everyman: Back to the Edge*.

The British Journal of Psychiatry for 'Major genes for major affective disorder?', Peter McGuffin, and 'Which depressed patients will respond to electroconvulsive therapy?', Allan I. F. Scott.

Sidgwick and Jackson for *A Century of Childhood*, S. Humphries, J. Mack and R. Perks.

Faber and Faber for 'Little Gidding', from *Collected Poems 1909–1962*, T. S. Eliot.

Virago Press for *Punishment*, Anna Mitgutsch, and *My Father's House*, Sylvia Fraser.

Little, Brown and Co. for *Handbook of Drug Therapy*, Hyman and Arana.

American Psychiatric Press for *Review of Psychiatry*, Vol. 7, 1988, Martin B. Keller, James C. Ballenger, Jesse H. Wright.

The Guardian for 'Why can't men ditch the dirt?', Jayne Greenwell.

Human Sciences Press Inc. for *Cognitive Therapy: Applications in Psychiatric and Medical Settings*, A. Freeman

André Deutsch Ltd for *Reflecting Men at Twice Their Natural Size*, Dale Spender.

Inter-Continental Features for the *Bloom County* cartoon, 1989 The Washington Post Writers Group/Berke Breathed.

The New York Times for 'Working girl in Reagan country', Mona Harrington.

St Martin's Press for *Museums of Madness*, A. Scull.

United Feature Syndicate Inc. for the *Peanuts* cartoon.

WNET/Thirteen/New York/British Broadcasting Corporation for *The Mind: Portrait in Blue*.

New American Library for *Do You Have a Depressive Illness?*, Klein and Wender.

How to Use This Book

'I would rather have a physical illness – any physical illness – rather than be depressed. Depression is the worst experience a person can have.'

Anyone who knows what it is to be depressed would agree. It is not just that being depressed means feeling despairing, frightened, guilty, bitter, helpless, tired and ill. *It is the most terrible sense of being trapped and alone in some horror-filled prison.*

When we have a physical illness or have been injured, we can feel immersed in the pain and discomfort, but, equally, we can separate ourselves from that pain and discomfort. We can talk to other people, share a joke, take an interest in what they are doing, watch television, read a book, plan our future, and when someone shows us love, comfort and support we can feel warmed, cheered and supported, and give back in return our love and gratitude.

When we are depressed we can do none of these things. We are surrounded totally by the prison of depression. We cannot escape, even momentarily. Occasionally we can act normally. We can answer a telephone, or chat briefly to friends. We might feel slightly better in the evening or when we are at work, but all the time we know that the prison has not gone away, just eased its grip on us a little. Even when a course of antidepressant drugs (psychiatric, medical and psychological terms are explained in the section Technical Terms) or a series of ECT (electroconvulsive therapy) has made us feel more able to face life, we know that the prison is still hovering there in the background, waiting. One false word or action, one crisis, and its jaws will snap around us again, and we shall be trapped and helpless.

Inside the prison we are cut off from every other person. We know that we are physically with other people, but what we actually experience is a barrier between them and us. They offer us love, comfort and support, but nothing crosses the barrier to warm, cheer and support us.

Nor do we think it should. We know that we are wicked and do not deserve what people offer us. What we do deserve is this terrible, hateful prison.

Inside that prison our thoughts are not the thoughts that usually accompany pain (usually 'Ow!' and 'Help!') and discomfort (usually 'Yuk!', 'Groan!' and 'Help!'). Our thoughts are concerned with universal moral issues expressed in a personal way, variations of, 'I ought to have been a better person': 'I ought to have done more for other people', 'If I had been a better person I would not have been abandoned and betrayed', 'I must be wicked, otherwise these disasters would not have happened to me', 'I have obligations which I cannot meet', 'I have made unforgivable mistakes', 'I cannot forgive myself for what I have done', 'No one, not even God, could forgive me for what I have done'. With these feelings come the helpless, hopeless feelings of dread.

Inside the prison of depression we cannot escape from the turmoil of these moral issues, for everyone we meet, every newspaper story and television scene, reminds us of our unmet obligations, our unfulfilled duties, our inadequacy and sense of intrinsic evil. We cannot endure this isolation, but we fear other people, and feel that we must shut ourselves away. We long for death, but fear the aloneness of death and the punishments which could lie beyond it.

Alone though we may feel in the prison of depression, we are not alone in enduring such an experience. Across the planet, many millions of people are trapped in the prison of depression.

*   *   *

If you are reading this book then it is likely to be for one or more of the following reasons:

You are depressed

or

Someone you care about is depressed

or

In your work you have to deal with people who are depressed.

In order to find out about depression you have, perhaps, read articles on depression in newspapers and magazines. You might have read about depression in psychiatric textbooks or in books written for the public by psychiatrists and psychologists. You might have consulted your doctor, or a psychiatrist, or some other professional person. You might have consulted your minister, or perhaps a spiritualist or a faith healer, or tried one of the alternative therapies like homoeopathy or acupuncture. You might have talked to a therapist or counsellor.

You might have been told a great many things about depression, but out of all these sources one message has been given to you loud and clear. 'Depression is a genetic illness. It cannot be cured, but it can be controlled by drugs.'

This message seems simple, but in fact it leaves you even more confused and frightened.

Somehow, this explanation doesn't seem right. You can see how bodily diseases like haemophilia and cystic fibrosis could be passed on by a gene, but how could depression – this confusion of feelings, beliefs, passions, fears, wishes, actions and non-actions – be caused by a gene? You have seen how people who have inherited some disease can, provided they care enough about themselves, have friends and family to support them, and get good medical advice, rise above their disease and *get on with their lives*, whereas it is not possible for you to separate yourself from your depression. It seems to inhabit your very person.

Moreover, depression might seem to be inside a person, but you know that it is also *between* people. If you are depressed, you know that it has something to do with the people in your life. If someone you love is depressed, you know that that person's depression has something to do with other people, and you worry about what you might do – or refrain from doing – which would change how your loved one feels. If you are trying to understand why your clients or your colleagues are depressed, you get to know them, and you see the difficulties, losses and disappointments with which they are struggling. You know that depression does not occur, in the way that haemophilia or cystic fibrosis can, to an ordinary person leading a secure and happy life. When you look at all the depressed people you know, you can see that they have, over their lifetime, suffered many difficulties, losses and disappointments, that what success they have achieved has not always brought them happiness, and that when they achieve success and happiness, they cannot enjoy them, for they believe that they do not deserve such happiness and success, that happiness and success will soon be snatched from them, and that pain must follow joy as night the day.

How could a gene create all this?

Moreover, being told that all you are experiencing is *nothing but* the effect of a gene dismisses all you have experienced and know as being trivial and unimportant. It doesn't just dismiss your experience and knowledge, it dismisses *you*. It says that you are nothing but a defective body, carrying a defective gene, passed on to you by an equally defective ancestor, and that you are likely to pass this gene on to your children. You cannot be cleansed of this gene, but must strive to keep it in check by a daily ingestion of drugs which affect the operation of your brain.

If you are depressed, such a diagnosis does nothing to help you, for it simply makes you feel even more intrinsically bad, useless and worthless. Such a diagnosis does nothing to help the relatives of a depressed person, or indeed, any one of us, for we can all worry that at any time we shall produce the depression handed on to us by some ancestor, or that we have already, unwittingly, passed this dread disease on to our children.

However, some of you in your search to learn about depression may have read something which many psychiatrists and psychologists fail to read, namely, the actual research reports by scientists working on the problem of the biological basis of depression. Perhaps you do read the monthly issues of the *American Journal of Psychiatry* and the *British Journal of Psychiatry*, or the heavy tomes of the *American Psychiatric Review*.

If you do, you will know that the sentence 'Depression is a genetic illness' is a statement of a *wish*, not a fact. A hundred years ago the German doctor Kraepelin attributed the behaviour of some of his patients to the illness 'manic-depression', and since then psychiatrists have been searching for the cause of this illness. They talk of the 'gene for depression' and the 'gene for mania', and some of them even say that such genes have been found. They talk, too, of 'chemical imbalance', and of physical tests for depression, and some say that the precise chemistry of the imbalance and the tests is known. However, what is described as fact is actually speculation. An enormous amount of research needs to be done before any genetic factor can be shown for certain to play a part in depression, and, from the results of the research, it seems that, if there is a genetic factor, it is one which requires the presence of many other factors – physical, psychological and social – for it to be activated.[1]

One of the great difficulties of this research is that, even after a hundred years, psychiatrists still cannot agree on how many kinds of 'depressive illnesses' there are.[2] You will probably have come across terms like 'clinical depression', 'endogenous depression', 'reactive depression', 'neurotic depression', 'bipolar and unipolar depression', 'major depressive episode', and so on. If so, you are certain to be confused, particularly when you discover that different psychiatrists give different diagnoses. One might tell you that you are 'clinically depressed', another that you have 'endogenous depression', yet another that you have a 'schizo-affective disorder'. What you are not told is that all these words are just labels used in an attempt to put the people who get depressed into different categories. However, it does seem that, while there are certain things that depressed people do have in common, each of us gets depressed in our own individual way.

If you have read the research literature, you will be saddened and worried to find that what researchers call 'outcome studies' show that depressed people treated only with drugs and electroconvulsive therapy do not do well. Most find that the depression recurs. Many remain depressed, but cease to seek any kind of professional help. Many die, not just by their own hand, but through illnesses. Being depressed is physically debilitating.[3]

This is very troubling, because while psychiatrists talk complacently of 'managing depression' by using long-term medication in the way that doctors 'manage diabetes' using long-term insulin injections, we know that a person with chronic diabetes can lead an ordinary life, but a person with chronic depression cannot. To be told that you have inherited depression in the way that another person has inherited diabetes is of no help at all. It just makes you more despairing and confused.

If you are a woman and are depressed, no doubt you have been told that it has been caused not just by a chemical imbalance but that this imbalance relates to the functioning of the feminine hormones. This is puzzling, because you can see how the malfunctioning of a hormone could lead you to think, 'I feel sick', but how can a hormone, however it functions, cause you to think, 'I am a bad mother'? Nevertheless, many women discover that from puberty to after the menopause their own real, lived experience is dismissed with the words, 'It's your hormones, my dear'.

However, there *is* a genetic factor in depression. In that double helix of DNA there is a special strand which separates us from all other animals and marks us out as human beings. That special strand of genes not only determines our human shape, it gives us language, and with that the ability to conceive of the past and the future. Using these abilities we can look to the future with hope and courage, or fear and despair; we can remember the past in happiness or mourning, in gratitude or envy, in thankfulness or resentment. Using these abilities we conceive not just of 'is' but of 'ought', and create for ourselves two worlds of meaning – the world as it is and the world as it ought to be. Now we can trap ourselves in a tangle of ises and oughts. Now we can say to ourselves, 'I do not accept myself as I am. I ought to be a better person', and so lay the cornerstone of the prison of depression.

You might, in your search for an understanding of depression, have tried to make sense of it in terms of ises and oughts by reading books by cognitive or behavioural therapists. In many ways these books can be extremely helpful, for they can make you aware of how easy it is to think in extremes (like, 'Nobody cares about me', instead of, 'Some people don't care about me, but some do'), and they suggest some practical ways of re-organizing your life. But, when they tell you you are thinking and acting 'irrationally' or 'dysfunctionally', you can hear this as yet another put-down and feel that ever so familiar stab to the heart.[4]

Even if you can put this aside, you soon discover that these cognitive and behavioural therapists slide over, or ignore, the implacable truths and dilemmas of our lives. For instance, one such author chides his client for being so illogical as to say, 'I'll never find another friend like that again', and asks her to estimate just how many people she could meet and how many of these could become friends. He ignores the fact that we do have relationships which are irreplaceable, like those with a parent who gave us unconditional love, or with someone with whom we shared the greatest joys and tragedies of our lives, and when such relationships end we can do nothing but mourn their loss. When we do suffer such losses what we need are not people who tell us to 'look on the bright side', but people who can acknowledge and share our pain.

Cognitive and behavioural therapists ignore, too, the major questions which face us all: 'Why am I here?', 'What is the purpose of life?', 'What happens when I die?' They assume that all of us are concerned solely with making the most of our lives, when in fact many of us are chiefly concerned with the question, 'How can I be a good person?'

In your search for an understanding of depression, and in your concern about the great questions of life, you might have read some of the books on depression which give a religious or spiritual answer to the problem. Some of these books might just heighten your sense of badness and inadequacy, but others do offer consolation. However, most of them advise you to put your trust in God or some spiritual power, and this is precisely what a depressed person cannot do. When we have been repeatedly and deeply hurt by the people we trusted, we learn to be very careful about where we place our trust, and if we cannot trust the people whom we can see and know, how can we trust an unknown, unknowable God? Moreover, if you believe in God, then when you become depressed you find that God, like everyone else, seems far away, and, worse, the more you hate yourself, the more you feel that God will never forgive you.

Whenever we come across an author, or a therapist or counsellor, or a preacher who says to us, 'Believe as I do and all will be well', it is very tempting to say, 'Right, I'll do that'. However, we cannot change our beliefs about the purpose of life and the nature of death in the way we can our beliefs about the best breakfast cereal. Our beliefs about the purpose of life and the nature of death relate to our own inner truth, and even though we may hide or deny our own inner truth, it never disappears, and it speaks to us clearly. You will know this if ever you have been in analysis and your psychoanalyst has given an interpretation which your inner truth knows is wrong. The respectful, fee-paying part of you can be saying, 'Yes, I see what you mean', while your inner truth is saying, 'No'.

This is where therapists can be dangerous. They can use their position, power and mystique to persuade us that what we know as truth is mere fantasy and that because we are anxious and depressed and having difficulty in coping with our lives we are intrinsically inadequate. If you have read any of the psychoanalytic texts on depression you will have discovered how little respect psycho-analysts have for a person's own experience and how belittling to the client the psychoanalytic jargon is.

So, whatever you have done to try to discover what depression is and how you might bring it to an end, all that has happened is that you have become more and more confused, and when we are confused we feel powerless and helpless.

The aim of this book is to help you sort out your confusion and regain that which is rightly yours, the power to understand yourself and the society in which you live, so that you can make the best decisions about how you should live your life. With such power we can not only understand the causes and the purposes of depression but, more importantly, free ourselves from its prison and live life joyously, hopefully and freely.

To do this, we begin by understanding our own real, lived experience.

It is our own real, lived experience which leads us into the prison of depression. It is not a gene, or our hormones, or our dysfunc-tional and illogical thinking, our lack of faith, or our complexes and inadequacies which have brought depression upon us, it is what has happened to us and, most importantly, what we have made of what has happened to us; it is the conclusions we drew from our experience.

That set of conclusions which leads us, finally, into the prison of depression was not drawn illogically, or fantastically, or crazily, but were the correct conclusions to draw, given the information we had at the time.

If, when you were a child, all the adults whom you loved and trusted were telling you that you were bad and that if you didn't mend your ways terrible things would happen to you, you wisely and correctly drew the conclusion that you were bad and had to work hard to be good. If, when you were a child, all the people you loved and trusted left you or disappointed or betrayed you, you wisely and correctly drew the conclusion that you must be wary of other people and that you should never love anyone completely ever again. You were not to know that if we grow up believing that we are intrinsically bad, and that other people are dangerous, we shall become increasingly isolated, the joy will disappear from our life, and that we shall fall into despair. Even if you did know that, you had to protect yourself. We all have to protect ourselves when we are in danger. The business of life is to live, and this is what we all try to do.

The reason we get into a tangle, be it by becoming depressed, or finding it hard to get on with other people, or any of the multitude of unhappy situations we can get into, is because we fail to go back and check whether the conclusions we drew as children still apply in our lives. We *all* fail to do this, simply because there is not enough time to be forever checking our conclusions. When we were children we drew the conclusion that we should not put our hand in a fire because fire burns. When we grow up we don't every day say to ourselves, 'I'll just check whether it's still not safe to touch a fire'. We simply go on acting as if fire will still burn us.

Similarly, many of us when we were children drew the wise and correct conclusion that we should not say what we think because the adults around us will punish us if we do. When we grow up we can fail to check this conclusion, and thus go on acting as if other people will punish us if we dare to say what we think. Never daring to say what you think leads inevitably to missing out on many things which would give you pleasure and confidence, and prevents you from discovering how joyous it is to share your thoughts and feelings with another person. As a child, your conclusion to keep your thoughts to yourself was a wise conclusion. As an adult, all you need to do is to check whether this conclusion still applies, or whether it can be modified – for instance, in conversations with your parents you might still need to be careful about what you say, but with close friends you can speak openly and freely.

What I have put in this book are the conclusions I have drawn from my experience of talking to people about themselves, and I keep checking these conclusions because I go on talking to people about themselves. So much of what people have talked to me about over the years has had to do with the problem of depression.

The problem of depression was first presented to me when I was a baby. I didn't know it was depression. I just knew that sometimes my mother was loving and caring, sometimes she was silent and unreachable, and sometimes she was wildly, dangerously angry. It was not until I was in my thirties that I realized that my mother had been depressed for most of my childhood. By that time I was involved professionally with people who were depressed, for I was working in a psychiatric hospital in Sheffield, where there were many depressed patients and where the professor of psychiatry, Professor F. A. Jenner and his team were researching into the metabolic basis of depression.

Professor Jenner thought that there might be some interesting, though not important, psychological aspects of those patients whose mood changes seemed to follow some pattern, and suggested that I take this as the basis for my doctoral research.

So I began observing and talking to people who were sunk in depression or, less frequently, fiercely active in mania. I sat in case conferences, and in the staff dining room and lecture rooms, observing and listening to the psychiatrists, all of whom believed most firmly that depression and mania were physical illnesses. I read exhaustively every book and article I could find on depression and mania. Slowly I drew three conclusions from my experiences.

These were

1. From all the possible observations they could make about their patients, the psychiatrists selected a very narrow range of observations.

2. The scientific literature on depression, whether written by psychiatrists or psychoanalysts, described depression only from the point of view of the onlooker. Nowhere was what it feels like to be depressed actually described.

3. When depressed people talked about what it was like to be depressed, they described as central to the experience something which the psychiatrists and psychoanalysts completely ignored, namely, the strange but unmistakable sense of being isolated, of being trapped in some kind of prison whose walls were as strong as they were invisible.

The psychiatrists, I found, spent very little time actually talking to their patients, so there was a great deal about them they did not know. When they did talk to their patients, or about their patients, they were busy turning what the patient said into what the psychiatrists called the symptoms of depressive illness. If the patient said, 'I no longer enjoy love making', the psychiatrist marked this down as 'loss of libido', and did not enquire as to whether the marriage itself had become flat, stale and unprofitable. If a patient with a deep religious faith said, 'I feel that God will never forgive me', the psychiatrist marked this down as 'irrational guilt', and did not enquire as to how central to the life of this person a belief in God was. If a patient said, 'I feel I'm trapped in a sea of mud and the more I try to get out the more I get sucked down', the psychiatrist marked this down as 'lowered mood', and made no attempt to understand just what the person was experiencing.

There is a good reason why psychiatrists, both then and now, do not enquire too carefully into what their patients think and feel. The reason is that people ruin theories. Psychiatrists and psychologists go to a great deal of trouble to create their theories about why people behave as they do and they want all people to fit these theories. We can make up all kinds of theories about people simply by making a few observations of what a few people do, and our theory can seem very good, but as soon as we make a few more observations, or, worse, ask people what they think, we find that our theory is ruined. People are so diverse they just don't fit into theories.

Every time I run a workshop where I talk about my theories about why we behave as we do, people in the workshop are sure to say, 'I'm not like that', and 'I don't see it that way'. So I can understand why psychiatrists prefer not to put themselves into situations where their patients can challenge their theories.

It is not just that people are so individual that they don't fit theories, it is also that each of us is so complex that no single label can ever describe us accurately. We are complex because we can always think, feel and believe two opposite things at one and the same time. Recently, one of my clients, a man in his thirties who had told me frequently and at some length how he was so timid and shy, how bad he was at his job, how he had got his qualifications only by the sheerest of chance, said to me, 'I'm really very arrogant. I always believe I could do the job much better than the people I work for'. And so he is, both humble and arrogant.

I have found, as you must have too, that no matter how well you know a person, there is always something more to be discovered about that person. No one ever tells his life history completely; no one ever reveals all of his thoughts, feelings and desires; no one behaves in exactly the same way with each person he meets. No category can ever encapsulate an entire person, no theory can ever explain completely why any one of us behaves as we do.

Thus, to maintain their theories, psychiatrists have always had to avoid talking to their patients. This is why in psychiatric hospitals patients and staff are kept so separate. It is not simply, as so many patients have been led to believe, that patients are inferior creatures who could contaminate the sane and superior doctors and nurses.

However, by not talking to their patients psychiatrists have failed to learn from them just what the experience of depression actually is.

What the patients in Sheffield told me, and what depressed people have gone on telling me, is that being depressed is very different from being unhappy. When we are unhappy we still feel a connection to the rest of the world, but when we are depressed we are cut off, enclosed in a strange isolation. People describe this experience in vivid images: 'I'm in a dark tunnel, and beyond the tunnel is another tunnel', 'I'm at the bottom of a black pit and no one can reach me', 'I'm stumbling lost in grey, swirling mist', 'I'm trapped beneath a dome of glass and the people outside appear like shadows'.

As the people in Sheffield and later in Lincolnshire were telling me this, they were also describing how their experiences had led them to draw conclusions which served to cut them off from other people, conclusions like, 'I am bad and unacceptable', 'I must not forgive', 'I must not trust other people'. I described this research in my first book, *The Experience of Depression*.[5]

In my conversations with people who were depressed, we frequently talked of death, of the losses they had suffered and the fears they had about their own death. Talking about death meant talking about religious beliefs. I realized how important all this was, and I knew how psychiatrists and psychologists ignore the whole question of belief. So I wrote my next book, *The Construction of Life and Death*,[6] where I described how the people who coped with their lives held beliefs which gave them courage and optimism, while those who did not cope held beliefs which made them frightened and pessimistic. For instance, among those people who believed in God, those who coped believed in a loving and benevolent God, while those who did not cope believed in a God who noticed them only to punish them and who did not forgive.

By then I had come to see that the beliefs which cut us off from ourselves, from others, and from our past and future can be summarized in six basic beliefs. If you have never been depressed and want to try it out, you will find the recipe for depression in my book, *Depression: The Way Out of Your Prison*.[7]

Depression is not a state of passive misery. It is an experience of tremendous fear. Just what this fear is and how we try to deal with it was the subject of my next book, *Beyond Fear*.[8] How we can use our understanding of this fear to develop ourselves and become the person that we want to be was the theme of my following book, *The Successful Self*.[9]

Because I have been talking to depressed people now for over twenty years and have kept in touch with many of them, I have been able to follow how these people changed themselves and their lives. In the second edition of my first book, now called *Choosing Not Losing*,[10] I added postscripts to the chapters about my depressed clients, describing how, ten years later, they were living their lives. In this present book I have brought together what I have discovered about how people can take charge of their lives and so change.

With all that I have written about depression in my earlier books, I do not feel that I have said everything that could be said or ought to be said about depression, because depression is not a problem which strikes just a few unlucky people. Depression is a problem from which no one is exempt.

It is impossible to estimate in any way accurately just how many people are depressed. It has been estimated that in the USA some four per cent of the population is depressed at any one time, and for around the world, an estimate of a hundred million has been given, but these are likely, for a number of reasons, to be underestimates.

Many people, when they consult a doctor, feel that they should speak only of physical complaints. It is very easy for the doctor to give just physical treatments and overlook the unspoken misery of depression. Julia West, an American psychologist working in Saudi Arabia, found that her women clients would describe their aches and pains, tiredness and illness, but not their personal misery of depression. This may have been because they experienced their depression only in physical terms, or it may have been because, in their discussions with Julia, they were always accompanied by their menfolk.[11] There are many of us who feel that our relatives, even when they are present only in spirit, prevent us from speaking freely about our misery.

Many depressed people do not seek any kind of medical help. It may be that they do not wish to reveal their misery to a doctor, or it may be that they do not realize that their dull, grey, lonely, cramped, trapped way of living can be called depression.

Amongst those people who lead apparently happy and successful lives, there are many who would say, 'I'm not depressed', but who know that depression, like a great black bird, hovers above them, ready to settle with a heavy, smothering weight upon their shoulders should they act, or speak, or even think without due care.

Such people often ask me, 'Doesn't being with a depressed person make you depressed?', and they look disbelieving when I answer, 'No'. They are convinced that depressed people are dangerous because their depression can magically and malignly call forth the depression lurking in themselves. Rather than confront their own depression, they spurn all contact with depressed people, or strive to isolate and confine them. If you are depressed you might have had experience of such people, perhaps even your own doctor, treating you as if you had the plague.

This fear of depression can prevent us from realizing that no matter how fortunate and far-sighted we may be, not one of us can be certain that the circumstances of our life will not change and all that supports our way of life vanish. Neither by hard work nor by goodness can we control every aspect of our life and ward off all tragedies. It may be that at some time all the people we love and need abandon us or reject us, or that the projects which gave our life meaning and purpose crumble or fail. When such disasters befall us, we feel great fear, and if we do not understand the nature of this fear we can defend ourselves against it by turning against ourselves, despairing, and locking ourselves in the prison of depression. On the other hand, if we do understand this fear and ourselves, we can, when disaster strikes, become appropriately unhappy but not depressed, courageous and not defeated.

Generally in the following chapters I use the pronoun 'we' when referring to something we all do, and, when I want to speak of the things which depressed people do, I use the pronoun 'you'. There is a difference between the way we think, feel and act when we are laying down the foundations of the prison of depression or living in the prison, and the way we think, feel and act when depression plays no part in our lives. However, I could have used 'we' throughout, for we are all capable of doing all that I describe if we are not wise.

By 'wise' I mean knowing what we fear most, and why; knowing what we need most, and why; and knowing how to defend ourselves in ways inexpensive of time and strength, and how to get and hold what we need in ways that enrich our life and our relationships.

Thus this book is for all of us.

*   *   *

The book is divided into five sections.

Section One, *The Meaning of Depression*, describes how we create the world of meaning (that is, our beliefs, attitudes, conclusions,

xxviBreaking the Bonds

opinions, expectations, wishes and fears) in which each of us lives. We live in meaning like a fish lives in water. Creating meaning is what each of us does all the time, but while we are very good at doing this, we often have difficulty in understanding just how we do it. As the ancient Chinese philosophers said, 'The fish is the last to discover the water'. Yet an understanding of how we create meaning is essential to an understanding of ourselves.

The world of meaning we each create is like a landscape in which we live. The landscape has limits, so in a sense we all build ourselves a prison, a prison made up of 'This is where and how I live, this is the kind of person I am, these are my obligations, duties, attachments and responsibilities, these are the rules I must follow'. However, some of us create landscapes which are vast and open, full of interesting and exciting possibilities, while others build landscapes which are cramped, monotonous and confined. The most cramped and confined of these is the prison of depression. In Section One I show just how we create such a prison.

Section Two, *Why Is It So Hard to Change?*, is concerned with why we so often do not want to leave our cramped prison, or re-structure it into something open and various. Depression is such a horrible experience that at first it seems that no one would want to remain in it, yet if you are depressed you know that being depressed does have advantages. As a university student said to me recently, 'My depression is like an old sweater. It's comfortable, so I keep it on. I think it's risky to change it for something new.'

The fear of change keeps many of us from changing; so does our pride, and the way we take things personally and hang on to hopes. Then there are the people who do not want us to change. Our loved ones do not want us to be unhappy, but, equally, they do not always want us to change the way we live our lives. What would happen to them if their depressed wife or mother gave up being depressed and went to college instead, or their depressed husband or father gave up being depressed and instead of battling on as a captain of industry became an opera singer? Even if, in giving up being depressed, you do not change your way of life, you do behave differently, and that means that your loved ones have to respond to you differently. They might not want to make the effort of thinking about you differently, and they may not be all that pleased when you no longer play the role of the martyr, sacrificing yourself for them, and instead insist that there are times when your needs must take priority. So it can happen that while you are making valiant efforts to unlock your prison of depression your nearest and dearest are resolutely barring the door.

You have to face these issues before you begin what is the subject matter of **Section Three**, *The Journey Out of the Prison of Depression*.

Here I tell you what the experts' secret is, and what preparations you need to make for the journey. Since at some time when you are depressed you will think of suicide, I have presented my argument that suicide is not a solution. I list some of the things you will need to find on your journey, and, since loneliness is such a problem, I give some suggestions as to how you might leave it behind. Before reaching journey's end, I show how some people have helped one another and tried out something new.

The key to the prison of depression is the discovery that you are not the bad, worthless, unacceptable person you thought you were, but that you, with all your strengths and weaknesses and peculiarities, are a person you can love and accept wholeheartedly. This discovery sometimes comes like a flash of blinding light, but more frequently it comes slowly, through a process of understanding which we can undertake like a journey, preparing for it beforehand, and then making sure that we visit certain places along the way. As with all such journeys in search of wisdom and understanding, we realize when we reach our goal that what we sought was in our possession all the time.

As you read this book you might at different points exclaim, 'Aha!', or think, 'I wonder how that applies to me?' It is a good idea to make a note of the Aha! experiences in case you forget. Sometimes, underlining the passages in the book is not enough, especially if you want to comment and the margins are not wide enough. So you might like to use a separate notebook where you can put your Ahas!, as well as do any of the Discovery exercises I suggest as ways of answering the question, 'I wonder how that applies to me?'

These exercises I have put in **Section Four**, *Discoveries*. Whenever in the first three sections it might be useful to do a relevant Discovery exercise I have marked this with the letter **D** and the number of the exercise.

The Discovery exercises are NOT compulsory, and there are no right answers except those which are *right for you*.

Occasionally, in the first three sections, I refer to what might be called technical matters, things which you might like to know more about. So, in **Section Five**, there is a series of *Technical Footnotes*. You might want to dip into these while reading the main part of the book.

Thus, if you want to know more about the research and arguments about the biology of depression, this is presented in Section

Five under 'Is Depression a Physical Illness?' Whether or not to use antidepressant or tranquillizing drugs is discussed in 'Drugs – Friend or Foe?' Since, try as I might to write only in ordinary, everyday language, I sometimes have to use the jargon of psychiatry and psychology, the glossary, 'Technical Terms – Keys to the Jargon', gives the definitions of these words. Whether or not to seek the help of a therapist and, if so, how can you tell if someone is a good therapist are questions which I have attempted to answer in 'Choosing a Therapist'.

All too often in life we neglect to take proper account of the stuff of our heart, our own inner truth. All too often other people tell us that our own inner truth is wrong, crazy, unacceptable. If you are depressed, perhaps some people have silenced you by saying, 'That's not you speaking. It's your illness'. To be silenced in this way is the utmost cruelty. Jill Tweedie, novelist and journalist, once wrote:

> Ex-depressive as I am, with only the occasional lapse, I cannot dismiss the idea that the vision of life seen in depression has the truth in it, the bare-boned skeletal truth, and an intrinsic part of depression is knowing this and being told that it is not so. Reality, however terrible, is bearable if others allow its reality. When they refuse you that, when they skip around you pretending you've got it wrong, that's rock-bottom time.[12]

Somehow, if we can face 'the bare-boned, skeletal truth' we can find the courage to go on with our lives. We can find that courage because, as the ordinary people that we are, we are *brave*. We know that life is full of uncertainty, not just the uncertainty we all face in terms of nuclear war, or of the destruction of the ecological balance of the planet, or of huge national debts, or of terrorism, or of Aids, but the uncertainties we each face in our own way: 'Will the firm I work for go bust?' 'Will my child get to school safely?' 'Is the lump in my groin cancer?' 'How will I manage if my husband dies?' We each have to live with our own uncertainties.

We are brave in the way we keep on going. We get up and go to work, no matter that our work is dull and unrewarding or demanding and stressful. We go on cleaning, cooking and looking after our children, knowing that many of the things we would like for ourselves and our children are not going to come our way. We go on trying to make our children brave by telling them that they are wonderful and that the future is opening up before them full of promise. We try not to tell them that their future might be tough and miserable, even though we fear it may be so. We go on loving one another, even though we know that out of that love will come the terrible pain of separation and loss.

Sometimes we lose our nerve. Sometimes our courage falters, and then we feel great fear. This happens when we lose confidence in ourselves and we find that there is an unacceptable discrepancy between what we thought our life would be and what it actually is.

Such a discovery is made by just about all of us at some point in our lives. When it does, we feel an immense fear which threatens to overwhelm and annihilate us. One way of dealing with this fear is by locking ourselves in the prison of depression. In there we can shut out other disturbances and give ourselves time to think things through and so come to terms with the discrepancy between what our life is and what we want it to be.

For some of us, coming to terms with the discrepancy and building another life is not too difficult, and so our period of depression is brief. However, for others of us the task is much more difficult. So much more has been staked and lost, so much time and effort has been wasted, and so few alternatives for the future are on offer. Most of all, if you have grown up believing that you are bad and unacceptable and that you have to work hard to be good, then in the prison of depression you can doubt that you have the right to change your life and to claim something for yourself. Thus your sojourn in the prison of depression goes on, until you can discover in yourself that sense of intrinsic acceptance and worth with which you were born.

This is not an easy thing to do because you have been told so many confusing things, not just by psychiatrists, but in the past by your parents and teachers, and in the present by people who want you to be the sort of person they want you to be.

Many people, not just psychiatrists, want to believe that depression is a physical illness.

If you are depressed and believe that it is a physical illness you may be holding this belief because it allows you to be irresponsible – no matter what you do, you can say, 'I cannot help what I do, I am ill'. Or perhaps you believe depression is a physical illness because you are trapped in an impossible situation and being depressed is the only form of escape that you can find. Or perhaps you have been brought up to believe that you must never question what anyone in a position of authority says, and so if psychiatrists, backed by the whole medical profession, say that depression is a physical illness, you believe them without question.

Many people want to believe that depression is a physical illness because that allows them to ignore the suffering of other people and the complexities of life. It requires very little mental effort to think, 'Depression is a physical illness'. Whereas to understand how we think, feel and act, how we affect and are affected by the people around us, how we respond to and are affected by the customs and beliefs attached to our gender, class, race, religion and nationality, and how we respond to and are affected by the propaganda that we are subjected to and the political, economic and ecological changes in the world we live in requires considerable mental effort and a tolerance of uncertainty. To say, 'Depression is a physical illness' requires one sentence. To describe the multitude of matters which are relevant to our experience of depression requires many sentences, indeed, a large book.

The aim of this book is to help you sort out this confusion and to be a signpost for your journey out of the prison of depression. *Depression is not an illness. It is an experience out of which we can gain greater understanding of ourselves and other people.*

My friend Pat Wakeling, a psychiatrist who, having found that the treatment his colleagues gave him for his depression did not work, had to find his own way out of the prison, wrote:

> Depression is not – as I have eventually and painfully learned – something to sweep under the carpet: to deny, to forget. It is an experience that brings great misery and causes a great waste of time, but it can be, if one is fortunate, a source of personal wisdom and worth more than a hundred philosophies.[13]

This book is a distillation of my work not just on depression but on all the suffering which we can encounter. In it you will hear the voices of some of the people who have talked to me over the last twenty years, people living in the United States, Britain and Australia. To them I give my gratitude and love.

I

The Meaning of
Depression

1

An Ordinary Story

'My family insisted I see a psychiatrist. So I went along expecting to have to tell him all about my life, but all he said was, "We don't need to go into all that. You're obviously depressed", and he prescribed me some pills. That wasn't what I wanted at all.'

Pat looked tired and much older than her forty-five years. She had read my book, *Beyond Fear*, and had written to me to say that she would like to talk to me because in that book I had described what she was going through – experiences of terrible fear and a sense of despairing and painful isolation.

So now she sat on my sofa and diffidently and simply told me her story.

She was a doctor's daughter and had wanted to be a doctor too. But her father had said that medicine was not a profession for a woman. So she trained as a nurse and met Simon, a medical student, and fell in love. They planned to marry, but Simon was killed in a car accident.

Later she married one of her patients, a Korean veteran who had acquired the habit of drinking to maintain his courage, a habit which he did not relinquish after the war. For ten years Pat tried to maintain her marriage for the sake of her son, but eventually had to admit failure. She was offered the chance to train as a teacher and, even though this, like all the jobs she had done previously, in no way stretched her ability, she was glad to have a secure job which allowed her plenty of time for her son. Soon, though, there were other demands on her time. Her parents were now old and infirm, and her sisters had compelling reasons why they could not look after them. So Pat nursed her father and then her mother through long, painful, and finally fatal illnesses.

When Pat was a child she had enjoyed drawing and painting, but her parents and teachers discouraged her. Her parents had belittled her efforts, and her teachers told her she could not study both art and science. Though she had put aside this interest, she was delighted when her son showed artistic talent, even though he went to Paris to study. Pat had plans for herself.

Pat said, 'All my life I've been looking after other people. But I'd always told myself that when Peter was grown up I was going to travel. I intended to go absolutely everywhere. I felt that I deserved that.'

So, at long last, Pat could begin to fulfil her ambition to travel. In the summer holidays she and a woman friend went to China. In Peking Pat fell dangerously ill and was rushed to hospital. An immediate operation was necessary. She survived, but her friend had to return home before Pat was well enough to travel. So Pat found herself weak, in pain and alone in a foreign hospital whose standards of care and cleanliness were far below what she had expected.

Pat told me how she had summoned up every iota of strength to travel home. Then she had to go into hospital again, and there she was told that she should plan to take early retirement, for now she would need to lead a quiet life with little physical effort and certainly no stress.

All this she endured in the same stoical way she had endured the troubles of her life. She left hospital and returned home feeling tired and uncertain about what she would do. Her son had returned from Paris to be with her, but as soon as she could Pat urged him to go back to his studies. She assured him that she would be quite all right.

However, when the taxi taking him away had disappeared down the road and she closed her front door behind her she was assailed by the most terrible fear. She felt that her very being was shattering. She clung to the coats hanging behind the door, trying to get from their softness a sense of being held, but knowing that they were only coats. She hoped that if this were death it would come quickly.

Eventually, the fear ebbed and she made her way carefully upstairs. She sat on the edge of her bed, hardly daring to breathe lest an untoward movement brought back the fear again. She saw it as a dark, foreboding ocean whose tide at any time would rise and engulf her.

Much later she lay down on the bed, and much, much later she slept. When she awoke it was to a new world, a world from which all colour had been drained and where the familiar

objects of her bedroom had taken on a strange, sinister meaning. She lay in bed all morning, fearing to traverse the vast
distance between bed and door and to face the impossible tasks
of bathing and changing her clothes. She longed for someone to
come and rescue her, but when she heard her neighbour
knocking she buried her head under the pillow. Her kindly
neighbour now seemed to her as someone she must fear.

Only the thought that her neighbour might well call the
police got her from her bed and into a semblance of living. As
the days passed she discovered in herself a facility for lying,
declaring to all who might ask that she was well. She gave all
kinds of reasons why she could not accept their invitations out
but never the true one, that she was frightened to leave the
security of her own home and venture into the company of
people who, in the guise of friends, threatened injury. She felt
exposed and vulnerable and needed to hide away, yet that
isolation was near unendurable. She said, 'I feel that I'm in jail
and they've thrown away the key.'

Some friends were not deceived. They contacted her son, and
he came again to see her. He told her to consult a psychiatrist.
Her friends and sisters said the same. She felt that she could not
refuse, and so heard her life of striving, hard work, devotion
and self-sacrifice dismissed as unimportant and her profound
experiences reduced to a label and a pill.

Pat's experience of fear and painful isolation is very common. For
many people it comes towards the end of a life of hard work,
self-sacrifice and disappointments bravely born. For many others it
comes in the middle years, when the rewards for hard work,
unselfishness and devotion do not materialize, or, if they do, prove
to be a disappointment. For many women the experience comes in
their twenties and thirties when, after childbirth, they do not
discover in themselves the bountiful fountains of mother love which
society assures them resides in all good, natural women. For many
teenagers the experience comes when they face the insecurities, the
hurdles and the dangers of adult life and they doubt that they have
the strength and ability to deal with these. For many children the
experience comes when the world which they took to be solid and
secure is shattered by the death, defection or disloyalty of someone
on whom they depend.

So terrible is this fear and the painful isolation that follows that few people have the courage to talk about them as they actually are. Instead we conspire to pretend that the fear and the isolation do not exist. Some of us maintain the pretence by remaining silent about our experiences, and others conspire to deny the fear and the isolation by ignoring, belittling and redefining them.

The aim of this book is to break the silence and to show that the fear and the isolation are not shameful aspects of inadequate people but are central to our experience and understanding of ourselves and our lives. Through understanding our fear and isolation we find courage and relationships.

Let's begin with the isolation, for we have a word for that – depression.

2

Depression – the Painful Isolation

'Depression' and 'depressed' are very common words. We often use them, and usually when we mean something else.

We say, 'Isn't it a depressing day?', when we mean, 'I don't like this weather'.

We say, 'This job is so depressing', when we mean, 'I'm bored with this job'.

We say, 'I'm really depressed about having to spend Christmas with my in-laws', when we mean, 'I'm angry'.

We say, 'I'm depressed about my child's exam results', when we mean, 'I'm disappointed'.

We say, 'I feel really depressed', when we mean, 'I'm unhappy'.

Until we have actually been depressed we do not realize that there is a great difference between being depressed and being unhappy. When we are unhappy, no matter what terrible things have happened to us, we still feel in contact with the rest of the world. When other people offer comfort and love we can feel it warm and support us.

When we are depressed we feel cut off from the rest of the world. When other people offer us comfort and love that comfort and love does not get through the barrier and we are neither warmed nor supported.

When we are unhappy, even if there is no one there to comfort us, we comfort ourselves. We are kind to ourselves and look after ourselves. We are close to ourselves. We are a good friend to ourselves.

When we are depressed we do not comfort and look after ourselves. Instead we hurt ourselves and make life even more difficult. We become cut off from ourselves. We become our own worst enemy.

Tom described the difference between his experience of unhappiness and depression. He said, 'The time of my greatest unhappiness was in early 1976. I had a good chance of being selected for the Olympics in the long jump when I was knocked down and run over by a car. It smashed my right leg. I was in hospital for weeks, and most of the time I was miserable and angry with the guy who'd done it to me. But one of the best things that ever happened to me happened then. I knew Dad cared a lot about my going to the Olympics, but when he came to see me in hospital straight after the accident I could see he was upset about *me* and not about the Olympics. He put his arms around me and gave me a big hug and said he was so glad I was alive. He came to see me every day in hospital and we had some great talks. I felt really close to him.

'That memory's very precious to me because he died about five years after. At least he wasn't here to see what a fool I made of myself when my firm let me go. There I was, thinking I had this great job for life, then one afternoon, no warning, the message, clear your desk and go. I should have realized that something like that might happen. The firm had been taken over by a large conglomerate, but then I didn't think about it, and afterwards I blamed myself. If I'd been any good they'd have kept me on. At first I couldn't believe it. I wandered around in a daze, thinking that at any minute I'd wake up or there'd be a message from my boss saying they'd made a mistake.

'When it started to get through to me that I'd actually been let go I felt that I'd lost my identity and that was terrifying. For years I'd thought of myself as Tom McPherson, accountant with Intercel Inc., and now I wasn't an accountant with Intercel Inc. I felt I wasn't anybody. I got so scared I didn't know what to do with myself. I holed up in a hotel room and phoned my wife and told her I had to go on an urgent business trip. I stayed in that hotel room for three days. I couldn't speak to anyone and I didn't want anyone to see me. Finally, when the hotel management were getting suspicious and making a nuisance of themselves, I went home. My wife was beside herself with anxiety. Someone from the firm had phoned her, so she knew.

'I couldn't talk to her and I didn't want her to touch me. Her sympathy just made me feel worse, and when she got angry with me I'd get so angry inside that I thought I might hit her. So I'd stay in my room or go for long walks. Walking didn't make me feel any better. Most of the time I felt I was in a dark tunnel under the earth, but when I was walking I felt that that tunnel was going down deeper and deeper. It didn't level out until months later when an old friend came and literally dragged me off to a group for executives who'd been let go. I hated it at first. I was so scared I couldn't speak, but once I realized that everyone there had been through what I'd been through, I could open up and talk. That group saved my life.'

When Tom spoke of walking in a tunnel which was going down deeper and deeper, and Pat of being in a jail where 'they've thrown away the key' they were describing vividly and accurately what they were actually experiencing. They did not say, 'I feel *as if* I am . . .', but 'I feel *I am* in a tunnel, in a jail'. When we say that experiencing something *is like* experiencing something else, we put a distance between ourselves and the similar experience. For instance, if we say, 'Listening to Beatles music is like being a teenager again', we know there is a separation between 'me now' and 'me as a teenager'. When we say that experiencing something is *the same as* experiencing something else, we make these two experiences into one and show that the experience is important and intense. To say, 'When I listen to Beatles music I am a teenager again', gives an account of a profound and absorbing experience.

Thus it is that when depressed people speak of what they are experiencing, they say, not 'It is like . . .', but 'It is . . .', and what it is is something fearful.

These images can stay with us all our lives. One elderly woman, describing an act of betrayal by her father when she was twenty, said, 'I felt that I had been skating on thin ice and then I fell through into utter blackness, and afterwards I always knew that I was skating and the blackness was always underneath.'

Each of us experiences depression in an image which is idiosyncratically our own, and yet which shares a meaning with all other people's images of the experience of depression.

'I'm at the bottom of a black pit.'

'I'm trapped inside a black balloon.'

'I'm in a glass cage. The glass is blurred and I can see people only vaguely and they can't see me.'

'I'm wrapped in a thick black cloth that I can't undo. I'm trapped and helpless.'

'I'm alone, immobile and weighed down by a huge black bird

sitting on my shoulders. Even when I'm not depressed I can feel that bird hovering over me.'

'I'm trudging across an empty desert and I can't find water. The desert is endless.'

'I'm lost in a swirling black mist.'

'I'm in an empty boat on an empty ocean. No sail or oars, and night is coming on.'

'I'm locked in a tomb and no matter how much I cry out nobody hears.'

'A hole, grey, very grey, a closing greyness like a cave, a hole that goes down for ever and it holds on like crazy. The hole is inside me and I'm inside the hole.'

(D 1) What would you say if I asked you, 'If you could paint a picture of what you are feeling what kind of picture would you paint?'

Does your image have the same meaning that all the images mentioned here have, namely,

I am alone in a prison.

If you are simply unhappy, your image would not have the quality of you being alone and trapped in some kind of prison. For instance, an unhappy person might say, 'I feel that I'm at my attic window looking out on a cold, wet day'. If asked, 'Can you leave the attic?', the unhappy person will say, 'Yes, I can go downstairs and be with my family', whereas the depressed person will say, 'No. The door is locked on the outside and in any case the house is empty'.

It is this *sense of isolation* which is the essence of the experience of depression.

It is a powerful and compelling sense of isolation which is different from all other experiences of aloneness and isolation. In those other experiences you could, if you had chosen, have contacted other people. From your camp in the woods you could have gone back home. From your lonely college room you could have found a phone and called home. But from the prison of depression there is no path, no telephone that will connect you with others. All paths peter out, all telephone lines are down. You are surrounded by a wall which, though it is invisible, is impenetrable.

Outside the wall those who know you realize that the wall is there. They reach out to you and, though their hands may touch your flesh, what they feel is the wall which resists all their love and entreaties. Their cries of, 'You're shutting me out', and 'I can't get through to you', are not empty clichés but reports of real experience. To them the wall is as palpable as it is invisible.

Banging our head against a wall is frustrating, but what makes the wall around a depressed person doubly frustrating is that the person inside knows and the person outside senses that in some way the person inside wants to be there.

The prison of depression is so terrible that it seems inconceivable that anyone would choose to enter it.

Yet, as anyone who has been there knows, inside the prison of depression you are safe from all those forces on the outside which threaten to destroy you. All the horrors and the disappointments of the outside world lie far beyond the walls of your prison and have less power to frighten you or even claim your attention, and all the demands, importunings, expectations and criticisms from your loved ones do not penetrate the walls to inflict their usual hurt.

So, as the prisoner and the jailer, you stay safe in your prison.

However, life in such a prison is not pleasant.

Your only company is your jailer, and you are a cruel jailer, taunting yourself with even worse criticisms than those you have shut outside. 'You're bad,' your jailer says. 'It's your fault everything has gone wrong.'

With only the cruel jailer for company you start to feel the worst torture human beings can ever experience – complete isolation. As torturers the world over know, courageous people can withstand the greatest physical pain, but the one torture which will eventually destroy the strongest person is complete isolation. We all need other people just as we need air food and water. Without other people our body aches, then ceases to function properly and becomes vulnerable to illness, while our mind, without the encounter of other minds, loses its capacity to distinguish its own contents from the contents of the world around it. Visions in the mind's eye seem like objects in the real world, while objects in the real world take on sinister, persecutory meanings.

Thus the isolation of depression begins as a place of safety and goes on to become a place of torture.

What leads you to seek such a place of safety and to remain in it, even through such torture?

It is fear, the greatest fear we can ever know.

3

Our Greatest Fear

Beautiful though our world is, it has many dangers about which it is appropriate to be anxious. The earth quakes, hurricanes blow, blizzards freeze. Necessary as other people may be to us, there are many dangerous people about whom it is appropriate to be anxious. Banks crash, wars start, cars collide, guns fire, fists smash, sex becomes hate instead of love. So we maintain an appropriately anxious guard and we teach our children to feel an appropriate amount of fear.

A certain amount of fear is necessary for our survival. We need to be alert to possible dangers and to respond to them with a spurt of fear which both focuses our attention and prepares our body, by increasing heart rate and adrenalin flow, to take the necessary action for fight or flight.

Some time ago a New York editor rejected my book *Beyond Fear* on the grounds that I did not instruct my readers how to give up feeling fear. I was amazed that he had never considered how essential for survival an alerting fear response is, especially in New York. What I was trying to do in *Beyond Fear* was to show how our fear response can go past the necessary alerting and mobilizing response and actually prevent us from dealing effectively with the danger. However, it is possible for us to become aware of such overlarge fear responses, to understand why we feel such fear, and, through such understanding, reduce the fear to appropriate levels.

In doing this we can come to realize that what we are afraid of is not something in the world around us but something inside us, and that what is inside us is nothing to be frightened of at all.

Until we do this, we all, to some degree, experience a fear which seems to have no object.

Sometimes we experience this fear without an object as *anxiety*, a persistent alerting to unspecified dangers and a kind of physical shakiness; or as *worry*, a persistent round of thoughts which project bad outcomes for all events, large or small; or, as Pat and Tom felt it,

3

12

as an *overwhelming dread and terror*, our greatest fear. This fear can come upon us at any time, but it most often comes as we wake out of sleep where all the defences we have created to keep the fear at bay have dissolved.

Our most popular form of fear without an object is worry, where we create objects for our fear. The world is full of *expert worriers*. There is no situation, no matter how blissful and secure, about which expert worriers cannot worry. The sun shines, and they worry about drought; the rain falls and they worry about flood; spring comes and they worry about winter; dawn breaks and they worry about night. They hoard worries like a squirrel hoards nuts, and, like Charlie Brown, they see an absence of worries not as happiness but as evidence that something dangerous has been overlooked.[14]

Lisa laughed when I described her as an expert worrier. She had never thought of worrying requiring any expertise. It came to her as naturally as breathing. She described herself as 'an anxious person', with 'anxious' being an attribute like her blue eyes and blonde hair. She saw herself as inheriting her anxiety from her mother, in the way that she had inherited her blue eyes and blonde hair. She was at first astounded when I suggested to her that feeling anxious about many small things was a way of dealing with a much greater sense of fear, but she went on to reminisce about times when she was especially fearful – when her husband was away, when her mother was dangerously ill, and, remembering her childhood, when she would be punished for being naughty by being sent to bed and she would sit with her ear to the door, straining to hear the sounds which assured her that her parents were still in the house. Later, in another conversation, Lisa mentioned that whenever her parents had quarrelled her mother would always scream at her father, 'You take me for granted. One day you'll come home and I won't be here', unaware that the person she terrified with this threat was not her husband but her child.

Lisa and I looked for the common element in her husband being away, her mother being ill, her mother's constant references to leaving home, and the little girl with her ear pressed to the door, and we found her greatest fear was her fear of being abandoned. (She feared death, but for her the terror of death was that all the people she needed might die before her, or that she might die first and so find herself alone.)

Lisa said, 'I always have this fear that everyone I depend on will go away and leave me. I couldn't cope with that. It would finish me.'

'What do you mean, "finish you"?', I asked.

'This sounds crazy, I know, but inside I feel I don't exist without other people. If they all went, I'd just disappear.'

What Lisa had yet to discover was that this was terror left over from childhood, baggage that she no longer needed to carry with her. Until she discovered that when she was alone she would not disappear, she would go on dealing with her fear of being abandoned by always feeling anxious and by worrying that every person she knew would one day reject and abandon her.

Not everyone experiences the greatest fear as *fear of being abandoned*. There are just as many people who experience it as *fear of loss of control*. One way of keeping anxiety, worry and fear at bay is to work hard and keep everything under control.

Dan said, 'I never worry. I just make sure that I've got everything organized and under control.' Dan and his wife Mary had come to consult me, not about themselves (there was nothing wrong with them – Dan had seen to that), but about their 24-year-old son, Danny, who was depressed and unable to work. Actually, the problem they were presenting to me was not the absent Danny but their difficulties in dealing with Danny. Mary felt that Danny needed looking after, while Dan thought that such molly-coddling was wrong. The boy should pull himself together, find some goal, and go for it. Organizing your life around goals was the right and proper way to live. Dan had always done that, and see where it had led him – a flourishing furniture business, a handsome house, and a fine family (with the present exception of Danny).

Mary bore out Dan's claim that he never worried. He just worked extremely hard. 'He always knows what's best for us', she said, drawing a picture of a kindly but authoritarian man who abhorred disorder and doubt and who kept his staff and family firmly under control. His staff and family always obeyed him, even Danny, until this dreadful depression had made him so difficult and disobedient. For Dan, the worst feature of Danny's depression was that he was no longer open to Dan's guidance.

Six months passed before I met Dan and Mary again. Two terrible disasters had befallen them. A fire had destroyed Dan's furniture emporium and the police suspected that it had been started by a disgruntled ex-employee. Then the stress of the fire and the arguments with the insurance company led Dan to have a heart attack, not a severe one, but severe enough to face the fact of his own mortality.

Dan had changed. He had become older, and much less secure and controlling. He described how even as he had watched the fire engulf his business he had been busy planning how to deal with the consequences, beginning with contacting the insurance company through to selling the site and rebuilding in a more advantageous part of town. It was not till a few days later when the police were talking of sabotage and the insurance company were delaying in living up to their promises that the full horror of his situation hit him. He had thought that he had everything in his life under control when in fact he had not. Now he felt that everything was slipping out of his grasp, that his world was crumbling, and that instead of having his feet firmly planted on solid ground he was falling through bottomless space. This terror and a sharp physical pain suddenly became entwined.

The ambulance and hospital seemed like a dream, and it was not until later that he saw with absolute clarity that he had encountered death. Again he felt that fear, for all his life he had told himself that he had death under control and now he knew that he did not. 'I felt,' he said to me, 'that my whole being was shattering. I hadn't felt like that since I was a kid and my father died.'

Good fortune had not entirely deserted Dan. It was while he

was in his most frightened and shattered state that Danny came
to see him and, for the first time in his life, Dan asked Danny for
help. For once, instead of ordering Danny to do something,
Dan said, 'Please would you help me? I can't manage the
business on my own.' Danny, instead of going silently away,
said, 'Yes, Dad', and took over the running of the business.

Mary said to me, 'Now Dan's getting better he's showing
signs of slipping back into his old ways of working too hard and
bossing us around. I have to remind him to take things easy and
to say, "Please".'

Dan and Danny still had many things to sort out individually and
together, but one thing Dan had realized was that all his life he had
felt that to keep himself safe he had to have everything organized
and under control. If he did not do this his outside world would
become chaotic, dangerous and strange, and he would feel that his
very self was shattering. He would become nothing but a pile of
rubble. The fire and his heart attack showed him that his organization and control were nothing but an illusion.

We can think we have everything organized and under control,
but in fact everything that exists in our universe is in constant
movement and change. If we fail to recognize this then one day our
universe will show us that it is so.

Dan was faced with three choices.

He could go on being terrified by the discovery that the world was
not the way he thought it was. Such terror is physically exhausting
and, in his case, would almost certainly lead to further heart
attacks.

or

He could do what Pat had done, bring the terror to an end by
locking himself in the safety of the prison of depression.

or

He could accept that everything is in constant change and that we
can control and organize very little of the universe, and then only for
a little time, and that this is not something to fear but something to
welcome and enjoy, for it is out of this constant movement and
change that we gain what makes our lives splendid – spontaneity
(including the spontaneity of love and forgiveness), hope, freedom
and our capacity to change.

Each of us in the way we experience *our sense of self and the threat of the annihilation of our self* is either like Lisa or like Dan. Each of us experiences our greatest fear, the fear that our very self will disappear or shatter, either as being rejected or abandoned and being left entirely alone, or as losing control and falling into chaos. Each of us experiences our sense of self either as being a member of a group or as the development of individual clarity, authenticity and achievement.

Most of us would say that we want both to be a member of a group and to achieve as an individual. It is often not until we are in situations of danger that we realize what is most important to us and how we see the greatest threat.

Finding the Source of Our Greatest Fear

Whenever someone consults me I try to establish in our first conversation how that person experiences his or her sense of existence and perceives the threat of the annihilation of their self. When somebody tells me something that sounds important I ask, 'Why is that important?'

When I was in California I met two people, George and Ruth, each of whom had encountered many difficulties in their lives.

George was sixty-two and recently retired. He was very courteous, ready to tell me his story, but his eyes looked tired. He had been diagnosed as having 'dysthymic disorder', but an inability to have a good night's sleep and to concentrate were, he said, his main problems.

George told me how his first wife had left him. That, he said, 'was not the kind of thing I could take easily. I don't think I ever got over it. With my present wife things have worked out quite well, except that there's a total lack of affection. Life is difficult for me. The reason I can handle all these things, and the reason I haven't said forget it, is because of my religious belief. That allows me to cope with all these things.'

'Can you tell me what your religious belief is?'

'We're Christadelphians. I believe that God is who He says He is, that there is a God. I can't, try as I might, see any sense in Darwinism. I feel that there's a power behind all of us. The Bible is His instruction to us and therefore we must find what He wants of us and what He's promised to us without preconceived ideas or having someone tell us what to believe. The promises were given early on to Abraham and Isaac and Jacob. Those same promises were repeated to King David. Those promises include anyone who encompasses those beliefs. We all have basic sinful ways inherited from Adam. Christ's purpose was to give us a way out. He was the Son of God and he therefore, being perfect, was able through his sacrifice to save all those who would come to him. Those promises will come to pass when he returns to earth and then there'll be a thousand-year period of shaping up the earth, bringing people into alignment, and we're told nothing beyond that, God being the be-all and the end-all. Christ will turn everything over to Him. Along with that, we believe that marriage is something which you should respect and hold to. My present wife has taken up my beliefs strongly. For many years she didn't give religion the time of day. She started to like what she saw and the people we associate with. Finally she went to a class and she liked that.'

'Did that draw the two of you closer together?'

'In a sense, but not in so far as affection is concerned. I've just decided that this is not in my life. In my own family we were never affectionate. I don't recall my mother and father, or my brothers and sisters having a hug between any of us, ever. With this group now, that's something I've had to get used to, always that's the greeting, a big hug, and, my goodness, with that something passes between you. It's like something bad goes out of you. It doesn't go into them, but you share something. I had never had that during my life. That's something I appreciate about this group. But as far as depression is concerned, the way it shows up now, I feel that life is no big deal. I don't think it's all that worthwhile, short of what I believe in. I'm trying to improve myself as best I can for as long as I can – that precludes any notion of doing away with yourself. I don't think I'd ever consider that. I simply don't think that life's all that great.'

'Would I be right in thinking that when you think about your life you feel disappointed?'

'In some ways yes. I've never had any great aspirations. I've never wanted great wealth. I'm possibly disappointed in what I've accomplished. It's possible to do a lot better than I did with the job. But I wasn't able to do that. Concentration was always a problem, and another thing was my personality. Even though I wasn't a boss, when people were doing things wrong I'd get after them. I was really acid about it quite a few times.'

'So you wanted the jobs done properly?'

'I felt it was all I could handle to do my own job.'

'My grandmother always said, "If a job's worth doing, it's worth doing well". Does that apply to you?'

'Well, my friends tell me that it does. I don't like to be tagged with being a perfectionist. But yes, generally speaking, if I want to do a job, I want to do it well.'

'Why is it important to you to do it well?'

'Because of my pride in what I've accomplished. I'm not interested in doing it any other way.'

'Why is it important to accomplish?'

'Maybe I can give you a for instance. The shower in our house, I considered was a poor design. I decided I wanted a nice tiled shower. I bothered everyone in town until I had quite a good knowledge about how to build a tile shower. The result is very nice. I enjoy it. I wouldn't enjoy it if it was a mess.'

'You don't enjoy mess at all?'

'I have mess around me, but I don't enjoy it. It bothers me.'

'What would happen to you if you couldn't accomplish anything, if everything around you was a mess?'

'Oh my God! I'd never considered that. A lot of it has to do with what other people think. I take other people in and show them the shower.'

'It's important that other people approve of it?'

'Approval, now there's a thought. That's something I seem to seek all the time. I wish I didn't. I have a cousin I really look up to. He couldn't care less about what anybody thinks he's done. If they pick on him about it it just rolls off his back. He never makes any effort to organize anything.'

'You're a good organizer?'

'Yes, if I'm motivated.'

'There are a lot of people who want to get things organized and under control. I call them What Have I Achieved Today Persons.'

'I'm sure I'm that way. Every night I'm frustrated if I haven't done something during the day. Other people just seem to do nothing all day long. They're happier than I am. My memory is such that if I have half a dozen things which need to be accomplished in a day, I write them down and I cross them off, and if I cross them all off I feel pretty good.'

We talked about his problems in not sleeping, and then George said, 'I wonder what I should be doing that I'm not doing. I think I should be quite excited about the prospects of my religious beliefs. There really are an awful lot of proofs. There's enough there to get a person excited, but there are also the things that prevent me from doing what I want. There are the physical problems like sleeping and aches and pains, and you wonder who you could talk to who could guide you so you correct some of these things, and that bothers me a lot. I just don't know who to talk to. Things like this medication. I don't know whether I trust my doctor. A lot of medical changes have come to pass because of things that I've suggested to him. I guess they don't know everything about what they're dispensing.'

George talked about some of the difficulties his children were experiencing, then said, 'These kind of things don't inspire confidence. I feel partly responsible because I didn't keep the family together and give them a better basis. Anyway, my biggest problem is the lack of sleep and the lack of concentration and ability to recall. Our belief requires, or I feel it requires, I study a lot. But if you can't keep your mind on what you're studying, what good is it? So that was probably my biggest problem, because it relates to my spiritual belief. The sleep just adds to that problem.'

'Why is it important to you to do this kind of study?'

'One reason is that all the people around me have been doing it all their life. But they can say verses all day long. I'd like to have some ability, just a little bit, enough where I can function in my own group. I won't even stand up and offer a prayer, let alone give a talk, because I can't seem to remember. Part of it is I'm afraid and part is that I haven't applied myself well enough. That bothers me too.'

'Whenever we're frightened, it's hard to remember something we've learned.'

'That's happened to me for many years now, and it's really common. When I'm forced to think of something, there's a blank. If I'm off by myself my own prayers are satisfactory. I know if I stood up in front of the group a wall would just cover me, and I don't want that to happen.'

'You won't risk it happening, and so you won't let yourself
discover that you could get up and it will be all right.'

'I can't believe that.'

'The problem with us being wonderful organizers, we like to
get everything organized beforehand. People like us always
have problems in being spontaneous. We don't have enough
trust in ourselves, in life, to act spontaneously. That's when we
become our own worst enemy. We stop ourselves from being
spontaneous.'

'How do you start?'

'I think one part is not to worry about making a fool of
ourselves.'

'That's easier said than done.'

'It's important to come to realize that it's not the end of us if
we do make a fool of ourselves. When we were children, that
did feel like being wiped out; as adults we can realize it's not the
end of everything, and that people like us to make mistakes, not
in a nasty way but –'

'So we seem human.'

'Yes. You must have a tremendous knowledge of this
material because you've studied it for so long and because it's so
important to you.'

'I want to know it even better, so it will become even more
important, that's what I'm striving for. I feel that I'm only just
beginning, that I'm really not at the point where I feel that I
could be acceptable.'

'Acceptable to whom?'

'To God.'

'So you still doubt that God accepts you?'

'Well acceptance, according to the Bible, takes place at the
Judgement Seat. That's the final acceptance. Whereas, I don't
begin to say who He will or will not accept. I wouldn't dream of
it. He's put down certain guide-lines. They're only guide-lines.
I don't say that you can ever be Christ-like, you can't, but you
should strive for that intended goal, realizing that you'll never
make it, but forgiveness is there. But I still think this Judgement
has a purpose, it's there to judge. So there has to be a line, a
certain demarcation, and it will be different for each individual,
according to their abilities and circumstance. But it's possible
not to be on the right side of that line. It's got to be, otherwise
why the Judgement? I'm concerned that I haven't progressed

far enough. And this is good to a degree, for it keeps you striving, but I'm quite concerned about myself at this point, that I need to progress further. Now the people around me don't tell me that. They say of course you'll make it. You're hanging in there until the end and that's what counts and perhaps they're right. But I don't want to play the odds in the wrong direction. You want to stack your deck the best you can.'

'If you were God would you forgive you?'

'No.'

'So, if you can't forgive yourself, you can't expect God to forgive you?'

'No, there are things that I wouldn't even begin to tell you about me that have me convinced that I'm a pretty poor character. They're in the past, but they show what I've been. These thing bother me a lot. I have worked on myself as a result, and it's my great hope that that will count for something.'

'That is what counts, what our intentions are and that we recognize our mistakes. In the past we acted in ignorance. We can't change the past but we can come to understand why we did what we did and try not to make similar mistakes, but if we go on punishing ourselves we actually prevent ourselves from becoming wiser.'

'I just wonder if there are things that I should be reading. I've started going to classes that are free, some things that will occupy my mind, a couple of financial classes, one a self-esteem class, a very popular class. I'm hoping that attending that class will help too.'

'Feeling yourself to be bad and inadequate and then have your conscience come after you, that's what you need to work on, and coming to feel better about yourself and turning your conscience into a good friend.'

'I need to learn how to avoid my inadequacies.'

'Until we accept our inadequacies, we can't change them. If we can accept our own inadequacies we can accept other people's inadequacies and then we can love them.'

'That's a big problem too, being critical.'

'What you turn on yourself you turn on other people.'

'I expect them to be much better than me. I think that they should be. I don't know why I lay that on them. It's something I'm trying to come to terms with.'

Thus George in this conversation showed that he experienced his sense of existence in the development of individual achievement and organization, not just in getting things done, but in gaining greater clarity of understanding. All the things that had gone wrong in his life he experienced as being mess and chaos, the circumstances which threatened to overwhelm and annihilate him.

When we experience our sense of existence in terms of individual achievement we need some standard to measure our achievement against. We look at what other people have achieved, and, if we approve of their achievements, we then seek their approval of our achievements. George set himself very high standards, and when other people failed to live up to his standards he was most critical of them. The one person whose standards he approved of was God, and so he sought God's approval.

This would have been a satisfactory way of living, except for one thing. George did not value, accept and forgive himself, and so he did not believe that God would value, accept and forgive him. He was drawn to his fellow believers because they gave him the warmth and acceptance his family had never given him, but to belong meant to believe in God's Judgement, and until he could see himself as worthy of God's forgiveness his nights of restless torment would continue.

Not all of us are like George, experiencing our sense of existence in individual achievement, and the threat of annihilation as the loss of control and chaos. Many of us are like Ruth.

When I went into the waiting room to meet Ruth she smiled at me and we began talking like we had known one another for years. She had that immediate, wonderful talent for easy conversation, laughter, and making people feel that she is interested in them.

Ruth was fifty-two and had had a very sad life. She had been diagnosed as having 'recurrent major depressive disorder' and had made two serious suicide attempts. Once we were settled in the consulting room Ruth began to tell me about her desire to die.

She said, 'I came out here and fell in love with the wrong man and decided to go to Washington and that's really where the trouble began. The boyfriend from here, who had never been able to say the words "I love you", suddenly sent me a tape which ended with "I love you". That didn't help. He finally came to see me and never uttered the words, and when he left it was with the announcement that it was all over and he did not expect to see me again. I went straight downhill.

'A few weeks after that, I made my first suicide attempt. Very spur of the moment. One grand and glorious evening I decided I'd had it and, talk about the foolishness of American doctors, I called a doctor I had seen only once and right over the phone he gave me a prescription for a hundred phenobarb, quarter grains, and I took that whole bottle that night. I very carefully disposed of all the things I didn't want anyone to find. Unfortunately, I woke up and found myself in hospital. Then I had to see a psychiatrist. My mother came to visit me and so he decided to discharge me. I discovered that I was terribly angry. I never knew I was angry. Somehow through that experience I discovered enormous anger and I still don't know what with. I'm not as mad now as I was then, but there's an awful lot of anger still in me. I don't know why.

'I got better. Did a lot of crying and a lot of talking. I found I could say almost anything to my mother. Only one subject I do not discuss with her, and that's that my father sexually abused me. I don't say that to her because she thinks he was God on earth. So we talked a lot and I cried a lot. We came back out here and I called the man in question and told him what I had done and said I'm planning to come back and I don't want to run into you in the neighbourhood and feel this horrible constraint. I want to feel we can just say hello to each other. I realize that's not really what I was doing but I thought that's what I was doing, and he of course got an enormous case of the guilts and said I should come and live with him.

'I had some questions about that, but I wanted it so badly that I decided to do that and got back out here and moved in with him and for about a year it went quite well, and then it began to go wrong and I began to get depressed again. I went to talk to a therapist who was a great help to me, but it was not enough. It didn't solve the problem and so one afternoon I decided, okay, that's enough. I'm going to check into a hotel and take every pill I can find and that's that. It's not fair to my therapist, but I'm a fairly good actress. She knew that something was wrong, but she didn't know how badly wrong. So I checked into my hotel and I had three litres of wine. I drank almost all of that and took all the pills and went to bed.

'The hotel maid found me the next morning. So I ended up in a psychiatric hospital. I was quite annoyed. Stayed there a few days, saw my therapist some more and started to function a bit better. I don't think it's really gone. I don't feel suicidal any more, but I've never got over the feeling of, "Gee, I wish it had worked". I don't function as well as I should. But it doesn't particularly bother me.'

'Are you working?'

'Oh yes. I spend my life working. I work a great many weekends and late nights. I know I should get out more. I'm a theatre person and I should go to the theatre. I'm a music person and I should go to concerts. But I'm not interested in them. I don't care about anything, except my job. It consumes all my energy. I couldn't get the motivation to do anything else. Basically I work and come home and turn on the television and go to bed. That doesn't really bother me. It seems to me that if that's the state I'm in that's okay.'

'Do you have friends outside of the people at work?'

'No, I don't. I'd like to, but I don't do anything that allows me to meet people outside of work. I haven't made friends and that I'm sorry about. I do like being with people. My best friend is in Washington, but I feel constrained when I'm with her and her husband. I spent a few days with them and we had a good time, but there's some constraint since we live so far apart. It worries me that my only real friend here is my mother. She's now seventy-eight and one of these days she's going to die and that scares hell out of me. When she does that I'm sure I'll be back with my therapist for a while.

'I want to meet people, but I don't want to make the effort involved. I want people to come to me rather than me going to them. Someday I'll get over it and I'll be ready to do something to jar me out of my lethargy. It's been two or three years since the last attempt and I just float along. I'm totally involved in my job. People think I'm crazy the hours I work. The depression has left me not really a hermit, but something approaching that. I would like to get involved with something, but I can't find anything. I'd like to work with Aids victims, but watching people die would probably bring me down. But that's the kind of thing that appeals to me.'

'What is it that appeals to you in that?'

'Helping people. I find myself talking to people – I'm the

mother figure at work, I'm by far the oldest person there, and so sometimes they come to me with their problems and I find myself thinking, yeah, I've been down that road, I know what they're talking about.'

'You see helping people as important?'

'Oh yes, I enjoy that. I like to do that.'

'Why is it important to help people?'

'Gee, I don't think I've ever thought about that. It feels good. I suppose it's an ego builder that I can help solve someone else's problems. It just feels good. It's a warm feeling. Feels useful. I like to feel useful. That's why I like my job. I feel useful. It's not just a rote thing.'

'Why is it important to feel useful?'

'You're after something and all I can come up with is that it feels good. I suppose that the books would say that it's a question of having a poor ego and therefore one must feel useful in order to make the ego feel good. I don't know that I agree. At this point the ego needs some help. But I've always been that way. I've always enjoyed helping, long before I was depressed, so I don't buy into that. It may be part of the American work ethic. Possibly because I come from parents who were into helping people. That's what you do.'

'If we looked at the other end of it, what would happen to you if you were not able to help people and you became completely useless?'

'Then I'd be dead. If there's no "problem to solve", then there's nothing, mainly because – the word challenge comes in, but it's not quite the right word, but if there's no challenge to life, then what's it all about? Why bother?'

'Are you describing the challenge in terms of your relationship to other people? You're able to relate to them through helping them, that there's that connection, and it's a challenge to be able to do that sort of thing?'

'Yes, it's a *raison d'être*. Even when I wasn't in a helping mode, when I was married with children, I was always involved in a drama group, in church. We had a group of friends who did crazy things to each other, and we used to write operas, and that was a kind of a challenge. It wasn't helping anybody, but it was having a hell of a good time.'

'You were part of a team.'

'Oh yes. It was creativity. And there's a creativity to helping people. That's a big part of it, to exercise the creativity, being able to come up with the right questions and the right solutions and possibilities. Yes, there's a creativity to it, and though I don't draw or do artistic things, it's essentially artistic.'

'So your reason for living is to be with other people in a creative way, whatever form that creativity might take? The greatest threat is finding yourself in a situation where there are no other people?' [I meant that if there were no other people, then there would be no one to help.]

'No, in a great many ways I'm a loner and I enjoy my privacy. In fits and starts I enjoy having company, having friends, but I'm not willing to go out of my way to get them. If someone throws me into a situation where there is a problem, I enjoy it, but I don't need to have other people constantly.'

'Having them around means that you're in danger of being hurt again?'

'I was an only child, so I've been in a lot of ways a loner. I've never liked crowds. At work we have a great many social activities and I generally don't go. I don't like big groups. I like to be with small groups. I don't feel I need a lot of people. I need two or three friends, I like to share good times. They feel better when they're shared. That's why I don't like to go to the theatre alone.'

We went on talking and I said, 'I expect you and your therapist have talked about how angry you were with those who didn't protect you from your father.'

'I don't think we ever talked about that. My mother left when I was ten. The abuse had been going on for a couple of years. Maybe I am angry with the old girl. But I like her enormously. We're great friends.'

'That's the great problem. It's much easier to be angry with someone you don't like. When we're angry with someone we love it's a terrible conflict, and when it's somebody we care about and feel sorry for – as we get older, we see our mothers as frail little old ladies – we wouldn't want to do anything to hurt them. But there's still that anger.'

'You may have found something. Maybe I am angry with her. It doesn't ring any bells, but maybe it's part of it.'

'When we're little, what we expect from our mother is that she's going to be there all the time and that she's going to solve all the problems and she'll look after us properly. We come into the world with the belief that that's what mothers do. I suppose we get it initially when we're in the womb because then our mother is actually doing that. She is being the perfect protector and is always there. So when we emerge we think she's still going to do that. But, of course, she fails to do that and then we get angry with her. Just in the ordinary run of things we all as children get very angry with our mothers because they fail us. They've got to fail us, otherwise we would never separate from them, but that doesn't prevent us from being angry. We want to be independent while being secure, and so we get angry when she prevents us from being independent and we get angry when she fails to provide us with total security. But if there's something more that happens, then we can't but help ask the question why didn't she protect me? It's this problem that it's not possible to have one good parent and one bad parent. Because if you've got a parent who is bad to you and the good parent does not protect you, then in fact you have two bad parents.'

'Yes, it's making sense. She left and I wasn't even aware of being angry with her for leaving. At the time she left I didn't throw temper tantrums.'

'You were left with your father?'

'Yes. I didn't express anger, hurt, yes, but not anger. Later on I went to boarding school for a year and she would come every single Sunday to see me. I think that's the main reason I never got angry with her.'

'There's another reason for not getting angry. When you're a People Person, as I sometimes call them, anger is a dangerous emotion because that's the emotion which will drive people away from you. So with People Persons not experiencing anger, or labelling anger as something else, labelling it as fear, is common.'

I said to Ruth, 'If you could paint a picture of what you feel when you're depressed, what sort of picture would you paint?'

'Because I don't visualize well at all that's a very difficult one for me. Can I paint you a word picture? It's an emptiness in the pit of the stomach, and an inability to concentrate on anything, and a jumble of thoughts, a great deal of lethargy. I'm now beginning to get a picture of a bloated child with a hole down the middle of her stomach, sort of one of those starvation pictures with a big bloated belly, but there's a hole. That's the best I can do visually. It's an emptiness. It's a feeling of lack of control about my own life. I can't make it better. I can't make it work. I can't solve the problem.'

'I get a picture of a child, when you said emptiness, there's emptiness around the child. There's also that lack of control in that when you were a little girl having these things done to you, you weren't in control of that. That's complete helplessness.'

'I like to believe that, but I think I could have controlled it if I'd tried.'

'How old were you?'

'I think eight. I certainly could have controlled it later on and I certainly could have controlled it then simply by saying go away. Maybe I didn't know that then, but I know that now.'

'That's the difference. When we're children and in the power of adults we experience a terrible helplessness.'

Now I asked Ruth how she imagined death would be.

'Peace. It's just peace. I have no fear of it at all. If we decide to have an atomic war I want to be right under it when it falls. Death is peace, an end to all the hassle.'

Ruth clearly understood that she experienced her sense of existence as a relationship to other people, and hence other people were essential to her. But other people had hurt her badly, so to protect herself she had withdrawn from people, and maintained only those relationships, like those at work, where she was in control. Her feeling of being used, rejected and abandoned, and her suspicion that this was what she deserved created in her a sense of emptiness, mirrored in her image of herself as a starving, empty, lonely child.

As a small child Ruth knew that she needed other people to give her her sense of existence. So when her father used her as an object to relieve his own sexual needs, she dared not refuse, even though she hated him for what he did. Such an experience has been described by Sylvia Fraser in her autobiography *My Father's House*:

My arms stick to my sides, my legs dangle like worms as my daddy forces me back against his bed. I love my daddy. I hate my daddy. Love hate love hate. Daddy won't love me love me hate hate hate. I'm afraid to strike him with my fists. I'm afraid to tell my mommy. I know she loves Helen because she is good, but she doesn't like me because I am dirty dirty. Guilt fear guilt fear fear dirty dirty fear fear fear fear fear.[15]

Like Sylvia, Ruth dealt with her rage against her father and her disappointment and anger with her mother by blaming herself and by trying to deny her anger. Again, like Sylvia, to recover her sense of being a whole, valuable and acceptable person she would need to let herself feel her anger at being so badly used, and through that find forgiveness for herself and those who took advantage of her innocence.

To an outside observer, George's depression, sleeplessness and inability to concentrate, and Ruth's depression and suicide attempts seem inexplicable, crazy even. But once we know the *reasons* which gave rise to these actions it becomes clear why they lost confidence in themselves and why George cannot sleep or concentrate and Ruth seeks the peace of death. Not only can we understand *why*, but we can see how change is possible. Reasons are not fixtures. They are ideas which we have created, and since we created them, we can change them.

However, quite often we create our reasons without bringing them clearly into consciousness. Often we take our basic reason – how we experience our sense of existence and see the threat of annihilation – so much for granted that we never think about it. What we all need to do is to make our basic reason quite clear to ourselves. We need to know what our priorities are.

If you don't already know this about yourself, you can work it out by choosing something that is important to you and asking, 'Why is this important?', and, with the answer, asking again, 'Why is this important?', until you can go no further, for you have arrived at

(D 2)　your reason for living.

For example, take the statement, 'I like to keep my home clean and tidy'. Lots of us do, but we differ on the reason why.

To the question, 'Why is it important to keep your home clean and tidy?', some of us would answer in terms of other people. We might say, 'I think a clean and tidy home is always inviting, and I want my friends to like coming here', or 'I wouldn't want people to think I was dirty and untidy. They wouldn't like me if they thought that about me.' To the question, 'Why is it important to you that your friends visit you/like you?', we might say, 'Because having friends/ being liked is what life is about.' If asked, 'What would happen to you if everyone rejected you and no one liked you?' we might say, 'That would be the end of me', or 'I would cease to exist', or 'I would disappear, just wither, fade away'.

To the question, 'Why is it important to keep your home clean and tidy?', the rest of us would answer in terms of control, organization and fear of chaos. We might say, 'A clean and tidy home is an efficient home, and I need to be efficient to achieve', or 'Mess makes me feel nervous. Once I've tidied up and got things under control I feel better.' To the question, 'Why is it important to achieve/get things under control?', we might say, 'That is the purpose of life'. If asked, 'What would happen to you if you could not achieve anything and everything got out of control?', we might say, 'I'd fall to pieces, I'd shatter, I'd crumble to dust'.

Sometimes I call the first group *People Persons* and the second group *What Have I Achieved Today Persons* (that is, to sleep soundly after reviewing their day, they have to feel that they have achieved something, even if it was no more than tidying the kitchen cupboards).

Sometimes I use the words 'extravert' and 'introvert'.

Extraverts and Introverts

'Extravert' here is spelt with an 'a' and not an 'o', which is the more usual spelling. There is a very important reason for this. It refers to the way we live all the time in two realities.

Our two realities are:

External reality, that is, everything that goes on around us,
and

Internal reality, that is, our internal experience of our thoughts, feelings and images.

These two realities have a quality of *realness*. They can seem totally real, or less than totally real, right through to not seeming real at all.

To function efficiently we need to perceive both our realities as real and *equally real*. We need to be sure that, 'This is what is happening around and to me, and this is what I think, feel and imagine'.

Unfortunately, perceiving both our realities as equally real is not something that comes to us as naturally as breathing. It is something which comes only when we strive to understand the world we live in and to understand ourselves. However, no matter how efficient we become in maintaining our two realities as real and equally real, when we are under stress we find that we retreat to our original position where one reality was more real than the other.

Which reality is the more real relates to how we experience our sense of self and perceive the threat of the annihilation of our self.

Those of us who experience our sense of self as being a member of a group direct our attention outward to external reality. Hence the word *extravert*, where 'vert' is from the Latin 'to turn' and 'extra' means 'outward'.

Those of us who experience our sense of self as the progressive development of individuality direct our attention inward. Hence the word *introvert*, where 'vert' means 'to turn' and 'intro' means 'inward'.

(The word 'extrovert' is often used to mean lively, talkative, sociable, and the word 'introvert' to mean shy, quiet, reserved. It is important to remember that many extraverts are shy and unsociable, while many introverts, as I have defined them, are sociable and talkative. If, as an extravert, you do not think well of yourself, you are likely to be shy and unsociable, while, as an introvert, if you have realized the importance of learning social skills, you are likely to be lively and talkative.)

The reality to which our attention is turned seems to us not merely more real but safer and more trustworthy.

Extraverts never doubt the reality of external reality. It is internal reality they find unreal, and they often fear to journey inward. Extraverts who have not confronted their internal reality and made inward journeys of exploration will say of themselves, 'I don't know who I am', or, 'Inside me is nothing but emptiness', or, 'I play roles; I'm never just me', or, 'You can go into these things too deeply', or, 'I have examined myself too deeply'. The television producer Michael Grade, writing in *The Guardian* about 'Me and My Psyche' said:

> I don't internalize anything. I work and live all my relationships on instinct, which later takes me a long time to work out. Sometimes it doesn't happen for years. I know something is going on in my subconscious which leads me to make different choices, because life is all about choices of one kind and another, but what finally informs those choices – upbringing, experience, character – I just have no idea . . . I'm one of life's pacifiers. I can't work by diktat, I like consensus, but I'm bad at getting in touch with my own emotional feelings.[16]

Their profound dislike of being alone leads extraverts to develop ways of keeping people around them. Needing to be liked, they become extremely likeable and charming. Some extraverts are contented to get by with being charming and agreeable, but many others, wanting to give something of value in return for people's regard, work very hard and strive to achieve. Extraverts who have some doubts about their own self-worth believe that, if you cannot make people love you, you can make them need you. Helping other people 'feels good', as Ruth said, because it makes us feel better about ourselves and it creates a bond between ourselves and the people we help.

Extraverts whose doubts about their own self-worth are even greater, and whose fear of other people is thus as great as their need, people their life with other relationships. They keep pets, or surround themselves with objects like books, pictures, clocks or clothes, or they immerse themselves in a hobby, and in all these activities they turn the animals and objects into human beings. (We all have this imaginative capacity to turn animals and objects which are indifferent to our existence into human beings like ourselves. Doing this can make our world much more comfortable than it actually is, but, equally, we can make our environment seem humanly hostile.)

Sometimes the people to whom the extravert relates are characters from soap operas, or pop stars, or fantasy figures. Often, when ordinary life is boring or unpleasant, extraverts immerse themselves in fantasies. These fantasies always relate to external reality and are tales of daring, glamour and excitement where the extravert is the admired and loved cynosure of all eyes. Thus, in many different ways, extraverts seek to make sure that they never find themselves completely alone. They do all they can to avoid the feeling of their self withering, fading and disappearing.

Introverts never say they have examined themselves too much. Examining themselves is the very stuff of their existence. They may not be examining themselves in terms of id and ego, or how they construct their world of meaning, as we learn to do in the course of therapy. Instead, they may be examining themselves, like George, in terms of their relationship to God, or in terms of their moral duties, or in terms of achieving the goals they have set. Whatever terms they use in this moral inspection, their activity is concerned with setting themselves standards and trying to meet those standards.

Throughout this inward journey of inspection, introverts never doubt the realness of their internal reality. Under stress, when they feel that everything is falling into chaos, introverts feel themselves shattering, fragmenting, crumbling even to dust, but never

disappearing. Dust they may be, but dust is still there. Some
introverts, when they become depressed, describe their self as
becoming 'two-dimensional', like a piece of cardboard, but without
depth. This is a horrible experience, but the self is still experienced
as being there.

It is external reality which introverts find unreal. We (for I am one)
look on external reality as being a passing phantasmagoria whose
realness and regularity we have to take on trust. Those of us who
cope with living have learned to act *as if* external reality is real.
However, we still get tripped up by our doubts.

One New Year's Eve I was staying with my friends Ron and Diana
in New York. They were planning a New Year party, and Ron said
he wanted to invite a colleague who he knew lived in the same
apartment block. 'I meet him in the elevator often,' Ron said, 'but I
don't know his apartment number. I'll have to find out from the
doorman.'

I was with Ron when he asked the doorman about the apartment
number. The doorman searched his list and said, 'No, there's no one
of that name in the building.' At Ron's insistence he checked the
mailroom list, and there, too, there was no record of this man's
name.

I was curious as to how Ron was reacting to this. Ron, I knew, was
an extravert. When I ventured a question, Ron said, 'There's some
sort of mix-up. I'm sure he lives in this building.'

'Do you wonder that perhaps you might have just imagined that
you've seen him here?' I asked, knowing that in Ron's position I
would have immediately felt that I had got this bit of external reality
wrong.

Ron thought that this was a stupid question, barely meriting a
reply. He never doubted the evidence of his senses. Of course he
was right about where his colleague lived. The doorman's list
proved to be incomplete.

Introverts like me need extraverts like Ron to keep us in touch
with external reality. I was reminded of this a few days later when,
as I was preparing to leave the elevator on the fifteenth floor to let
myself into Ron and Diana's apartment, the key slipped from my
fingers, teetered on the edge of the elevator floor, and then disappeared down the gap between the elevator and the corridor.
Immediately my surroundings became unreal. I could not believe
that the key could disappear in this way. I looked at my empty hand,
the space where the key had gone, and did not believe it. It was not a

matter of intellectually not believing it. The actual quality of my surroundings had changed. I could not be certain where I was or what was happening.

Many introverts when external reality becomes unreal simply do not act. They stay still, or seek the least untrustworthy place they can find, like their own room, and resist other people's efforts to get them to act, for they dare not risk an action in a reality they do not trust and which might bring disaster. However, what some of us learn to do is to act *as if* what we see is as it is. This is risky, for we could get things badly wrong, but it does mean that we can have a chance of acting sensibly.

So I acted as if what I saw was real. I went down in the elevator and told the doorman what had happened. He was very kind and phoned the maintenance man to come and let me into the apartment. I waited in the foyer, then chatted with the maintenance man as we went upstairs and he unlocked the door. But all the time everything around me felt unreal, and it was not until I was back in the apartment that my surroundings became real again.

For extraverts, the loss of internal reality is terrifying and disabling. There is a sense of a playing of a role, or many roles, but without an actor, or of an internal emptiness like that depicted in Ruth's image. One woman told me how she feared to look in a mirror, lest when she did there would be no one there.

Rebecca, an immensely likeable, very intelligent, very successful graduate student, called her uncertainty about her internal reality 'the impostor complex', a term popular with graduate students at the University of California at Santa Barbara.

Rebecca told me how the impostor complex 'means somebody who is successful who feels that they are only pretending, that they are going to be found out eventually, that people will discover they're not as bright or as worthwhile as they're meant to be. I just worry that I will eventually reach a level where people will just decide that I'm not doing as well as I think I am, or that I'm not as bright as I think I am, or other people said I am. The more time goes on, the more intense this feeling seems to be, the more I seem to accomplish, the more intense the feelings seem to be. I guess it's just the natural fear of not being as successful as I want to be.

'Why is it important to you to be successful?'

'To make myself feel that what I'm doing is worthwhile, that

I'm making some contribution, and to make my parents proud of me. To feel that I'm the equal of people around me. I think a lot of it has to do with low self-esteem. I think that people maybe will like me better if I have accomplished all these things.'

'Why is it important that people like you?'

'It makes me feel good. It makes me feel unhappy if I think people don't like me.'

Later in our conversation Rebecca said to me, 'I don't feel that I am intellectually all that gifted. I think that I work very hard and I think I am successful because I work hard, and I think I should be proud of it. If I was very gifted and I could learn French or Latin because I had a gift for languages, I'd have no right to be proud of it, but because I work very hard at it I feel entitled to feel proud.'

This comment arose from our discussion about the fundamentalist religion in which Rebecca had been raised. In explaining how many of us grow up with the belief that we have to earn the right to exist, I said, 'Some of us are taught quite actively that we don't have the right to exist. There's a lot of Christian teaching which says that we have to be grateful to God for giving us the gift of life.'

'That's how I was brought up. It was that you were nothing and humans were wicked and you were totally unworthwhile. You were supposed to think of yourself as absolutely dead last and everybody else was more important than you were. You had to achieve for the glory of God. What you do is not for your own glory. You don't even do what you do. God allows you to do it. He gives you the strength to do it. If things were taken away from you this was something the Devil did, or it was God allowing you to be tested. Anything bad happening to you is probably your own fault.'

I commented, 'You're describing how, for all you've achieved, you haven't achieved it at all. It's simply that God's allowed you to achieve it, and that makes you a kind of impostor.'

However, Rebecca's uncertainty about what she had a right to claim for herself was rooted not just in her early upbringing but in how she experienced herself. She said, 'I feel that a lot of my concern about what other people feel about me, is that I feel I need to know what other people think of me so as to see what

I'm really like, that I'm not capable of making an accurate judgement of what I'm really like, that it's other people's cumulative judgement that decides what a person is like, what I am like. I just don't trust my own judgement. I always think that my judgement is going to be skewed because I can't see how I act. I can't see how I appear to other people. I worry that I do things not meaning to insult people, but I just act so that they feel insulted and so they don't like me. I worry that my own perception of reality is not the correct one.'

'Do you worry about your perception of external reality?'

'Not too much, no. I can have very definite opinions about what other people are like and make judgements about them, and feel certain that I'm right, but about myself I'm tentative, I guess. I'd like to see how I looked from the outside, because the way you perceive yourself can be quite different from the way that other people perceive you, and I really would like to know how I come across to other people.'

Earlier in our conversation I had asked Rebecca, 'Suppose you weren't able to achieve anything and you found that everybody disliked you, what would happen to you?'

'I think I would get very depressed. When I get depressed I quit eating, I get real lethargic, I sleep a lot, I just sort of break into tears, I wouldn't be able to function, and I think I would be an unpleasant person to be around. I think many people who know that people don't like them are unpleasant people to be around. If I became convinced on a long-term basis that I was useless and that nobody liked me, I suppose I could become one of those people who just sort of has a job and doesn't talk to anybody and has no friends and lives with her cats. If it went on I think I would want to go to sleep and not wake up.'

Now Rebecca said, 'I don't know that I felt I never had the right to exist. It was more like, there was no point to existence. It was more like a very empty existence, where nobody cared about you.'

I have written extensively about the different ways in which extraverts and introverts perceive themselves and their world, and I have lectured about this frequently, but, no matter how clear I try to be, I am never clear enough, for quite a few people still say to me, 'I don't know whether I am an introvert or an extravert'. (Equally, quite a few people have told me that they know precisely which of my descriptions apply to them.)

Part of the problem is a misunderstanding. I am not talking about types of people, but about different kinds of reasons. Extraverts and introverts can all act in much the same way, but they differ in the reasons for their actions.

For example, some introverts and some extraverts might all dislike being away from home. However, the reason introverts dislike being away from home is that in a new place they do not have the control and organization which they have at home, and the reason extraverts dislike being away from home is that in unfamiliar surroundings, where they have few connections with other people, they are driven into themselves, and this can be disturbing. (This problem with unfamiliar places was pointed out to me by my friend Jo, an extravert, who was about to set out on a journey through Botswana.)

Extraverts and introverts might all want to achieve but extraverts need for achievement is in terms of other people ('If I achieve other people will not reject me'), and introverts need for achievement is in terms of 'that's what life is about'. Introverts and extraverts all want to have good relationships with other people, but introverts need other people to keep them in touch with external reality, while extraverts need other people because 'that's what life is about'.

Another reason why some people are confused as to how they experience their sense of existence and perceive the threat of an-nihilation is that they have difficulty distinguishing *what they do feel* from *what they ought to feel*.

My friend Candida described this to me in a letter:

I have just finished reading *The Successful Self* and want to tell you that I found your book inspiring and challenging but, unlike your others, frustrating too. Frustrating because I found myself lurching from introvert to extravert characteristics! So much of what you said made sense: the expectations of others, for example. My birthday is at the beginning of August and ever since I can remember my mother has told me: 'You're a Leo. Leo's are warm and loving, and such extraverts!' Or 'Nonsense, you're just being silly – Leo's are *full* of self confidence'. Can you imagine how I felt at eight, eighteen, or even twenty-eight? Crippled by shyness in the centre of a crowd, but knowing I was supposed to be the centre of attention, I invariably said something stupid and made a fool of myself. If that was being the centre of attention, I didn't like it! Similarly, I have always been told that I am not musical (my mother, again): 'We're not a musical family and you're tone deaf.' Hence, no singing lessons or piano lessons at school and whenever I sang at home – in the bath, in my room – my parents clapped their hands over their ears in mock horror. My lack of singing ability is still a family joke. And still, many years on, I wonder whether I can *really* be as tone deaf as they thought: I *love* music, especially classical music and opera.

What didn't make sense in the book was the way I kept wavering between each category, introvert and extravert. I know, for example, that I experience my existence as a member of a group, but I feel I *should* experience it in terms of individual achievement. Am I a guilty extravert? I can certainly rush around, making myself busy, but I'm also brilliant at worrying about what might happen in the future, looking at every possibility and trying to work out in advance what I'd do. There were *so* many examples where I identified as an introvert then turned the page to find an extravert characteristic that fitted. Maybe I'm a reluctant extravert who admires, and therefore wants to identify with, introvert characteristics.

Knowing yourself is very difficult when you have always had powerful people around you telling you what they think you are.

Why We Need to Know Ourselves

As I travelled in the USA and talked with many different women I was struck by how frequently a woman would mention how she feared that she might become a bag-lady. I thought that only American women had this fear until I saw the British television series *Behaving Badly*, where the middle-aged heroine Bridget, played by Judi Dench, was spurred into living her life on her own terms (that is, according to her family, behaving badly) by the sight of an English bag-lady, though in this case the bag was an old pram.

We can all become bag-ladies, down-and-outs, or lonely, dissatisfied, unhappy people because we have failed to take account of what we need most in our lives and have failed to ensure that, at least to some significant degree, our needs are met.

However, to meet our needs we must first know what they are. We can all say, 'My needs are to achieve *and* to have strong relationships with other people', but what actually happens is that time and time again we have to make a choice between the two.

As a child, will you pursue your own interests or go along with your friends?

At school, will you study the subjects that interest you, or please your parents by studying the subjects they think are important?

In choosing your first job or your college, will you leave your family?

(D 3) What will you put first, your career or your family?

If you make your choices according to what you think you ought to do, rather than according to what is right for you, no matter how successful you might appear to others to be, you will be dissatisfied and unhappy.

If you experience your sense of existence as being a member of a group, but you feel that you ought to strive for individual success and achievement, then as soon as you reach a position of authority or individual success, you know that you are in danger. People will dislike you when you exercise your authority and will envy, often spitefully, your success. Of course you can decide most wisely that it is possible to survive without absolutely everyone liking you, but, until you do, choosing individual achievement before personal relationships will cost you dear.

If you experience your sense of existence in terms of the development of individual achievement, clarity and authenticity, but you feel that you ought to devote your life to your family or the care of other people, then as you discover that your devotion to the careers of your spouse and children does not make their success your success, or that the repetitious tasks of housekeeping and caring for others do not create a sense of achievement, you know that you are in danger. Until you clear a space in your life where you can cultivate some activity which does give you some sense of individual achievement, choosing personal relationships before individual achievements will cost you dear.

We need to know what our priorities are so that:

1. We can guard against our greatest fear.

2. We can enjoy what matters to us most.

Among those of you who are depressed, there are many extraverts who, having failed to maintain old friends and to make new ones, find yourselves alone, bereft of family and friends. Also, there are many introverts who, believing that you have no right to organize your own life, find yourselves in situations where you have no control and no sense of achievement.

Often we get ourselves into such unpleasant, debilitating situations because we are so frightened of our greatest fear that we never allow ourselves to discover that what we fear is not as fearful as we thought.

As extraverts we need to learn to make the journey inward, into our internal reality, so as to discover that there is nothing there to fear but something there to value, the capacity to be alone.

As introverts we need to learn that we do not need to keep the entirety of external reality organized and under control in order to make it safe, and that we can acquire social skills which enable us to act on external reality effectively and to relate to other people easily and without the need to control them.

Along with this is a task which we must all undertake. We must learn to value and accept ourselves.

The more we value and accept ourselves, the less we are under the threat of the annihilation of our self.

Extraverts who value and accept themselves know that other people will value and accept them, and that if death and disaster or just the changes that life brings take away the people whom they love and rely on, they can make other relationships because they have within themselves something of value to offer.

Introverts who value and accept themselves know that they are able to achieve what they want to achieve, and that if death and disaster or just the changes that life brings prevent them from achieving or destroy what they have achieved, they can change their plans and try again because they have within them the power to do so.

Extraverts who believe that they are bad and valueless believe that all other people will sooner or later discover this and so rejection and abandonment is inevitable, and they will be left completely alone.

Introverts who believe that they are bad and valueless believe that no matter how hard they try to organize, control and achieve, it is inevitable that they will fail and fragment as everything falls into chaos.

Whenever we lose confidence in ourselves the threat of the annihilation of our self comes upon us and we feel the greatest fear.

Why do we lose confidence in ourselves? Why do we feel that we are not good enough, not acceptable, bad, perhaps even evil?

4

Believing That We Are Not Good Enough

We all, as babies, entered the world knowing that we had the right to exist. We were there, so we had the right. We were there, and we accepted ourselves. We valued ourselves, so when we felt discomfort we did what we could to look after ourselves. Crying, yelling and thrashing about were usually effective in getting the relief we needed. We did not waste time asking ourselves, 'Do I have the right to exist?', and, 'Dare I ask for anything for myself?', questions which bedevil and sometimes ruin the lives of a great many adults.

As babies we could not have wasted time on such nonsensical questions because we were too busy doing something else – making sense of what was happening around us and to us.

Making sense of what happens around us and to us is like breathing – something we do every moment we are alive and something we cannot not do. Even when we have dulled our senses with alcohol or drugs, or when our brain has suffered injury, we still go on making sense of everything, even though the sense we make in dreams, or stupor, or confusion is not very sensible.

We start making sense of everything when, in the womb, our little, developing cortex begins functioning as a cortex. In the womb we make some kind of sense of the warmth and darkness, being held and having our needs met, but when we make our journey into light we have a great deal more to make sense of.

When we are born we have to learn quite complex things, like what is close to us and what is far away. However, while we cannot tell whether a round object is a ball close enough to touch or the moon shining through the window, there is something we know straight away. We know what a face is. Indeed, if some psychologist shows us cartoon drawings of faces and other things when we are only five days old, we can tell which are the faces, and we go on

42

looking at them because we find faces the most interesting things in our world.

Faces are the most interesting to us as babies because they respond to us. We engage them in conversation, and we are very good at this when we are babies because we know that we need continuing conversations in the way that we need air, food and water. Conversations are fascinating, exciting, and, in making sense of everything, the most challenging. A rattle is a rattle, but what does Mummy mean?

The process of making sense of everything happening around us and to us can be called the making of meaning. We each create our own world of meaning, and there is no way while we are alive that we can step out of this world of meaning. Even when we say that something is meaningless we give it a meaning, that is, 'The meaning of this thing is that it cannot be fitted easily into my world of meaning'. We live in meaning like a fish lives in water.

The way we make meaning is that we divide the seamless, moving, changing limitless *everything that is* into sections. We label these sections, and then evaluate them.

For instance, at present I am looking at the scene outside my window. According to the way I have divided this scene, it comprises trees, and, beyond that, cars and students going by. My division of the scene into trees, cars and students obscures the fact that the trees, cars, students and me are all linked together by a substance I cannot see but can sometimes feel, the air which we each take in, use and let out. The ways in which cars, people and trees take in, use and release air are intimately related in chemical reactions sometimes to their mutual benefit and sometimes not. Moreover, this scene has much more meaning for me than just being made up of objects and people. Everything I look upon has some special value for me. The leaves are turning yellow, and so the scene appears to me to be both sad and beautiful. I am pleased that the old almond tree in my garden has survived an unpleasant disease, and each car and each student suggests a multitude of associations with experiences I have had at other times and in other places.

The meanings we create are not just descriptive and evaluative. They are *predictions* about what we expect our future will be.

Every time something happens to us, or we do something, we draw a conclusion. Then we use that conclusion to guide us in the future.

For instance, this morning I needed to do some shopping in a particular part of town. I decided to park my car in a garage that I had never used before. Since it was early morning I predicted from the conclusions I had drawn from my past experience of garages that I would be able to park on one of the lower floors. However, when I drove in, I found that most of the floors were reserved for the government offices next door and that I had to park my car on the roof. I drew the conclusion that this was too inconvenient a garage to use when shopping and resolved never to use it again.

Like everyone else, I have been creating meaning and thus predictions ever since my brain started working. Our first conclusion, formed when we were a foetus, must have been, 'I'm alive!', though, of course, we drew this conclusion in feelings and images and not in words. The prediction we formed from this conclusion was, 'I intend to stay alive', little knowing what dangers would assail us and what stratagems we would have to devise to stay alive. Staying alive was not just a matter of keeping our body alive. Our 'I' had to stay alive, for to be a body, however lively, without being an 'I' is not to be alive.

We draw conclusions from our first sight of the world that we are born into. My friends, Deborah and Scott, decided that their baby should be born into, not the clinical coldness of a hospital, but the warmth and friendliness of the Birth Center in Philadelphia. As they described it to me, Scott was there, ready to receive the baby when the top of her head appeared. Another push, and Scott found himself being appraised by two steady blue eyes. He was quite sure that he was being assessed, and it was not until the baby decided in a look which clearly said, 'That's all right', that she became free of her mother and was lifted to meet her mother's astonished gaze and smile. Even when little Hannah was busy nuzzling her mother's breast, she continued to gaze at her adoring, enchanted parents.

If we are lucky, like Hannah, in our choice of parents and the time and place of our birth, the first conclusion we draw about the world we have entered is that it is warm, loving and ready to meet our needs. We carry this conclusion with us for the rest of our lives, although as we get older we need to modify this conclusion so that it is now, 'The world is only sometimes warm, loving and ready to meet my needs'.

If we are unlucky, like babies born in times of war and famine or to mothers who are too distracted by their own problems to envelop the baby in love, our first conclusion about the world is that it is cold, hostile and unable or unready to meet our needs. It is hard to maintain our sense of self-worth in such a world, and so a baby drawing such a conclusion soon loses the self-confidence with which he entered the world. He becomes frightened and, if he continues to feel that he is punished and defeated by a hostile world, he finds that the only way he can protect his sense of 'I' is to isolate himself in the prison of depression. Thus many children, born in unhappy circumstances, live their lives in a state of depression.

The cure for such children, as it is for adults, is to help them discover, through experiences of joy, kindness and love, that their conclusion that, 'The world is always cold, hostile and unable or unwilling to meet my needs' is just as wrong as the conclusion, 'The world is always warm, loving and ready to meet my needs'. The first conclusion leads to fear and the second to disappointment.

The conclusion that we need to draw is that the world is some-times cold, hostile and unable or unready to meet our needs, and sometimes warm, loving and ready to meet our needs, and that we should develop efficient ways of assessing and dealing with the dangers and opportunities that the world presents.

Our biggest handicap in reaching this conclusion is that we do not always go back and check our conclusions. I am certainly not going to visit that garage every week or so to check whether those government cars still have priority. Even more so, when our con-clusions are drawn from especially happy or especially sad or dangerous situations, we do not want to go back and reassess. If you as a child have concluded that your grandfather was a great guy you don't want to look back and see that he was a miserable old man who gave your grandmother a bad time. Similarly, you don't want to recall the events which made you so frightened of the world.

There is another important reason why we do not want to go back and reassess our conclusions. We don't want to be constantly reminded how chancy and changeable our world is. We like to feel that some things stay the same.

When we wake up in the morning we don't want to have to check the conclusion we made years ago that, 'If it's snowing outside I'd better put on something warm.' When we make our morning coffee we don't want to have to check the conclusion we made as a child, 'Don't put your hand in boiling water.'

There also isn't time to check our every conclusion to see if it still applies to the new situation. Yet we have to use our conclusions constantly to make sense of every new situation and deal with it. It is strange how many people question whether our childhood has any influence on us in adult life. If they thought about it they would realize that:

All we can bring to a new situation is our past experience.

The past experience which we use all the time includes our experience as a child.

So, while we do abandon some of the conclusions we drew in childhood – like believing in Father Christmas or thinking that our 23-year-old teacher is very, very old – there are many conclusions that we never check and which we go on using to make sense of a new situation and to deal with it.

So, just as we, when we wake up, don't see any need to check the conclusions we drew, years ago, about the weather and clothes, or about taking care with boiling water, so we don't see any need to check the conclusion we drew about ourselves when we were children.

Now some of us had parents and teachers who were always kind and supportive, and some of us had parents and teachers who were demanding, critical and punitive, some of us had a happy and secure childhood, and some of us had an insecure and unhappy childhood, but, whatever, we each drew the same conclusion about how a child and an adult must try to behave.

This conclusion which each of us drew as a child and which underlies everything we think, feel and do is:

Because I am not acceptable as I am, I must work hard to be good so I can live with myself and not have other people criticize and reject me.

These are my words. Each of us feels, expresses and acts upon it in our own individual way.

We each differ in what we mean by *being good*.

Some of us would not use the words 'being good', but instead think in terms of setting goals and achieving them. Nevertheless, failure seems like badness and weakness. Tom blamed himself when his firm let him go. George sets himself goals in studying the scripture so as to be acceptable to God. Ivan Boesky set himself the goal of gaining great wealth and, while being tried and sentenced for illegal stock exchange dealings, explained, 'I think greed is healthy. You can be greedy and still feel good about yourself.'[17]

Some of us would not talk of 'being good', but of meeting our responsibilities and doing our duty. Nevertheless, failure to meet our responsibilities we see as wickedness. Pat did not think of herself as being good when she nursed her sick parents, but she did feel she was wicked to be angry with her sisters for not helping her.

Some of us would not talk of 'being good', but of being helpful to other people. Such helpfulness, as Ruth said, 'feels good'.

Some of us would not talk of 'being good', but of being acceptable to other people. This can mean always striving to be well groomed and properly dressed or, most frequently, always going along with what other people want and never simply pleasing yourself. Lisa, who worried about her appearance constantly, always tried to please other people and considered doing anything to please herself as selfish and therefore wicked. If she did dare to do something to please herself – like eating a cream cake – she felt guilty.

So here we all are, each in our own way, striving to be good.

Most of us are extremely good at being good. We work hard, achieving goals and immediately setting new ones, we meet our responsibilities to others, we consider other people's wishes before our own, we try to make our appearance attractive, we keep our homes clean and tidy, we strive to be unselfish, unaggressive, kind, loving, loyal, modest, generous, friendly, cheerful, understanding, patient, and punctual, and we try to teach these ways of being good to our children.

Most of us are so good at being good that we generally forget that all this striving to be good is in an effort to overcome our feeling that *as ourselves* we are not good enough, that we are bad, even evil, and certainly unacceptable to ourselves and to other people.

Nevertheless, if someone comments on how good we are, we must instantly disclaim it. We feel that we have to say, 'Oh, not really', and go on to talk about how incompetent we actually are, or how dependent we are on other people, or how we ought to achieve more, or how it is luck and not virtue or competence which enables us to do what we do. A few of us have learned to respond to a compliment with simply, 'Thank you', but even then the 'Thank you' must be said modestly, lest we be punished by those people who see it as their duty to humble the proud. Thus, no matter how good we are at being good, we can never be good enough.

No matter how good we are at being good, whenever we fail to be good – when we do not achieve our goals, when we make a mess of things, or let people down, or fail to please people, or people criticize, reject or abandon us, or when life does not turn out the way we expect it would – even if we do not directly blame ourselves for our failure, we become aware of a sense of badness and unacceptability. Then we feel very frightened, and we have to strive hard to put things right.

Where does this sense of badness and unacceptability come from? After all, when we were small babies we were pleased with ourselves. We existed, and we did not doubt that we had a right to exist. How was it that later we drew the conclusion that we were bad and unacceptable and that we had to spend our lives working hard to be good?

Drawing the Conclusion 'I Am Bad'

Sometimes we draw conclusions slowly, amassing evidence little by little, and gradually becoming certain that something is as it is. Sometimes something sudden and dramatic happens, and we know instantly and clearly what our conclusion is.

Sometimes someone says something to us and we realize that we are not as good as we thought we were. Anna told me how, when she was a small child, her mother contracted tuberculosis and so was in hospital for much of Anna's childhood. She said, 'When I was sent to boarding school I used to go to chapel and pray for my mother. This was during the Second World War and there was this other little girl and her father was in the navy. So we'd go and pray. She'd pray for her father and I'd pray that my mother would get well, and her father came home on leave. So I went to one of the nuns and I said, "Mary Jane's father's home but my mother's still in the hospital", and she said, "I guess you didn't pray enough, dear." How can these people say such things to children! They probably think it's good for your character. I just had a double worry then, that my mother was sick and that I hadn't prayed enough. I continued in that attitude, that I wasn't good enough.'

Pat accumulated the evidence that she was bad and unaccept-able slowly. She does not remember being a baby, but family photographs show her with her parents who look as though they loved her and were proud of her. Her first clear memory is of being shut out of her mother's bedroom and later being told that she had a baby sister. Her father is not present in this memory. She cannot remember ever sitting on her father's knee.

'He wanted a son,' she told me, 'I was a great disappointment to him. In later years he was very fond of my youngest sister –

she was very pretty, not like me – but I think he just felt uncomfortable in a house full of females. He spent all his time working, and when he took up golf we never saw him at weekends. Mother was affectionate to me, but she was always busy. The only way I could get any attention from her was to be useful. I've been doing housework for as long as I can remember.'

So Pat gradually formed the opinion that as herself she was valueless. Only what she could do for people had some value.

'I never consciously thought, "I am valueless",' she said. 'It was just something I *knew*, like I knew the sun would rise each morning. It was a fact of the universe. What I did think about was how I could please my mother and father. I thought that if I tried really hard to please them then they would be proud of me. I knew they loved me, but it was in a distant sort of way, like I loved my great aunt. She was a relative, so you were supposed to love her. I wanted to make them notice me and be proud of me. That's why I wanted to be a doctor.'

'Your father stopped you from being a doctor?' I said.

'Not stopped, like saying, "You can't". He just let me know in different ways that he didn't think that medicine was a suitable profession for a woman. And he told all of us that he couldn't afford to put us through university.'

'Were you angry with him?'

'Angry? Oh, no, I wouldn't dream of being angry with him. I was sure he was doing what he thought was best for me.'

Dan remembers very clearly the day he concluded that he was bad. It was the day his father died. Dan had just turned seven.

Dan said, 'My father was a great believer in "Spare the rod and spoil the child", and he was always taking a stick to me. My mother would get upset, and she and my grandmother especially would always try and make it up to me with some sort of treat. They usually made me feel I wasn't as bad as he said. Of course there were times when I deserved a beating – as a kid I was always getting into mischief – but sometimes I didn't. He had a quick temper and he'd just hit out. And you couldn't reason with him. Once he'd made up his mind he was going to give you a thrashing nothing you could say would make him change his mind.

'Well, it was just a week before my seventh birthday, and he came home on the Saturday evening and found a whole bed of young tomato plants all trampled down. He decided I'd done it. I hadn't. I'd been at a neighbour's house all afternoon because my mother and grandmother had gone to visit an aunt who'd had a baby. When he saw me coming in the front gate he just grabbed me by the collar and dragged me inside. Then he got his razor strop – do you remember those heavy leather straps that men used to use to sharpen their cut-throat razors on? – well, he just started in on me. I thought he was never going to stop. I was sure he was going to kill me. When he did stop, he shoved me in my bedroom and locked the door. I was crying and hurt, and I was so mad at him. When I knew he couldn't hear me I said out loud, "I hope you die. God, make him die." A week later he did. Had a heart attack and keeled over, dead. I knew I'd done it. I knew I was wicked. After that I just had to make up for being so wicked. That's why I've always worked so hard and why the place burning down really got to me. I thought that at long last I was being punished for my wickedness.'

When Dan had first come to see me, many months before he told me this story, his wife had said to me that she thought Dan had been too strict with their son Danny when he was a child. 'Nonsense,' Dan had said, 'children, especially boys, need a firm hand. My father often took the stick to me and it never did me any harm.'

We all, like Dan, have very convenient memories, or, rather, forgetories. We all can forget something that is too painful to remember. Thus many of us who concluded from one traumatic incident that we were bad have forgotten all about the incident.

Lisa had done this. When she first came to see me she described her childhood as idyllic and her parents as perfect. Months went by before she could tell me about her parents' quarrels, and many more months before she could allow herself to remember a terrible incident when she was five and her grandfather had undressed her, explored her genitals with his fingers, and then put his erect penis in her mouth. Lisa found it impossible to describe this clearly, but when she said, 'I thought I was going to choke to death', I guessed what had been done to her.

She told me that her grandfather was a minister and that her parents were very proud of him. He lived in another state, so a visit from him was a special occasion. On that particular day, her parents had to go out and her grandfather had offered to mind her. Her parents had instructed her that she had to be very obedient and do whatever her grandfather wanted her to do.

'I was very confused,' Lisa told me. 'I knew it was wrong to take your clothes off like that, but I didn't dare be disobedient. I thought that perhaps this was something ministers did and that I was stupid, that I wasn't doing it right.'

'Did you tell your parents?' I asked.

'I didn't dare. I thought they'd blame me. I hated him, but I wanted him to like me so he wouldn't turn my parents against me. I already knew they thought more of him than of me. He took over my bedroom when he came to stay and I slept on a couch on the back verandah, and they always served him first at meals and gave him second helpings. So I just kept it to myself and tried to forget it.'

My friend Jill had a similar experience and, like Lisa, did not tell her parents.

'I kept my mouth shut, until I was about nineteen or twenty. It was my mother's father. Everybody was reminiscing about him and deifying him. I'm not sure when it started, I might have been eight, it certainly was between when I was ten and twelve. It was just sick. I kept saying to my mother, "I don't want to go there, I don't want to go there." I finally got him caught by my grandmother, but then, of course, my grandmother would have nothing to do with me.'

These experiences left both Jill and Lisa extremely frightened and disgusted with themselves, but they each expressed this fear and disgust in different ways.

Lisa, being an extravert, 'ran away' from what was happening in her internal reality into her more real external reality. She always kept herself very, very busy. She had a full time job, kept her house perfect, and was a superb cook and dressmaker. She sought and made friends, and was a popular, sociable woman. The fear inside her could not be denied, however, and she located the source of her fear as being in the world around her. Lisa feared spiders and all creepy crawlies, she feared ugly people and anyone who was deformed in any way, she feared crowds and open spaces, and, most of all, she feared that everyone she loved and needed would reject her. She believed that no matter how hard she worked to make people love and need her, sooner or later they would discover that 'inside I'm foul and disgusting'.

Jill, being an introvert, was always concerned with achieving, and this she managed to do, even though from her earliest childhood she was always afraid.

She told me, 'I think I could be scared pretty easily as kid. If someone strange came to the door, I would hide under the bed.'

'What did your parents think about this?'

'They weren't picking it up. School was just hair-raising. I'd vomit every morning before I went to school. I was frightened about my ability to achieve.'

Jill did achieve. She took two degrees, became a university administrator, and married. But she was always anxious, always somewhat defensive with other people. She said, 'I was going all right until I was thirty-seven and then the bottom just dropped out. I remember being awakened at night. I knew something horrible was going to happen. I made the mistake of going to work that day and things got all out of proportion. People were looking at me, and I don't think I was acting too well. That night I came home and I couldn't sleep. There were cars coming round and I could see their lights and I thought they were checking on me. After that I went into hospital, altogether five times, and each time I was just given drugs. I'd get into these panic states and I'd go back in. I'd be running up and down the hall. I couldn't sleep. I'd get more and more frightened. I'd be thinking a lot of different things very fast, interactions I've had with my brothers and with my dad, a lot of different things, all frightening things. Then I'd get even more frightened. In hospital they'd have four, five, six people dragging me down in order to shoot me with something. And they put me in isolation. That was the worst experience. Suddenly people were following me and I was put into a locked ward. I don't know how long I was in there. I haven't been in hospital now for eight years or so. But it's terrible, I just stay in bed. I'm immobilized. I don't know what the drugs are doing for me. I guess I'm suicidal because not a day goes past but I think of ending it. The psychiatrist sees me about once every three months for a change of the pills. He just asks me how I am. It's terrible being at home day in and day out, but unfortunately I don't think it's terrible enough for me to try to get out of it.'

When terrible things happen to us we can find ways of coping with them and coming to terms with the results of them if the people around us acknowledge what is happening to us, allow us to talk about what is happening and how we feel about it, and confirm our value by giving us love and support. When bad things happen to introverts they need the people around them to help them sort out the confusion and to maintain the sense that external reality is real. Once external reality seems unreal, it becomes more and more difficult for introverts to distinguish between the thoughts in their internal reality and the events in their external reality.

All of us can have difficulty in distinguishing the enemies we actually have from our feelings of being persecuted. Introverts, when they find themselves in danger, can feel themselves persecuted by strangers or people with whom they have little connection. After all, it is better to see a stranger as an enemy that to see yourself as betrayed by those who should have cared for you.

Jill's experience was of parents who did not see what was happening to her, of a grandfather who exploited and despoiled her, of a grandmother who rejected her, of a mother who, though loving, says, 'That was long ago. You should be over it by now,' and a psychiatrist who has never listened to her story but who says, 'Keep taking your tablets. Psychotherapy is not appropriate for you.'

Although Jill and I had been friends for nearly ten years and had had some good times together, it was only on my last visit when her inactivity was impossible to hide that she told me about her childhood and her time in hospital. I had met a psychotherapist in Jill's home town who I knew would understand very readily what Jill had gone through, and I urged Jill to talk to her. But Jill refused. She expected, as she had always done, that once someone knew about her past that person would reject her. She risked telling me because I lived far away, but she would not reveal what she saw as her intrinsic badness to someone in her home town.

To talk about how Jill and Lisa felt about themselves and, similarly, how all of us, to some greater or lesser degree, feel about ourselves, I have to use words like 'bad', 'evil', 'worthless', 'unacceptable', but these do not convey what the experience of badness actually entails.

These words are simply outward signs of a very powerful internal experience. We each give this experience a structure by turning it into an image which we locate somewhere inside ourselves. There are, I guess, as many images for badness and unacceptability as there are people to hold them. The *kinds* of images I have come across are of:

a pit or swamp of utter foulness and blackness;

a translucent centre of purity, besmirched and befouled with black filth;

a small child, naked and alone, consumed by shame, encircled by contemptuous eyes;

a raging torrent of crimson and black fire which will devour all it touches, or a wild, primitive, raging beast which, when loosed, will hack, slice, smash, lay waste, and devour.

I have found that people who have no memory of ever being accepted and valued and whose depression is profound and long lasting have an image of their badness and unacceptability like the first kind, a foul pit or swamp.

People who have brought from childhood some sense of being valuable and acceptable but to whom hurtful, ugly things have happened have images of badness and unacceptability like the second kind, a besmirched pure centre.

People who in childhood have suffered intense shame and humiliation have an image of their badness and unacceptability like the third kind, a humiliated child.

People who in childhood have suffered the kind of experiences which aroused in them murderous hatred but which gave them no opportunity to discharge and resolve this murderous hatred in non-destructive ways (for instance, being punished for shouting, 'I hate you Mummy!') have an image of the fourth kind, a raging torrent or a wild beast.

No doubt there are many other kinds of images, just as there are many different kinds of conclusions we can draw about our childhood experience, and certainly our images can change. The first kind of image, so powerfully present in the immobility of deep depression, could, under provocation, change to the fourth kind, and the second kind, with a further series of crushing events, could change to the first kind.

Equally, the images change as we discover that what we saw as undiluted badness and unacceptability was nothing more than the conclusions we drew about ourselves in childhood and which no longer apply, and that those forces inside us which we were told were wicked are actually among our most valuable possessions, for they are the source of our strength, courage, creativity and our joy at being alive. The black swamp becomes a cavern filled with riches, the translucent centre is washed clean, the child is comforted and admired, the fire becomes a flame of purity and hope, and the beast a cuddly pet – or perhaps the images change in ways as many and various as the stars in the sky.

To change your image of your badness and unacceptability into an image of your worth and acceptability, it is helpful if you make the badness and unacceptability image clear. You might like to bring it clearly into your mind, or, going beyond that, describe it in words, or in a poem, a picture, a sculpture, or music. Whenever we bring something clearly into consciousness and then put it outside ourselves in words or in something we make, we take control of it and thus reduce its power.   **(D 4)**

Now it is much easier to ask, 'How did I acquire this image?'

What Pat, Anna, Dan, Lisa and Jill described of their early childhood is something which, to some greater or lesser extent, happened to all of us.

As small babies we were pleased with ourselves and we pleased ourselves. We slept when we were tired, were active when we felt active, emptied our bladder and bowels as soon as they were full, and, when we felt hunger or any discomfort, we voiced our displeasure and demanded that the world make us comfortable again. If we felt angry with our mother we bit her, and if we did not want to engage in conversation we turned our head away.

Some of us were lucky enough to have mothers who let us go on being ourselves for many months, but some of us were unlucky enough to have mothers who very soon stopped us from being ourselves. However, sooner or later, all of us as babies were shown that we could not go on pleasing ourselves and being pleased with ourselves. We had to conform to what society expected of us.

For some of us the first lesson came when we cried in hunger and were not fed. Perhaps we were not fed because our mother had no food, or perhaps because our mother had been told by people who considered themselves to be child care experts that babies should be fed according to a clock and not according to the baby's need. As we lay there, our little body creasing with hunger pangs, we drew the conclusion, in images if not in words, 'If I ask for something the world will not give it to me'.

Some of us were lucky enough to have mothers who met our need for food, but even we, sooner or later, encountered society's demands that we empty our bladder and bowels at special times and places. Some of us were lucky enough to have mothers who knew that we could not achieve this until our sphincter muscles were strong enough, and so they let us discover at our own pace that society's rules about cleanliness have some sense to them and can yield a feeling of achievement. However, some of us found that when we could not learn these rules quickly enough to please our mother we were called 'dirty and disgusting' and we were punished and humiliated. Whatever experiences we had, we all drew the conclusion that, 'No matter how I feel, I must make my bowels and bladder conform to what society expects'. For many of us 'what society expects' dominates our life, making us carry out rituals of cleanliness and trapping us in a sorry round of constipation and diarrhoea, all of which adds to our worry about how acceptable we are.

By showing us that we cannot expect to be fed just because we are hungry and that our bowels and bladder must conform to society's rules, our families force us to draw the conclusion that other people's wishes and needs must be met before our own. If we want something for ourselves we find ourselves being called 'selfish', and if we want what others have we are called 'greedy and envious'. Anyone who is selfish, greedy and envious is bad. If we observe that our families are expecting us to be unselfish in order that they can be selfish, we must keep that thought to ourselves, for if we do not we are punished and humiliated.

Rebecca said, 'I always felt manipulated. My father would want me to do something and I wouldn't want to do it, and he'd say, "You're thinking only of yourself". I'd think who do you think you're thinking of? There was one time when I was at college and I was at home and I had an argument with my brother and my mother would not intervene and I went to stay with my grandmother for several weeks because I was having a hard time at home. Then my mother called up and said, "I want you to come home. I feel abandoned. You're just thinking of yourself." I thought who the hell are you thinking of? I'm unhappy there. I'm happy here. What right do you have to ask me to be miserable so that you can be happy? I think that was pulled a lot on me as a child. Everything is justified by saying that your parents love you, your parents know best. If your parents love you, does that mean that they're asking you to do what is best for you? I wanted to be an anthropologist and my father thought that that was ridiculous. He would say I wouldn't get a job, I should go to medical school, or do accountancy, or something practical, and when I'd ask why he'd say, "I'm only thinking of you". I don't think he was thinking of me at all, but so many things were justified by him with "I'm thinking of you", "I'm doing it for you", "It's for your own good", "After all I've done for you".'

We all learn, too, quite early in life that we have something else bad inside us. This is anger and aggression. As a toddler we live in a world of giants who act in unpredictable ways, who continually put us in new and often frightening situations, who say things which we cannot understand, and who expect us to do things which we cannot do. Sometimes all of this overwhelms us and we can do nothing but fling ourselves down in despairing rage. If we are lucky the adults with us remember what it is like to be only two and they treat us kindly, but if we are unlucky (and many of us are) we get punished. We are hit, or locked up alone in a room. As well as frightening us, this puzzles us, for while the adult is saying, 'It is wicked to be angry', the adult is angry, and while the adult is saying, 'It is wicked to be violent', the adult is violent.

Adults may believe that they are teaching small children to be clean, considerate of others, unaggressive, and not to be selfish, greedy, envious or angry, but what children are actually doing is drawing the conclusion, 'I am not acceptable'. The child's birthright of self-confidence has begun to dwindle.

Sometimes parents, seeing one of their children in need, fail to see the conclusion another of their children is drawing.

Rebecca said, 'I have two brothers younger than me. I think my father valued Jimmy, the older of the two. He was like my father. My father never got along with my younger brother, Nick. He was an accident and he was ten days old when my father went to Vietnam for a year. They never seemed to bond and my father has never got along with him, but my mother has always defended him and paid a lot of attention to him, so I always felt that Jimmy was Dad's favourite and Nick was

Mother's favourite, because he was persecuted, and that left me out, although I know that as I'm a girl my mother feels close to me, but I never felt like anyone's favourite.'

One of the tasks of parents is to define aspects of the world for the child. They say, 'Don't eat that dirt.' 'That's hot. Don't touch it.' 'That dog might bite you.' They also define aspects of each child, like, 'You're a boy.' 'That's your bum.' 'As you get older you get taller.' Often in this defining they go beyond factual information and add their own value judgements, like, 'You're a bad boy.' 'Be careful how you touch your bum. It's dirty.' 'Big boys don't cry.' When, like Candida's mother (pp. 38–9), they define the child in ways which the child finds do not fit with her own experience of herself, the child, unable to reject what a powerful parent says, feels inadequate and unacceptable, just as Candida did when she could not be the outgoing, centre-of-attention person her mother insisted she was.

Many children find themselves being defined by adults in negative, rejecting ways. Pat, like many girls, found herself being defined as 'not valuable like a boy'. Dan found himself being defined as an object on which his father could take out his rage. Lisa and Jill found themselves being defined by their parents as being of less value than their grandfathers, and by their grandfathers as objects they could use to satisfy their sexual needs. Out of these experiences of humiliation the child draws the conclusion, 'I am of little value'.

These conclusions, 'I am not acceptable' and 'I am of little value', prepare the way for the conclusion 'I am bad', which we drew when we found ourselves trapped in a dangerous situation from which there was no escape.

The dangerous situation was one where we were helpless and in the power of strong adults who were inflicting pain on us and on whom we depended.

Perhaps, like Dan, we were being beaten, or, like Lisa and Jill, we were being sexually abused, or perhaps, like Pat, we were neglected and used. For some of us the adults were deliberately inflicting pain and humiliation on us for their own ends, although for others the adults could do nothing else, for they were starving, or in mortal danger, as in a war, or they were ill, or overburdened with their own troubles. Or perhaps they had died, or left, and we needed them desperately and they did not come.

For those of us who were born to parents who loved us and wanted to do the best for us, the situations where we were helpless and in the power of adults who inflicted pain on us were those where our loving parents were beating us to make us good.

Over the years I have met many people whose parents beat them to make them good, and many parents who believed that the only way to make children good was to beat them. The most vivid description I have ever come across of what it is like to be so beaten and the conclusions a child draws from such beatings is in Anna Mitgutsch's book *Punishment*.[18] She calls this book a novel, but she writes, it seems, from her own experience.

A beating: it never meant a spontaneous burst of anger, which might be followed by awkwardness and reconciliation. It began with a look which transformed me into vermin. And then there was a silence in which nothing had been decided yet and which nevertheless was past escape. The offence was swallowed up by the silence; it was never discussed. There were no alibis, explanations, excuses. There stood the misdeed, whether it was a banana stain on a dress or food refused – unatonable – and suddenly the misdeed was only a symbol for such an enormous wickedness that no amount of punishment sufficed. 'Get me the carpet beater,' she commanded; 'get me the cudgel.' This was a wooden stick the thickness of an arm, which split in two in the course of my education. The broken cudgel was itself significant evidence of a culpability so great that it could never be punished fully. Had she been completely just, she would have had to beat me to death. I owed the fact that she continued to let me live to her sacrificial mother love, which, like the Grace of God, was not earned and could never be repaid.

Even when I had learned that it was a senseless gesture, I threw myself down in front of her each time, my arms clasping her knees, begging, *Please, please dear Mama, my dearest Mama, I'll never do it again, I promise, I swear, you can take everything away from me, only please, don't hit me.*

She never bent down to me; her face remained remote, as if she were carrying out the work of a higher power. I never dared disobey her command; I always went whimpering behind the curtain to the side of the stairs, where the cudgel and the carpet beater were hung from hand-crocheted loops; they had their special hooks. What happened when I handed her the instrument of chastisement I don't remember; I only know that all hell broke loose. This is what hell must be like: pain and pain and pain in a rhythm that the body recognized almost instantly and against which it could not protect itself, neither by turning aside or by running off, because the pain simply struck another part each time.

Blind, I never saw her or the cudgel during the beating, only the smacks of wood on flesh, of metal-reinforced rubber on flesh, could be heard. Could it really be heard? Do I believe now that I heard it? How could I have heard it when I screamed, screamed as loudly as I could, from the first blow to the last? For sooner or later there was a last blow. Why this or that blow should be the last, I could not guess. It was God's will, it was her will: she didn't beat me in anger, after all; she beat me for my own good and to drive out my abysmal wickedness. The last blow was a well-considered temporary end of an atonement that would never end.

And then she would let herself fall to the floor, breathing heavily and stretching out full-length, exhausted as from the completion of hard labour, and I stood there terrified, with my heart racing and the pain suddenly gone numb. Was she about the die of exhaustion, had she fainted, all because of my guilt, the hard work I had caused her? She had told me so often that I would be the death of her. 'Take the cudgel away,' she said weakly, almost gently, and her slack voice gave me hope that she would survive . . .

My sense of my own worth depends on my defence of her honour. I cannot betray her, because if it should turn out that she never loved me, then I am a monster, something that should not be permitted to exist.

Therefore I don't say what I know and have known for a long time: that she is one of those who make our skin crawl and stop our imagination cold when we read about them in history books and documents, one of those who are expert in all branches of torture. She had the talent, though she was limited in scope; she had the tools, stored in an orderly fashion and always at hand; she had her mute sacrificial lamb, helpless and willing; and she had her secret, voluptuous pleasure, which released itself into a state of unconscious exhaustion after the execution of her task. She rarely allowed herself to be overcome by anger. She gave her victim notice – 'Just wait until tonight' – but in the meantime I had to go to bed, where my fear would escalate into suicidal fantasies. Where did she learn that? What handbooks had she read? When the punishment began she expected self-control; crying and pleading just made it that much worse; self-humiliation set her off. Beating was a ritual surrounded by other rituals. Even her inspection of the red welts and blood-shot bruises, after the work was done, was part of it. Was she, in other words, one of those people whose careers are made in torture chambers and concentration camps? How shall I answer that question about her who was also my mother? The word *Mama* also meant the broad lap on which I was allowed to sit, the soft face you could kiss if you were good and brought home all A's. *Mama* meant the pet names I never heard again in later life: 'bunny rabbit' and 'sugarplum'; it was the smell of Christmas cookies when I got home from school, out of darkness into the warm, bright living room in December. *Mama* meant safety and peril; she could protect me from just about everything except herself.

Many of us had parents who would not think of beating us to make us good. Instead, the situations where we were helpless and in the power of adults who inflicted pain on us were when our parents gave us just a few sharp slaps, or were locking us up, or threatening never to love us again, or saying that we had caused them terrible pain or were making them ill, or were criticizing us in contemptuous and degrading terms.

Whatever the circumstances of the situation, we were small, helpless, trapped and in pain.

We may not have had the words to describe that situation but we knew that the meaning of the situation was, in essence:

'I am being punished by my bad parent.'

We were, for a while, angry with our bad parent, but then a most terrible realization dawned on us. We were little and weak and dependent upon the parent who was inflicting pain on us. We realized that we were in double jeopardy.

What could we do?

We could do what all people do when we cannot change what is happening. We redefine it.

It is dangerous to suffer pain, but it is even more dangerous to be in the total power of someone who is bad. We could not stop the pain, but we could redefine our parent.

Our parent was not bad, but good.

Why do good parents inflict pain on their children?

Because the child is bad.

So we redefined the situation. It was not, 'I am being punished by my bad parent', but:

'I am bad and being punished by my good parent.'

Now we were safe. We were still in pain, suffering, feeling guilty, but at least safe in the hands of a good parent. Just like Feiffer's little

(D 5) girl,[19]

  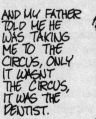 

Why did we feel we had to make this sacrifice of our sense of goodness and worth? What was there in that situation which threatened us so much?

Saving Our Self

Whether we are an adult or a child, whenever we find ourselves in a situation where we are totally in the power of other people we face the greatest threat we can ever know. It is the threat to annihilate us *as a person.* Even if the people in whose power we are are kind to us, we are still in danger, for if they insist that we feel, think and act solely in the ways that they wish then we will cease to be ourselves. We will become an automaton, a puppet, not just a thing, but a no-thing.

To preserve our self we will make all kinds of adjustments and rearrangements. We try to be as disobedient as we dare. No law-abiding citizen is a hundred per cent law-abiding. No one wants to be taken over completely by the government. Some of us in the situation of being completely in other people's power will decide that if we cannot live as ourselves we will die as ourselves, either in heroic defiance or in suicide.

When there is little we can achieve by action in preserving ourselves, we make alterations to the way we operate as a person. These may not be healthy alterations, but they enable us to survive. In the same way, when our body is starving, we will eat anything which will enable us to survive, no matter how noxious or unpalatable such food may be.

There are many things we can do to ourselves to preserve our self. Frequently we choose one of the following:

We can shut off our feelings and operate calmly, not letting our feelings come through to disturb us, perhaps even denying that we have feelings.

Or we can insist that everything is perfectly fine, and resolutely forget every bad experience inflicted on us.

Or we can split ourselves in two, making one part the person who lives an ordinary life and the other part the person who suffers horrible experiences.

Or we can define ourselves as bad and deserving the terrible things that are done to us.

Shutting off our feelings and operating calmly, not letting our feelings come through to disturb us, perhaps even denying that we have feelings

What gets us into most trouble when we are children are our emotions. If we get angry, we are punished. If we are frightened we are told not to be silly, not to be a coward. If we are envious or jealous, we are told we are wicked. Even when we show our love we can be told that we are soft, or silly, or too clingy and dependent. The only emotion adults encourage us to feel is guilt.

So we have to find ways of keeping our emotions under control. For introvert children, irrespective of what the adults around them might say, emotions pose a particular threat. They are disorganized and disorganizing, and so threaten a complete loss of control. So introvert children need to develop ways of organizing emotions and keeping them under control.

What better way than denying that you feel any emotion?

If you are an introvert you know how readily you can make yourself feel utterly, utterly calm while the crisis rages around you. You may have realized, too, how essential it is, once the crisis is under control or you have a chance to be alone, that you let the emotions out, cry your tears of rage or sorrow, or shake with fear, or curse the instigator of your anger.

However, such calmness can get you into trouble. Extraverts can scorn you for, apparently, having no feelings. Worse, if you never allow yourself to feel and express your feelings you cease to be able to make proper sense of what is happening to you.

By 'proper sense' I mean striving to get as close to the truth as it is possible to be. Discovering what the truth of any situation is is always difficult, but we, both introverts and extraverts, make it impossible to get anywhere near the truth if we lie to ourselves.

There are times when for our own safety or for the welfare of others it is beneficial to lie to other people. But,

Never, never, never is it beneficial to lie to yourself.

Unfortunately for us, this is the kind of lie all of us use most frequently.

In times of crisis, there is a world of difference between saying to yourself:

'I'm going to keep calm. I'll get upset about this later,'
and
'I'm not upset.'

The first statement is a recognition of what is happening and a plan for dealing with it effectively. The second statement is a lie, and if we do not let ourselves know what the truth of the situation is we can never deal effectively with the situation.

Neither in our external reality nor our internal reality do things disappear simply because we say they do not exist. When you are about to be run over by a bus, you cannot save yourself by saying, 'I'm not about to be run over by a bus.' When you are consumed by emotion, you cannot save yourself by saying, 'I'm not upset.'

Emotions, like buses, will not disappear when we deny their existence. They go on doing what they are doing whether or not we acknowledge their existence, and, if we do not acknowledge their existence, we cannot deal with them appropriately. Instead, the emotions deal with us in ways which are not appropriate.

Denied anger can burst forth in uncontrolled rage, often against inappropriate objects, like our children.

Denied fear and anger can interfere with the effective functioning of the auto-immune system, and thus make us prey to all kinds of diseases.

Denied fear, anger and murderous hate can reappear in compulsively repeated fantasies which threaten to be acted upon and so have to be guarded against with repeated obsessions. Thus a woman, haunted by the fantasy that she might injure her family, will go on and on obsessively cleaning her house. A man, haunted by the fantasy that he will kill someone, will return, again and again, to a place where he thinks that, while driving home, he has knocked down a pedestrian, and, despite all the evidence to the contrary, he will not be able to convince himself he has not injured anyone.

In our society, many men, both introverts and extraverts have been taught to lie to themselves in order to become 'a real man'. The lie which such men tell themselves is that they do not have tender, or artistic, or nurturing feelings, and that they never feel afraid. Thus they feel sex without love, anger without compassion, and, since they cannot feel part of the world and other people through their creative and nurturing feelings, they treat the world and other people as objects to be used and abused. Such men can become politicians, government officials, businessmen, criminals, soldiers, terrorists, torturers, and the kind of scientist who believes that all human experience can be understood solely in terms of chemical change.

Insisting that everything is perfectly fine, and resolutely forgetting every bad experience inflicted on us

If ever you have been in a situation where you have had nothing to do for a long time, like being in bed ill or on a boring journey, you will have discovered how all sorts of memories come back to you concerning events which you may not have thought about for many years, if ever. You can see how, if you gave yourself the time and were not always attending to things in the present and planning, or worrying, about the future, you could recall most of your past life. You might not remember names (psychologists say that the name remembering bit of our brain has a capacity for only about forty names, which was all that we needed when, in our tribes or villages, we met not more than forty people in our lifetime) but the events and people are recalled, and those from childhood come back with exquisite clarity. You can be amazed at just how much you can remember.

It is tremendously important that we remember our past life, because it is our past which gives us our sense of identity. If you woke up one morning and could not remember anything of your past, how would you know who you were? Some people do have this experience of forgetting all their past life, and when they ask someone for help, they do not say, 'I've forgotten how to read,' or 'I've forgotten how to get dressed.' They say, 'I've forgotten who I am.'

So we need to remember our past. However, what we remember of our past needs to fit in with what we believe is our identity. There has to be a consistency between the story our past tells and who we say we are. If an inconsistency does occur, which do we change, our identity or our history?

I once had two clients, Annette and Mick. Annette came to see me because she was depressed, and Mick because he was depressed and had had such terrible panic attacks that he hardly dared to leave his house. They had never met, but, as I discovered, they as children had had similar experiences which left them with the dilemma, which shall I change, my identity or my history?

When they were five years old, had they been asked to give an account of their identity and their history, each would have said, 'I live with my mummy and daddy and my brother who is ten. Mummy and Daddy love us very much and they are always kind.'

Then one day Annette and Mick each saw something which destroyed the consistency of their history and their identity. They saw their father, hitherto a kind and gentle man, become enraged with their older brother and punish him.

Annette described to me how her father had suddenly seized a broom and beaten his son around the head and back, and, when the broom stick broke, he pushed the boy to the ground and kicked him repeatedly. When the mother tried to protect her son, the father pushed her away and she fell against a cupboard and split her face open.

Mick saw his father strike his brother across the face and then order him to take down his trousers and bend over. Then he heard the whistle of a cane through the air, the crack of it against bare flesh, and the cries of his brother, which, as the whistle and crack went on and on, turned to whimpers.

How could Annette and Mick reconcile their identity and their history?

Each scene that they had witnessed was horrible and immensely disturbing. Yet, when I asked, 'What was it about this scene which made it *especially* horrible and disturbing?', each gave a different answer.

Annette said, 'It was my father going out of control.' Annette was an introvert.

Mick said, 'It was my brother being shamed and rejected like that.' Mick was an extravert.

Annette reconciled her identity and her history by changing her identity. She would no longer respond to events spontaneously. She would get everything about herself, and especially her anger, under control. No matter what happened, she would say to herself, 'I'm not upset.' She would keep her father's anger under control by becoming extremely good and obedient. If he should become angry with her, then it would be her fault.

Thus, whenever Annette remembered the scene, she did not feel the helpless fear and anger with her father which she had felt then. Instead she felt guilt. 'If I had been really good that wouldn't have happened.' Not allowing herself to feel anger lest her rage go out of control, she never defended herself when people treated her badly. She married a man who did treat her badly, and she blamed herself for all his misdemeanours. She lived a life of misery until she could cease telling herself the lie, 'I am not angry.'

Mick reconciled his identity and his history by changing his history. He forgot that he had seen his brother beaten by his father. 'It didn't happen,' he told himself.

For a lie to be effective it needs to contain a kernel of truth and certainty. I suppose this is why when we lie to ourselves we do so in the reality which is most real to us. Introverts' lies to themselves are about internal reality – 'I'm not upset' – and extraverts' lies to themselves are about external reality – 'It didn't happen.'

Lying to ourselves about events in external reality may make external reality appear to be nice and wholesome, but we cannot deal with emotions by forgetting them. Mick might have forgotten what he saw, but the emotion the scene aroused in him stayed with him. From then on he was afraid of his father and did not know why. In dreams and in fantasies he found himself in situations where he was naked and ashamed, exposed to humiliation and contempt. When, in his thirties, some business reverses and marriage difficulties made him lose self-confidence, the fear of exposure and shame turned into overwhelming panic.

For the first few months in therapy Mick would say, 'I had a happy childhood. Couldn't have had better parents. Do people remember much of their childhood? I don't.'

Therapists, like generals, have to be lucky, and here I was. Mick was just starting to be interested in his forgotten childhood when his brother, who had left home in his teens and lived abroad, came back for a brief business trip and stayed with Mick. When Mick asked him, 'Why did you leave home so young?', his brother told him, and in listening to his brother's history, the memory of this terrible scene came back to Mick.

Mick's process of reconstructing a history and an identity was by no means completed by recovering this memory, but the memory was a key piece in a large jigsaw.

Splitting ourselves in two, making one part the person who lives an ordinary life and the other part the person who suffers horrible experiences

Sometimes, the lies we tell ourselves like, 'I'm not upset,' 'That didn't happen,' are not enough because the horrible things that happened to us happen not just once or twice but over and over again. Then we might have to resort to a lie which aims to split our self into pieces. This lie is, 'This is not happening to me. It is happening to someone else.' Sylvia Fraser found that this was the only way she could deal with the sexual abuse she suffered as a child.

'When the conflict caused by my sexual relationship with my father became too acute to bear, I created a secret accomplice for my daddy by splitting my personality in two. Thus, somewhere around the age of seven, I acquired another self with memories and experiences separate from mine, whose existence was unknown to me. My loss of memory was retroactive. I did not remember ever seeing my daddy naked. I did not remember my daddy ever seeing me naked. In future, whenever my daddy approached me sexually I turned into my other self, and afterwards I did not remember anything that had happened.

'Even now, I don't know the full truth of that other little girl I created to do the things I was too frightened, too ashamed, too repelled to do, the things my father made me do, the things I did to please him, but which paid off with a precocious and dangerous power. She loved my father, freeing me to hate him. She became his guilty sexual partner and my mother's jealous rival, allowing me to lead a more normal life. She knew everything about me. I knew nothing about her, yet some connection always remained. Like estranged but fatal lovers, we were psychically attuned. She telegraphed messages to me through the dreams we shared. She leaked emotions to me through the body we shared. Because of her, I was always drawn to other children whom I sensed knew more than they should about adult ways. Hers was the guilty face I sometimes glimpsed in my mirror, mocking my daytime accomplishments, forcing me to reach for a counter illusion: I was special in a good way. I was a fairytale princess.

'Who was my other self?

'Though we split one personality between us, I was the major shareholder. I went to school, made friends, gained experience, developing my part of the personality, while she remained morally and emotionally a child, functioning on instinct rather than on intelligence. She began as my creature, forced to do what I refused to do, yet because I blotted out her existence, she passed out of my control completely as a figure in a dream.'[20]

Of course we cannot actually split ourselves into different selves, dividing like a cell divides into many cells. Such splitting is always *as if*. All we are doing is not acknowledging all the various aspects of ourselves and their interconnections. We can think of ourselves as being made up of 'father's sexual partner' and 'me', or of 'my dutiful and obedient self' and 'my wicked self', or of 'mind' and 'body', or of 'emotions', 'thoughts', and 'desires', but indeed every part of us is in continuous and continual relationship with all other parts, and in continuous and continual relationship with our surroundings. If we could remember this we would find it so much easier to experience ourselves as a whole person in close and satisfactory contact with other people.

Defining ourselves as bad and deserving the terrible things that are done to us

(D 6) By telling ourselves the lie, 'I am bad, evil, unacceptable to myself and other people', we lay down the cornerstone of the prison of depression.

The business of life is to live, and so all these ways of preserving ourselves are wise and practical things to do in order to survive when we are living under the most terrible threats. If our ancestors had not used such methods of preserving themselves, not just against the devastating things done to them by other people but against the devastating things done to them by floods, droughts, fires, earthquakes, hurricanes, plagues, illnesses, accidents and death, then we would not be here today. The human race would not have survived.

What is unwise and impractical is to go on using these ways of preserving ourselves when we are actually not in danger.

Where we get ourselves into a tangle as adults is when we continue using unnecessarily in adult life the self-preserving defences which were so necessary in childhood. We fail to go back and check whether the conclusions we drew as a child still apply in our adult life.

Why do we fail to check our conclusion that 'I am bad'? After all, believing that you are bad makes you feel guilty, and guilt is a most horrible feeling. It is the fear of retribution, the punishment which you are sure you deserve.

Becoming an Expert in Feeling Guilty

Believing that you are bad makes you an expert in feeling guilty. There is no situation about which you cannot feel guilty once you put your mind to it. The starving children of Africa? 'I ought to do something about them and I haven't.' The hole in the ozone layer? 'I've used aerosols and I drive a car, so it's my fault.'

Closer to home you as the expert in guilt feel responsible for ensuring the total happiness of all of your family, or for the total success of the organization for which you work. Thus, when your adult child has an unhappy love affair, or your cousin twice removed fails to send you a Christmas card, you feel guilty. Or when your organization does not reach the over-optimistic targets the directors set, or your colleague has a drink problem, you feel guilty.

As an expert in guilt you cannot live in the present. You are constantly worrying about the past and fearing the future. As an expert in guilt you cannot enjoy happiness when it comes, for you believe that as night follows day, suffering will follow joy. When good fortune does come your way, you know it will not stay, for you are the guilty one and you will be punished.

Why do we go on feeling guilty? Why do we inflict such pain upon ourselves?

Because by feeling guilty we are declaring that we are not help-less.

By feeling guilty we are declaring, 'In the past I could have acted differently. I had the power to act one way or another, and I chose the wrong way.'

By feeling guilty we are declaring that we had the situation organized and under control, or could have done, and that we had the power to relate to and care for other people.

Feeling guilty is a denial of helplessness.

Feeling helpless can take you back to the time when you were weak and helpless and in the power of dangerous adults. Rather than experience again that most terrible terror, you prefer to feel guilty.

Alas, because you will not risk the terror to reappraise your conclusion that you are bad, you prevent yourself from discovering that your situation has changed. Your situation now, as an adult, is that your self is secure and cannot be threatened by other people *unless you let them*.

If you insist on saying to yourself, 'I'd be finished if my husband left me', you have given your husband the power to threaten your self. If you insist on saying to yourself, 'I just fall apart whenever my boss criticizes my work', you have given your boss the power to threaten your self.

However, if you say to yourself, 'It would be tough going if my husband left me but I'd survive', your husband cannot then threaten your self. If you say to yourself, 'I'll take account of reasonable and constructive criticism of my work, but I'll reject criticism from people who are fools or are being malicious, and I'll remember to distinguish criticisms of my work from criticisms of me', then you are no longer helpless and in the power of other people.

If we do not go back and check our conclusion that 'I am bad' we make this and the constant feeling of guilt into our way of living. It becomes the basis of our whole way of living, and it spoils not just our life but the lives of those we love.

My friend Gregory, who lives in California, and I keep a regular correspondence. Recently he wrote to me:

'I have come to realize how much I played the role of The Guilty One from childhood on.

'As is typical of introverted children of alcoholic parents, my unconscious feeling as a child was that if only I were a better boy my father would stop being drunk and abusive and my parents would love each other. As none of that happened, it was clear that I was not a good enough boy and that I must work harder. And as working harder didn't make things any better, then I must be a Failure: I was The Guilty One responsible for my family's misery.

'I transferred this neurosis right over into my marriage, and it fitted Anna's beautifully. Deeply unhappy since childhood, Anna quickly found (unconsciously, not deliberately) that I was willing and able (and probably sickly eager) to be The Guilty One responsible for her unhappiness. And this, of course, made me very angry. What can make us angrier than situations that we put ourselves into?

'My shrink thinks, rightly I'm sure, that my 'moderately severe' depression was my latest effort to punish myself (and a very successful effort it was too).

'I am simply refusing to play this game any more. It means changing a behaviour I have had since I was five, and of course it isn't easy, but I'm doing fairly well, I think.'

When Gregory claimed that he 'was The Guilty One responsible for my family's misery', he was making a claim to great power. His parents were not responsible for themselves. He, a small child, was.

Feeling guilty with its claim to great power is one of the compensations for drawing the conclusion 'I am bad'. There are others.

Compensations for Believing 'I Am Bad'

When we concluded that we were bad, we immediately set about working hard at being good. We became very obedient. We tried to do what adults told us to do. Not that we were always successful, because adults often make conflicting demands on children and expect them to do what is beyond their powers to do. Of course we did not want to be totally obedient. Whenever we thought we could get away with it, we pleased ourselves in order to preserve ourselves, but often these self-preserving activities were marred by fear of discovery or by our own sense of guilt.

Each of us specialized in a particular way of being good. Gregory worked hard at school and became a great scholar. Pat became very competent in organizing and in looking after people. Tom became a good team man, first in athletics and then in accountancy. Dan became a good achiever and a successful businessman. Lisa became very good at being attractive and pleasing people. Rebecca became a most likeable person and a very successful student. Jill became a very sweet, gentle and competent person. Some of us, having been told by our parents and teachers so often that we were bad, obediently fulfilled their expectations and became very good at being bad. One of my clients, Caroline, as a child was told constantly by her parents that she was both mad and bad, so in her teens she proceeded to fulfil their expectations by having affairs with unsuitable men, losing jobs, and becoming so frightened and depressed that her parents put her into a psychiatric hospital. It did not occur to her that in telling a child that she was mad and bad her parents were treating her cruelly. She just blamed herself.

Whichever form of goodness we chose, we all became very good at being good. This was hard work because we could never stop trying to be good. Occasionally we might take a break, but underneath always was the conviction that 'Because I am bad, I must work hard to be good'.

Because everything we did was based on the conviction 'I am bad', we were left feeling that no matter how hard we tried, we could never be good enough. No matter what we achieved, we would denigrate our achievement. We felt anxious, guilty and driven.

For some of us, the sense of being anxious, guilty and driven was only occasionally present, for we had parents and teachers who set us goals which were in our power to achieve, who encouraged us rather than punished us, and who showed us that they cared about us and would not desert us. Even so, our safety was in the hands of adults, and thus the happiest of us would, from time to time, feel anxious and guilty and think, 'I must do better'.

Living like this, we could so easily lose heart and fall into despair.

(Small children can despair, just as adults can.) We had to find ways of bolstering our self-esteem and giving ourselves hope. We needed to believe, 'Even though I am bad, I am not *that* bad, and one day everything will come right'.

Some of us devised a way of feeling better about ourselves by believing, 'No matter how bad I am, I am better than other people'. Taking pride in our skills at being good, we criticize, gossip about, and reject other people because they have not achieved the standards of goodness which we have achieved. We look at our precisely mowed lawns and say, 'Wouldn't you think the family across the street would get their son to mow their lawn properly?' We look at our thin, athletic body and say, 'Wouldn't you think my sister would go on a diet and get some exercise?' We look at our quiet, orderly family and our immaculate house and say, 'We cannot have blacks/Pakistanis/squatters living in this street. They are noisy, dirty and dishonest.' (Whenever you find yourself at the receiving end of this kind of criticism, remember that the faults that the people are criticizing are not yours but their own. They are using you to overcome their own sense of inadequacy.)

Some of us go beyond simply criticizing and rejecting other people in order to make ourselves feel better. Some of us become very strict and controlling of others, very punitive, even cruel.

Those of us who do this had, as children, prolonged experiences of being helpless and in the power of adults who were inflicting great pain on us.

In families where the parents are very strict and controlling and demand, using severe punishments and sanctions, complete obedience from their children, the child is put again and again in the situation where the realization, 'I am being punished by my bad parent', creates such fear that the redefinition, 'I am bad and am being punished by my good parent', is not enough to stem the terror. So the child performs a second redefinition. It is:

I am bad and am being punished by my good parent, and when I grow up I shall punish bad people in the way that I was punished.

This is the way that cruelty is handed down from one generation to the next. By inflicting on others a form of the cruelty which was inflicted on us, we deny that the cruelty which was done to us harmed us, and we take pride in our own striving to overcome our sense of badness by punishing those people who could remind us of the circumstances whereby we drew the conclusion that we were bad.

Those of us who did this would, as adults, say, 'I was beaten as a child and it never did me any harm', not realizing that the harm it did us was in thinking that it did not do us harm. Hence, when the opportunity offers, we can punish our children cruelly, while claiming it is for their own good, and we can work as jailers, policemen, soldiers, concentration camp guards, terrorists and torturers, and feel no sympathy for the people in our power.

Similarly, while some victims of child abuse perform just the first redefinition and believe themselves to be bad, others make the second redefinition, and then, in adult life, claim that, 'I was sexually assaulted as a child and it never did me any harm', and go on to do to children what was done to them.

Most of us would say that we hate cruelty and that we do whatever we can to protect and help anyone who suffers cruelty. We may not realize that while we are very good at recognizing cruelty which is far away from us, we are also very good at ignoring cruelty when it happens right before our eyes.

I was running a workshop on the theme of psychological therapy for the major psychoses. Half of the people there knew what it was like to be psychotic, either in the schizophrenic way of an introvert or in the mania of an extravert. The other half were professionals, social workers and psychologists who listened, interested, as the others described their experiences.

At the beginning of the workshop we each described what had brought us to the workshop and what we hoped to get out of it. One young man, Mervin, just said simply, 'I've been allowed out today to come with my friends. I'm psychotic.'

Mervin listened to the discussion and commented, but he often felt restless and got up to wander around the room. In the afternoon he changed his seat to come and sit beside me.

There had been much discussion about the insensitive way people are treated in the psychiatric system. Now I wanted to bring this discussion closer to home, to focus on how the cruel treatment of a child has such long-term effects, and how, while we are very adept at recognizing cruelty far afield and being shocked by it, we are equally adept at neither recognizing cruelty close to home nor being shocked by it.

I began to talk about this and Mervin, as he had done before, interrupted.

'When I was six,' he said, 'I got belted for throwing an ice cream on the floor. I'm the youngest of five, and they all had bigger ice creams than mine. I thought it wasn't fair, so I threw mine down.'

I put my hand out to pat him. 'My word, that was a wicked thing for a six-year-old to do, wasn't it?'

He recognized my irony and nodded. 'Yes, and then my father picked up his belt with a great big steel buckle and he whacked me with it.' He drew back his arm to demonstrate how a man would wield a buckled belt, 'and he whacked me, right across here,' and he showed how a small child would crumple under such a blow.

Now he crouched forward, his head on his hands. I put my hand on the nape of his neck and stroked him.

'I love my father,' he said.

'How do you feel about this now?' I asked, thinking it to be a fatuous question, as just the way he crouched there showed the pain.

'Terrible,' he said.

Through all this I had been looking at Mervin. Now I turned to the group, thinking that they would want to offer some comfort and support to Mervin.

There was a silence. Then David, one of the social workers, spoke. He was addressing Ingrid who had earlier been describing the inadequacies of the care she was being given. He said, 'I think it's very important that the gaps in the service be recognized and that the co-ordination of the delivery of the different services be improved.' He continued in this vein for some minutes, never looking in the direction of Mervin and me.

Should I, I thought, point out that we were witnessing what earlier I had declared to be so common, our inability to recognize cruelty when it is close to us. Yes, I thought, and did.

The discussion between David and Ingrid went on for some time, but finally there was a pause, and I pointed out what had happened. I said that not only had Mervin shown us his pain, but he had also shown us how children sacrifice themselves in order to preserve their parent as a good parent. All the people in the workshop who experienced themselves as intrinsically bad had, in one way or another, gone through this experience.

There were a father and son in the group, John and Peter, who had each been given the diagnosis of manic-depressive. John told me very firmly that what I had said did not apply to him. 'I had a happy childhood. It was during the war years, but it was happy even so. And I can say the same for my son. He had a happy childhood. He can say the same for himself, can't you, son?'

'Yes, Dad.' Peter was leaning forward, his elbows on his knees. His father could not see his face. As he said, 'Yes, Dad,' he grinned and winked at me.

His father went on, 'Of course I had to chastise him. Parents have to hit their children in order to rectify them. My father hit me, and I had to hit Peter. He needed to be rectified.'

The smile had vanished from Peter's face. He looked very sad.

Brian, who had organized the workshop, said, 'Parents can be cruel to children in more ways than by hitting them. My parents used to talk about me as if I wasn't there. We'd be sitting at the table and they'd be saying, "He did this", and "He did that", as if I wasn't even in the room. Also, they expected me to achieve for them, all that academic success, just for them and not for me in any way at all.'

After the workshop, over a cup of coffee, Ingrid and I talked about her discussion with David. She said, 'I knew that we shouldn't have been talking like that, that we should have been paying attention to Mervin. But I wanted to go on talking because I couldn't bear the pain.'

Whether we remain forever fearful that we are not good enough and painfully vulnerable to hurt and to hurts done to other people, or whether we try to hide our sense of badness by taking pride in our efforts to be good, and criticizing, even punishing cruelly, those who do not reach the standards we have set ourselves, we have, if we are to survive, to give ourselves *hope*.

We hope that our efforts to be good will be rewarded.

When we were small children we discovered that there was a law of the universe, 'If you are bad you get punished'. True, there were times when we were bad and didn't get punished, and sometimes we got punished when we had done nothing wrong, but once we had concluded that we were intrinsically and always bad, we knew that whatever punishment we got, we deserved it. Even if we had not done something wrong, we knew that we could have done something wrong.

Even as small children we were logical, and so we could work out that if, 'If you are bad you get punished', is a law of the universe, then its opposite must also be a law of the universe. So we concluded that, 'If I am good I shall be rewarded'.

Some of us simply worked this out for ourselves, but others of us were taught this explicitly by adults at home, at school and at church. If we had parents who believed in using behaviourist psychological principles in raising us, we got gold stars for cleaning our teeth and lost our pocket money when we answered back. At school we won prizes for achieving and were punished and humiliated for failing. At church and Sunday School we were told that God knew and kept an account of everything we did and thought. Some of us were warned of the tortures of hell fire, and some of us were promised that if we were good Jesus would save us from all harm, but, whatever, the message was clear. If you are bad you will be punished and if you are good you will be rewarded.

The threat of punishment made us frightened, but the promise of reward gave us hope. It was on that hope that we built our life story.

When we were small children learning about badness and goodness, punishment and reward, we were also busy constructing the story of what our life would be.

Our story begins with who we are and where we live, and goes on to tell how we intend to fulfil our ambitions and to be loved by all, or at least by one significant other. It might be, 'When I grow up Prince Charming will come along and fall in love with me. We'll get married and live happily ever after.' Or it might be, 'When I grow up I'm going to be rich and famous and greatly loved.'

Our story contains, too, scenes where we have our revenge on those who have injured us, and scenes where our true worth shall be revealed and all those who have criticized and humiliated us will be ashamed, astounded and lost in admiration for us. Best of all, there are scenes where we receive an abundance of rewards for all our strivings to be good and for all our sacrifices. Indeed, our whole story is a recompense for what we have suffered in childhood.

In that time when we are creating our story we are also making the greatest sacrifice, short of death, that we can make. We are giving up being ourselves.

In learning to be clean, we had to learn, not just the rules about bowels and bladders, but about washing hands, changing underwear, polishing shoes and so on and on. Left to ourselves we would not have bothered about such things, but to be good we had to give up pleasing ourselves, just as we had to give up pleasing ourselves in order to become unselfish and considerate.

In learning to be responsible and hard-working we had to give up a great deal of our desire to play. It is only in the last fifty years or so that adults have recognized how important play is in a child's development, but this has led many parents and teachers to become involved in organizing and directing children's play instead of simply letting children play. The children are directed into learning all sorts of arts and skills, into joining children's organizations like the Scouts and church groups, and into a highly organized social life. They have no time to themselves, either in blissful solitude or just hanging out with their friends. So while poor children are deprived of the freedom to be themselves in play by the necessity of working, children from affluent backgrounds are deprived of the freedom to be themselves in play by interfering adults who believe that children should always be achieving and improving, that is, being a credit to their parents.

As babies, we laughed when we were happy, cried when we were sad, and yelled when we were angry. As children, we had to give up being ourselves as we learned to hide our emotions. We had to learn not to laugh in the wrong places, to look cheerful no matter how sad we were, and to be calm and quiet no matter how frustrated and angry we were. Since our emotions are spontaneous, learning to inhibit them is tremendously difficult, and so we often failed. The phrase 'being in touch with one's emotions' has become a cliché in therapy because all therapists, of whatever persuasion, recognize that for us to live happily and confidently with ourselves we have to recognize, correctly label, accept and appropriately express our emotions, which is a way of living very different from what we were taught as children.

Again, as small girls, we were shown that we had to give up much of that assertive, active part of ourselves so as to become 'feminine'. We were told that if we were not feminine we would not be loved. As small boys we were shown that we had to give up much of that gentle, nurturing, artistic part of ourselves so as to become 'masculine'. We were told that if we were not masculine we would be scorned.

All this sacrifice of ourselves would have been intolerable if we could not, in constructing our story, believe that sooner or later we would be rewarded for all our efforts to be good.

Living Our Story

Having prepared our story, we then proceeded to live it. We had the plan. We simply tried to follow it.

Our story, as we live it, becomes the structure of our life. If we are lucky, our hopeful story and our actual life remain close together. We plan to marry Prince Charming and live happily ever after, and this is what we do. We plan to be rich and famous, and we achieve this.

So long as our story and our life go along together, we forget that our story is nothing more than some ideas in our head. We take it to be an order of the universe. We believe that there is an order in the universe, one of justice where the good are rewarded and the bad punished. We work hard at being good so as to avoid punishment, and we feel secure in a universal Grand Design of which we and our lives are a part.

If we are lucky, if we are very, very lucky, nothing happens to us to make us question our belief.

Few of us are so lucky. Over time, our story and our life diverge. This might be a gradual divergence, as we slowly discover, perhaps, how unsatisfactory Prince Charmings can be, or how riches and fame do not necessarily lead to happiness, or it might be a sudden divergence, caused by some loss, or death, or failure.

Whichever, once we see the divergence we realize that we have got things wrong. We see that our story is nothing but our imaginings, and that reality is something very different from what we thought it was.

We had gone around thinking that we were an individual in our own right, and we discover that we are not. We find that we are neglected, abused, and treated as an object of no importance.

We had gone around thinking that we had secure and loving relationships, and we discover that we are wrong. The people we love and rely on abandon, desert, reject, and betray us.

We had gone around thinking that other people relied on us, and we discover that they do not. The people we thought needed us show us that they do not need us, and the people we thought regarded us as indispensable show us that they can manage without us.

We had gone around thinking that we had organized a secure life for ourselves, and we discover that we have not. Our security is destroyed and our livelihood and possessions are swept away.

We had gone around thinking that we were succeeding in gaining our goals, and we discover that we have failed. We are shamed, humiliated and thrown into chaos.

We had gone around thinking that we were meeting all our responsibilities, and we find that we have not done what we ought to have done. We are overwhelmed by guilt.

We had gone around thinking that we lived in a just world where our goodness would be rewarded, and we discover that no amount of goodness prevents disaster. We therefore feel betrayed, resent- **(D 7)** ful, and terrified.

Such discoveries destroy the structure of our lives. Everything which we thought was solid and secure becomes fragile and ephemeral, even the structure we thought of as our self.

We are consumed by the greatest terror.

What can we do?

5

Constructing Our Prison
of Depression

As Pat crouched on the edge of her bed, her heart thudding with fear, one thought kept repeating over and over, 'I have wasted my life'.

That most precious thing, her life, had slipped from her fingers and had gone, and what lay ahead was nothing but emptiness and futility, a path she had to tread until she died. She cursed herself for being such a fool, for wasting her opportunities, for not acting differently, for not seeing what was happening.

'I kept thinking next year, later, when this is over, then I'll do something, I'll achieve something – I must have thought I was going to live for ever, and now it is too late.'

As she lay on her bed, staring into the darkness, she saw scenes from her life in all the exquisitely painful clarity of memory.

There was Simon, coming towards her across a field. He was wearing a yellow shirt, and her heart leapt up at the sight of him and she was suffused in joy. 'That was the only time in my life I was happy,' she thought. 'I knew it was too good to be true. I was never happy again, and I never will be.'

Even her childhood had been unhappy. She saw herself at five, standing at the front door and holding a picture she had drawn, eager to show it to her father who was coming up the path. But he just pushed past her and went into the study and slammed the door.

She saw herself at seven, bringing her mother a cup of tea, and her mother saying absently, 'Put it on the table', and smiling down at the baby on her lap. Pat found herself burning with the same hatred she had felt then for her youngest sister, hatred which turned into bitter, previously unacknowledged, resentment for the sister who had offered no help when their parents were ill. She thought of all the effort she had expended in keeping in friendly contact with her sisters, and how they just took her for granted.

'They never phone me,' she thought. 'I always have to phone them. Well, I've had enough. That's the last they'll hear from me. They didn't even come to my wedding. They thought I was marrying beneath me.'

She remembered her wedding, a quiet affair, with her husband pale and shaky from a night's hard drinking at his bachelor party. 'All that drinking was supposed to be funny,' and she remembered cleaning up after him and trying to prevent her son from seeing his father drunk. She remembered how she would tell herself that he was a war hero, and that if she was patient he would soon be all right and that she must try very hard not to upset him. Now she burned with anger and disgust, both for him and for herself, and she thought, 'I'll never forgive him', and then, 'I'll never forgive myself'.

She thought of her son growing up without a father he could be proud of, and she felt the sharpest, most excruciating pain that we can ever know, the pain that we feel when someone we love is suffering and there is nothing we can do to protect and save him.

She tried to ease the pain by thinking what a fine person he was, and then she thought, 'I don't want to be a burden to him. He tried to do his duty, but he doesn't want a bad-tempered, sick old woman around. I'll tell him not to come here any more, and I won't go and see him.'

Somehow, the thought of curling up, clutching her hurts to herself, shutting out and punishing everybody whether they had hurt her or not, had a certain bitter satisfaction. So, too, cutting herself off from the people she loved the most in the world seemed to be a fit punishment for a woman who had spent her whole life telling herself that all she had to do was to be patient, good and kind and look after other people, and one day, when she had met the needs of all these people, it would be her turn to look after herself and please herself. Obviously she had failed. Obviously, if she had tried harder and been a better person, kinder, more caring, less angry and resentful, she would not now be alone, old, ill, unwanted, too tired to struggle any more. Even if she were offered another chance, she was too worn out to take it. If this was all there was to life, then she had wasted it and deserved to be punished, and punishing herself now might be better than burning in hell's fires. Whichever way, it made no difference. She was alone, and wanted to be alone, and deserved to be alone.

These thoughts and images went round and round for many wakeful hours, and in her dreams they coalesced into the prison walls of the depression into which Pat awoke.

How Thoughts and Images Create a Prison

Depression does not come upon us by chance. It is not a random aberration of the mind any more than it is a random aberration of our body. It is a defence which we build for ourselves when we are in danger, and, just as we can all move with surprising speed when we find ourselves in the path of a runaway bus, so we can jump into the defensive walls of depression with such speed that the prison seems to come upon us like a cloud descending out of the blue.

Also, so long as we live our lives believing that we are bad and have to work hard to be good, we have already built most of the prison. All we need to do is to set a few more bricks into place and we have walled ourselves in.

To understand just how we do this, we need to think about how we actually experience getting along with other people, experience being in a particular environment, and think about our past and future.

When we talk about getting along with other people, we use words like 'in touch with', 'relate to', 'being close to', 'communicate with'. These words mean more than just talking to someone. They relate to a very powerful feeling which we all know but rarely describe.

We are all aware of the sense of being alive. It is much more than just breathing and moving. It is a sense of life which is inside us and which streams from us, joining us to other people, the world in which we live, and to ourselves.

That is, the sense of life streams from us to join us to other people and to the environment only when we feel safe. As soon as we feel in danger, we put up a barrier which holds in that sense of life and protects us from danger.

For instance, suppose you are invited to a party and you go along believing that everyone there is your friend. When you arrive you greet everyone warmly and you feel your sense of life streaming out, joining with the sense of life coming from your friends. (I am not relating anything mystical and mysterious, just trying to describe with an inadequate vocabulary something that we all find everyday and obvious and immensely pleasurable.)

Now, suppose, in the midst of this, all these people whom you thought were your friends suddenly turn on you and attack you. Immediately, even before you can work out what has happened, you stop that sense of life going out to them. You put up a barrier. You defend yourself. You try not to let what your erstwhile friends are sending out to you get past your barrier and hurt you.

Alternatively, suppose you get a memo from your boss, saying that he wants to discuss your work with you. Your boss has a reputation for being very critical, and so you prepare yourself by stopping your sense of life from streaming out to greet him by putting up a barrier. However, when you get to his office, he greets you warmly and tells you that he wants to congratulate you on a job well done. As soon as you realize that you are safe, you whisk away the barrier, and let your sense of life stream out to join with his. You share a joke with him, you tell him about your family, about your personal plans. You enjoy the sense of being open to another person.

The same experience of feeling joined to or cut off from relates to our environment. When we feel safe, we feel, as we say, 'at one with nature', or, 'at home in the city'. But as soon as our environment seems to threaten us, we cut our sense of life off from it. We feel alien in an alien land.

Similarly, our sense of life can stream out, joining us to our past and future. When we remember our past with happiness and satisfaction, our sense of life joins us to that past, and when we anticipate the future with joy and satisfaction, our sense of life joins us to our future, even when we think of that part of our future which is certain, our death. If our sense of life streams out to visions of our death, we see ourselves dying a peaceful death, surrounded by our loved ones, after a life well lived. However, if we fear death, our sense of life does not stream out to greet our version of what it might be, and if we remember our past with regret and resentment, our sense of life does not join us to our past.

When our sense of life streams out to our past and future we experience our life story as being a proper story which has a beginning, a middle and an end. When we cut ourselves off from our past or from our future, our story is incomplete, and incomplete stories always make us feel uncomfortable and dissatisfied.

It is our sense of life which can, if we let it, keep us whole. When we say, and believe, 'I accept and value myself', our sense of life joins 'I' and 'myself' together. 'I' and 'myself' are then the best of friends. But when we say, and believe, 'I am bad and unacceptable', 'I' and 'myself' are divided by a barrier. They are enemies who become, once the prison of depression is built, the prisoner and the cruel jailer.

Everything we believe, every construction of meaning we make, can be categorized as joining us to other people, to our environment, to our past and future, and to ourselves, or as cutting ourselves off from other people, from our environment, from our past and future, and from ourselves.

'I like other people' joins us to other people. 'Trust nobody' cuts us off.

'I love gardening' joins us to our environment. 'I'm scared of flying' cuts us off.

'I had a great time at school' joins us to our past. 'I could never please my parents, no matter what I did' cuts us off.

'I'm really looking forward to our holiday' joins us to our future. 'I dread Monday mornings' cuts us off.

'I enjoy my own company' joins us to ourselves. 'I hate to look at myself in a mirror' cuts us off.

When we were babies we had a set of beliefs which joined us to everything. Everything we encountered was interesting. Every person we met was a friend. We were our own best friend.

Then we started to find that there were parts of our environment which were dangerous to explore. We found that sometimes our most wonderful mother disappeared and a most dangerous person came in her place. When we worked out that this dangerous person was actually our mother being angry or unhelpful, we were confused about when it was safe to be close to her and when not. We found, too, that sometimes we were not our own best friend, because we would get ourselves into trouble. So, gradually, we collected quite a number of conclusions which served to cut ourselves off from other people, our environment, our past and future, and from ourselves.

Thus we discovered one of the great dilemmas of life.

If we go around allowing our sense of life to stream out indiscriminately in all directions, we make ourselves vulnerable to hurt. If we put our hand in a flame or try to cuddle a cobra, we get hurt. If we don't guard ourselves against those people who would take advantage of us, we get hurt. If we don't learn from past mistakes, and don't assess what perils might lie in the future, we get hurt. If we accept uncritically everything that we do and give ourselves unstinted, total praise, we are unaware that there is a gap between 'what I am' and 'what I could be', and so we never fulfil our potential.

On the other hand, if we cut our sense of life off completely from all other people, from our total environment, from our past and our future, and if we become our own worst enemy, we have put ourselves in complete isolation, a place where we cannot live.

This dilemma of life is one which cannot be solved once and for all, but needs to be dealt with day by day, as we make careful, informed judgements about where we should allow our sense of life to stream out, and where we should place a barrier. When we do need to put up a barrier we should remember that it is a flexible defence useful for the time being and not an Eternal Truth of the Universe, unalterable for all time. 'I'll keep out of her way for the time being,' rather than 'I'll never speak to her ever again.'

If we do not do this, when we feel ourselves under great threat, we can put up too many barriers, and so lock ourselves into the prison of depression.

How Pat Built her Prison of Depression

It was in those hours of darkness, as Pat lay on her bed, that she fitted the last pieces of her prison together.

She had already built much of her prison. She believed that she was bad and unacceptable. She looked to other people to give her the appreciation she would not give herself, and so she was frightened of other people, for she had given them the power to hurt her. She resented those people who had taken advantage of her, but, since she believed that it was wrong to be angry, she never expressed this anger and instead continued to be unforgivingly resentful. She remembered nothing happy from her past. Only her hope for the future had kept her connected to something outside of herself.

Ever since she was a little girl with parents who noticed her only when they wanted something from her, she had hoped that if she tried very hard to be good, helpful, considerate and hard working, people would appreciate and love her, and that one day, once all the people she had to look after no longer needed her, she could fulfil her own ambitions. She had given up her childhood interest in art, and then her teenage interest in medicine, but she had kept her interest in travel, and being able to travel she had seen as her reward for years of hard work and sacrifice.

When Pat realized that such a reward was not forthcoming, she faced with mounting terror the choices we all have in trying to explain why it is that sometimes goodness is not rewarded.

When any disaster occurs there are only three ways that we can explain why it happened. We can say:

It was my fault

or

It was someone else's fault

or

It happened by chance.

If we have grown up believing that if we are bad we shall be punished, but if we are good we shall be rewarded, then when disaster befalls us we are faced with:

Blaming ourselves for not being good enough, and so feeling guilty.

or

Blaming others, and so feeling angry and resentful that the system of rewards and punishments has operated unfairly.

or

Deciding that there is no system of rewards and punishments, that disasters can happen to anyone at any time, and so feeling frightened.

Thus, if we believe that goodness is rewarded, when disaster befalls us and we see a discrepancy between our script for our life and what reality is, we have a choice between feeling guilty, feeling angry and resentful, and feeling frightened.

When Pat faced this dilemma, she rejected the choice of feeling angry and resentful for she believed that anger and resentment are wicked. When she allowed herself to see the possibility that she had based her whole life on something which was not true, everything fell apart and she was overwhelmed by terror. To combat this terror, as she lay there in the darkness, she decided that the system of rewards for goodness was true, and that she was the guilty one whom she would never forgive.

Guilty people must be punished, and, rather than wait for some unpredictable punishment, she would punish herself. She would cut herself off from everyone, her friends, her sisters, and her son.

Now the system was restored. There was pattern and stability. The stability of complete isolation. Pat had, within the space of a few hours, followed successfully the recipe for becoming depressed.

The Recipe for Depression

Over the years, as I listened to people telling me about the conclusions they had drawn from their experience and I asked, 'Why is that important?' and 'How do you feel about this?' to find the reasons that lay behind the conclusions, I found I was collecting the kinds of conclusions which cut us off from ourselves, other people, the past and the future, and the world. I gradually came to realize that these conclusions can be grouped under six basic beliefs.

So, if you have never been depressed and you would like to try it out, this is what you do.

You must hold these six beliefs, but you must hold them totally, without doubt or question, as Axiomatic Truths, Laws of the Universe, Absolute Verities of Nature.

The six beliefs are:

1. No matter how good I appear to be, I am bad, evil, unacceptable to myself and to other people.

2. Other people are such that I fear, hate and envy them.

3. Life is terrible and death is worse.

4. Only bad things have happened to me in the past and only bad things will happen to me in the future.

5. Anger is evil.

6. Never forgive, and never expect to be forgiven.[21]　　　　　　(D 8)

These six beliefs mesh together in one composite, enclosing whole.

How the Six Beliefs Fit Together

The starting point, the foundation of the prison of depression is the belief, 'No matter how good I appear to be, I am bad, evil, unacceptable to myself and to other people.'

We have seen in the previous chapter how we can come to hold this belief. If this is what you believe about yourself, it follows that:

Other people are such that I fear, hate and envy them.

If you are intrinsically bad, you can never be at ease with other people but must always be frightened of them, lest they discover how bad you really are, and then criticize and reject you. Thus you always fend people off, for fear of them getting close and discovering what you are really like.

If you believe that you are bad and unacceptable, then, no matter what kindness and love people may show you, you hold fast to your belief that, 'When anyone says they like me, I know that person is either a fool or a liar.'

This attitude prevents any therapist, however talented, from helping you. If the therapist can't see how bad you really are, he's a fool, and you don't want a fool for a therapist. If he does see how bad you are and still keeps displaying warmth and positive regard, he is a liar and you don't trust liars.

Indeed, you don't trust people generally, for how can you tell whether a person is really good, or, like you, bad and pretending to be good?

If we fear anybody for long enough we come to hate that person. As much as you try to hide this from yourself, you are aware that, if you have grown up fearing your parents as well as loving them, you also, at least from time to time, hate them. You feel very guilty about this and try to hide your hate by not daring to criticize your parents, or to oppose them in anything, and by trying to do all you can for them. However, the hatred does not go away. It makes its presence felt in your physical illnesses, or in nightmares, or, if you are an extravert, in panic attacks, or, if you are an introvert, in frighteningly cruel fantasies and rituals of cleaning and checking. Some people who get depressed are well aware of their hatred for their parents, but they cannot tolerate this hatred, for it is a constant reminder of how disappointed they are that their parents failed to be good parents.

A measure of just how many people there are who believe that they are bad is the amount of hatred there is in our world, not just that expressed in wars and atrocities, but in the day-to-day interactions of ordinary people going about their business. If you believe that you are bad, then someone who is simply rude to you, or inefficient, or who fails to live up to the high standards you have set yourself, arouses in you not merely annoyance but hatred.

When we fear someone we keep well away from that person. We do not get to know them, and so we do not learn of the difficulties with which they are struggling. Most people, from a distance, seem to cope with their lives really well. After all, few people stand at a bus stop telling passers-by of their troubles. So, if you are frightened of other people, you do not learn of their difficulties. You think they are having an easy life, and you envy them.

Over the years, I have been told by many depressed people how puzzled and envious they are, for, in all their family, they are the only one with any worries, the only one to get depressed. Brothers and sisters, uncles, aunts and cousins all lead happy and untroubled lives. Later, when my depressed clients decide to value and accept themselves, and the prison walls of their depression vanish, they start to talk to their relatives and what do they find? They find that everyone has burdens and disappointments, everyone has their share of suffering, and no one should be envied. Indeed, it is one of the benefits of depression that it protects us from seeing just how much suffering there is in the world.

Not that being depressed prevents us from seeing *all* the suffering in the world. If you believe that you are bad, and that other people are dangerous, then you must conclude that:

Life is terrible and death is worse.

When we are small children our parents show us, not just in what they say but in what they do, what meaning we should give to life and death. Some of us are lucky, for we have parents who show us in word and deed that life is wonderful and death not to be feared. Some of us are not so lucky.

Lynette wrote to me to say:

'To most people I probably seem a very capable lady with three small, exciting children, someone who is really very sensible and is ready to wade in and do all kinds of work concerned with children's activities and sport, but in myself I carry such a burden of deep misgiving and lack of self-confidence that I spoil life for myself . . .

'My father was a sea captain and therefore I was brought up by my mother. Life seems to have been normal until I was about seven, when my mother's mother died. Then my mother was left without support. Poor thing. She was so scared her life would shatter that I think she would rather have done nothing that venture doing anything. Like the introverts you describe in your books, she built massive walls of defence around her life. I remember the rituals of hand-washing, the locking of the doors (in which I had to take part until my late teens, when I went to university), the refusal to wear underclothes because they might be tainted in some way, the wearing of old dirty clothes because they were safer than new clean ones, the counting out of pound notes, the placing of traps in front of her bedroom door to ensure that no one went in and touched her clothes, the walking back along the road to check that no one was following her on her short trips out, the ritual once-a-week shopping trip with a special bag to bring home the sanitary towels so that they didn't touch the other shopping – so many rituals, these are just a few, and I was privy to them all . . .

'The fear of death has haunted me since I was a little child. I remember once, when I was quite small – perhaps ten – lying in the back of the car as we drove home at night through some warehouses and I remember thinking that it must be like this lying in a coffin. I remember screaming out but not daring to tell my parents of what I was afraid. I remember later, when I was about thirteen, sitting beside the fire at home and experiencing the feeling of total annihilation. It was like a giant wave coming to envelop me and after that 'I wouldn't be there'. That phrase has haunted me on and off all my life. I'll die and 'I won't be there'.

'My fear of death has lessened since I have had children. Yet when I was younger, I remember thinking that death made a mockery of life. What sense was there in life when death annihilated everything in the end? What was the point of doing things when you died in the end? Life with the children has changed that for me and I've outgrown my fear of death. What I feel now is sadness that this lovely thing can't go on and on. I remember my mother's terrible fear of death and I remember her saying to me one day just as I was going to school, "Don't forget you'll die one day too." What a way to start a day at school!'

We discover death when we are small children, and, as soon as we discover the fact of death, we have to give death a meaning.[22]
There are only two meanings we can give to death. Either it is the

end of my identity or it is a doorway to another life. Once we have decided which of these two meanings we shall give to death, we have determined the purpose of our life.

If we decide that death means the end of my identity, our purpose in life is to make our life satisfactory. There are many ways in which we can define 'satisfactory'. As introverts, we can define it in ways which mean developing our individuality and achieving many things. As extraverts, we can define 'satisfactory' in ways which mean that we are surrounded by loving people. Or as Successful Selves, people who, as extraverts or introverts, have developed themselves fully and live easily in both their internal and external reality, we can define 'satisfactory' as individual achievement and being surrounded by loving people.[23]

If we decide that death is a doorway to another life, we are immediately confronted by the question of justice. We can imagine life after death as being much better or much worse than life on earth. If there is a life after death which is much better than life on earth, is it fair that everyone should go there, irrespective of how bad they have been? Should Heaven open its gates to Hitler as well as Mother Teresa? Our answer is usually 'no', and with that 'no' we try to work out what are the rules we must follow in this life in order to qualify for a better life after death. Thus, if we see death as a doorway to another life, we have to live this life according to the rules of the next.

As we work all this out, we are working out our set of religious or philosophical beliefs by which we explain the purpose of life and the nature of death.

If we accept and value ourselves and see death as the end of our existence, we can feel reasonably sure that we can make our life satisfactory and that death will not be something to fear. If we accept and value ourselves and we see death as a doorway to another life, we can feel reasonably sure that we shall meet the standards of the next life.

However, if you believe that you are bad and unacceptable, and you see death as the end of your identity, you expect that you will fail to make your life satisfactory, and that your death will be a punishment for your failure. If you believe that you are bad and unacceptable and you see death as a doorway to another life, you see yourself failing to meet the standards of that other life and being punished in the afterlife as you were punished in this life.   **(D 9)**

Some of us, at least for part of our lives, are unsure whether death is the end of our identity or a doorway to another life. If we value and accept ourselves, we can cheerfully say that it doesn't matter which it is, because for us life is good and death not something to be feared. We can say cheerfully, 'If death's the end, then I won't know anything about it, and if there's something after, I'll deal with that when I get there.' But if you are uncertain of which meaning to give to death and you believe that you are bad and unacceptable, then you face the worst of both possibilities, an unsatisfactory life and a Hereafter of punishment. Life is indeed terrible and death worse. You cannot but help feel that:

Only bad things have happened to me in the past and only bad things will happen to me in the future.

If you believe that you are bad and unacceptable, if you fear, hate and envy other people, and if you see life as terrible and death as worse, then what you remember from the past is coloured (sombred would be a better word) by these memories. Every scene from the past is one of loss, disappointment, regret, even if it is not also one of humiliation and fear.

Similarly, when you look to the future, you can see only misery, the punishments you deserve for your badness and inadequacy. Good fortune is something you dread, for you believe that good fortune can only be followed by bad, and if you are blessed by good fortune you could be doubly punished by bad. Like Opus in *Bloom County*, you can draw a pessimistic conclusion out of every event.[24]

Many of the people who later become depressed have always held a pessimistic view of life. Such people regard optimists as fools. After all, if you go along expecting good fortune, you are bound to be disappointed, and the pain of disappointment is very great.

Whereas, if you go along in a kind of low level misery, always expecting the worst, you can be surprised by joy.

I have had many arguments with my depressed clients about the relative merits of optimism and pessimism, and they have each derided my foolish optimism. They have rejected my argument that we can make a great deal of our life a self-fulfilling prophecy. You can go along to a party expecting not to enjoy it, and you can make sure that you don't. Where other people were concerned, two of my father's favourite sayings, 'You only get back what you give away', and, 'You catch more flies with honey than you do with vinegar', turn out to be true in most cases.

However, no amount of honey, I have found, can wrench suffering away from people who want to hold on to it, and to the satisfaction they feel when doom and disaster prove them right. For them the greatest satisfaction is in being able to say, 'I told you so'.

Somehow, we have to find a wise balance between optimism and pessimism, along the lines of 'Hope for the best but prepare for the worst'. This works all right when we see 'the worst' as things which might happen in the world around us, but, if you see badness inside you, 'the worst' can arise at any time, especially if you believe that the evidence that you are bad is anger which, no matter how much you try to eradicate it, you still feel inside you. You hold firmly to your belief that:

Anger is evil.

As children, the way that we got ourselves most frequently into trouble was by being angry. When we were toddlers, if another child snatched our toy, we would assert our right to the toy and snatch it back, often giving the other child a hit, only to find that the adult who saw us do this would punish us. If we found ourselves overwhelmed by our feelings, and in despair and rage we flung ourselves on the floor and screamed and kicked, our mother, embarrassed by our bad behaviour, would speak to us sharply and perhaps hit us.

As we got older we continued to be punished for fighting with our friends and siblings, just as we were punished for 'answering back' an adult, no matter how insulting that adult had been to us.

As often as not, it was our anger that got us into those situations where we were forced to define 'I am being punished by my bad parent' as 'I am bad and being punished by my good parent'. Thus our anger came to be the essence of our badness.

What made coping with our anger so difficult was that all too often we were not shown by our parents and teachers ways of expressing anger which were not disruptive and dangerous and which actually improved communication and understanding between people. We found that adults were allowed to get angry with us, but that we were not allowed to get angry with adults. We found that adults were allowed to be violent with us, but that we were not allowed to be violent with adults. We saw adults shouting, threatening, swearing, hitting people, throwing things, slamming doors, killing people (and perhaps not just on television), and angry adults refusing to speak, shutting themselves away, sulking, threatening to leave, leaving and not coming back. We saw, and felt, adults being angry with one another but taking that anger out on a child.

Rarely did we see adults arguing fiercely with one another and ending the argument with a laugh and a compromise. Rarely did an adult show us how anger can be thought about and fashioned into a response which gets your point of view across but does not create unbridgeable rifts in the fabric of society.

What I have described here are the ordinary experiences which all children have. Alas, many children have extraordinary and terrifying experiences of adults' anger.

Many of you who have grown up believing that anger is evil have witnessed scenes of terrible anger. One of my clients described how, as a child, she would step between her parents as her father threatened her mother with a knife. This would give her mother time to run out of the house. 'I always thought,' she told me, 'that one day he would put that knife in me. I still have nightmares where he's chasing me with that knife.'

Others of you who have grown up believing that anger is evil have, as children, lived in a home where nobody ever got angry. Discord was expressed by silence, cold, unending silence. Perhaps your mother spent all her time trying to please your father, and if she ever tried to complain or argue the slightest look of displeasure on his face would reduce her to silence. Perhaps your parents never spoke directly to one another, but communicated only through you. Perhaps, if you offended your parents, you might be told, quietly, to go to your room and remain there until your parents would allow you back into their presence again, or perhaps you might, apparently, just have ceased to exist for all the notice they took of you.

Meryl, who is an extravert, told me how this silence made her feel that she had disappeared. 'I'd look at myself in the mirror, just to make sure that I was still there. I got so I would do anything, absolutely anything, for my parents so they wouldn't ignore me.'

Extraverts can be enormously afraid of anger, for anger means the rejection and abandonment which threatens to annihilate them. They can become very skilled in denying their own anger, and say, 'I never get angry', when what they mean is 'I daren't get angry lest I drive away the people I need for my sense of existence.' Often they label their anger as fear, and often the fear they feel is guilt for their unacknowledged anger. Sometimes this anger labelled fear, the hatred that comes from being continually afraid, and the fear of punishment culminate in that most horrible experience, a panic attack.

Introverts can fear anger, or the expression of anger, for that can be the chaos in which the introvert sees the threat of annihilation. Introverts are very skilled at isolating their feelings of anger and separating them from the experience which gave rise to that anger. They then deny that they are angry, or they label their anger 'righteous anger' and use it in a way to make themselves look virtuous. When James was telling me about his father, he suddenly realized that the reason his father, a cold, obsessional minister, regularly beat him on Sunday afternoons was not, as his father had always said, because a conscientious and loving father had a duty to chastise his wayward son, but because his father was disgusted and angry with himself for preaching God's word and knowing what a miserable sinner he was.

Thus, by isolating their anger and then denying it or 'virtuously' relabelling it, introverts do not have to feel afraid of their anger. On the whole, introverts dislike being afraid more than they dislike being angry.

However, whether we call our anger by another name, or pretend to ourselves that we are not angry, or deny the real cause of our anger, our anger does not go away. How could it, when our anger is as much part of us as is our breath?

Without our anger the human race would not have survived. This planet, fertile though it is, is not particularly hospitable to us, and, compared to the animals with which we had to compete, we are quite puny. Certainly, we had our intelligence, but intelligence does not create courage. It is anger, that anger which says, 'I am here, and I have the right to be here, and I will survive.' We rarely say these words when we are angry, for there is no need to say them.

'I am here, and I have the right to be here, and I will survive' is what anger means.

The dilemma that anger presents us with every day of our lives is that if we always assert ourselves and our courage and our anger by expressing our anger, we cannot live with the people whom we cannot live without. On the other hand, if we *never* assert ourselves, our courage and our anger, we lose ourselves, we cease to be a person, and we become a no-thing.

How can we find the right balance between asserting our anger and not asserting our anger?

The answer to this depends on individual circumstances. For instance, if you live in a country where free speech is valued, you can express your anger with your government by writing to the newspapers, but if you live in a country where free speech is punished, expressing your anger with your government is much more dangerous.

However, working out the right balance between asserting and not asserting your anger becomes impossible if you believe that anger is evil. How can you think carefully and logically about something which you reject and fear?

So long as you go on believing that anger is evil, you will go on see-sawing between denying your anger and thus denying yourself and having your anger burst out in uncontrollable ways like being violent, or having panic attacks, or becoming ill.

Many people have tackled this problem by joining assertiveness training classes where they learn to see themselves as having the right to assert themselves, that anger is an acceptable and necessary part of themselves, and to find efficient, appropriate, and socially acceptable ways of expressing that anger.

However, while some of us have learned better ways of dealing with our own anger, many of us still find the most difficult part of the anger dilemma is in dealing with other people's anger. We might feel all right about speaking angrily to another person, but we don't feel at all right when that person speaks angrily to us. We take personally what that other person says, and we feel hurt.

Those of you who get depressed are experts in taking other people's anger personally. You cannot say, 'He's just had a bad day and he's letting off steam. I just happened to be the convenient one to cop it.' You say to yourself, 'He hates me', and you withdraw, feeling hurt and unforgiving. You must do this, because you believe that you must:

Never forgive and never expect to be forgiven.

When we are weak and helpless in the power of people who are injuring us, we may not be able to escape from this terrible situation, but there is one thing we can do to protect ourselves. We can vow never to forgive.

Making this promise to ourselves makes us feel stronger. We affirm that we are a person in our own right who has secrets which our enemy cannot penetrate and who, though lacking strength now, will in the future be strong. By not forgiving we give ourselves hope.

So, as a small, weak child in the hands of domineering and cruel adults and older children, we were wise to draw a conclusion which gave us courage and hope.

We turned our conclusion not to forgive into scenes in our story where we would triumph over our adversaries. When our anger and hurt were great, we imagined vanquishing and destroying them. When we felt shamed and humiliated, we imagined returning in the glory and having them grovel at our feet. When we felt rejected and abandoned, we imagined ourselves as rich and famous, and our adversaries begging for our recognition.

Such day dreams cheered us up enormously, and, if our adversaries had ceased their attacks on us and returned to being loving parents and siblings, we might find it in our hearts to forgive them.

However, if we continued to find ourselves attacked, abused, shamed, humiliated, rejected and abandoned, no mere day dream of revenge could purge our emotions and reconcile us to those around us. In the attempt to keep ourselves safe we had to go on not forgiving.

Thus do many children become adults who believe that it is wrong to forgive. They will argue, quite correctly, that if you forgive you leave yourself open to further hurt. Some adults who believe that it is wrong to forgive still experience forgiving as giving up part of themselves. Forgiving makes them feel less of a person.

Not forgiving can become a way of trying to control other people. There are many parents who, perhaps, would not dream of hitting their child but who do not hesitate to use that most cruel admonition, 'Mummy won't love you if you do that'.

Provided your spouse and children have a strong sense of guilt, you can manipulate and control them by threats to withdraw your approval of them until such times as they make amends. Being unforgiving can make you quite powerful and, eventually, very lonely. Sooner or later, everyone you have ever known is on your list of the unforgiven, even those adult children on whom you have expended so much effort. I always feel sad when I talk with parents who, like Dan and Mary, come to ask me about their adult children who are in difficulties, but I am much more saddened by those people in the prison of their depression who tell me how they have fallen out with their adult children and will have nothing to do with them. What a waste, when our children can become, as adults, our best and closest friends.

Not forgiving we injure ourselves. Ruth Fuller, whose son was murdered, was asked on television whether she had forgiven the young man who had killed her son. She said,

'I don't want him hurt. I just try to write him out of my life. I feel very bad saying I can't forgive this boy. I feel very badly about it, but I don't suppose I ever will. It's a destructive thing. The only person being hurt by me not forgiving is me. It does hurt you inside. You are not the person you are. You can never be, because there is this other thing there all the time.'[25]

Even without using not forgiving as a way of controlling people, taking other people's thoughtless slights and bad temper personally and vowing never to forgive them soon leads to loneliness. Since each of us is so wrapped up in our own affairs, we often do things which other people find hurtful. Here I am, working away on a book which I hope will help some people, and I forget a dear friend's birthday. Will she forgive me?

Will I forgive myself?

If you see forgiving as something which you ought not do, then when you do something wrong, you must not forgive yourself.

This is where you become the cruel jailer in your prison of depression. Your prisoner cannot expiate his guilt. Your sins are unforgivable.

George believed that his sins were unforgivable, so he expected that on Judgement Day God would not forgive him. Like George, if you believe in God and that you are bad and that it is wrong to forgive, you will feel sure that God will not forgive you.

This is why many people with a strong religious faith have, when they are depressed, a powerful sense of being damned. Psychiatrists call this 'irrational guilt' and say that it is a symptom of endogenous or psychotic depression. They fail to see that a sense of being damned is the logical outcome of the person's beliefs and that the feeling of being damned is extremely real. It is the person's own truth.

Jesus talked a great deal about the necessity of forgiveness. He told Peter that he should forgive his brother, not seven times, but 'seventy times seven', and He taught the prayer, 'And forgive us our debts as we forgive our debtors'.

Jesus explained:

> For if you forgive men their trespasses, your heavenly Father will also forgive you. But if you forgive not men their trespasses, neither will your Father forgive your trespasses.

So, if you cannot forgive yourself or other people, you know that you are damned. But if you do forgive yourself and other people, you will be forgiven.

However, Jesus did speak of one unforgivable sin, and that was the sin against the Holy Ghost. There has been much argument about what this means, and interpretations have been expressed in many different ways, but what these interpretations have in common is the sense that if, when we glimpse some profound and awesome aspect of our existence as an individual and as part of the universe, an aspect which we know without the necessity of proof is true, and then we deny that truth, we do ourselves damage. We have, in fact, not been true to ourselves, and that is unforgivable.

But not for ever unforgivable. We can find our way back to our own truth.

We were born with a sense of our own truth, of being ourselves, and with a sense of belonging, of being at home in the world. Then, bit by bit, we were forced to deny our own truth and to give up being ourselves. As we gave up being ourselves we lost our relationship to the world. We and it became alien, 'A stranger and afraid, in a world I never made'.

In order to survive, we gave up the most valuable thing we could ever have. No amount of fame, sex, riches, and power can compare with the joy of being yourself at home in the world.

No wonder we cannot forgive ourselves for such a loss.

No wonder we feel we have been asked to pay too high a price for our survival.

No wonder we feel cheated and bitter.

Yet, if we stop for a moment and cease feeling unforgiving, resentful, bitter and guilty about not being good enough, if we can just be still, we can discover something which we have always known.

Our own truth is always there. We are always ourselves. The world is there and we are part of it. We had simply hidden this knowledge from ourselves. All we have to do is to find it again.

Why don't we rediscover this knowledge?

Why do we stay locked in the prison of depression?

II

Why Is It So Hard
To Change?

6

Fearing Change

Change is always frightening. Even when it is something we want – such as our wedding, a better job, a splendid holiday – before we embark on it we feel scared. Perhaps we feel just a shiver of nervousness, or perhaps we worry about something going wrong, or perhaps we feel the greatest fear of all, and find ourselves falling, helpless, through empty space, or watching, helpless, as all the people we need disappear.

So it is that if we are to make changes in our lives we must be courageous.

Such courage can be found relatively easily in two kinds of situations:

When we are certain that the new situation in which we shall find ourselves will bring us every advantage and happiness.

When we are certain that the situation we are leaving is totally and absolutely bad.

Thus, if the new situation promises perfection, or if the old situation is totally imperfect, we have certainty, and, if there is one thing you crave when you are depressed, it is certainty.

The certainty you crave when you are offered a chance of giving up being depressed is that you will be perfectly happy for ever and ever. After all, you know that all those people who are not depressed are always perfectly happy.

This idea is a version of the self-deluding comfort we each give ourselves, *anyone who hasn't got my problem hasn't got any problems at all.*

Mothers of small children think that childless women have no problems. Stockbrokers think that anyone who isn't a stockbroker has an easy life. Nurses think that anyone who isn't a nurse doesn't know what hard work is. And so on.

These ideas are just part of the comfort blanket we each snuggle into when we feel disheartened. However, when we do look at other people without the aid of our comfort blanket, we can see quite clearly that every person has troubles to bear.

So, when you are depressed you want to believe that all non-depressed people never have any troubles, but, if you look clearly, you see that they do. You might ask your therapist, as many of my clients have asked me, 'If I give up being depressed, does that mean I shall be perfectly happy?', but you will find that your therapist will give you no such guarantee. You would not believe any therapist who did. You know quite well that no one is perfectly happy all the time.

Thus the uncertainty of what might befall you if you give up being depressed can stop you from changing.

Surely, though, the completely terrible situation in which you find yourself, that of being depressed, would make it easy for you to change.

But is it *completely* terrible?

Whenever we find ourselves in a situation which is totally and absolutely bad for us, unless we are being constrained by other people, we leave it immediately. Whenever we remain in a bad situation it is because it is not totally bad for us. It contains some advantage which we are reluctant to give up.

Many people, finding Beirut to be a totally bad situation, left, but others stayed, because for them that bad situation has advantages. Perhaps they make money out of trading arms and drugs, and see this as a major achievement for themselves. Perhaps they see their purpose in life as caring for other people, and where could there be people more in need of their care? Or perhaps they feel that, while the agony of war is great, the agony of being away from their family is greater.

So it is that many people, finding themselves in the Beirut of depression, or perhaps only glimpsing it on the horizon as a possibility, see this situation as totally and absolutely bad, and will get themselves out of it immediately. They change their lives and their attitudes and flee that war-torn city. But others stay, because their prison of depression contains certain advantages.

It is the advantages of depression which keep you depressed, not the pain. If depression were totally and absolutely bad you would not stay within its walls.

To give up being depressed you have to give up the advantages of being depressed, and that can be difficult.

The first step is to make very clear to yourself what these advantages are.

Of course, since you hold firmly to the view that everything in your life and in you is totally and absolutely bad, you will insist that there is *nothing* in your life which confers on you the slightest advantage. However, if you take a careful look at what goes on in life generally, you will see that everything that happens has good and bad implications.

An aeroplane crashes. The bad implication is that some people die. The good implication is that the airline improves its safety procedures, thus saving the lives of many more people. You believe that you are basically a bad person and have to work hard to be good. The bad implication of this is that you always feel unhappy, stressed and needing to work harder. The good implication is that your achievements or your concern for others help other people.

Everything in life is a mixture of good and bad.

Even depression.

So, *what advantages do you get out of being depressed?* **(D 10)**

In this Section I have outlined some of the possible advantages – certainty, pride, taking things personally, and hanging on to hopes.

Depression for you does have advantages, but it is not just your advantages which keep you depressed. It is also the advantages that other people get out of your being depressed. What some of these advantages are I have put in the chapter called *Other People*.

Let's begin with the advantage of certainty.

7

Wanting Certainty

The unknown is always uncertain. So we say to ourselves, 'Better the devil you know than the devil you don't know'.

At least with an old devil you feel you can predict what he will do to you and you have well-tried ways of protecting yourself from him. With an old devil you feel you know what is the very worst he can do. Perhaps any change will mean jumping out of the frying pan and into the fire.

Consoling yourself like this, you can stick with a boring job, an unpleasant partner, a long-standing depression, and, even if you are not happy, you are secure in your misery.

What can be more secure than the prison of depression, where every day is the same and nothing can get in to upset you further?

The shutting out of all uncertainties, disturbances and uncontrollable threats is the essence of the defence of depression. You cut yourself off, you throw up a wall, surround yourself with a barrier, and you are, you hope, safe and certain. Of course the prison walls are not impermeable. Some things do break through to disturb you, and there are things inside yourself which you cannot shut out, and they will plague you, just as the continuing isolation will bring increasing pain. But the defence of depression will shut out the great uncertainties, and, though you feel miserable, you feel secure.

You know that outside the walls of your prison are all sorts of matters which need your attention. But to give these matters your attention means encountering pain, and the pain of loss and disappointment is far, far sharper than any physical pain. I remember when my son and I left Australia after my divorce I needed to complete my tax forms for that year in order to have some of the tax I had paid returned to me. Desperately short of money though I was, I could not bring myself to fill in those forms because that meant reviewing the events of the past twelve months. I was no stranger to physical pain. I had given birth to a child and had had four major operations, including the removal of part of one lung, but the pain of these was as nothing to the pain of my loss and disappointment. I lacked the courage to face that pain, and I have never, to this day, completed those taxation papers.

Inside the safety of depression you can refuse to confront all the situations that you find difficult. You can avoid seeing people, going to places and, most of all, making decisions.

Psychiatrists regard a depressed person's statement, 'I can't make decisions', as a symptom of an illness, when really it is a reasonably effective defence.

If you are trying to shut out all those matters which you find uncontrollable, threatening and confusing, you cannot give those matters the careful scrutiny they need if you are to make a decision about them. They create such turmoil in your mind that you decide that it is best not to decide. You can say, 'I am depressed. I cannot make any decisions.'

By deciding not to decide we can feel that everything that is bothersome will vanish and everything else will remain the same. But, of course, things do not disappear just because we ignore them, and nothing does remain the same. Everything is changing all the time, and we are always part of that change.

We all like to pretend to ourselves that there are times and places in our lives where we do not make decisions. We say, 'I won't make a decision about that', and overlook the fact that we have *decided not to decide*. Spending the day in bed with the blankets over your head is as much a result of a decision as is going out and facing the world.

Decisions are much easier to make when you know what the consequences will be. The consequences of spending the day in bed with the blankets over your head are fairly easy to predict – you'll miss a day's work, your home won't be cleaned, your family will complain, there'll be nothing in the fridge for you to eat, and so on – while the consequences of going out and facing the world are much harder to predict.

Especially since the world is no longer what you thought it was.

Depression is one of those defences we can use when we see that there is a major discrepancy between what we thought reality is and what it shows itself to be.

As we realize this discrepancy, the solid certainties of our life turn to matchwood, breaking and splintering round our head as a bottomless chasm yawns beneath our feet.

Depression is an attempt to shore up the splintering, brittle timbers, an attempt to catch on to something solid as you fall into the abyss.

Once you have shored up some brittle structure or have placed your feet on a fragment of rock, you dare not move lest what little safety you have crumbles.

I often think of this situation as being like that of a person who, having fallen over a cliff, catches on to a projecting tree root and manages to press his toes against a tiny crevice in the cliff side. Even when someone from the safety of the cliff top throws down a rope, he dare not reach for it, lest an untoward movement loosen the tree root and he plunge down into the bottomless abyss.

Once, when I was describing this image, one of my listeners commented that this image was of a far safer situation than the one where she felt herself to be when she was depressed. On those occasions, she felt she was in a wooden cage where she could not sit, stand, nor lie, but could only crouch, fearing to rock the cage, for it is suspended by a fraying rope over a bottomless pit.

Thus, making a decision whose consequences you can neither predict nor control could release the tree root or snap the fraying rope.

Or so it seems to you, because you so doubt yourself and mistrust change. When such images come upon you, you dare not work on them to change them, to imagine how you could take the chance to seize the rope which would pull you to safety, or even, with one mighty bound, become free to soar up in the air, and so find the chasm but a gentle valley and the earth warm and welcoming beneath your feet.

Why regard change as dangerous?

Why not regard change as opportunity, adventure, freedom?

However, to come to this joyous way of regarding change you have to give up something very important to you.

You want security and you want freedom.

What you have to give up is believing that it is possible to be both secure and free.

We all want to have our cake and eat it too.

We all want to be completely secure and completely free.

We do not want to recognize that the more security we have, the less freedom, and the more freedom, the less security.

We can work hard to get ourselves a secure income, we can marry someone steady and reliable, we can fit our home with secure locks and burglar and fire alarms, we can live in a secure, law-abiding neighbourhood, and we can feel ourselves to be secure. But we are not free. We have obligations and responsibilities arising out of what we have done to make ourselves secure. We have to obey the laws of the community which keeps us safe. We have purchased security with our freedom.

If we do not understand the complementary nature of security and freedom, if we go on believing that we can be both completely secure and completely free, we make ourselves very unhappy.

Many people who live in luxurious security feel that they ought to be free and behave as if they are, thus creating havoc for themselves and those around them, as well as material for the gossip columnists. Many people, having opted for the secure job and the secure marriage, find themselves bored and suffering inexplicable anguish.

Those people who do understand the complementary nature of freedom and security know not to pay too high a price for security. They opt for just a moderate amount of security and keep as much of their freedom as they can. They know that in the insecurity of freedom we can feel anxious, but we can also feel the bliss of letting things take their course, of going with the flow. In the insecurity of freedom they can view alternative possibilities, change the way they think and act, and, most importantly, they can hope.

Hope can exist only in a state of uncertainty.
Total security means total certainty.
Total security means to be without hope.

The prison of depression is built with blocks of total certainty. 'I am bad, evil, unacceptable to myself and other people. Other people are such that I fear, hate and envy them. Life is terrible and death is worse. Only bad things have happened to me in the past and only bad things with happen to me in the future. Anger is evil. Never forgive.'

Certainty. Security. No hope.

To hope means to run the risk of disappointment.

Avoid disappointment. Stay depressed.

To be insecure means not to be in control.

Stay in control. Stay depressed.

To be uncertain means to be unsure of the future.

Predict the future with certainty. Stay depressed.

Deciding to be depressed has consequences far and wide and quite beyond your control.   **(D 11)**

For instance, you might, by being depressed, be putting off facing up to the discrepancy between what, according to your story, your marriage should be and what it actually is, but once you give up being depressed you have to make a decision about your marriage, whether to accept the discrepancy and live with it or reject the discrepancy and leave your marriage. Whichever you decide, your decision will have consequences for you, your partner, your children, and all your friends and relations. There is no way you can predict and control these consequences.

Every decision that we make alters the world of meaning which we have created. Deciding to eat Puff Wheat instead of Corn Flakes for breakfast may not be a major change, but abandoning 'I am bad and unacceptable' and replacing it with 'I accept and value myself' is. Every decision you have made since you decided that you were bad and valueless was based on that decision. Now all those conclusions need reviewing and changing. Now all new situations demand a new response from you.

Now your history has to be revised and a new future planned. Now you have to think about a meaning of life that is not built just on punishment and reward. Now you have to find other ways of dealing with anger. Now you have to review all that unforgivingness and desire for revenge. Most of all, you have to reconsider how you will get along with other people.

All the time you considered that you were bad and unacceptable, you had to keep a barrier between you and other people. You dare not let other people close in case they discover how bad you are, but at the same time you had to find ways of holding on to them because none of us, neither introverts nor extraverts, can live alone. You had developed all sorts of skills in hanging on to other people, but at the same time keeping them at a distance.

Perhaps you had decided always to be the parent in your relationships. You were authoritarian, dominating, controlling, perhaps in a very nice way, but, nevertheless, all your relatives, lovers, friends, colleagues and acquaintances were pushed by you into being the child in your relationships. Because you were so very good at being good, you told yourself that you always knew what was best for other people, and so you did not hesitate to tell other people what to do. Because you were in a position of power over some people – perhaps your employees, or your children, or your partner – and because there are always many people who like being told what to do since that absolves them of personal responsibility, or because you were so skilled in making people need you and since there are always many people who want to be dependent, you could surround yourself with people who behaved towards you like obedient children towards a parent. If they tried to be disobedient you could threaten them with your displeasure, or you could make them feel guilty. Of course you often felt burdened by all the responsibilities you had, and often you felt lonely when your family, friends and colleagues treated you like children treat an adult, that is, they tended not include the adult in their play and jokes, but in being the parent you could keep people around you and not let them dangerously close.

Perhaps, instead, you decided always to be the child in your relationships. You looked around for people who were willing to be the parent in your relationships and who would accept your dependency. You could find a boss who never wanted to be challenged but always wanted praise, a partner who wanted to be in charge, friends who never felt more virtuous than when they were being sympathetic and supporting. You could even turn your children into being your parents. Wherever possible you avoided people who had failed to develop an exquisite sense of pity and guilt, because making other people feel pity and guilt became your special way of keeping people around you, and as you were always a child they could not expect you ever to behave as an adult. Of course, you often were annoyed that other people made decisions without consulting you, and you did not like being treated as an immature fool, but in being a child you could control others, be looked after and rarely be challenged.

Perhaps you specialized in being the parent with some people and the child with others, or perhaps with your nearest and dearest you alternated between being the parent and being the child, choosing whichever one seemed suitable at the time. This could be aggravating for your partner, but perhaps your partner alternated in roles as well. Such a relationship might work reasonably well, except for when you both wanted to be a parent or a child at the same time. However, from time to time, you might suspect that there could be more to a relationship than playing mummies and daddies.

Deciding that you are acceptable and valuable means that you do not have to go on controlling your relationships. Instead you can simply be yourself. However, if you have spent all your life controlling your relationships, you have few skills in dealing with people when you are simply yourself. How do you deal with people when

you are not forcing them into being a parent or a child? Relationships where there are no barriers and no controls are risky,
(D 12) challenging and unpredictable.

Perhaps it would be better to stick with what you know. And, after all, you have your pride to consider.

8

Pride

So far in this book I have been stressing how the terrors, uncertainties, losses and disappointments of childhood force us to give up so much of ourselves and how we come to think of ourselves as being bad and unacceptable. How then can we have pride? Surely the belief that we are bad and unacceptable would make us humble?

Ah, yes, but when we are at our most humble, we are at our most proud. We have to be, for it is our pride, like our anger and our refusal to forgive, both aspects of our pride, which enables us to survive. Come what may, so long as the force of life is in us, we want to survive. Even as we cry, 'I've had enough, I'm giving up', our determination to survive as ourselves works out another means of survival and our pride carries it through. (Suicide is always an act of pride. When we feel that to live as other people expect us to live is to give up being ourselves and that there is no possibility that we shall obtain the conditions we need to be able to live comfortably with ourselves, forgiving ourselves, we can choose suicide as a way of continuing to be ourselves and thus maintaining our pride.)

So, as the terrors, uncertainties, losses and disappointments of childhood force us to draw conclusions which make us give up being ourselves, our pride says, 'If this is what I have to do and to believe, then I will take pride in it'.

You can take pride in knowing how bad you are, and you can scorn those people who think they are good. You can take pride in knowing what people are – untrustworthy and contemptible. You can take pride in knowing and facing up to the bleakness of life and the fearsomeness of death. You can take pride in never getting angry, and pride in showing only righteous anger. You can take pride in the strength of your determination not to forgive, and the tenacity with which you seek revenge.

You can take pride in the way you expect nothing from life. You can take pride in your capacity to suffer. You can say to yourself, 'My burdens are greater than anyone else's', and 'Anyone who hasn't got my problems hasn't got any problems at all', and, since you know that something would be amiss if you weren't suffering, you can take pride in your suffering. Some depressed people regard their depression as their cross and take pride in bearing their cross as Jesus bore his. If you take pride in your suffering you will resist anyone who offers to take that suffering away. If you see your suffering as a way of ensuring reward, if not in this life, then in the next, you will prefer to store up treasure in heaven than to be happy on earth.

Best of all, you can take pride in your high standards. You have set yourself these standards, and, even though you never quite reach them and you are constantly berating yourself for your failure, you feel nothing but contempt for those people who do not share your standards.

You lay a trap for any unwary therapist or friend who might, out of concern for your health and strength, urge you to take things easily. 'Don't work so hard', we might say, or, 'There's no need to clean your home right through every day', and to prove our point go on to say that we never take work home at weekends, or that we give our home a thorough cleaning no more than once a week. You murmur agreement, for you are always polite, but you are thinking, 'How lazy!' and 'How dirty!'

When we live just being ourselves, accepting ourselves, we live comfortably within ourselves, enjoying a sense of wholeness. We have standards about how people ought to behave and how things ought to be done, but these standards and ourselves are not separate. We are all of one piece. But when we regard ourselves as being bad and unacceptable, the standards we have about how people ought to behave and how things ought to be done are separate from our beliefs about ourselves.

There is:

> *the bad you, always expecting and always hurt by criticism,*

and, quite separate,

> *your high standards, criticizing, judging, condemning you
> and other people, your conscience.*

The trap you lay for any friend or therapist is that the friend or therapist cannot tell in advance which part of you is going to hear and respond to advice.

I might want, as I often do, to comfort that part of you which I see as a lost, lonely, suffering child and what you call 'me who is bad and unacceptable'. So I say, 'Be kind to yourself. Don't push yourself so hard. Relax. Enjoy yourself,' but my message does not reach that part of you. My message reaches only those judging and condemning standards, your harsh and punitive conscience, and so you see me as dangerous and contemptible. You say something along the lines of, 'Do-gooders like Dorothy Rowe encourage laxity and vice.'

On the other hand, you might have consulted a psychologist who uses the techniques developed by cognitive or behavioural therapists. These therapists believe in speaking to that part of you which is interested in getting things done, making some kind of progress. The therapist clarifies some issues you want to work on, say, tackling a certain job or learning to talk to yourself in more positive ways, and then shows you how you can do this systematically by setting goals, carrying out some regular activity, and keeping a written record of what you achieve. He sets you homework and expects you to report back at the next therapy session.

All very sensible and laudable. Your conscience would approve. Only your conscience doesn't hear any of this. The therapist's sensible advice goes straight to the 'bad you' who hears it, not as encouragement, but as wounding criticism and persecution. You say to yourself, 'I can't do this. Why does he expect me to do this? I've never been able to do this sort of thing. It's hopeless.'

Therapists are supposed to know about you and your conscience and to have ways of manoeuvring through the minefield you set, but friends and relatives who aren't therapists don't. So you hurt and confuse them. They try to comfort you by telling you to relax your standards, and you turn on them with contempt and outrage. They try to help you sort out your confusion, and you blame them for persecuting you.

And all of us, friends, relatives, therapists of all persuasions, each of us in our own way, try to convey to you that we care about you and that we know that you are a valuable, lovable, likeable person. But you can confidently sweep aside all these protestations. You know without reminding yourself that, '*If anyone says they like me, that person is either a fool or a liar.*'

Obviously.

If we know what a bad person you are, then when we say we like you, we are lying.

If we don't know what a bad person you are, then when we say we like you, we show that we are fools. We are too stupid to see what is before our eyes.

Who wants a liar or a fool for a friend or therapist?

Not you. You have high standards.

Thus you keep your therapist and anyone who might try to help you in a no-win position. This, of course, is another aspect of your pride. If you accept their advice, they will win, and you will lose, and you cannot let that happen.

The standard which your conscience demands is perfection. You who believe that you are irredeemably imperfect will accept nothing less than perfection. Only perfection, you think, will overcome your sense of badness. Your disgust with yourself is mirrored by your disgust with the world. The world, you believe, ought to be perfect.

You, your work, your home, and your family must be perfect. If you, your work, your home and your family are not perfect then you feel that your very self is in danger of being annihilated. As an introvert you see imperfection as everything going out of your control and falling into chaos, and as an extravert you see imperfection as the reason everyone will reject and abandon you.

Your demand for perfection drives a wedge between you and your family. Although you know how the slightest word of criticism cuts you to the heart, this does not stop you from criticizing others sharply and cruelly. Fearing imperfection, you become angry. You might hurl against the people you love the epithets you use against yourself. 'This room looks like a pig lives in it,' you say, as you tell your child to tidy his room. 'You're hopeless and disgusting,' you tell your loving partner. Or you refrain from abuse and instead withdraw into guilt-arousing silence, shutting out your loved ones who, if they are well supplied with guilt, grow miserable as their attempts at placating you fail, or, if they refuse to feel guilty, ignore you and leave you. Or, relying on the fact that the people you love love you, you say, 'If you don't do what I want you to do, I won't love you.' Such a threat, when put into practice, makes your extravert loved ones terrified and your introvert loved one grow cold towards you.

You will protest that in demanding perfection you are simply trying to do the best for your family. 'The best' you see as perfection, not what might realistically be achieved. You demand that your children should not only be perfectly good and perfectly educated, they should also be perfectly happy. 'I only want you to be happy,' you say to your family, and they, being ordinary people in an ordinary world and so having their own difficulties and disappointments, have to hide these from you. In your presence they strive to appear to be happy and content, and they live their lives away from you.

> Laura wrote to me, 'I'm twenty-two and I have had bouts of depression since I was about ten. It is an awful feeling, and was at its worst in my late teens, when I had serious thoughts of suicide. However, I have brought myself out of the suicidal stage of life, and now have learned to have some control over my depression. Astonishing though it may seem, your book has made me realize that my mother has had some bad patches of depression and I never knew. Hers shows in such different ways that I never recognized it. Imagine that – twenty years living together and we were really living alone! My parents both had such troublesome early lives that they want everything to be perfect and wonderful for me. How can you tell them you've thought of suicide when their first reaction will be to think that *they've* failed – that *they've* done something wrong. I've heard my mother cry – in great gushing sobs – and I couldn't take it if she cried because of me.'

This crazy notion that we and the world can be perfect is presented to us by the media every day. All women are slim, attractive and cheerful. All men are slim, attractive and manly. All children are healthy, properly fed, well mannered, attractive and enthusiastic. Everyone lives in a beautiful home, has a well paid job, lots of friends, and leads an interesting life. If you don't fit this picture, so our media say, then there is something wrong with you.

Why do the media do this to us? If you ask yourself this question you will find yourself being led away from your immediate concerns of yourself, your job, your family and friends, and into questions about politics and economics, how we live in a society which depends on the manufacture and selling of more and more goods. The economy, so our governments say, has to grow. If the media gave us the message, 'You're all right as you are', we would not go rushing out to buy ourselves new clothes, a new house, a new car, a new fitness course or a new beauty treatment. At weekends, instead of rushing out to buy paint for the house and new plants for the garden, we would sit around talking to our friends and playing with our children. When we took part in sport, instead of buying the latest equipment each year, we would go on using the stuff we liked year after year, just as we would wear the clothes we liked rather than the clothes we think we ought to wear. We would purchase goods simply because they met our needs and gave us pleasure, and not because we thought we should strive to buy more and more so as to conform to other people and appear to be successful.

To think about politics and economics is very difficult, for not only are these subjects full of inconsistencies and unanswerable questions, they can also make us feel insignificant and helpless. So, rather than think about why these pictures of perfection are presented to us every day, you simply see these pictures as the standard you ought to reach, and you berate yourself for your failure. Why aren't you slim, attractive, successful, with a multitude of perfect friends and a perfect family? Why aren't you perfect?

The idea that we can actually make ourselves and our world perfect is another of those fancies with which we like to delude ourselves. We forget that the only way we can know anything at all is when there is some kind of contrast or differential. We know light only because there is darkness, heat only because there is cold, life only because there is death, and perfection only because there is imperfection. In Heaven we shall need to remember our life on earth if we are to be aware of the perfection of Heaven. If all that we know in Heaven is perfection, we shall not be able to recognize perfection. It would mean, too, that in Heaven there would be no humour, for we invented humour as a life-enhancing way of coping with imperfection.

However, humour presents a problem to you, because while you might be very skilled at using humour to get along well with people while keeping them at a distance, and you might be even more skilled at turning your wit against yourself and lacerating yourself, you are frightened of other people's humour lest they hurt you, and you are very sensitive.

'Sensitive' is a word which many people who get depressed use with pride about themselves in such a way that they can then take pride in being depressed.

'Sensitive' can mean that you are a caring person, sensitive to other people's feelings and needs, and, of course, being sensitive to other people's needs and feelings is a virtue in which you can take great pride. However, being sensitive also means for you being easily hurt, and to defend yourself against the pain of such hurts you put up the prison walls of depression. Thus to you, being sensitive can mean both being good and being depressed.

If you believe that *by being depressed you show that you are good*, then being depressed becomes a source of great pride. 'If depression is a punishment for my badness, I accept it.' After all, good children who have been naughty hold out their hand for a slap, and good adults who have been caught speeding pay their fines. 'If suffering shows that I am good, then I will suffer.' 'Because of my concern for other people, I suffer and am depressed.'

Of course the argument that being sensitive shows that you are both depressed and good is a fallacious one. 'Sensitive' is being used here with two very different meanings, namely, 'easily hurt' and 'having empathy'. However, we do not always think clearly about matters where our pride is involved.

The kind of argument which leads to you seeing sensitivity as both the source of your depression and your goodness is often used by people who extend their notion of sensitivity to include their artistic ability. Here, such people see their creativity as arising from the same source as their depression. Thus they must resist having their depression taken away from them, for to do so would destroy their creativity.

Sometimes this argument is used to allow the person to claim artistic talent without having to put that claim to the test and risk being revealed as untalented ('I could have been a great artist but my depression prevented me'), and sometimes it is used tragically, in the way that Virginia Woolf and Sylvia Plath used it. They saw their creativity inextricably linked with their depression, and even though they each knew that their childhood experiences were linked to their adult pain, they did not want to uncover this link through therapy, since they believed that such an exposure would sap their creativity. Alas, when they felt that they could no longer live with their depression, they chose to die.

The pain that other people inflict on us can be very great, but the pain that we inflict on ourselves can be even greater. While many of the people who get depressed, despite the temptation, do not kill themselves, many inflict on themselves the long, drawn out pain of taking pride in *keeping yourself to yourself*.

This is how you can turn being frightened of other people into a virtue. You can claim that you have much more important things to do than waste time on mere people. Concentrating on the virtue of not wasting time stops you from remembering the breathtaking, paralysing fear you feel whenever you have to join a group of people.

As a child, you had good reason to be afraid of other people because they had hurt you in many different ways, and, to protect yourself and give yourself hope, you dreamed of becoming a marvellously extraordinary person. You imagined that you were a very special person, an ugly duckling about to turn into a swan, a hero yet to do an heroic deed, a star that would outshine every star that has ever been. One day your very specialness would be revealed and everyone would gaze at you in total love and admiration.

Such a dream stood you in good stead when you were a child, bolstering your courage and your pride, but as an adult these dreams played you false. These dreams made you quite unable to accept yourself as someone who was ordinary. Your pride would not allow you to be ordinary. So you decided that if you could not be the Most Perfect, Wonderful, Intelligent, Beautiful, Admired and Loved Person the Entire Universe in the Whole of Time Has Ever Seen, you would become the Worst, the Most Despicable, Confused, Evil Failure and Outcast the Entire Universe in the Whole of Time Has Ever Seen.

One of the most difficult things you have to do in dismantling your prison of depression is to come to see yourself as ordinary. Not humbly ordinary, taking pride in your ordinariness, but ordinary ordinary, part of the human race and everything that is. (You'll know when you come to see yourself as ordinary, because then you are gently and lovingly amused by your idiosyncrasies and you no longer take yourself a million per cent seriously.)

Sylvia Fraser, having faced up to what her father had done to her and having uncovered something of the sad and sordid history of his family, wrote:

'All of us are haunted by the failed hopes and undigested deeds of our forebears. I was lucky to find my family's dinosaur intact in one deep grave. My main regret is excessive self-involvement. Too often I was sleepwalking through other people's lives, eyes turned inward while I washed the blood off my hands. My toughest lesson was to renounce my own sense of specialness, to let the princess die along with the guilt-ridden child in my closet, to see instead the specialness of the world around me.'[26]

Pride is tricky. It can assert itself in a multitude of ways. It can save us, and it can destroy us.

The medieval Christian Church did not recognize how pride can save us. Instead, the Church saw the destructiveness of pride, and called it the deadliest of the seven Deadly Sins because *pride stops us from changing*.

The pride which stops us from changing is contained in those beliefs we constructed to shore up our self-esteem and self-confidence when, as children, we were being shown by the people around us that we were not acceptable and valuable. We pretended to ourselves that we *really* were very important, and we told ourselves how one day our true worth would be rewarded. If, as we got older, we regained our self-esteem and self-confidence, we could relinquish these comforting beliefs, but if we do not learn to care for and to value ourselves, we continue to cling to the beliefs which bolster our pride. (D 13)

These beliefs have to do with how important you really are and how, one day, your hopes and wishes will be fulfilled. Just how important you feel is contained in how you always take things personally.

9

Taking Things Personally

Harry was telling me about his problems at work. 'With my old boss, Ken,' he said, 'you could talk to him straight. You could argue with him and tell him where he'd got things wrong. We'd have some really big arguments and get steamed up, but all the time we knew we were arguing about work. Afterwards, when we'd got the thing sorted out, we'd just go on talking as usual, real friendly. But this new chap, it's impossible to have a reasonable discussion with him. Anything you might say that could be a criticism of him, he takes personally.'

To take things personally you have to do two things.

First, you have to interpret another person's words and actions as being intended to hurt you.

Second, you have to grant that person the right to hurt you.

Harry's old boss did not take things personally because, first of all, he interpreted Harry's arguments as being directed at a work problem and not at him, and, second, when Harry pounded the table and called him a stupid old goat, something he was wont to do in times of stress, Ken would not grant Harry the right to hurt him. He would brush Harry's abuse aside with 'that's just Harry letting off steam'.

Harry's new boss did not have such self-confidence. He suspected that Harry resented him, and so he interpreted Harry's criticisms about work as criticisms of him. He would not brush these criticisms aside because he was afraid of Harry, and so he granted Harry the right to hurt him.

Taking things personally begins as one of the measures we can take to protect ourselves when we are small and weak and feeling that we are being both overwhelmed and neglected by the people who should care for us. When we are in this situation we can feel ourselves to be totally and utterly unimportant. All other people

124

have turned their attention away from us. As extraverts we can feel that sense of abandonment which threatens to annihilate us, and as introverts we can feel a sense of aloneness like that of the sole inhabitant of an empty universe. We have to do something to cope with such desperate feelings.

So we redefine the situation by turning it into its opposite.

'Everybody ignores me,'

becomes

'Everybody takes notice of me.'

Now we have to ask ourselves, 'What kind of notice?'

It would be nice if the notice people took of us was to praise us, but to say to ourselves, 'Everybody notices me to praise me', is stretching it a bit too far. Of course, some of us in this situation who are feeling a very powerful threat of annihilation do try telling ourselves that we are as powerful as Napoleon, as desirable as Cleopatra, but once we disclose such fantasies to others we are likely to be called mad and then dealt with in unpleasant ways.

So what most of us do is to say to ourselves, 'Everybody takes notice of me to criticize, reject and hurt me'. This is in line with reality. As children, we do receive a great deal of criticism, rejection and hurt. All we have done is to change 'Many people take notice of me to criticize, reject and hurt me' into:

'Everybody takes notice of me to criticize, reject and hurt me.'

Now our pride has made us the centre of attention. But our sense of inadequacy remains.

As children, we recited the rhyme, 'Sticks and stones will break my bones but names will never hurt me', and we knew that it could be true, but so long as we saw other people as being bigger and more powerful than us, we went on giving their words the power to hurt us.

'Taking things personally' is a statement of both our pride and our sense of inadequacy. It is also a sign of a refusal to accept reality and of laziness in thinking.

The reality is that, as much as we want people to notice us and to take account of us, most people will not do this. People are involved most of all with their own lives. Most people, like Sylvia Fraser, sleepwalk through other people's lives. Most of the things which other people do and say which can hurt are not said and done with the *intent* to hurt us, and the people who do such things are, like Calvin, surprised when we show that we are hurt.[27]

Calvin and Hobbes   by Bill Watterson

Most of the things which other people do and say which hurt us are done for reasons that have nothing to do with us at all. The reason that your husband forgot your birthday was not because he wanted to hurt you, but because all his interest was wrapped up in his football team. The reason your parents ignored you was not because they wanted to hurt you, but because they were involved in their own affairs. It is sad but true. We are more involved in ourselves than in one another.

The laziness in our thinking is our refusal to make the effort to discriminate when people are actually trying to hurt us and when they are not. It is foolish to go through life thinking that no one is your enemy. Being a warm, wonderful human being is no protection against other people's enmity and spite. It is foolish to go through life thinking everybody is your enemy. That way you are endlessly, wearyingly on guard. You have to make careful discriminations, and that requires careful perception and thought.

Having identified those words and actions which are actually intended to hurt, you then have to decide whether you are going to give them the right to hurt you. Sometimes the words and actions arrive so swiftly or unexpectedly that they slip past your guard and stab you to the heart. Then you have to do your thinking retrospectively.

Here, again, your thinking has to be perceptive and thoughtful. Most of the hurts which are directed towards you you can dismiss as the other person's foolishness. But there are some which you must take account of, for their message, though wrapped in anger and hate, is, 'Notice me! Help me!' If the message comes from someone who is important in your life, you ought then to take account of the message, not in terms of your own hurt, but in terms of what is happening to the person from whom the message comes.

Caroline, who had once been depressed for a very long time, was minding a friend's young son, a most difficult boy, while her friend was in hospital having a baby. She told me how, when she visited her friend in hospital, the friend was angry with her and complained that Caroline was not looking after her son and her house properly. Caroline said, 'If that had happened to me a year ago I'd have got upset and I wouldn't have spoken to my friend again. But now I feel better about myself I could see it differently. I did feel a bit hurt, but then I thought, well, it's the third day after the birth. Women do get upset and angry then. So I just let her say what she wanted to say. When I went to see her the next day she was quite all right and thanked me for all I was doing.' (D 14)

Giving up taking things personally makes life so much more pleasant. But to give it up can be as hard as giving up certain hopes.

10

Hanging On to Hopes

Rose had been reading my books and one day wrote to me. She said:

'I have for years been to many therapists and some have had a sympathetic ear, but none have really understood my religious fears, and so much of what you have written concerning God, the fear and pain with Him and with religion itself, is exactly how I feel.

'I have known some people who have feared death and all it contains, but I have never known anyone who has felt frightened of God and what He may do to me, not only in this world but after. I so fear this. To fear death, I know many people feel like this, but I also face the fear of God pressing on me all my life and I am nearly sixty-two. I don't know how I have lived through all of this. I have not really lived. I have always wanted to die, but I can't die either. I say, oh God, how can you do this to me? How could you allow all this to happen to me? Most people have some sort of trouble in their lives, some sort of calamity and they are devastated for a time, maybe for years, but to suffer for a lifetime like I have is too much. I don't enjoy anything. I don't trust anyone. I am in constant fear that God is watching me, for everything I do is no good. I so envy Christians their faith in God, praising God. I am jealous of their love of Him, of their trust in Him, of their hope and peace in having Him at their side. I cry bitterly when I see this on television and in places of worship that I have tried to attend, but in great pain I leave behind the believers whom God loves, but not me.'

A few months later we got together for a talk. She told me of the torture she had suffered all her life, feeling guilty and fearing God's punishment. In her gestures and posture she showed herself as being weak and frightened, cowering beneath the gaze of an all-powerful, wrathful God.

Then she talked of her childhood. Her parents had been members of the Pentacostal Church and had forced her to attend. 'I was frightened of my father,' she said, adopting the same posture as when she spoke of God. 'His hand,' and she held her hand up, palm outstretched, 'would come down on my bare leg, and it would leave a palm print of blisters, the blow was so hard.'

Her mother never protected her from her father's wrath. Instead her mother demanded that Rose serve her, and this Rose did.

> 'Every weekend I scrubbed the house from top to bottom,' she said. 'My father would give me a halfpenny a day, and I would save it up and go to the market to buy fruit. I'd carry it home and give it to my mother. She'd just say, "Put it down there." Never thank you. She never thanked me. Only once in all my life did she even acknowledge what I'd done for her. When my daughters were little, one day she said, "You've looked after me and now your daughters will look after you." That meant a lot to me. But it was all that she said. Not even when she was dying did she say anything caring to me. Her last words were for my sister-in-law, not for me. All my life, she never forgave me for anything I'd done wrong. When I was a little girl, I'd be there, pulling at her skirt and saying, "Mummy, please forgive me, please forgive me", but she never would. She'd just say, "Go to your room", and I'd go there and cry and cry, but she never came. She never hugged or kissed me. Neither of them did.'

It is easy to see the similarity between Rose's experience of her parents and her image of God as angry and unforgiving. The question was why Rose clung to this image. Many of us, presented with a picture of God as a bad-tempered, vain, selfish, unpredictable, unforgiving old man, decide that such a deity is not for us, and either give up the belief in God altogether or opt for a God or an Ultimate Power who is benign, accepting and all-encompassing.

Rose said that she would never attempt to leave God, for, if she did, he might punish her more. So she remained, immersed in the guilt for sins which she might have committed and for which she felt unforgiven, fearing she had unknowingly committed the sin against the Holy Spirit, the unforgivable sin, and certain that she would spend eternity in Hell.

She begged for God's forgiveness, and even with the thought that He might forgive her came another fear, the fear that having forgiven her He might then expect something more of her, something which she, in her weakness, could not do. No doubt when

Rose was a child her parents, having punished her, would allow her
into their presence again by giving her another task to do, and she,
weary with terror and tears, would find the task threatening to be
beyond her powers and to invoke her parents' wrath again.

Nevertheless, Rose remained locked into this relationship with
her vengeful, unloving God not just out of fear but out of hope. For
all of us, whenever a situation is totally bad and utterly hopeless, we
do what we can to escape from it. Thus we try to leave a war-torn
city, end a completely unhappy relationship, cease to think such
totally painful thoughts. Whenever we remain in a bad situation it is
because we have some hope. We hope the war will end, that the
relationship can be improved, that the hope which underlies our
tangled, painful thoughts will come into being.

The hope that underlies Rose's tangled, painful thoughts is the
hope conceived when she was a tiny child, that one day her parents
will show their unconditional love for her. If they would love and
forgive her, then she could love and forgive herself, and so know
that God loved and forgave her. To give up the hope that God will
forgive her means giving up the hope that her parents will love and
forgive her. She has spent all her life being obedient and good in
order to earn her parents' love and forgiveness. Her hope for this
reward has been the mainspring of her life. How can she now give it
up?

This is the dilemma which faces many of you who are locked in
the prison of depression. When you were a small child you conceived the hope that one day your parents would give you the
unconditional love that you needed to feel confirmed as a valuable
and acceptable person. Will you go on hoping that one day they will
do this, or will you come to accept that your parents can never do
this?

Sometimes our parents cannot fulfil our hopes for unconditional
love because they are not, and can never be, physically present in
our lives. Sometimes our parents cannot fulfil our hopes for unconditional love because of their own limitations. To give unconditional
love, a person must have a certain generosity and wisdom, and
many people do not have these qualities. To be a child of such
parents is unfortunate, but you should not take it personally. After
all, they would not have been able to give unconditional love to *any*
child born to them at the time you were born. That is sad, but it is
better to be sad and in contact with other people than to be
depressed and alone. It is better to accept the sadness and relinquish

the hope than to go on, year after fruitless year, trying to get from your parents something which is not in their power to give.

To accept the sadness, relinquish the hope, and free yourself from the prison of depression you need to have greater understanding of both your parents and yourself. This means coming to see your parents as fallible human beings, and coming to recognize in yourself something which all animals do when they find themselves in a situation where sometimes they are rewarded and sometimes punished. Psychologists call this the *principle of partial reinforcement* and can demonstrate it with all kinds of animals, including us.

Imagine a situation where a white rat is in a cage that contains a lever which the rat can press to make something happen. If every time the rat presses the lever he gets a painful electric shock, he very quickly gives up pressing the lever and simply ignores it. If every time he presses the lever he gets a pellet of food, he soon loses interest in the lever, returning to it only when he is hungry. If, when he presses the lever he sometimes gets a pellet of food and some-times gets a painful electric shock, each occurring in a random way which he cannot predict, he keeps returning to the lever to press it again and again, enduring the shocks in the hope of gaining the food.

Similarly a child will behave with his mother. A child who finds that every time he approaches his mother she slaps him very quickly stops approaching her. A child who finds that every time he approaches his mother she smiles at him and kisses him soon takes his mother's love for granted, occupies himself with other interests, and returns to her for a cuddle and a kiss only when his interests lead him into something which upsets him. A child who finds that when he approaches his mother sometimes she slaps him and sometimes she kisses him, each occurring in a random way which he cannot predict, cannot leave his mother, but stays near her, risking her slaps in the hope of her kisses. Psychologists call this last situation *anxious attachment*.

The child who grows up in this state of anxious attachment can neither live happily with his mother nor apart from her. He is also likely to transfer this way of relating to all his important adult relationships, for it may be the only form of attachment that he knows.

Rats put in a situation of a series of rewards and punishments that they cannot influence may not be able to reflect upon their situation, but we can reflect on the situations in which we find ourselves. We are not the helpless victims of a psychological principle, although we might like to argue that we are in order to absolve ourselves of responsibility for what we do. When we find ourselves in a situation where we are sometimes rewarded and sometimes punished, be it when we are gambling or seeking love, we can recognize that our hopes have been raised by the rewards, can calculate the odds that the rewards will outweigh the punishments, and decide on how much punishment we can endure in the hope of receiving the rewards. If the reward is certain to be great we might be prepared to suffer much, but if the reward is trivial or an illusion fed by our hopes, then if we are wise we know when to say, 'Enough is

(D 15) enough'.

We think and talk about pride, and taking things personally, and hoping for our parents' love as if they are attributes inside us, when in fact they each exist only in relationship to other people. It is other people who cause us to bring our pride in its various forms into being, other people who cause us to use our pride as a defence, and thus other people who make it so difficult for us to change.

11

Other People

When you are on the path that leads to the prison of depression and while you are locked in that prison, you are completely absorbed in yourself. You become oblivious to what is going on around you, not just what is happening to family, colleagues and friends, but to what is happening in society and the world at large. You find it hard to concentrate enough to read a newspaper, while television brings only pictures of horrors you cannot bear to watch. This self-absorption makes you unaware of the influence that other people have on you, but this influence does not go away simply because you are unaware of it. Rather, this influence becomes all the more strong because you are unaware of it and so do not question it. Not questioning, you do not attempt to change those influences from other people who wish you to remain as you are. And remaining as you are means going on being depressed.

When we look at the world we see it divided into separate things – sky, earth, mountains, clouds, cars, houses, dogs, shops – and we think that these things are in reality separate, but they are not. They are in continuous contiguity and change with everything else, and what we see are the categories and divisions which we have created.

When we look at the world we see in it separate persons – men, women, children, friends, strangers, family – and we think that these people are in reality separate individuals, but they are not. They are in continuous contiguity and change with everyone else, and what we see are the categories and divisions we have made.

So you think of yourself as an individual, and I write about you and me as if each of us is an individual, when in reality we are in continuous interaction with other people, trying to make sense of what they say and do, responding to them according to the sense we have made of what they say and do. These other people can be in contact with us directly in space and time, living in the same house, working in the same job, walking down the same street. Or they can be represented in other forms, in the newspapers, magazines and books we read, on television and radio, in the conversation of those people in contact with us directly. Or they can be represented in our internal reality by *images* which are not merely pictures of people we once knew or of people far away, or of the people created by us in fantasy, but images which act within us with all, or even more, of the force and power which the persons themselves might have.

My father died twenty-five years ago and my mother seven years ago, and I lead a life very different from what I did when they were alive, yet I know exactly what they would say about every situation I find myself in. When I come across something funny or ironic in life or politics, I long to discuss it with my father, and I never buy a dress without knowing whether or not my mother would like it. The first thought saddens me, and the second amuses me, when I think of all my efforts as a teenager to reject all my mother's views.

So here we all are, with all of those people inside us and all those people around us. We are never separate, never alone, even though we may tell ourselves that we are. We are in constant, continuous relationships with other people. Constantly, we are affecting other people, and other people are affecting us.

We may think of depression as being something located inside us, but we are wrong.

Depression arises out of our relationships with other people. It is a response to our relationships. It is a way of trying to organize and control our relationships. It is a way of negotiating our relationships.

You cannot understand why you need to be depressed and you cannot dismantle your depression until you understand what is happening in your relationships with all the people who play a part in your life. By doing so, you can see the pressures that are on you not to change. The pressure not to change can come from yourself, because you believe that changing will have adverse effects on your relationships, and from other people, who gain some advantage from you staying as you are. These other people can be the society in which you live, your family and, if you are part of a couple, your partner.

Ourselves and Society

To describe all the ways in which society can thrust us into a role which does not suit us and insist that we should not change would be a vast undertaking in itself. Instead, I shall describe the issues that I have come across many times in many different ways in therapy and ask you to use them as triggers to remembering and understanding your own experiences.

My account of the ways in which the roles of men and women are defined does not set out to be an exhaustive one, but simply asks you to consider your own experience, *to question whether you see the roles of men and women as something fixed and unchangeable, and what aspects of your own role you would be reluctant to change.*

Similarly, I shall describe some aspects of an important function of society, the division of people into classes. Class is usually not a topic in therapy, yet our beliefs about the class we belong to affect our actions most profoundly. I shall describe class differences solely from my own biased point of view. Please, again consider your own experience and *question your beliefs about the class to which you, however reluctantly, belong.*

Part of the continuous interchange which we have with other people is that interchange which we have with the concept we call 'society'. We can never see at one time all those people who make up 'society', but we are sure they are all somewhere and together hold a set of beliefs which are very important to us. We believe that we know what these beliefs are, and we can feel society imposing these beliefs on us. We feel ourselves to be under great pressure to accept the imposition of society's beliefs, for, if we do not, we can find ourselves ostracized and punished by society's representatives.

When we are small, children's society representatives are our parents. They teach us society's rules and, by encouraging, warning and punishing, they impress on us the necessity of following society's rules. This we try to do, but we often fail, because society's rules are inconsistent and frequently beyond our capacity to achieve. Our society says that it is wrong to kill, and then expects young men to become soldiers and kill people. Our society says that we should earn our own living, and then fails to provide many of us with the education necessary for us to do so.

Society, so our parents instruct us, expects that we shall assume the roles appropriate to our sex and class. So little girls are taught that their most important role is of wife and mother, while little boys, although apparently offered a wide range of roles, soon find that they should fulfil only those roles which are described as masculine. Twenty-five years of the Women's Movement has

brought but few changes to what is regarded as the traditional roles
of men and women.

Jane Greenwell, in her article *Why Can't Men Ditch the Dirt?*,
wrote:

Women have struggled long and hard for independence but
they remain skivvies in their own homes. How can this be?
How can feminism have allowed this paradoxical state of affairs
to go unchallenged?

A recent survey revealed that while more women have taken
up work outside the home during the last twenty years, an
overwhelming majority of them still do the lion's share of the
housework.

Only 22 per cent of men with working partners take on an
equal share of domestic chores. Of course, there will always be
men who wouldn't be seen dead holding a teacloth, let alone
mopping a floor. But there is a third category. I know several
men who belong in it, including my husband. They are middle-
class, middle-aged, thinking and intelligent: they have matured
beside feminism and espoused its causes; they would argue
sincerely against feminine oppression; they are married to or
live with working women and have supported their partners'
efforts towards equality. They change nappies, push prams,
deliver children to school, cook meals. But when it comes to the
basic, daily, business of keeping grime at bay, our so-called new
men simply opt out.

On one level it is mystifying. My husband will talk rationally
and justly about the fallacy of prescribed gender roles but when
I raise the knotty subject of housework and voice discontent he
will either fall silent or get out the vacuum cleaner and push it
pointedly (and inefficiently) over the sitting room carpet. When
the discussion/demonstration is over we are back to square one;
I still do the chores and he doesn't . . .

So by what inexplicable logic are women still deemed by
universal appointment to be the clearers of mess?

One crudely simple explanation is that challenging this long-
held notion would have uncomfortable consequences for men.
They have too much to lose. After all, cleaning is hard work. It is
boring, frustrating, time-consuming, energy-sapping and ultimately futile since it always has to be done again. What man,
encouraged by his upbringing and by contemporary society to

be an achiever, would consider wasting his valuable time on such an activity? . . .

There are many ways in which men who have embraced the various aspects of feminism, who have supported women's fight for the option to work outside the home, have thereby made personal gains and have enriched their own lives.

An equal partnership is emotionally more satisfying than if it were less balanced. A man can take pride in and enjoy vicarious status from his partner's career success and increased self-esteem; there is the added financial bonus of two incomes. An active role in child care has many payoffs, not least a closer and more rewarding relationship with one's offspring. Even cooking dinner can be pleasurable and affords the chance to show off and win praise.

But housework? What's in it for him? There lies the rub.[28]

Who does the housework in your home? (D 16)

In Britain, the USA and Australia, over the last forty years, it has been fashionable for people to declare that class distinctions no longer exist, but anyone who cares to look can see that this is nonsense. (Miles Kington once commented that, 'There are people who think that Britain is a class-ridden society, and those who think it doesn't matter either way as long as you know your place in the set-up.'[29]) In the USA and Australia, class depends on money, so people move up and down the classes according to their fortunes, while in England class continues chiefly to relate to family, accent and manners, but in all three countries the class into which a person is born carries certain expectations about the role a person should fulfil. The same applies to all countries, be it the rigid class structure of the Hindus in India or the egalitarian structure of the USSR, where, in the words of George Orwell, all people are equal, but some are more equal than others.

Where membership of a class depends on the person's financial status, the pressure to achieve is enormous. Thus young Americans and Australians are told that, whatever class they have been born into, they should work hard and do better than their parents. In this situation those of us who value and accept ourselves can interpret this instruction either as an exciting challenge where winning is certain or as a ridiculous notion which can be safely ignored. Those of us who do not value and accept ourselves feel that, even though we are sure we shall fail, we must try to achieve to avoid criticism and rejection. So we strive endlessly to achieve, and no achievement is enough, or, having tried and failed, despise ourselves even more.

Up until the Second World War, the working-class people in Britain were taught that wealth and possessions were 'not for the likes of us', a class distinction which led many people to emigrate. In the last forty years, and for the first time in British history, working-class people in Britain have enjoyed some prosperity. They have abandoned the foolish notion of riches being 'not for the likes of us' and see no reason why they too should not enjoy the pleasant things in life. At the same time, encouraged by government policies, many members of the middle- and upper-classes have set themselves the goal of gaining more wealth and possessions. So, in Britain today, many people enjoy and endure the best and the worst of both kinds of class structure. They have to be concerned with achievement, family, accent and manners, and so have a much wider area in which to fail.

In this situation those of us who value and accept ourselves can interpret the instructions about achievement, family, accent and manners as challenges and rules to be accepted or rejected as we see fit. Those of us who do not value and accept ourselves dare not risk rejection and criticism, and so, despite being certain that we shall fail, strive to meet the requirements of our class and despise ourselves when we fail.

Into whatever class we are born and no matter how much we chafe against the rules of that class, we can always bolster our fragile self-esteem by taking pride in our class and despising those who do not belong. We can use our nationality, race and religion in precisely the same way.[30]

We can gain security and pride in the role our sex, class, nationality, race and religion has given us, and this security and pride can prevent us from changing.

The roles which society impose on us in terms of sex and class set limits, if we allow them, on what we can do and how we can change. If you see the role that has been imposed on you not as an idea in people's minds but as a Fixed Reality of the Absolute and Unchanging Universe, you can see neither the part that your role has played in creating the situation in which you find yourself nor that the rules of this role can be broken.

Tracey lived in a cold, damp flat in a huge tower block which overlooked the dereliction of a once wealthy industrial city.

When her husband abandoned her and her two school age children, she discovered how terrible poverty is. Through her childhood and adolescence her father had worked as a foundry-man and her mother as a factory cleaner, and, while there was never anything to spare, there was never any doubt that she would be adequately fed, clothed and housed. Now she feared for herself and even more for her children.

A social worker interviewed her to decide what government help she should receive and talked of 'one-parent families' and 'the poverty trap'. She asked Tracey what kind of work she could do and obviously regarded Tracey's answer as unsatisfactory. Tracey said she hadn't worked since she was married. When she was at school she had learned to type and liked it, but she hadn't touched a typewriter for over ten years. When she had left school her mother had got her a job in a hairdresser's. No, she didn't get training. She left soon after to get married. Yes, she had been pregnant. That's why she got married.

After the social worker had left Tracey despaired, and, as the days went by, she felt worse and worse. Her son got an ear infection and she took him to the doctor. She was so ashamed of herself when, in the doctor's surgery, she started crying. The doctor said, 'There, there. You're having a tough time. I'll give you something to help you sleep. Come and see me again in a month.'

So each month she went back to see the doctor and each time he asked her how she was and wrote out another prescription. Within six months she was taking something to help her sleep, something to cheer her up, and something to stop her being anxious. But she still didn't sleep properly, she felt dismal and worried, and she hated herself. She often thought that if she didn't have the children and her parents she would take all her pills at once and never have to face the world again.

Her father, jobless when the foundry closed, grew vegetables on his allotment and was always pleased when he could give her a pound of potatoes or a bunch of spinach. Then one day he was knocked down and killed by a drunken driver.

Tracey arranged his funeral and comforted her mother. It was six months before the fact of his death really hit her. When the doctor saw her he knew that something more needed to be done. He said, 'I'll get the community nurse to visit you.'

Tracey still remembered the social worker's visit with horror, so the thought of some nurse entering her flat and seeing the dirt and chaos filled her with dread. Just the sight of a competent woman made her feel even more insignificant and useless.

However, when she opened the door to the nurse's ring there was no bossy woman standing there. It was, in her words, 'a gorgeous fella'. He was the community nurse and his name was Jim.

For the first few visits Jim just sat amongst the squalor of her flat, drank coffee, let the kids be cheeky to him, and listened to her. At first she just poured out all her complaints and worries, but as time went by it became more of a conversation between the two of them. He asked her advice about a technical problem one of his patients had with the Social Security, and, since she had much more experience with this government department than he had, she helped him draft a letter for his patient.

Eventually, when keeping the flat in order and shopping and cooking were no longer totally impossible tasks for her to do, Tracey found that they were talking about work. 'I'd like to get a job,' she said. 'I'm sick of being stuck in this place, day in, day out. But I'm not trained for anything. I suppose I could go cleaning, but that's early morning and I need to be here for the kids.'

'You could go on a training course,' said Jim.

'Like what?'

'Word processing. You've done typing. There are plenty of excellent jobs for women who understand word processing.'

However, when Jim brought along some glossy brochures about the word processing courses, illustrated with pictures of elegant women looking serene in a beautiful office, Tracey found herself shaking with an emotion she could not name. 'No, no,' she said, 'there's no way I could do that.'

Jim could see she was upset, so he put the brochures away. As he was leaving he said, 'Perhaps you might ask yourself just why you got so upset.'

Tracey thought about this and the first word that came to her was 'loyalty'. She saw her mother's gnarled and roughened hands, the cold, red hands of her neighbours as they plodded up the stairs carrying their loads, and the smooth, slim hands of the women pictured in the brochures. The second word that came to her was 'belonging'. She hated the tower block where she lived, and her mother's tiny terraced house seemed smothering now that her father was not there, but this was where she belonged.

She prepared all her arguments as to why she could not attempt the word processing course so as to be ready for Jim's next visit. She was too nervous, she had no decent clothes to wear, she was not clever enough, what if the kids got sick, and so on.

On the morning of Jim's visit she called to see her mother and mentioned the course. Her mother said, 'That sounds wonderful. I'd have given anything to work in an office. Your father was a good man, but I would have been better off working and not getting married. In my day a woman was expected to get married.'

This was the first time her mother had ever said such a thing, and Tracey was astounded. Somehow Tracey felt that she had been given permission to change what had seemed to her the unchangeable limits of her sex and class. And so she did.

If this were a romantic story, Tracey would have married Jim and done a little word processing on the side. But it isn't a romantic story. As Tracey says, 'Who needs romance when you're running your own word processing business?'

As an Australian observing the English, I sometimes think that, despite the limitations of the lack of money and adequate education which working-class people suffer, working-class people are not so much bound by these limitations as middle- and upper-class people are bound by theirs. Many working-class people can *see* their limitations and realize that these are not Fixtures in Absolute Reality, but the outcome of certain politics and economics. Whereas middle- and upper-class people do not always see their limitations in this way.

Many middle- and upper-class people are so bound by the rules of conduct of their class that they see working-class people as being a different race, if not a different species, and so they are frightened of them. In the same way, many English fear their Pakistani, Indian and West Indian neighbours, many rich Americans fear poor Americans, many white Americans fear black Americans, and many white Australians fear black Australians. Such fears significantly reduce the number of options they have in their activities and relationships. If, for instance, you regard tenpin bowling as a working-class pastime, and your pride and fear would not allow you to take part in any working-class activity, you prevent yourself from having what can be a very enjoyable experience.

Similarly, the rules of conduct which define the middle- and upper-classes prevent people from changing.

Richard, a delightful young man who had all the best character-istics of a yuppie, told me of the unhappy years he spent in one of the best boarding schools, and finished his account with, 'When I have a son I'll send him to the same school.'

'Why?' I asked, feeling immensely sorry for this unborn child.

'You make good connections there. It's a matter of knowing the right people.' Never mind that the thought of having to meet these 'right people' in any situation other than business created in Richard the most heart thundering, sleep destroying panic.

Over the years, as I have listened to many people from what are usually described as privileged backgrounds talking about how they are trapped by the demands of their sex and class, I have come to realize why, given the benefit of some education, it is easier for working-class people to throw off the demands of class. Being working-class confers no privileges other than a feeling of belong-ing. The privileges of the middle- and upper-classes are great, and so even as these people describe the terrible tragedies and miseries of their lives, they show that for them it is unthinkable that they should ignore the demands of their class. An aristocratic woman wept as she described the torture it was for her to carry out her social duties, especially those which involve entertaining relatives who were astoundingly rude to her, but when I tentatively suggested that she should be kind to herself and simply refuse to have such badly behaved people in her home, she laughed so as to humour me for having such a foolish and impossible notion. A man, heir to a title and a substantial fortune, having witnessed the violence of his parents' marriage and fearing the violence within himself, found himself unable to feel anything but mild friendship for the young women of his class. He told me of his aching loneliness, and of a girl he had known at college. 'Why didn't you marry her?' I asked. 'My father would never accept her,' he said.

Certain Australian aborigines, so I have been told, when expelled from their tribe for breaking the tribe's rules, go into the bush alone and die, not from any act of suicide, but from the loss of all that they saw as real. Without their tribe they simply could not exist. There are many people who experience their class in this way and who therefore fear even to question its rules, much less to break them.   **(D 17)**

Society, having given us our role and class, does not want us to change them. All societies are in the business of keeping everything the same, whether they are proclaiming conservatism or continuous revolution. Occasionally, usually in times of crisis such as war, society will redefine certain roles. Young men who in times of peace are regarded as aggressive, dangerous hooligans become, with the outbreak of war, 'our brave boys'. The media spread the message that the role has been changed.

During the Second World War women worked in all kinds of jobs which traditionally had been seen as men's work, but after the war government policy was that men returning from the war should be given jobs. So, after seven years of being told how wonderful and right it was for women to be farmers, bank managers, engine drivers and aeroplane pilots, women were now told that their role was to be no more than a wife and mother. Any woman who did not accept this was unnatural.

Women's magazines immediately became devoted to women's domestic concerns and pictures of Rosie and Riveter were replaced by pictures of Rosie the Mum. Popular songs were solely about romance – lovers coming together, lovers so painfully separating. A woman's fulfilment could be only through a man. One popular song, still often heard today on BBC Radio 2, was *Dance, Ballerina, Dance*, about a ballerina who foolishly put dancing before the man who loved her, and who now, no matter how successful she might become, would always be lonely.

One of the most admired films of the fifties was *All About Eve*, which told the story of how a successful actress, played magnificently by Bette Davis, was used by a younger woman, played by Anne Baxter, to further her career. The setting was stylish, the dialogue brilliant, the pace gripping, but the moral was clear. The older woman triumphed because she recognized that what mattered most in her life was her man, while the younger woman, successful actress though she may have become, was condemned to a life of loneliness and bitterness. *All About Eve* was called 'a woman's picture', and it certainly was a picture of what women were supposed to be. Men could be greedy and ambitious, but women should be self-sacrificing and ever mindful of the needs of others. Indeed, their main role was to be *responsible wives and mothers*.

Our media are still giving women the same message. The 1989 film *Working Girl* is, as Mona Harrington wrote in the *New York Times*, one of 'a run of hot box-office movies gunning down powerful women'. She went on:

> It's an attack on a woman holding power of her own. Here she's an investment banker with a corner office in Manhattan. She lies, she cheats – all for the unpardonable purpose of promoting herself.
>
> Worse, in the course of a love affair with the hero, she appropriates the sexual initiative. Even Katharine Hepburn at her sassiest knew better than that. But happily for the established order, this outrageous creature gets slapped down. By the end of the movie her job is in jeopardy and the hero withdraws his love.
>
> In case we miss the point about true womanhood, the movie gives us not just a bad example but a good one. The point of the plot is not the defeat of the wicked woman but the rise of modern-day Cinderella: the secretary of the monstrous banker. This daughter of the working-class pops herself out of the secretarial ranks into an office of her own and, of course, wins the love of the hero.
>
> And why does the system so lavish its rewards on her when it so relentlessly punishes her boss? Because, unlike her boss, the rising secretary offends none of the more serious rules for women. In her first meeting with the hero she passes out and has to be carried, helpless and senseless, to safety. Her voice is soft, whispery, almost childlike. 'I have a head for business and a body for sin,' she tells the hero – before losing consciousness.
>
> Her business acumen is also suitably feminine. Where does she get the idea for the big investment deal on which the plot turns? From analysis of stocks? No. From the gossip columns, where she picks up tidbits about the wealthy and turns them into ideas through hunches and intuitive leaps of the imagination. But who does the analysis of figures, and races around making the connections between buyers and sellers? The hero.
>
> Furthermore, her rise out of the secretarial ranks into the lower reaches of the financial world depends at crucial points on powerful men. Because the drama focused on the competi-

tion between two women for power and love, the issue of sex seems foremost. But the movie is also a morality tale about class and about the American dream, the promise of change, of upward movement to greater fortune. Indeed, our secretary-heroine does move up and the secondary moral of the story explains how.

The answer is hard work: five years of night school; assimilation of middle-class business culture – hair style, clothes, accent; but most important, *gumption*. This is what finally did it: spirit, daring, risk-taking. It logically follows why the poor remain poor: lack of gumption.

So there you have it – a movie straight out of Reagan country. The system is fine as it is. We have no class injustice; anyone with gumption can make it. And women can make it so long as they play within the old male-female hierarchies, which were the right ones after all. We know this because women who challenge them are crazy or nasty, and certainly unlovable.[31]

It is not just women who are told by the media what they ought to be. Millions of men grew up believing that John Wayne was the ideal which they should emulate. Many men have come to hate themselves because they could not be like John Wayne, and many more, modelling themselves more or less successfully on John Wayne, have failed to realize the limitations of this character. This was a figure which could operate only in a setting where there was absolute distinction between good and evil. Since none of us lives in such a setting but only in a world where issues of good and evil are always confused and ambiguous, we require a greater breadth and subtlety of understanding than John Wayne could ever supply.

Unfortunately, many of us, both men and women, have, as children, accepted the figures portrayed by the media as ideal, have striven to be like our ideals, and, when we failed, or when our emulation of the ideal failed to deal effectively with the issues of our life, we blamed ourselves.

We are loath to give up these ideal figures because they promise so much. Didn't John Wayne make you feel so *safe*? So when society says, 'This is the kind of person you should be', we do not always question this. **(D 18)**

Thus, in many and various ways, society, like our families, can be very effective in preventing us from changing.

Families Against Change

There are many ways in which our families, both in the flesh and as their internal images, can prevent us from changing.

There is *our loyalty to our family*. Even if we admit to ourselves that our relatives cause us problems, loyalty to our family will stop us talking about this.

When I was a child, my mother used to warn me about discussing family business with strangers, and when, years later, I worked in psychiatric hospitals, I realized that there were many parents who gave their children the same warning. I saw many psychiatric patients assuring their psychiatrists that they had a good marriage, got on well with their in-laws, and had the best possible parents. Again and again I felt that anyone with eyes to see and ears to hear would know that the person was speaking out of love and loyalty and was leaving much unsaid, but then I realized that, in the way that we see and hear only what we want to see and hear, the psychiatrists could not see anything which conflicted with their belief that depression was a genetic illness. For them, all of the problem lay within the patient. (Here, of course, the psychiatrists were being loyal to *their* parents, for if it is true that what parents do does affect their children, then this must apply to the psychiatrists' parents as well.)

Often our loyalty to our family prevents us from even admitting to ourselves that we have problems with our relatives. Even just acknowledging in the privacy of our own thoughts that our partner and, worse, our parents, have faults and have hurt us makes us feel guilty. So, in striving to be good, we can maintain that our marriage is excellent and our parents paragons of virtue.

Moreover, if we are parents ourselves, we become very wary of criticizing our parents, especially if we have chosen to bring up our children in much the same way that we were brought up. We don't want to start feeling guilty about our children. So we decide that what happens to us in childhood has no effect on us in adult life.

Deciding this does not stop us from expending much time and effort in getting our children educated and trying to train them to be clean, tidy, unaggressive, unselfish, hard-working, respectful, responsible and obedient. Instead, we hold two opposing beliefs simultaneously. We believe that a child will remember how to be clean, tidy, unaggressive, unselfish, hard-working, respectful, responsible and obedient, but will forget how it feels to be used as a sexual object, or beaten, humiliated, abandoned, rejected, bereaved, or treated cruelly in any way.

Thus, when our children turn out well, we can claim the credit, but when they turn out badly, when they mistreat their own families, when they take drugs, or become depressed or schizophrenic, or when they turn to crime, we can deny all responsibility and say that their actions are the result of their genetic inheritance – from the other side of the family, of course, or from a far distant ancestor.

We much prefer to think of any difficulty arising in our families as coming from a gene belonging to a far distant ancestor rather than from what is happening in the family now and what has happened in the past, in the history of the family.

It is not that we do not want our family to have a history, but that we want it to be a history which fills us with pride. We need a family history because that is what fastens us in time and place. Otherwise we feel, as refugees can come to feel, that we belong nowhere. So whatever our family's history, we extract from it something to make us proud. Thus the descendants of the people who crossed the Missouri to settle on the treeless plans of Nebraska erased the shame of being called Soddies, (because they had to construct their homes out of sods of earth) by saying of the first Nebraskans, 'The weak ones didn't make it and the cowards didn't try'.

Every family history has its pride and its secrets. That pride and those secrets are part of the reality into which each of us was born.

When my mother used to forbid me to tell our neighbours and my teachers anything about private matters in our family I thought she meant anything to do with money. We were not at all well off, but my mother had the greatest contempt for anyone who, as she said, 'cried poor'. It was not until I was an adult that I realized that my mother had something far more important to keep secret. This was that she was the granddaughter of a convict transported to Australia in 1828.

Nowadays, Australians who can trace their ancestry back to the first white settlers feel as much pride in this as Americans whose ancestors came over on the *Mayflower*. My sister has explored our family history to uncover the story of our great-grandfather who, as a lad of seventeen, was transported from Donegal in Ireland to Botany Bay. We know that his crime must have been trifling, for in those days people were hanged for as little as stealing a sheep, and we also know that he would have been uneducated. He never saw

Breaking the Bonds

his family again, and he was wrenched from his religion, since the British government forbade Catholics to practise their religion in the convict settlement. Much later in life he married and had two daughters who were soon deserted by their parents. One of his daughters became my mother's mother.

These three generations of my family suffered great hardships, just as generations of families all around the world suffered great hardships. The effects of these hardships were passed on to succeeding generations.

Often we do not recognize how the history of our family has affected us, because the legacy of our family is something we are born into, and we accept it in the way that we accept air and sunshine. Every family has its story and its secrets, and we draw conclusions about ourselves from what we learn of the story and the secrets.

As a child, I did not recognize that my mother's black moods, fearsome temper and fear of other people resulted from her belief that there was something intrinsically bad about herself, something which she had to keep secret. Neither did I recognize that her contempt for the English came from her father, who at seventeen had to leave Scotland to find a means of livelihood in Australia, and from her Irish grandfather. She might have doubted her own value and worth, but she certainly had her pride.

So the legacy my ancestors left me included a sense of blackness and uncertainty with which I struggled and which I turned into the question, 'Why did my mother behave as she did?' The legacy also included an inability to be impressed by people in positions of authority. Now I know that my mother was depressed and I know why, and I know that we should not accept people in authority simply because they are in authority, for people in authority are often unkind and unjust to those in their power and use them for their own selfish gratification.

Something else which I inherited from both my mother's and my father's family was obsessive cleanliness. I came to understand this legacy once I studied social history and learned how many people in the nineteenth and early twentieth century, condemned by poverty to work unceasingly and to live in appalling conditions, struggled to better themselves. In those days the means of keeping clean – soap and hot water – were very expensive, and so the rich were clean and the poor dirty. When the poor people struggled to better themselves and wanted to show that they were bettering themselves, they tried to be as clean as they possibly could be. They created rules about cleanliness which were absolute, and any infringement of the rules brought severe punishment, for family pride was at stake. Their children grew up believing that 'Cleanliness is next to Godliness'.

Thus my family, like millions of working-class families, while struggling out of poverty, worked hard at being clean and teaching their children to be clean.

Certainly personal and public cleanliness did more to improve health than medicine ever did, and a clean and tidy environment, if not carried to stultifying excess, is pleasing to the eye, but those of you whose rituals of cleanliness and tidiness absorb much of your time and energy and make you anxious should ask yourself how much of all of this is really necessary, and how much are you, like your ancestors, trying to show that you have bettered yourself. Are you still fighting your great-great-grandparents' battles?

Another battle which many people fight on behalf of their ancestors is that of needing to achieve. Most of us had ancestors who found themselves as strangers in a wilderness or struggling to survive starvation and poverty, and who had to strive unceasingly to achieve lest they failed and fell into destitution and death. They had to give the message, 'Achieve or die', to their children. However, those of you whose every moment is filled with effort to achieve should review your family's history and ask, 'If I ease off and take time just to *be*, instead of always worrying about becoming more and more successful, will the virgin earth I'm tilling yield no crops, or will I lose my job and become homeless and starving? Am I still fighting my ancestors' battles?'

When psychiatrists draw up family trees and mark the members in succeeding generations of a family who became depressed, they do not ask what hardships those people were enduring. A television series called *A Century of Childhood*,[32] which drew on film and photographs as well as the reminiscences of many people, showed how only in very recent years has it become accepted practice for adults to treat children kindly.

Poor children, as soon as they were old enough to fetch and carry, were expected to work. In the book accompanying the series, Frances Sherlock, eldest daughter of a family of twelve brought up in Chester in the 1920s, remembers how important her work was to the family's survival.

'Every other year as I grew up my mother had a baby, which meant that being the eldest I had lots of chores to do and four kids to look after. I had napkins to wash, messages to run, I had to find anything I could to keep the fire going – old shoes, anything that would burn. I'd go along the railway track looking for coal that had dropped off the wagons: more often than not we helped it off. And I don't ever remember having a chair: mother and father had a chair but we just stood around the table. Everything was hard work then.'

Rich children were sent away to school. Lord Bath, born Viscount Weymouth in 1902, recalled:

'I suppose the first time I was really unhappy was when I had to leave home and go to my prep school in Kent. It was a very good school, but the discipline was very strong. The headmaster was a great disciplinarian. I remember whenever we played football one had to hang one's jacket on the peg which was allotted to you, and if you hadn't hanged it properly it would fall to the floor, and the houseman or houseboy used to go around and collect them, take the name of whose it was, and give them to the headmaster. And you never knew you dropped anything until breakfast the next day, and the headmaster would say, "Weymouth, you left your pants on the floor". And you had to go up there and you had to hold out your hand. I remember it so well, I mean he used to give you a hard one on each hand. It hurt like hell: it was really agonizing. The same thing went on at Harrow and the discipline was probably more severe than it was at my prep school. There were prefects and there were fags. I, of course, was a fag to a prefect. And they used to call, "Boy!", and then there was a mad rush by the two boys to get there first, and the last one had to do the job. And I remember once I was twenty minutes late for a run and the senior prefect had me up and he gave me three on my behind, very hard, which hurt like hell. They really do beat boys when they say beat. Being very thin you feel it much more. But I was never late again.'

Suffering does not always make us kind. In 1987, when I was researching for my book *The Successful Self*, I met Lord Bath's son Alexander Thynn, the eleventh Viscount Weymouth.

He described to me how he had been born into a family which was organized into a strict hierarchy with his father, the Marquess of Bath, at its head. His father expected complete obedience from his children and, for the early years of his life, Alexander was an obedient child who tried to please his father, and, like so many obedient children, he became, as he described himself, 'a shy, sensitive little boy'. He did quite well and decided to go to university.

This did not suit his father at all. The Thynn family, his father declared, were not intellectuals, and no son of his was going to university. But Alexander insisted, and off he went to Oxford. He hoped to get a good Second Class degree and prove his father to be totally wrong. But he got a Third, and his father said, 'I told you so.' Some very bitter quarrels followed.

Alexander said, 'It was an identity crisis. Mine was a bullying upbringing and there came a point where I was not going to be told what my identity was going to be. University gave me the tools to destroy the attitudes which had previously been imposed on me.'

The battle with his father was for Alexander more than a simple disagreement between two people with different points of view. His father attacked Alexander's basic judgements about himself and what he could achieve, and Alexander began to doubt his own judgement. 'I felt a great deal of doubt. Could he be right? Could it be that I'm not fitted to be what I thought, ambitiously, I could go on to be? In the uncertainty of my own assessment of myself, the uncertainty of the feeling I gave to others when I was in their company, I was withdrawing and cutting off from previous contact. I became a recluse. But later, as my confidence was gradually found, and, as the battle was won against my father, or at least he'd stopped trying to enforce his attitudes on me, and then, gradually, I emerged in what could be regarded as my natural self.'

Alexander found his confidence through painting. His murals fill some sixteen rooms, vast, colourful, and highly individual. He divided them into 'cocoons, therapies and fantasies', but altogether they form Alexander's attempt at a total explanation and a philosophy of life, perhaps summed up in a banner which runs the length of one long room, 'Heaven and Hell are what we experience here on Earth, in the relationships between our fellow human beings.'[33]

It is not difficult to see a connection between Lord Bath's experiences as a child and his desire that his children conform to his

wishes in the way he had been forced to conform to the wishes of his
father who had sent him away to school. After all, most of us, like
Lord Bath, follow the rule, 'Treat others as you have been treated',
rather than the rule, 'Treat others as you would like to be treated'.

When we, as children, have parents who demand total obedience
we are faced with a choice. We can decide to obey them to the point
of identifying with them and becoming even more like them than
they are themselves. A strict father can have a martinet for a son. Or
we can try to maintain our own identity.

Maintaining our own identity in the face of powerful and demanding parents is very difficult, as Alexander found. We need,
then, to be able to trust our own judgement, for, if we doubt
ourselves, we shall, like Alexander, feel our very sense of self
shatter and disappear. It was only by having the courage to risk
trusting himself that Alexander was able to hold himself together
and go on living his life on his own terms. His children live at home
and attend the local school.

The treatment which Lord Bath had received at school was not
unusual. A survey of secondary schools in England in 1977 showed
that eighty per cent of the schools used corporal punishment, while
in Scotland the use of the tawse was even more common. In one
Edinburgh school in just one term the tawse was used 10,000 times.
But the banning of the use of the cane in schools in Britain in 1987
was not without protests from many parents and teachers.

Nor was the treatment which Lord Bath gave his son unusual. The
authors of the book which accompanied the television series *A
Century of Childhood* commented, 'Many old people we have spoken
to said that their parents never kissed or cuddled them or told them
they were loved.'[34] Unfortunately, the belief that being loving to a
child 'spoils' that child is still held by many people because that was
the reason their parents gave for not showing their love to their
child.

Parents hand on to their children much more than a set of genes.
They hand on ways of seeing, sets of beliefs and habitual ways of
behaving. These ways of seeing, these sets of beliefs and these
habitual ways of behaving can give us courage or fear, happiness or
sadness.

It is over twenty years since I first met Jean. She was a patient in
a women's ward in a large psychiatric hospital and we used to
go for walks around the hospital grounds because both of us

were appalled at the lack of privacy and the dirt on this ward. I had nothing useful then to say about depression, but I did comment that writing things down helped to sort things out when life was very confusing. Ten years later Jean got in touch with me to say that she had taken my advice about writing and that in the intervening years she had left the hospital, gone back to work and was living not far from me. We kept in touch.

In one of her letters to me Jean wrote, 'Virtually since I can remember I have been unable to speak about any problems I had, but now I feel that gradually I am overcoming this pattern. This habit is the same as that of my mother. I never in my life remember her complaining, and her load was heavy. My father was physically violent with the animals on the farm and very threatening and verbally abusive to us children, all of whom seemed designated by him to fulfil the role he chose, that is, to do as he said without question instantly. I was terrified of my father. My late brother and I, as we grew into our early teens, decided upon public service, my brother went into the RAF and myself into nursing. Total opposition from my father. Our teachers, knowing what work we wished to do, sought that we should have education further than that which we had gained at the local village school. This father would not let us have. He would not allow us to take up the scholarships we had won. Decades later, my father told me himself that he had wanted to become a teacher, but his father had denied him the chance to go on to grammar school. My father's father, I have gathered from what I heard as a child and from various relatives who knew him, was a morose and angry man. He felt forced into a marriage he did not want (grandmother was pregnant), sought thereafter only to pay the rent and see that his requirements were met, and beyond this seemed not to take any notice of his wife and children. But to the villagers and the Church he was all sweetness and light. I think, also, that the isolation in which my family lived, out of sight or sound of other human beings, did not help.'

Jean concluded her letter with, 'I have long been convinced that most of the psychological afflictions we suffer are caused by acquiring disadvantageous habits, and that I, as an individual, had to recognize this and modify such habits.'

One day when I had called at her home for tea, Jean said, 'Depression is a bad habit. You pick up habits from your family, and such habits are hard to break. There's been the habit of depression in my family for at least three generations. My generation was the first to recognize that this habit was depression. You have to recognize that it is a habit and break it.'

So long as we do not review and come to understand our family's history and the legacy of secrets and imperatives which succeeding generations have passed down to us, the longer we go on fighting battles which are not our own and using, without thinking, the habits which generations of our family have passed on to us like the family jewels.

(D 19)

So, too, we need to review and come to understand a history much closer to us, the history of our relationship with our parents.

Now this is where sanctions come down thick and fast, from inside us and from society. 'Honour thy father and mother' the Commandment instructs us. Good children never criticize their parents.

When we found ourselves, as small children, trapped in that situation where the only way we could give ourselves some sense of security was to define it as 'I am bad and am being punished by my good parent', we needed to affirm very strongly to ourselves that our parent was good. One way was to insist that our parent's goodness was beyond question. Of course it must be, else the sacrifice of ourselves which we had made was in vain.

However, so long as we remembered the first situation and our first, and truthful, interpretation of it, 'I am being punished by my bad parent', our redefinition and our self-sacrifice could always be questioned. What we needed to do, and what we did, was to forget the original situation, our original interpretation and our redefining. All we remembered was, 'My parents are perfect and I am the guilty one. Their suffering is my fault.'

Unfortunately, many of us find that, for all our redefinitions and selective forgetting, one of our parents goes on inflicting so much pain on us that no amount of redefining and selective forgetting will allow us to see this parent as good. So we come to see this parent as a Bad Parent, and, to stop ourselves from being too frightened, we turn our other parent, ordinary, fallible though he or she is, into the Perfect Parent. This way we can turn against our father and worship our mother, or cling to our father and reject our mother, and so feel safe.

Sylvia Fraser, in summing up her life, addressed her mother thus:

> Since my father was an obvious and dangerous villain it was necessary for me to believe that you were a saint, even if that meant blackening my own character to keep that myth going. It was safer to be a bad child with a perfect mother whom I failed to please, than to be a frightened child with a flawed mother who failed to protect me. And yet, and yet, now that I have rescinded the legend of your saintliness, you too are released to become more human, to be worthy of understanding and love.[35]

Nevertheless, so long as our Bad Parent goes on persecuting us, we cannot have a Bad Parent and a Perfect Parent. All we have are two Bad Parents. No matter how angelic our Perfect Parent is, so long as our Perfect Parent does not protect us from our Bad Parent, we have two Bad Parents.

This is a truth which we, as children, have to hide from ourselves in order to feel secure. Unless, as adults, we rediscover this truth and come to terms with it, we go on and on feeling nothing but anger and resentment towards our Bad Parent, and nothing but concern, obligation and guilt towards our Perfect Parent.

It took me years to recognize this in myself. My mother's black moods, fierce temper and constant criticism of me were too frequent for me to deny. So I made my father over into my Perfect Parent. This was easy to do because he was a gentle, kindly man who loved me unconditionally. He would never, as he would sometimes say, 'turn his daughters down', that is, reject us, and he never did, no matter what mistakes we might make. I remembered this as his total loyalty to me, and thus hid from myself the fact that my father was not the Perfect Parent I wanted him to be.

The truth was that my father was afraid of my mother because, whenever she was angry with him, she would reject him. She would retreat into angry silence, or declare that she had finished with living and would kill herself. To my father, an extravert, this rejection was the greatest threat, and so he would placate her and try to avoid disagreeing with her over anything. Thus, when my mother and I fell out, which happened often when I was in my teens, my father did not dare take my side against her. He would speak to me privately and give me good advice, but if matters came to a head I was on my own.

In our determination to keep at least one of our parents as the

Perfect Parent, we forget part of our own history, and so have a life story full of gaps. As an adult, I remembered myself as a small child being very close to my father, and, as an adolescent, being quite alone in my family, yet I would never question how the first memory led to the second. It was only when I began talking with many depressed people and listened to what they were saying about their parents that I began to understand my need to protect my father. My teacher then was Colin Woodmancy, a psychoanalyst and child psychiatrist, and he remarked one day, 'No child can have one good parent and one bad parent. They are either both good or both bad. If one parent treats the child badly and the other parent does not protect the child, then the child has two bad parents.' I found this truth very painful to accept.

Some people dare not acknowledge that their Bad Parents are as frightening and destructive as they are, nor the degree of murderous hate they feel for their Bad Parent. Instead, such people allow themselves only to express a little of their anger against their other parent. Adele was one of these.

Adele was a Californian girl, but she had not had the kind of carefree life that Californian girls are supposed to have. She told me, 'I started being depressed when I was going into puberty, and it lasted for more than twenty years. I was very withdrawn and still am, or, at least, I'm very much a loner. I was always mopey, but through all that there were times when I hit rock bottom and I thought of suicide. I even tried it once, not real strongly, but enough. I overdosed and threw up.

'I've been to quite a few counsellors over the years. The last one about three years ago. We got to the root of some major problems and I've been doing pretty good since then. When I was at my lowest point it was hard to put one foot in front of the other. I didn't know what to do with myself. I would play with these over-the-counter medications and put myself out of it over the weekend. I must have been a real bummer to be around.

'About five or six years ago, I hit a real slump and overdosed. I was seeing a psychiatrist then and he gave me antidepressants and none of them worked. That was when I found out about the therapist that helped me. Right now I think I'm doing pretty good. My depression stems from my low self-esteem and a total feeling of hopelessness. I thought, "Nothing is going to get any better, I can't do anything to make it better, what difference does it make?" I have to use my memory to relate all this. When I have a bad day I think, "It used to be like this all the time. How did I stand it?"'

I asked Adele if she could paint a picture of what it was like to be depressed, what sort of picture would she paint?

She said, 'I don't know if I could describe a scene. It would have a lot of black in it. I'm very much into colours – an abstract with a lot of black – when I'm depressed nothing has form. It's just a big jumble or blob. You can't see any straight lines. A very dark abstract painting.'

She went on, 'My depression was due to psychological problems. My father was very abusive and from day one I thought I was half an inch high. I didn't have any self-esteem. I didn't think I had any brains until I started college. He was more physical with my sister. With me he was verbal. He was always giving me messages. One of my earliest recollections was like being in an aquarium and it was very dark inside and all the tanks were lit. There was a pit, with an octopus or something at the bottom, but he picked me up and held me over it, and I remember just screaming and carrying on. Likewise, being at the ocean and standing on a cliff and him pushing me and grabbing me, pretending to push me over. He would put fake dog shit on my plate at the dinner table. He also put a firecracker under my chair at dinner time. He would introduce me to his friends as the dumb one of the family. But when you're growing up with that – his term for me was "You dumb shit" – when you hear this all the time, you're not going to think you're worth anything. You think you're dirty, you're no good. Thank God nobody can see it.

'He also had a belt with rhinestone studs in it and my mother said he used to hit my sister with it when she was little so that she had big welts on her legs. I don't remember being hit with it, but I remember a kind of dread fascination with that belt, so maybe he hit me too. My mother wasn't very supportive. She was one of those long-suffering types. She was beat down too and it was her "Oh, poor me" attitude. Though every once in a while I'd hear her say, "If you do that again I'll divorce you."'

Neither of Adele's parents thought that there was anything wrong with her, even though, 'When I was in high school all the time I was at home I would spend in my bedroom. Watch television, think about movie stars. It was all fantasy. Occasionally my mother would tell me to come out. I'd go and lock myself in the bathroom. I felt exposed. I never stayed home from school. I had about three best friends. I've never been entirely friendless. I wasn't nasty. I was just very negative, insulting myself so as to beat them to the draw. I like to think of myself as getting along well with other people. Why my mother didn't get me help then I don't know. A few times when she tried to get me out of the bedroom I locked myself in the closet. It wasn't until I was twenty-one and I had a fight with my boyfriend and I ran away – I was afraid I was going to lose him – that she got me into therapy.'

With her first therapist Adele made a momentous discovery. 'I always thought it was my mother I had the problem with. I remember calling my friend and I said, "Guess what, it isn't Mom I dislike, it's Daddy." It's like this big revelation and it floored me. It wasn't until I had finished seeing my first therapist that I realized what verbal abuse was. I don't think he ever used the term but the connection was made.'

What Adele learned from her first experience of therapy enabled her to leave home. 'I was glad to get out. I moved out when I was twenty-three and left him for a year. Then I moved back home and within a week my mother moved out and left him so I was stuck there. This was a man I can't stand. I used to envision he'd be sitting at the kitchen table and I'd envision taking a gun and just letting him have it on the back of the head. Of course I never did. It used to be very difficult for me to even sit in the same room as him.'

Adele said that she was always amazed when her friends told her that they liked their fathers. 'To me fathers were alien creatures. I feel that way with most men. Of course with a role model like my father, my relationships with men have been awful. I have crummy taste in men, just like my mother. I've at least been smart enough not to marry any of them so far. I was always looking for somebody else to improve my self-esteem because I couldn't do it for myself. I was very much dependent on men. I haven't had a date in about ten or eleven years, and when that first started I was so depressed I felt I wasn't worth anything. Men scare me so much. Now the men I work with, there are some creeps, but there are also some very nice guys, and so I'm trying to learn from them as role models so I can really say there are some decent ones out there somewhere. It's finding them that's difficult. My first therapist once asked me if I thought anyone had ever loved me, and I thought for a long time, and then I said one person, my grandmother, and she died when I was eleven. So I always hoped maybe I would get some warmth from my relationship with men, but they all turned out to be goofballs and losers. But I remember telling my first therapist if I wasn't married by the time I was thirty I was going to commit suicide, and here I am forty-three. Thank God I didn't do that. To me men are alien, they're not human, they're like creatures from another planet, and I have to work through that.'

Adele now had a clear idea of what she needed to change about herself. She said, 'It took four or five therapists and off and on therapy from the age of twenty-one before I finally felt that I had a handle on my life. One of the things my last therapist did was to help me get rid of my anger towards my father. He said, "As long as you get angry with him, he still has control over you. Until you get rid of it you won't be able to grow and change."'

Adele had the opportunity to test this out when she decided to buy a new car without asking her father to help her make the choice. Then the car was in an accident. 'I told my father and he said, "That car's a worthless piece of shit. Come down here and I'll sort it out for you." I had bought that car on my own and it was a real learning experience for me. I said, "Thanks, but no thanks." I was nice about it, but at least I could say, "No, I don't want you to rule me any more." That was the feeling behind it.'

'So in previous years, he was helpful to you?'

'Yep, but when he was trying to be helpful, if you didn't understand what he was talking about, then you were stupid. And he was always one of those that if you ask him a question which could be answered with a yes or no he'll give you the background, the whole history. You don't care to hear that. So we always had to be careful what we asked him.'

'But he could relieve you of responsibility.'

'Yes.'

Thus giving up her anger with her father so as to free herself from him also meant giving up the advantage of having him do things for her.

Giving up the anger we have with the people who have hurt

us is certainly easier when something happens which allows us to feel the sweetness of revenge. Her father's first wife had never dared to oppose him, but his second, to Adele's great amusement, had him right under her thumb.

'His current wife said he's the coldest man she's ever met. I thought, "You had the nerve to say that to him!" I've learned that that's the way he is. That's his problem. He still occasionally throws out rude comments, although he has mellowed. I live far away so I don't have to deal with him. Maybe once, twice a year I'll see him.'

'Can you shout at him and criticize him like his present wife does?' I asked.

'No.'

'What would happen if you did?'

'I really don't know. I don't think he realizes he's being as cruel as he is. I don't think I would have the nerve, even after all these years, to come back at him.'

Even though she still would not answer her father back, Adele has changed. She said, 'I don't get depressed now, I get angry. The one thing that I have come away with as a result of living alone for so long is the realization that I come first. When all's said and done, when you check out of this life, you're the one that you have to account for. It's all very well to say that other people come first but they don't really. You come first. You can help other people and do as much as you can for them, but you have to put yourself first because nobody else is going to.'

Some people find it extremely difficult to let go of the anger they feel for the parents who treated them so badly. They complain, quite rightly, about how they were abused, neglected, humiliated, and abandoned by their parents, and yet the pain that they feel is not just the pain from such terrible experiences. It is also the pain of disappointment. They feel that they ought to have had Perfect Parents, and they cannot forgive their parents for not being perfect.

Their complaints are not simply against their parents, but against the world which has treated them so unfairly. They want to believe in a world where goodness is rewarded and badness punished, yet it seems that neither are their parents being punished for their wickedness nor are they themselves being rewarded for their suffering and their goodness. They say to themselves, 'One day justice will be done', and they go on, year after miserable year, locked into an angry, hurtful relationship, not just with their parents but with the images of the parents that they carry inside them. 'I ought to have had perfect parents' becomes their refrain of unforgiveness, which is all the more difficult to resolve because they cannot determine who or what they are not forgiving for such an injustice.

We all, as small babies, expected our parents to be perfect, to meet our every need, and to protect us from all harm. When they failed to do so, we felt rejected and betrayed. We, as babies, could not know that we needed parents who would fail us, for if we had parents who met our every need, we would never grow and develop. It was our mother's failures which led us to explore ourselves and our world and to develop skills in dealing with our world. What we needed was not a Perfect Mother, but, in Donald Winnicott's phrase, a 'good enough' mother, someone who would feed us and keep us warm and safe from major harm, and let us get on with being and becoming ourselves.

What we need are not Perfect Parents, but parents we can outgrow so that we can return to our parents as friends, adults and equals. To achieve this we need to go through a period of rebelling against our parents, not just in the teenager way of doing things our parents disapprove of, but in looking very closely and clearly at our childhood and from two perspectives, that of the child we were and that of the adult we are now. That way we feel again the pain of the child, but from our adult point of view we know that we are not helpless in the way that the child was helpless. Out of such a review we can see our parents as the ordinary people that they were, and the kind of people they have become, for as adult children we often persist in seeing and reacting to our parents in the way that we did as a child. In such a discovery we might also find forgiveness.   **(D 20)**

Remember always that *forgiveness, like love, is spontaneous*. It cannot be willed into existence. Resolving to forgive someone is no more than resolving not to persecute that person, just as resolving to love someone is no more than resolving to be kind to that person. Forgiveness, love and happiness are not things which we can achieve, but graces which come upon us when we live as ourselves at home in our world.

You who get depressed find such a rebellion against your parents extremely difficult because when you look with an adult's eye at the child you once were, you look without pity or sympathy. The plight of every other child in the world tugs at your heartstrings, but of the child you once were you say, 'I was a bad child and deserved to be punished'.

Loving and feeling sympathy for the child you once were is not weakness and self-pity. It is acknowledging the vulnerability of children to which adults should respond with concern, sympathy and protection. If you give concern, sympathy and protection only to those children you define as 'good' and not to those you define as 'bad', then you are not genuine in your claim to be a caring person. You are simply using your concern, sympathy and protection to reward those children who behave as you want them to behave, that is, to meet your needs. If you regard your love as a reward to people who please you by meeting your high standards, then what you call love is not love. It is merely, like money, a means of barter.

Perhaps you have never thought about this because all the love you have ever known has been this counterfeit love. If you pleased your parents by being good, they showed you love. If you failed to please them, they withdrew their love. If you were an extravert this withdrawal of love was terrifying, and so you built your whole life around the necessity of keeping your parents' love. If you were an introvert the withdrawal of your parents' love did not threaten you with annihilation for you knew how to be on your own, but you found the only way you could assuage the ache and longing for your parents' love was to exchange love for approval. You gave up wanting your parents to love you. You simply wanted their approval, and, if they failed to give you that, you could try to get approval from other people. However, no matter how much approval other people might give you, if your parents did not approve of you, you were not satisfied.

Many parents use their love as a weapon to make their children behave as they wish. Some parents do this because they do not love their children but see them simply as their possessions to be manipulated as they please. However, most parents do love their children and, if left to themselves, would show this love uninhibitedly to their children, but they have been taught by their parents and by society that to love your child simply because your child *is* is to 'spoil' your child. So many parents hide their genuine, accepting love from their child, and show instead the counterfeit love of rewards and punishments. Because of this, many children grow up believing that their parents do not really love them.

Real love loves us for what we are. Counterfeit love loves us only for what we can do.

The tragedy of so many people's lives is that they never discover that underneath their parents' counterfeit love was genuine love, and that, despite all their foolishnesses and failure to be the Perfect Child, a Credit to Your Parents, their parents had always loved them unreservedly.

It is my great good fortune that I avoided such a tragedy in my life. This came about through my mother's deplorable habit of secretly reading other people's letters. My sister had written to me for some advice about a mutual friend who was depressed, and in my letter to my sister I spoke of how I never doubted my father's love for me, but how I always knew that my mother did not love me because she withdrew her affection whenever I displeased her. My sister found out only by accident that mother had read this. My mother never spoke about it directly to me, but from then on until she died my mother never again criticized me. Everything I did was wonderful, and in every possible way she showed her love for me.

The tragedy of never knowing that your parents really loved you can come about because you will not risk reviewing your life and questioning the reality of the figures you have created of the Bad Parent and the Perfect Parent. You find this hard to do if, like your parents, you dare not question the expectation common in our society that children should always be respectful and obedient to their parents and never challenge them in any way. This expectation is built upon the bargain in which, in return for obedience, the parents give the child security. For many of us the price we pay in terms of obedience is extremely high.

Fiona came to interview me for a women's magazine, but we talked more about her than about me. Laughing, really, because Fiona was one of those people who describes the conflicts and difficulties they encounter as hilarious jokes. What more hilarious joke could there be than the terror she felt every time she drove her car? She had to drive often, for her work required it, and each time she launched herself into London traffic she was sure she was going to die. She knew all about the techniques for controlling panic – she had been interviewing psychologists for years – but no amount of measured breathing and positive self-talk could stop the terror mounting.

It was not until we were comparing our mothers' favourite

warnings (all mothers have favourite warnings, and we know them better than the sound of our own heartbeat) that she mentioned what her mother said whenever she knew that Fiona was about to drive her car. 'Fiona,' she would say, 'whatever you do, don't have an accident. If you died that would kill me.'

So it was not that she herself might die in a car accident that terrified Fiona, it was that if she did she would cause her mother's death. Her mother had been giving her this kind of warning all her life. If she didn't eat properly, or empty her bowels regularly, or keep herself scrupulously clean, or behave nicely, then the result of her disobedience would be her mother's death. No allowance was made for chance mishaps. If anything went wrong, it was Fiona's fault, and her mother would pay the price.

In laying this burden on Fiona her mother was not simply trying to keep Fiona safe. She was also, and perhaps more importantly for her, trying to spare herself the pain and guilt she might otherwise feel if Fiona was injured, or sick, or died, or, even worse, failed to become a credit to her mother. By making Fiona chronically anxious and guilty, her mother

(D 21)   promoted her own self interest.

Even as I spelled this out to Fiona, she agreed that it was so, but said there was nothing she could do about it. 'My mother's old now,' she said. 'What if I did have an accident and the shock of it killed her? I'd never forgive myself.'

Most parents are very skilled in making their children feel guilty (they learnt how from their parents), as Calvin once observed when he lost his friend Hobbes.[36]

To give up being depressed you have to give up this persistent, apparently automatic feeling of guilt which you use as a way of assuring yourself that you are good and not helpless. However, as much as you try to do this, your parents, who might not be wanting you to be anything but the child they want you to be, can continue to use the same methods that they have used all along to keep you in line. They might want the best for you, but they want to define what is best.

At a workshop on depression which I was running Judy told the story of how it had taken her years to see clearly the guilt arousing tactics which her mother used to get her to be the daughter she wanted. Her mother, while promoting Judy's sense of guilt, did not leaven this painful teaching with love, as wiser parents do, and so as soon as Judy was old enough she went in search of love and found it in the arms of a man her mother deemed to be a scoundrel. When he did behave as scoundrels do, Judy, well trained in guilt, took the blame upon herself and fell into a depression. Then through her misery came a glimmer of an idea, the thought, at first a sin, a sacrilege against her perfect mother, that this paragon of virtue was actually pleased that Judy's marriage had failed. She would rather be right than see her daughter happy.

This glimmer of an idea became a beacon, and Judy went in search of further enlightenment. Before long, when her mother uttered her usual warnings that Judy's inherent incapability and waywardness would lead to further disasters, Judy interpreted these warnings in the ways in which her enlightenment had shown her. Thus, when her mother, looking at Judy's small son, said, 'A boy brought up in a one-parent family always becomes delinquent', Judy did not, as she would have done in her unenlightened days, dutifully see in her son the seeds of delinquency, so that her vision and his desire to fulfil her expectations would combine to prove her mother right. Instead, she gave her son the kind of love her mother had denied her, and she encouraged him to be the wonderful person she knew he was.

Judy told us how proud she was of him now he was a young man, and how he was her best friend. Then she laughed and said, 'But sometimes I catch myself feeling guilty because I deprived my mother of having a delinquent grandson.'

The skills which Judy's mother and Fiona's mother used to create in their daughters a persistent, nagging sense of guilt are skills which many parents employ. These skills are based on the assumption that children must be grateful for being born and must spend the rest of their lives repaying their parents for their self-sacrifice in providing a home and caring for their children. 'After all I've done for you' is a refrain sung by many parents which sometimes makes us, as their children, weep with rage and frustration, but sometimes laugh, as we did when we watched the American television series *Rhoda*, about a New York woman who is continually reminded by her mother of her mother's sacrifices. One day, driven to desperation by her mother's reproaches, Rhoda cried, 'Will I ever be able to repay you?' and her mother replied, 'You should live so long.'

If you have been taught that you are for ever in your parents' debt, that you must go on and on paying instalments on a sum which never reduces, and that to question this is to be guilty of the sin of ingratitude, you can never feel adequate or valuable or free. It is in your parents' interest to keep you feeling guilty about their self-sacrifice, because then they can be sure that you will not leave them alone and uncared for, no matter what other responsibilities you as an adult might have.

How foolish we are to build our parent-child relationships on guilt, for guilt is fear, and fear drives out love! How foolish we are to think that we can compel people to love us by making them feel guilty!

Because of our foolishness, most of what goes on in a great many families has little to do with love and everything to do with control, compulsion and fear. The control and compulsion can operate by the promotion of guilt (let us not forget that children can become very skilled in making their parents feel guilty) and by rule making and supervision, which define each person in the family and limit what each person can be or do. In one scene in the popular soap *Neighbours* Scott said of his sister who has gone to Paris, 'She'll come back with a big head.' His grandmother replied, 'You'll soon cut her down to size.'

If you belong to a family who, whenever a family member does not conform to the role which the family has specified, cuts that person down to size, you will be anxious about making any change in yourself which would make you the butt of your family jokes and criticisms.

Your family might not want you to change because that will mean that they will have to change in how they think about you and treat you. If your family has always seen you as 'the quiet one' or 'the responsible one', and you decide to change and become sociable or pursue your own interests, this will upset their way of thinking and acting. They will actually have to think about you, instead of just responding automatically to the image they have of you. They will have to talk about you differently to their friends and make adjustments in their lives. People don't like change. It makes them nervous. So, if you start to change, your family is quite likely to try to keep you where you are. Ask any fat person who, after slimming successfully, put the weight back on again. Family remarks like, 'Being thin doesn't suit you', 'You look a lot older now you're thin', 'Have another cream cake. I made them just for you', can be very difficult to withstand.

Having a defined role in your family can give you a sense of security, so it can often seem the simplest and wisest course of action to give up being, or striving to be, the person that you want to be. Doing this you forget that if we are to live comfortably with ourselves our lives must have significance to ourselves, even if not to other people. *When our family insists that we be what they want us to be and we comply with their insistence, our lives lose their significance, because in being what our family wants us to be we have to give up being ourselves.*

Sometimes when we are children our family offers us a choice of roles, but if neither of these roles allows us to be ourselves the choice is no choice at all. The choice which most families offer is 'to be good' and, since how to be good is specified in our family's terms, we know how 'to be bad'.

Caroline's parents spelled out to her very clearly how a good child in their family should behave. From her earliest days she was expected to be clean, neat, quiet, obedient, respectful to adults, well spoken, and to play nicely with the children of whom her parents approved; that is, she should be everything that middle-class parents would want in a daughter. Whenever she failed to meet these standards her parents called her 'mad' and 'bad'. Caroline remembers herself as being a quiet child who was very frightened of her parents. She also remembers when she became convinced that she was, in essence, bad.

When she was five and going to school, she noticed that whenever a child in her class had some little injury that needed a bandage the teacher was particularly kind and solicitous to that child. Caroline knew where there was a package of elastic bandage strips at home, and one day she took some of these strips and put them on her thigh, hoping that her teacher would notice her and comfort her.

When Caroline first told me this story she had not asked herself why she needed such comfort from her teacher. She was still at that stage of depression where she had no sympathy for the child she once was.

When her mother discovered that some of the bandages were missing she questioned Caroline who, fearing punishment if she confessed, denied that she had taken them. Some time later, again hoping for her teacher's attention and comfort, she took some more bandages and put them high up on her thigh, well hidden by her skirt.

It was a sunny day, and when she got home she found her young brother enjoying the water in an inflatable paddling-pool set out on the lawn. Caroline flung off her dress and leapt into the pool to join her brother. The bandages were revealed.

In the scene which followed Caroline remembers sitting on the lawn, twining blades of grass around her finger while her mother pronounced judgement, giving it a finality and reality which Caroline could never doubt or question. Reality was revealed to her, and it was that she was a liar and a cheat, that she was absolutely and irrevocably, for ever and ever, bad, wicked, an outcast, damned beyond redemption, the cause of all the pain and suffering that her parents had endured and would ever endure.

So Caroline's role in her family became confirmed as that of the mad, bad one. It was put on her by her parents, but she also chose it, not just because of her mother's pronouncements, but because she could not, in all honesty, be good the way that her parents defined 'good'. She observed that in her parents' relationships there was a certain hypocrisy – what they said to people was very different from what they said in private – and she wanted no part in that. She had an introvert's need for truth, for only in seeking truth can an introvert try to keep external reality real and keep chaos at bay.

Caroline had other reasons for rejecting the 'being good' role.
The 'being bad' role offered her some limited scope for being
herself, while the 'being good' role, which demanded con-
formity to all her parents' wishes, would turn her into her
parents' creature, a no-thing. Moreover, the 'being bad' role
offered her a way of getting back at her parents, a very expensive way in terms of her health and spirit as she found when, in
her late teens, her parents committed her to a psychiatric
hospital.

At first, Caroline accepted without question her psychiatrist's explanation that she had a mental illness which could be
controlled by drugs because it absolved her of responsibility for
her actions. Never mind that she oscillated between extreme
anxiety and profound depression, the pills, she hoped, would
cure all that.

But they did not, and the years slipped by while she went in
and out of hospital, losing job after job, drifting in and out of
one unhappy sexual relationship after another, and still, every
morning, waking out of a dream of terror and impending doom
into a consciousness of total guilt, wet with the perspiration of
fear, dreading to face the day. She would remain in bed, fearing
to emerge, and all the time worrying about tasks undone and
achievements lost.

Throughout her life Caroline's father had taken no positive
interest in her but had beaten her when she was a child and
criticized or ignored her when she became an adult. Yet it was
he who pushed her into changing. So anxious had he become at
the way she stayed in bed, the blankets over her head, profoundly depressed month after month, that he went in search
of a book to explain what was happening. He found my
Depression: The Way Out of Your Prison, and, so Caroline later told
me, thrust it under the blankets to her. It was a while before
Caroline could bring herself to read it, but once she did she
resolved to come and see me.

I remember Caroline as the most anxious person I had ever
met, so it took us some time to have a coherent conversation.
What we talked about was not just about her life but about her
work, or, at least, what her work should be, for Caroline is a
brilliant artist.

When there is something which we can do which is meaningful to us and which when we do it fills us with elation and the

joy of creation, all the trials and tribulations of our lives become simply the materials for our purpose or else fall away into nothingness. Unfortunately, most of us are so convinced of our lack of ability and creativity and have received an education designed to stifle our natural creativity, curiosity and expression, that this lifeline is not readily available to us. But Caroline knew that she could paint, and she knew that painting was important to her.

So I said to her – frequently – 'Paint, and don't let anyone tell you how or what to paint.' I had to say this frequently, for Caroline so doubted her ability that she would let other people tell her what to paint and to make ill-informed criticisms of her work. These criticisms inhibited her and sometimes stopped her from painting altogether.

With many stops and starts Caroline began painting consistently, and soon it became apparent that she would be able to make her living from painting and free herself from economic dependence upon her parents. The anxiety about such a change drove her again and again back into depression.

There was the straightforward anxiety about a totally new way of life, financially independent, taking responsibility for herself and all the unknowns that that would bring. But there was also another, perhaps greater, anxiety. Would she, in becoming a successful painter, become the 'good girl' her mother wanted her to be? Her mother took a great interest in her work and spared her no criticism. Did this change mean that, in the end, her mother had won?

Caroline's battle with her mother had been conducted with the ammunition of guilt. Her mother made her feel guilty. Caroline withdrew into a depression. Her depression made her mother feel guilty, for she genuinely loved Caroline, even though she hid this love behind a barrage of complaints and criticisms. Her mother tried to assuage her guilt by giving Caroline presents. Caroline felt guilty for taking such gifts and became more depressed, her mother responded with more guilt and more gifts, Caroline became more depressed, and so on and on.

Caroline had to discover that in becoming an independent person managing her own life she was neither playing the 'being good' role nor the 'being bad' role, but had discarded both roles in favour of being herself.

One of the greatest difficulties Caroline had in doing this was in dealing with the dreams which left her with such powerful feelings of guilt and dread. Most people who have gone through bad experiences have such dreams, for in our sleep we are trying to master those experiences which all but overwhelmed us. These dreams threaten what self-confidence we have, yet it is the self-confidence that we establish in our waking life that can resolve the issues in our dreams. We need to tell ourselves that such dreams are nothing but memories which we can use as a resource for greater understanding of ourselves and other people and other than that have no relevance in our present lives. The problem lies not with our dreams but our fear of helplessness, and we can overcome this fear by realizing our strength.

Caroline's battle was with her parents and her dreams. Though she regrets that she has not yet had a child, she is fortunate that as she prepares to change she is free to do so. She is not, as many depressed people are, entangled with a partner who may not want her to change.

Partners and Power

Living with someone who is depressed is very difficult. Coming close to that person we can actually put out our hand and touch the prison wall which surrounds the depressed person. It may be invisible, but it is impenetrable.

Hitting a wall whenever we offer comfort and love is very frustrating, and frustration creates anger. So when we offer comfort and love to someone who is depressed it is likely that very soon we find that our loving, concerned feelings are replaced by anger. That anger can make us feel ashamed and guilty. How can we be angry with someone so obviously suffering? Moreover, the way the depressed person ignores or turns aside our offers of help and wise advice can make us feel helpless, which in turn can make us feel frightened, especially if we pride ourselves on our ability to be helpful.

It is not surprising that, feeling this anger and fear, concerned family and friends say, 'Why don't you pull yourself together?', that doctors reach for the prescription pad to bring the consultation to an end, and therapists deem the depressed person 'not suitable for therapy'. It is not surprising that we look for explanations of depression which will enable us to deny or justify the frustration,

anger, shame, guilt and fear which a depressed person provokes in
(D 22) us.

On extremely popular method of dealing with the anger we feel
when someone resists our help is to cease taking that person
seriously and instead categorize them as bad or mad, not in their
right mind, ill. Hence the popularity of the belief that depression is a
mental illness.

Women as well as men will readily proffer the opinion that anyone
who does not agree with them is mad, but it is men who have
elaborated the notion that a depressed person is mad into a theory of
genetic inheritance. The part that women have played in this
development is that they have been the patients whose behaviour is
supposed to have been explained by this theory. The majority of
depressed patients are women, and of these most are married. Some
epidemiologists even have the uneasy feeling that women's depression has something to do with the institution of marriage.[37]

Indeed, the epidemiological evidence shows that it is single men
and married women who are more likely to receive a psychiatrist's
care. Marriage, it seems, suits men but not women. The solution I
suggest is that men marry men, while women follow Katharine
Hepburn's advice that men and women should live as neighbours
and visit occasionally.

The epidemiologists I have read seem somewhat relieved that
they do not have to go on and examine the question of why marriage
does not suit women when society and the Church, that is, men,
have always decreed that all a woman needs to be happy and
fulfilled is a husband, a home and children.

I have always found it curious that men are always so sure about
what a woman needs and how the deficiencies of the female form
make her man's inferior (in the last century it was a woman's weak
brain, in this century it is her hormones) when men so commonly
declare that they do not understand how women think. When the
film producer David Puttnam was interviewed by *Time* journalist
Eugene Linden and asked, 'Why have you never used a woman as a
central character?' David Puttnam said, 'Maybe I should worry
about this, but I don't understand women's motivations, which
means that I don't know how to address the script, the castings, etc.
Women's reactions are extremely arbitrary to me.'[38]

Women, on the other hand, usually say that they understand
men, and, when they do not, they, like Adele, usually know why
they don't understand men. They know that they lack the appropri-

ate experience in which to get to know men. The only time women use a biological theory to examine the behaviour of men is when they wonder about how much of a man's aggression can be attributed to hormones. I have never heard a woman say that men are not responsible for their aggression since it is a result of their hormones, yet men will quite frequently categorize women's behaviour as nothing but the result of their hormonal or genetic make-up.

Thus it is that when a married woman becomes depressed, her husband takes her along to the doctor, much in the same way as he would take his car to a mechanic, and says, 'Make her better, doctor'.

I have lost count of how many women I have had thus delivered to me. I know precisely how many wives have delivered their husbands to me in the same way. Just two, and they wanted me to keep their husbands occupied while they got on with their careers. Most wives come along with their husbands, or send messages that they will come too if I thought that would help. But then most women married to a depressed man, or depressed themselves, know that the depression has something to do with them both. A few men do understand this, and so come with their wives, ready to take part in the unravelling of life histories, but most see the situation in terms of the psychiatric theory: since the machine broke down, it needs to be mended. Why the machine broke down and how it can be mended has nothing to do with them, other than perhaps taking the broken down wife to a doctor and, where necessary, paying his bill.

Such an attitude saves men from self-inspection, which is to be avoided, since it might reveal, amongst other things, that there can be advantages in having as a partner someone who is depressed.

Such advantages are, at first, hard to imagine, but they are there nevertheless. One thing that can be said in favour of someone who is depressed is that, miserable and frustrating though you might be when you are depressed, you are *reliable*. You are not out gadding about, spending your partner's money, meeting other people who might entice you away from your partner. You are safe at home, and your partner knows where you are every minute of the day. Moreover, while you are safe and reliable, you do not make decisions on your own, and you do not try to impose your views on your partner. Most of the time you go along with what your partner wants.

Your being depressed can help to fulfil your partner's needs. Your partner might be an extravert who needs to be needed, or an introvert who needs to keep other people under control.

Your depression might be all that is holding the marriage together, and the marriage might be more important to your partner than to you. In your depression you are avoiding examining your relationship and facing up to the conflicts and disappointments there. Your partner might actually have more invested in the marriage than you have.

These advantages apply to whichever person in the partnership is not depressed. There is, however, one major advantage which accrues to the man when the woman in the partnership gets depressed.

Every marriage partnership is a sharing out of responsibilities and skills. Each partner does what he or she is good at, and the other partner benefits. He goes out to work: she looks after the children. He cleans the car: she cleans the house. He mends the fuses: she does the cooking. He takes the children to football matches: she visits his parents. He is quiet in company: she does the socializing. He is calm in a crisis: she gets upset.

It is not that they could not swap places in each of these situations. It is that they take up these places because this is how they see themselves and their capabilities. So one does for the other what the other will not do.

The last of these situations refers to an arrangement which many couples make. After all, it is approriate and expected in our society that the man be calm and strong and the woman show her feelings and be in need of his protection. So, in actuality, the woman expresses the feelings of both of them. This arrangement saves many men from getting depressed. Their wives do it for them.

It is not in the interests of such men that their wives should cease to be depressed, for that might mean that the man has to own his own depression.

If you are a depressed wife and you are wondering whether this is the situation in your marriage, listen carefully on those occasions when you feel less depressed and more inclined to present your own point of view and perhaps even argue with your partner. Does he say things like, 'If you make me angry I'll not be responsible for what happens', or 'If you keep carrying on like this I'll get depressed and where will you be then?'

Do you respond to these threats by shutting up and becoming depressed?

(D 23)

Such a withdrawal is both a retreat in the face of someone who is physically and, quite likely, economically more powerful than you, and a way of getting back at your partner. Such a withdrawal says, 'See what you made me do. Now I won't talk to you.'

Depression has a great many uses. Most importantly it holds us together in the face of threats to our sense of self, but once we have established it as a defence we can use it in our power struggle with other people, making them feel guilty and forcing them to behave as we want them to behave. It is a devious and dishonest weapon which we can use when we feel that we dare not confront other people openly.

Since we are all in the business of survival – the purpose of life is to live – we often, in our weakness, have to resort to devious and dishonest weapons. Since in most marriages the woman is physically weaker than the man and economically dependent on him, it is understandable that many married women use depression as a way of holding themselves together.

The power struggle – any power struggle – is concerned with trying to make our way of seeing the world accepted by other people as The One True Reality, and our beliefs and attitudes accepted by other people as The One Truth. Some people go to no end of trouble in trying to do this – becoming dictators, establishing religions – but no one has ever succeeded in getting everybody, or even most people, to give up their own way of seeing and believing and to accept his. We each have our own individual way of seeing and believing, and we each see and believe differently. Consequently, when two people come together in a marriage partnership they differ, and they struggle for power.

If the couple both understand that they have their different ways of seeing and believing, if they make their own ways of seeing and believing explicit, and if they take the other person's point of view seriously, they can agree to disagree. Then, in the interests of their partnership, they can make the aim of the power struggle the search for compromises which both find satisfying. Not all partnerships operate like this.

In partnerships where one person becomes depressed there is little or no open communication, neither is there a great knowledge of and respect for each other's point of view, nor is there a search for compromise.

This is hardly surprising, since few of us have the kind of upbringing which encourages us to be open with other people. Most of us are taught by our parents and teachers that we are not good enough, and so, believing that we have something to hide, we acquire conversational skills aimed at hiding rather than revealing ourselves. It is often said that women are more open than men, but this is nothing more than a difference in what we feel we are allowed to reveal. Men commonly feel that they are allowed to reveal their desire for dominance, and women feel that they are allowed to show their distress and guilt, but both men and women are reluctant to reveal their profound anger and hate, their envy and their shame, and their immensely vulnerable sense of weakness and helplessness.

The less we value and accept ourselves, the greater our sense of weakness, and the greater our sense of weakness, the more we feel the need to defend ourselves by imposing our ways of seeing and believing on to other people. When we value and accept ourselves we do not feel weak, and so we are not threatened by other people having points of view different from our own. *We actually reveal how weak we feel by the determination with which we try to get other people to conform to our ideas.* We can be putting on a great show of strength, but the very show reveals our weakness.

Thus, in a partnership where each person feels weak and vulnerable, the battle for power is fierce. In such a struggle communication is kept to a minimum, because by communicating you might reveal your weakness. So the couple develop a form of communication based on not disclosing information and using silence to make the other person silent. Certain topics, however vital to the lives of the couple, are never broached, since any attempt by one partner to mention such a topic produces in the other silence, be it the silence of 'the strong, silent man', the silence of someone ceasing to attend to the conversation, the silence of physical absence, or of retreating into a sulk, or the silence of a depression. Whichever form of silence, it silences the partner who initially ventured to speak.

This form of communication, aimed at not communicating, creates a threat to both people, for it fails to supply the confirmation that we need from other people that we exist and have significance. When to this is added the ferocious need of the other person to negate our way of seeing and believing, we can find our sense of self in great peril.

Once one member of the couple feels so threatened that, to hold herself (or himself) together she retreats into a depression, the other has, in a sense, won the battle. Now her way of seeing and believing is shown to be mad, that is, not having any relationship to reality. His way of seeing and believing has been validated. He is sane.

There are some men and women who, once their partner becomes depressed, see this as nothing but a victory for themselves and who, having found the ploys which make their partner lose all self-confidence, continue to use them to their own advantage. They have no sympathy for the suffering their partner undergoes.

However, it is possible to love someone we neither understand nor communicate with, and so most men and women, once their partner becomes depressed, do not want to see their partner suffering. Having had their own way of seeing and believing apparently validated, they now feel confident that they can say to their partner, 'See things the way I do', and their partner will immediately cease to be depressed. Instead, their partner proceeds to prove them wrong. The terrain and the tactics of the battle have changed, but the battle goes on.

The only way to end such a battle is to disengage. It takes two to fight, just as it does to tango.

Elizabeth now talks to me about how differently she responds to old situations, now that she understands why she spent so many years of her marriage being depressed. Now she no longer needs her depression as a defence, but she has to watch herself closely in case she slips back into her old ways of responding to her husband's tactics.

Elizabeth's marriage is, to an outside observer, ideal. Her husband is a successful doctor, her three children would make any parent proud. To her it was a marriage of tension and wariness, for one mistaken word or gesture by her and Roger, her husband, would retreat into an aggrieved silence which would last for many weeks. She had gone into her marriage full of confidence, an assured and happy young woman, but gradually her happiness drained away and turned to despair.

What Elizabeth is aware of now is the subtle ways in which her self-confidence can be undermined.

She told me how her eldest son and his wife had invited Roger and her to spend Christmas with them. She and Roger had talked this over and decided not to accept the invitation. They would prefer to spend Christmas in their own home with their daughter and her fiancé.

Elizabeth said to me, 'It would have been a lot less work for me if we had gone to Jim's place, but Roger, though he'd never admit it, loves Christmas and he always wants it to be exactly the same every year. He doesn't get on at all well with our daughter-in-law's parents, and I know he didn't want to spend two or three days with them there. When we talked it over and made our decision he said to me, "I think we've done the right thing. You'll feel better in your own home." Now in the bad old days I would have left it like that. I would have accepted that I was the weak one who couldn't cope. But now it's the good new days and I said to him, "And you'll feel much better too, won't you?"'

Roger did not withdraw into an aggrieved silence at this impertinence because over the last year he had discovered that his sulking no longer brought Elizabeth to heel. If he tries to sulk she tells him not to be silly, or she goes out and enjoys herself, leaving him to get his own meals.

Elizabeth went on, 'I've discovered something else. When I was depressed I used to think I was losing my mind because I'd start to tell Roger something and then I'd just trail off, unable to finish what I'd started to say. I would forget what I'd started to say. I'd sit there holding my head and thinking there was something seriously wrong with me. Well, the other day I was watching him when I was talking to him, and I saw what he does. When I'm saying something that he's not interested in or that he doesn't want to hear, he doesn't look at me. His eyes just slide away. That's what would stop me talking and make me feel that I was going crazy. The other thing he does is that he never hears what I say the first time I say it. He always says, "What was that?", and I have to repeat it. Now what I do is that I say to him, "Are you listening?" and that gets his attention.'

(D 24)

Because a couple do not communicate they can fail to appreciate how profoundly they differ, not just in matters like how they spend their money or what they do in bed, but on the very purpose of life.

In the way that we are always drawn to someone who appears to share our attitudes, yet is different from us in ways which we find attractive and admirable, extraverts are drawn to introverts and introverts to extraverts.

For many years now I have been diligently searching for couples made up of two introverts or two extraverts, but to date I have not found one. I know couples who thought that they were both introverts, but when I asked each of them the series of questions 'Why is that important?' one of the couple proved to be an extravert who is interested in what goes on in his or her internal reality but who still sees relationships with other people as being of prime importance. I know couples who thought they were both extraverts, but when I asked, 'Why is that important?', one of the couple proved to be an introvert who had acquired excellent social skills and who operated competently in external reality, but who still saw the need to achieve and to develop his or her individuality as being of prime importance. (Remember, we all want to achieve and to have good relationships with other people. The question is, when you have to make a choice, which, for you, *comes first*?)

Many couples, not just those in grave marital difficulties or with one member depressed, have never discussed how each sees the purpose of life, yet these assumptions underlie every decision they have to make and every misunderstanding and fight they have.

Take, for instance, the constant question of how they should spend their money. Shall they, say, spend the year's surplus cash on a new car or a holiday? The introvert in argument says things like, 'I see a new car as a real achievement', or, 'A new car shows that we are going up in the world', or, 'I need a reliable car to be sure that I meet my sales targets', or, 'What's the use of a holiday? When it's over you've got nothing to show for it', and each argument is based on the assumption that the purpose of life is individual achievement. The extravert says, 'Let's have a holiday. We need time together', or, 'We ought to do things as a family', and each argument is based on the assumption that the purpose of life is relationships with other people.

Or, the question of sex. Many introverts find sex frightening because it implies the loss of control which the introvert fears. Many extraverts are promiscuous, not because their sexual urges are greater than most people's, but because it is only in sex that they can find the relationships which maintain their sense of existence but in which there is neither the intimacy nor the communication they fear. Having sex is a great way of avoiding conversation.

Some couples are aware of each other's understanding of the purpose of life and despise it. Just as we can be racist or sexist, we can be 'vertist'. The prejudice extraverts have about introverts is that they have no feelings. The prejudice introverts have about extraverts is that they are histrionic and have no depth of feeling or understanding. These prejudices can come to the fore when a couple suffers a tragedy. A couple spoke to me separately when one of their close friends was killed in a car accident. The husband, an extravert, said, 'I haven't been able to work since the accident. This friend and I were very close. My wife's taking it well, but then she wasn't as close to him as I was.' When his wife, an introvert, spoke to me there was a hint of scorn in her voice when she said, 'My husband is making out that he's the only one affected by this death. Just because I don't cry in public he thinks I'm not affected. He forgets that I was as close to our friend as he was, closer perhaps.'

Because our way of seeing the purpose of life and the threat of the annihilation of our self is so basic to everything that we feel and do, when we are part of a couple we want to impose this on our partner and have our partner accept it. Yet, if we do not realize that our partner's way of seeing the purpose of life and the threat of the annihilation of the self is as vitally important as our own, we doom our relationship to pain and disaster.

If we do not realize this, we can, even when we want most to help our partner, inflict great pain and actively stop our partner from changing.

One morning I had a phone call from a husband greatly concerned about his wife who was depressed. He explained that his wife had been seeing a therapist for some three years and had been making steady progress. The previous evening the therapist had cancelled his wife's weekly appointment because all the therapists in that region were to hold a meeting the next day to discuss how they might best work with the victims of a recent national disaster. His wife was exceedingly upset about this cancellation and had become very depressed.

I guessed that his wife had seen the cancellation as a rejection and as evidence that she was not as valuable as the disaster victims. I thought that this was something between her and her therapist and certainly not something in which I should interfere.

The problem that I had to deal with was not the wife's but the husband's, a problem which he presented in terms of 'achievement', 'goals', 'making progress', and 'back to square one'.

I thought that he sounded like an introvert, but he could have been an extravert talking in the way that men's education teaches them to talk. That is, in terms of reducing every situation, however vague and amorphous, to a problem, and then acting so as to solve that problem.

A man at a Natural Childbirth Trust meeting where I was talking about depression told us how, when his wife became depressed and he was advised to show his love for her with plenty of hugs and kisses, he thought that X amount of hugs and kisses should produce Y amount of improvement in her. He was confused and angry when there seemed to be no mathematical relationship between how much he did for her and how much she changed. It took him a while to realize that in this situation thinking in terms of problem solving was, at best, irrelevant and, at worst, damaging.

My caller had not reached this point of understanding, and I did not think that I could create such enlightenment over the phone. So I concentrated on the paradox that being with a depressed person creates for all of us.

We become depressed because we believe that we are bad and unacceptable. To change this belief we need the people around us to value and accept us. This means *valuing and accepting our depression*.

There are many partners and many parents who do not wish their partner or child to be depressed. Their heart breaks when they see the person they love suffering so much, and they would give anything to bring this suffering to an end.

They think of the 'anything' they would do in terms of love, support and comfort, and, in practical terms, of accompanying the loved one to clinics and therapists, spending money and time. They do not always realize that what is needed are two things which are often hard to do.

The first is to show that you love the person as she or he *is*. If you say, 'I love you, but I wish you weren't depressed', the second part of the sentence negates the first. You need to show that 'However you are and whatever you do, I love you'.

The second is that you must give the person room to change and to become whatever she or he becomes. If you say, 'I want you to be the person I married', or, 'I want you to be happy', you are laying down conditions about how that person must change. You are showing that you want the person to conform to your wishes and that you do not accept that person's sadness. What you need to show is that your love is true love, which expects and demands nothing, but simply accepts. True love says, 'I love you and wish you well, even if that "well" does not include me and what I want'.

Only that kind of love can give a person the encouragement and freedom to set out on the journey out of depression.

III

The Journey Out of
the Prison of Depression

12

The Expert's Secret

When I was ten years old, my father took me to see *The Wizard of Oz*. My father thought it was the wisest film he had ever seen, and we often talked about it. Perhaps this is why whenever I think of how someone can cease being tortured by fear and depression I think of that person setting out on a journey along a yellow brick road.

Like Dorothy, they meet different people, and learn different things, but, most of all, they learn about themselves. In one way, their journey never comes to an end, for the gaining of wisdom is never complete, but at some point in their journey they discover that what they were searching for they already had. The Scarecrow was always intelligent, the Tin Man always had love and compassion, the Lion always had courage, and all that Dorothy had to do was to click her heels together and she was home. Or, as T. S. Eliot said:

> We shall not cease from exploration
> And the end of all our exploring
> Will be to arrive where we started
> And know the place for the first time.[39]

It is our failure to understand ourselves which causes most of our suffering. Certainly our planet is not particularly hospitable to us, and our bodies suffer illness, accident and death, but by far the greatest amount of suffering is caused by what we do to ourselves, and to one another. We are cruel and selfish, but most of all *ignorant*. Cruelty and selfishness are forms of ignorance, a failure to understand that the web of life is indivisible, and if we injure any part of it we injure ourselves.

This ignorance is not a lack of knowledge. We all have the requisite knowledge. Like Dorothy and her companions, we just refuse to recognize that we know. We insist that the only person with the necessary secret knowledge is the Wizard, except that nowadays we call our wizards Experts. We want the Experts to use their secret knowledge to take our pain away.

Speaking as an Expert on Mental Health and Mental Illness I can tell you that we Experts *do* have a secret. The secret is that there is no secret. We keep this secret because we don't want to go out of business.

You don't want to recognize that you already have the knowledge necessary to get you out of your misery because for most of your lives you have had people and yourselves telling you that you were stupid and ignorant, and deliberately confusing you and telling you lies. You have been bamboozled and you bamboozle yourself. Now, in order to discover what you already know, you need to go on a journey.

This is a journey without maps, for you are going into territory which no one person has ever explored completely. However, from time to time, you will meet someone who knows part of the way and can point a direction or accompany you for a mile or two.

Do not be fooled into thinking that any of these helpful guides represent the goal of your journey or that any one of them should accompany you all the way. You need to outgrow each of your guides and discover your own wisdom, for no one knows everything and for so long as you have a teacher you are still a child. This is why Sheldon Kopp called his book of wise stories *If You Meet the Buddha on the Road, Kill Him*.[40] Even Sheldon Kopp and his books, once studied, must be outgrown. Every good guru knows this.

A guru is a person or an object from which we learn and gain enlightenment. On your journey you will meet many gurus, so, even though you do not have a map, you will find many guides.

Every journey, however, requires some preparation.

13

Fitting Yourself
for the Journey

This journey, like every journey, requires some preparation. There are practical preparations and mental preparations.

The *mental preparations* are what we tell ourselves before we start on any journey which we think is risky. We say to ourselves, 'This journey is worth the risk. I shall succeed. I am not afraid.' Of course, we wonder whether we should attempt such a journey, and whether we shall be able to cope with the difficulties and dangers, and we feel afraid, but by saying to ourselves that we are right and strong and unafraid, we pack our bags and leave home.

You have been wondering whether the journey out of the prison of depression is worthwhile, and, if it is, whether you can cope with its difficulties and dangers, and, as ever, you feel afraid.

You tell yourself that you are weak. Have you the strength to make the journey?

You tell yourself that you are bad. Do you deserve to make the journey?

You tell yourself that you are frightened. Are you brave enough to make the journey?

To each of these questions you must answer, 'Yes!'

Life is for living. Let's make the most of it.

You may not *feel* that you are strong, valuable, acceptable and brave, but to start the journey and all along the way you should tell yourself that you are.

If you act as if you are strong, valuable, acceptable and brave, you will become so.

I learned this trick from my friend Margaret. I first met her years ago when she, reluctantly, came to see me on the advice of a counsellor. In my office she used to sit silently, hiding behind dark glasses. Even when she stopped wearing these glasses she still found it hard to look at me. This was because she knew, without a shadow of a doubt, that she was totally and absolutely bad. She thought that when I discovered how bad she was I would throw her out and tell her never to darken my door again.

Margaret thought that my idea that we learn to think of ourselves as being bad and unacceptable was utter nonsense. She had felt this way for as long as she could remember. She was certain that she had been born bad.

To prove me wrong she started saying to herself, 'Margaret, you're all right.' She would tell me, 'I say to myself, "Margaret, you're all right", but it doesn't make any difference. I still feel I'm bad and I'm still scared.'

However, she did keep saying 'Margaret, you're all right' to herself, and slowly she changed. At first she would not let on to me that she was changing, because she thought that the minute she said she was any better I would say I didn't want to see her any more. Finally, she had to admit to some change because she was no longer able to keep her regular appointment with me. She had joined a survivors' group, and she was learning rock climbing, canoeing, and how to live off the land and survive the extremes of climate.

When she told me this I was utterly astounded. She was an unhealthy, unathletic thirty-five-year-old who found just going to the cinema an impossible feat, and now she was running every day and doing weight training so as to be able to climb up cliffs and shoot rapids. Moreover, under the conditions the group worked in, there was no way she could hide from people. If she had all this badness inside her, her colleagues would be sure to find it.

But, of course, this badness had disappeared. Margaret had acted as if she was valuable and acceptable, and, lo, she had become so. One day, when we were chatting over a coffee, she said, 'I think I've become the kind of person I like.'

When I was collecting lists of books which people found helpful, Margaret wrote to me saying:

'Since I last saw you, I haven't forgotten to write. I just don't know what to say. I have thought about it lots since then, and how I can help, but I don't think I can. I am not a 'big' reader (apart from the works of D. Rowe and, of course, the gospels according to Quentin Crisp). What I have found most helpful is talking and listening to other people and learning how they see things differently to me (even though I don't find it easy talking about my feelings). I have you and Quentin Crisp on video and watching the videos I also find helpful. I still find it a struggle sometimes; I still have my neuroses but, to quote Quentin, "you have to push your neuroses around until they're in a place where they don't hurt", and, if I can do that, things get easier. The most difficult thing, I found, is accepting myself as I am. I am gradually getting to be someone I like, but sometimes it isn't easy. I miss talking to you – not perhaps that I did much, but I like being with you, and, when I finally get my thoughts out, it's a happy feeling.

'I'm sorry, but I haven't been very helpful, have I? All I think I can say is that for me, seeking wisdom in living, it is more useful to talk than to read.' (D 25)

Margaret knew that she was frightened of people. She had devised many ways of keeping her distance from people and defending herself against them. By doing things which required physical courage, she found the courage to deal more closely with people, and once she risked this, she found that people were not as dangerous as she had thought. If she liked herself, then obviously other people would like her. When we know that other people like us, we like them, and the more we like people the less we are afraid of them.

The first step in being brave is to identify quite clearly what it is that frightens us.

Avril gave me some good advice about this. In a letter to me she said:

'Part of my work is with unhappy children, and I am learning to attend closely to the language they use. Turning this on myself, I recently caught myself using a series of "formula" phrases such as "I hate driving to Bristol" or "I dread the first day of my period" or "I feel anxious when you shout like that". I tried substituting "I am afraid (of)" and found that I became aware of a depth of everyday fear which I was ignoring. Once upon a time I must have known I was frightened, and pretending not to be became an effective coping strategy. However, remembering that I am still frightened seems, paradoxically, to have helped. Perhaps I am not using so much energy in pretence.'

When we can acknowledge our fear and then name it we can work out something to do about it. Perhaps a fear of driving in city traffic could be ameliorated by doing an advanced driving course, and the fear of someone shouting by doing an assertiveness training course, and a fear of the first day of a period could be overcome by relaxing high standards and taking that day easily, instead of rushing about and working hard.

Dealing with nameless dread and terror which comes with the threat of the annihilation of the self is much harder, for it can come upon us unawares, usually as we wake from sleep. For so many people this happens in the early hours of the morning. At 3 am, all around the world, there are people alone, awake, and in terror.

Meryl described how when she awoke at this time it was out of a nightmare, a dream which might be set in many different places but always told the same story. She would be there, surrounded by her family, and then, one by one, ignoring her entreaties, they would slip away and she would be left alone. She would wake in terror, and lie there, listening for her husband's breathing to assure herself that he was still alive. Then she would ease herself out of bed and creep to each of her children's bedrooms to check that they were safe. Now wide awake, she would go downstairs, make herself a cup of tea, and pace about restlessly, waiting for first light. Occasionally, she would doze for an hour on the couch, but even then she would be tired and exhausted the next day.

When we were talking about this dream, I mentioned to Meryl that Freud had said that our dreams contain a wish, and from there we went on to explore how she tried to hide from herself the fact that, as much as she encouraged her family to depend on her and meet her need to be needed, at times she resented their dependency and particularly the way they took her for granted. Her dream represented her need for her family, her resentment of her family, and her guilt about her resentment. Meryl came to realize that, having been so disappointed in her own parents, who would punish her by refusing to talk to her, she had resolved to be the Perfect Mother who *never* rejected her children. Thus she would never admit to herself that she did, from time to time, feel that intense hatred which all parents can feel for their aggravating children.

Once Meryl could relinquish her impossible ambition of being the Perfect Mother and become, instead, a good enough mother, she dealt directly with her resentment of her family's demands by saying no to them on occasions and by insisting that they take account of her needs and wishes. She found that when she gave up being a martyr to her family they were much more appreciative of her, and she got the responses which she, as an extravert, needed.

If you have made yourself a martyr to your unappreciative family, remember the Principle of Partial Reinforcement and apply it to your family. If you are always at their beck and call, trying to meet their every demand, they will not appreciate you, but once they find that they cannot rely on you to meet their demands, they will appreciate what you do for them.

Not all of us have dreams of being abandoned. Introverts, waking into terror, are having the experience of everything becoming insubstantial and falling apart. I find that I come to half wakefulness with the discovery that I have got something wrong, or have acted rashly, thoughtlessly, and exposed myself to some danger as vague as it is terrible. The pain of a tightness under my heart wakens me completely.

A few years ago, when it was becoming clear to me that I should make a major change in my career, I was experiencing these terrified and terrifying awakenings frequently, and at the same time my clients were telling me about their troubled nights. Such matters are rarely discussed, for to describe them to someone who has not had such an experience might lead that person to think you were crazy, and if you mentioned such things to a psychiatrist he would slap on the label 'early morning waking, a symptom of endogenous depression', and increase your tablets or send you for ECT. So I decided to make the matter clearer to myself, and to other people, by writing about it. Hence what eventually became a big book called *Beyond Fear*.[41]

I still occasionally awaken in the night with the feeling that I have got something wrong or have taken an ill-advised step, but I no longer wake to terror. I just remind myself that *when we are asleep all the careful constructions and organizations that we have created in our world of meaning drift and dissolve. Once we wake up, they all go back together again*.

In order to give yourself these reassurances, especially when the world is dark and you feel all alone, it is always useful to have something special to say to yourself.

Some people find reassurance in a sentence or a few lines from a
poem which they say over to themselves, not in mindless repetition,
but in concentration, dwelling upon it, and absorbing the strength
and peace which comes from it. The words might have the power of
William Ernest Henley's poem:

> Out of the night which covers me,
>   Black as the pit from pole to pole,
> I thank whatever God there be
>   For my unconquerable soul.[42]

the peace and acceptance of the words of Julian of Norwich:

All shall be well, and all shall be well, and all manner of things
shall be well[43]

or that of the *Tao te Ching*:

> It is more important
> To see the simplicity,
> To realize one's true nature,
> To cast off selfishness
> And temper desire.[44]

Time spent looking through poetry books, perhaps finding again
the poems you studied at school, and copying into a notebook those
verses which speak to you, is never wasted. When you feel lonely
and afraid, you can read again those words, and remember that the
people who wrote them *understood*. When you spend your days with
people who don't understand, it is important to remind yourself
that there are people who do.

Some people pray, not God-bothering prayers, instructing Him as
to what He should do, but prayers which simply affirm trust and
acceptance, 'the love of God and the fellowship of the Holy Spirit'.
    And there is music.

When I asked my friend Stephanie for a list of books which she
had found helpful, she sent me a wonderful list, but asked:

'Have you considered a list of music? Once, when I was terribly
down, someone played me a record of Alfred Cortot playing
Chopin, and though I don't really like his rather sticky style, I
thought that day, if someone can play something like that with
so much love, life *is* worth living, just so that I can hear it, and
tears of relief came to my eyes (because life looked very much

unworth living just then). The Albinoni Adagio for Strings is
another piece, quite short, that I can hear again and again and
again, feeling release of mental and physical tension and a
stealing over me of twilit loveliness. I've watched it do that for
others. Some will find visual things helpful – a shaft of light, a
landscape, a flower, a tree, a picture. For some calm, and even
insight, may come via sensitive fingertips – worry beads are,
after all, pretty ancient as tranquillizers go. But, for me and for
many, music (or musical sounds such as chants or bells or
gongs) speaks most clearly and directly to the heart. When
music calls you to sing or dance or just bounce a little inside,
you know you are not alone. Knowing that, knowing you can
be reached and can respond, even if only a little (and even if the
response is a great wallow of weeping), is a tiny first step up the
treacherous black slope or the greasy pole or out of the thick
glass phone-booth or whatever.'

In her next letter Stephanie said:

'My mind wandered off on to those other things which seemed
to pierce the lukewarm pudding, the doughy depressed self,
and let in light and air and sweetness – if only for a moment –
and the fleeting conviction that there is something worth living
for. It is as if a window is opened upon a living inner world
inside the thick, dead rind of self, or, perhaps, upon a bright
and colourful outer world that has somehow been closed off by
a muffling, grey screen. Suddenly in that moment you know
that all along there has been this aliveness, this vitality, this
energy and that you – *you*, the nonentitous hopeless worthless
(etc) can touch it and make it your own. Out of a series of
instants like these, I think, comes the push to wellness.
    'For me, most of these bright instants have been musical.
The-I-am-alive-because-I-can-hear-this sort of thing and the
thump in the chest that says if I weren't alive I couldn't hear it
and I'd miss it, dammit. Much the same has happened when
playing or singing to myself – and this can be even more
exciting, because you do it for yourself, playing a phrase from,
say, Chopin (who had been there, listen to him, try the 4th
Ballade for instant recognition of the state) and repeating it as
many times as you like. You don't have to ask the orchestra or
the pianist to do it – you just use your hands or your breath or

whatever and keep evoking those wonderful sounds, that wonderful plangent sequence of notes or chords.

Remember as you do these things to bring you peace, that you are not running away from anything, the terror that you feel is the terror of the threat of the annihilation of your self, and that that threat is an *illusion*. If you're an extravert, remember that even if you are alone, you don't disappear, and if you are an introvert, remember that everything changes all the time, and you may as well define this constant change as splendid freedom and not dangerous chaos.

Now let us consider the **practical preparations** for the journey. If you have read the story of the *Wizard of Oz* as Frank Baum wrote it, you will know that Dorothy did not, as Judy Garland did in the film, just set off in red shoes down the yellow brick road. Dorothy made some practical preparations before she set off. She packed a basket of food, changed her dress, and, discarding her old shoes, put on the silver shoes that had belonged to the Witch of the East.[45] For you, some other preparations are necessary.

It is always a good idea to keep **a log of your journey**, a sort of diary. You might like to make an entry every day, or just when something important or very moving has happened, or when you have discovered something. You might like to write in prose, or you might prefer poetry or pictures.

The simple act of writing something down is tremendously helpful, because to do so we have to bring something clearly to mind. Instead of having half-formed thoughts and confused emotions crashing and fumbling around inside us, we crystallize these thoughts and feelings into sentences. Once we put these sentences down on paper we have taken something from inside us and put it outside. Now we can look at it, judge it, and **master** it.

By *master*, I mean the way in which we need in some way to complete an experience by giving it a meaning that we can live with. Some of our experiences are easy to master. For instance, we decide to learn to skate, we go along to the skating rink and, after a number of falls and much practice, we not only master the art of skating but give the whole experience a meaning which we can live with very nicely. We can say, 'I can skate.'

However, many of our experiences are not easily mastered because they arouse conflicting emotions and leave us feeling very uncertain and confused. Many of our unhappy experiences in childhood we could never master, and so they still trouble us in

many different ways. The process of reviewing our childhood
involves finding these unmastered experiences and mastering them
by giving them meanings with which we can live.

Repressing such experiences is not mastery, for they are still there
in forms with which we cannot live. Looking at our childhood
experiences from the two perspectives, that of the child we once
were and the adult we are now, can allow us to find a way of
mastering these experiences. Instead of trying to forget the pain our
parents inflicted on us, we can find a meaning which goes something like:

**'I can now understand why I came to believe that I was bad, and I
can see that I do not need to go on believing this. I can understand
why my parents did what they did, and I can see that they were
misguided, mistaken and confused, as people often are, and that
they usually thought that they were acting for the best.' By facing
something and seeing it clearly, we can master it.**   (D 27)

Keeping a diary also helps you realize that you are indeed gaining
in wisdom and coping better. Often, when you meet a crisis, you
can feel that you have made no progress at all. A glance back
through your diary will show how you have changed. When
Stephanie was writing to me about music she said:

> 'Music, part of my life since very early, became hateful at one
> point. My husband put on a recording of some Mozart in
> another room and I thought I would go mad with the violins
> sawing relentlessly at my nerves. That was the day he said
> gravely, "I think you'd better see someone after all", and I did.
> It was probably within a couple of weeks that I first went to my
> dear therapist: 1978 that was and it seems several light years
> away now.'

It is important to remember that you changed and how you
changed, for one issue you have to face when you finally dismantle
your depression is a sense of wasted time – all those months and
years when you could have been doing something much more
delightful and satisfying. The gaining of wisdom is never a waste of
time, for not only does life become more satisfying but you can use
your experience and the wisdom you have gained to help other
people.   (D 28)

The next practical preparation is that you should **take your health
seriously**. Disliking yourself meant that you did not look after

yourself. When you got sick you did not want to ask for help, and whatever help you did accept, whether antibiotics for your chest infection or yoga for your bad back, you were sure it would not work. Nothing, you were sure, would make you better. Since you were sure that nothing would make you better, nothing did.

Rita wrote to me to ask my advice about a new treatment for depression.

'Recently, I have read about the new light treatment available at the Maudsley Hospital in London and wondered whether you knew of anyone who has had this treatment and what were your opinions about it. "The treatment consists of looking at a box of full spectrum lights, designed to simulate daylight for two to four hours per day. The sufferer sits about four feet away from the light box so as to get an intensity of 2500 lux, and can read, work, watch TV, provided that he/she looks directly at the light several times a minute." I am quoting from the literature from the S.A.D. Association, of which I am a member. I seem to keep well during the late Spring and Summer months, but come October/November I start to feel depressed. I do believe I suffer from what is now known as Seasonal Affective Disorder.'

I wrote back to Rita, saying:

'Like you I have been following the reports on the success of S.A.D. and the improvements people have by sitting in bright lights.

'Everybody knows that human beings cannot live in total darkness all the time and that most of us feel a lot more cheerful and energetic on nice sunny days. I think that scientists have established that in bright light and sunshine there are various beneficial chemical changes going in in our body. After all, we all need sunshine to get Vitamin D to keep us healthy. Eskimos have to eat a lot of cod liver oil to make up for the fact that they do not see much sunshine.

'However, not everybody feels more cheerful in sunshine. People who are depressed can find sunshine very difficult, and there is always a rise in the suicide rate in spring. The reason for this is not the effect of sunlight on our bodies but the meaning that we give to such light. If you value and accept yourself and look forward optimistically, then spring is always full of promise, but if you don't value yourself and you expect that only bad things will happen to you because you are bad, then spring is not full of promise but only threats.

'The artificial light treatment probably does make some chemical change in the body of the person sitting there looking at the light. The person then has to interpret that change. They can interpret the change as being something pleasant, enjoyable, healing and potentially extremely helpful, or proof of the fact they are bad or sick, or something harmful and certainly not beneficial.

'So if you decide to try out this treatment, first of all practise saying to yourself that you are a good and valuable person, that you are your own best friend and that you are going to do everything possible to get yourself strong and healthy and to enable you to lead an enjoyable and happy life. While you are having the treatment you say to yourself, ''This treatment is doing me good and I deserve to have good done to me.'' After you have had the treatment, keep on talking to yourself in this very positive way. Don't slip back into the old ways of talking to yourself as if you are your own worst enemy. If you go along to the treatment believing that it will do you good and that you deserve it to do you good, then it will do you good, but if you don't, it won't.'

We hear a lot nowadays about *stress*. People talk about stress as if it is a kind of Darth Varda, ready to appear at any time and wipe us out. They make it seem like we have to have the Force with us if we are to combat stress.

Which is all nonsense. Stress is just a word which we use as shorthand for those experiences where we lose confidence in ourselves and feel that we cannot cope with the demands that confront us.

When we have confidence in ourselves we don't feel stress. We see demands as challenges which we intend to master. When we have confidence in ourselves we don't feel that we have to accept every demand that is made on us. We know what is important to us, and we can say, 'I'll accept this and this, but not that'. When we have confidence in ourselves we know how to say, 'No'.

When we don't have confidence in ourselves we always feel stress. We see demands as burdens which will crush us even further. When we don't have confidence in ourselves we feel that we have to accept every demand that is made on us, for if we refuse other people will get upset and we shall be criticized, rejected, abandoned. When we don't have confidence in ourselves we cannot work out what our priorities are, because we feel that we have no choice but to accept the demands that other people and our own conscience with its impossibly high standards make upon us. In a word, we feel *stress*.

(D 29)

When we are under stress, our auto-immune system, which fights off all the noxious agents which make us ill, ceases to operate efficiently. This is why people who are depressed get so many bouts of colds and flu, and worse. What makes any illness you have likely to be worse is that, because you don't value yourself, you don't look after yourself properly and you don't seek the help that you need.

How many times have I heard a depressed person say, 'I can't trouble the doctor again. He's tired of seeing me!' How many times have I said to a depressed woman plagued with premenstrual tension, 'If your doctor won't recognize that you've got PMT and help you, see another doctor', and she said, 'No, I can't do that. He'll be angry with me!'

Yet it is not possible for a doctor to diagnose and treat Premenstrual Syndrome, as it is now called, without him seeing his patient frequently. Dr P. M. Shaun O'Brien, an obstetrician and gynaecologist who specializes in this syndrome, listed all the different treatment approaches and wrote, 'None of these single approaches is correct because the requirements of women will differ according to age, desire for pregnancy, menstrual pattern, the patient's own view, and, most important, the specific nature and timing of the individual's symptoms. Unfortunately no two women seem to respond identically to the same therapeutic measures.'[46]

Women who value themselves do not suffer with premenstrual tension. Women who value themselves and who are not well at some point in their menstrual cycle persist in bothering their doctors until they get some satisfactory help, and they look after themselves, taking things easy when they don't feel well, accepting help and not feeling guilty about it.

Women who don't value themselves and who are not well at some point in their menstrual cycle find it difficult to get the help they need from the medical profession. Many men doctors do not take menstrual problems seriously, so sometimes a woman needs to find another doctor. Those doctors who do take menstrual problems seriously know that sorting out such problems requires much trial and error, with the woman taking an active part in what can be a lengthy scientific investigation. The woman and the doctor need to have a good working relationship. None of this is possible if the woman so little values herself that she fears that the doctor does not like her, thinks she is a hypochondriac, and is irritated by her demands.

Woman who don't value themselves and who are not well at some point in their menstrual cycle find it difficult to get the help they need from their families. Because they do not treat themselves with respect and dignity, their husbands and children learn not to treat them with respect and dignity. They ignore her suffering, and, if she complains or gets angry, they do not take her anger and her complaints seriously. They brush them aside with, 'It's the time of the month', or, 'She's always complaining about something'. The doctor may be telling her, 'You need to rest. Put your feet up. Let your family look after you', but she cannot do this because her family will not recognize and respect her needs. She knows that if there is no supper on the table, or clean clothes for the morning, her family will behave badly, as only families can.

If only we treated our loved ones with the respect and dignity we reserve for strangers!   (D 30)

Now that you are acting as if you value and accept yourself, you can both treat your loved ones with respect and dignity and you can demand that they treat you with respect and dignity. Many people who do not value and accept themselves are frightened that if they demand respect and consideration from their family, their family will leave them. If you are like this, remember that you can't get rid of your family as easily as that. Even when children grow up and leave, they still keep coming home.

It is not enough to decide, now that you are acting as if you value and accept yourself, that you will rest. You need to learn how to rest. As a baby, you knew how to relax every part of you. Now you need to re-learn it, perhaps by going to a *relaxation class*, or listening to a *relaxation tape*, or, best of all, joining a *yoga* class. (The correct name is *hatha yoga*.)

The aim of yoga is to create a sense of unity between the body and the mind, and with that sense of unity a greater awareness of oneself.

Whenever we feel under threat, our body, or some part of our body, becomes tense. When we are continually under threat we cease to be aware of just where that tenseness is, and so we can be surprised when our body starts to protest. Our clenched jaw and locked eyebrows produce a fierce headache. Our tightened lungs begin wheezing. Our rigid neck and clamped shoulder blades crunch in agony. Our stomach grinds itself an ulcer. Our pounding heart wearies and works less well. Our bowels knot in painful constipation and diarrhoea. When we do not value and accept ourselves we are always under threat, so we need to learn just which part of our body we always hold tense. Then we can learn the many ways that yoga has of releasing that tension and giving us peace.

In yoga there is no competition. No one fails and no one wins. It is a process of self exploration where, as my teacher Eric Gregory says, 'You go as far as you can go, and then a little further.'

In journeying out of the prison of depression, you should not try to get everything right all at once. Some people say to themselves, 'I'm going to stop being depressed, give up smoking and get thin.'

This is far more than anyone could achieve all at once. Many people have told me that giving up cigarettes is harder than giving up being depressed, while *learning to be kind to yourself*, an essential part of the journey, often includes eating well.

Perhaps one of the very high standards you have set yourself is that you have to be thin. Perhaps you think that to be good you have to be thin, and so you exclude from your life all the pleasure that comes from food. But to be valuable, do you have to be thin?

If you are carrying a bit more weight or smoking more cigarettes than are good for your health, it is *not* because you are a bad person. Eating and smoking are things that you do in order to protect yourself when you feel under threat. Food and cigarettes are your friends.

I do not use the word 'friends' lightly. If you think about the kinds of food you like and eat to comfort yourself, you'll see that they appear to you as friends, far more trustworthy and reliable than some people you know.

Similarly, if you're a smoker and I said to you, 'If your cigarette was a person, what kind of person would it be?' you could describe a particular person who is a friend.[47] Caroline, whose parents blamed her for everything that went wrong in their lives and who had told her from childhood onward that she was mad and bad, saw her
(D 31) cigarettes as 'loyal, constant, warm, loving, accepting friends'.

You cannot give up your friends of food and cigarettes until you start to accept and value yourself and so feel able to undertake projects where you have the chance of meeting people who can be good friends to you. However, what you can do immediately is to widen the range of presents that you give yourself.

You have spent a large part of your life being unpleasant to yourself. Now, as you prepare to set out on your journey, you must think of all the pleasant things you can do for yourself, and *do at least one pleasant thing for yourself every day*. You do these things not because you ought to, not because it's good for you, not because I told you to do so and you want to be obedient. You do pleasant things for yourself because they are pleasant. Discover the healing power of joy!   (D 32)

One of the pleasantest things you must do for yourself is to let yourself rest. When you are depressed you are plagued by *tiredness*; indeed, there are many people who experience the major part of their depression as tiredness.

Sometimes, what you call tiredness is actually *despair*. 'What's the use of doing anything? Why make the effort?' Instead of confronting your despair, you call it tiredness.

Tiredness that is despair comes from the tension of constant anxiety, the deleterious effects this tension has on the body, and the efforts you make to be good. If you are constantly saying to yourself, 'I must achieve and keep everything under control', or, 'I mustn't upset people. I must do what they want', or, 'I must meet other people's needs or they will reject me', then you are pushing your body when your body tells you to rest.

Depressed people often say that even when they sleep all night they do not wake refreshed. This could be because their body is not functioning efficiently because it is not being properly nourished or because some part of it reacts unfavourably to certain foods – what is nowadays called allergy. Many people have found that by being tested for allergies and from then on avoiding the food to which they are allergic has given them increased energy. Many people, too, have found that a course of acupuncture has restored their energy.

I went to an acupuncturist, Paul Franks, for help with a sore thumb. Paul measured my energy levels by taking subtle readings of tiny variations in my pulse in the way developed by Chinese medicine. Paul said that mine were out of balance, and that the course of acupuncture would be aimed at restoring the balance. What I experienced quite early in this course was an increase in energy and a feeling of well-being. Paul also treats people with depression. I can understand how, if such people feel such an increase in energy and a sense of well-being, this would enable them not only to get on and do what they want to do but would also give them hope.

However, neither specialists in allergies nor acupuncturists have a magic cure which will work for those people who believe that they are too wicked to be allowed to be well and that, 'I suffer, therefore I am'.

Another reason why depressed people are not refreshed by a night's sleep is because they achieved that sleep by using prescribed sedatives.

Sedatives to help us sleep are extremely important. Without sleep we cannot function properly. In periods of crisis, when we are greatly worried and cannot sleep, it can be sensible to take a sedative to assure ourselves of a few hours' rest. However, if we go on taking sedatives we soon create another problem for ourselves.

We sleep not just to rest our body. We sleep in order to dream, and dreaming is very important. In dreaming we sort out our impressions of the previous day and store them for future use. Some of this sorting out is no more than general tidying up, although some is concerned with problem solving.

Whenever I am writing something, before I go to bed I decide what I shall be working on the next day, and before I go to sleep I ask myself, 'How shall I start that chapter?' or, 'How shall I organize that article?' While I am asleep I work on these questions, and when I wake in the morning I have answers to such questions.

Sometimes I wake in the morning with an idea which is to do with my writing but unconnected with the questions I posed myself the night before. One morning I woke out of a dream and lay there thinking about it. My dreams, which seem perfectly sensible when I am dreaming, are, by the standards of waking life, too complicated and bizarre to be described in words, so often I know something of the meaning of my dream by the emotion it leaves in me and by a word or phrase that comes into my mind. On this particular morning the word was 'death', but I knew from the emotion I felt it was someone else's death, not mine. It did not feel like a premonition but rather like a piece of information.

It was Saturday morning, the day Dawn comes to help me with my correspondence. I thought no more about my dream but prepared for Dawn's arrival.

Later that morning I got Dawn and me some coffee and
settled in my big armchair to do some writing. But, instead of
working on what I had planned, I suddenly 'saw' or 'knew'
what later became the next chapter in this book, 'Suicide Is Not
a Solution'. It was a very easy chapter to write. Just a matter of
getting it down on paper.

What had happened was that my dream had forced me to
confront something which I had been avoiding. The reason I
had set out to write this book was because I had wanted to put
down all the things to do with depression which I knew to be
important. What I had written about depression in earlier books
had not been complete. Yet in this book I was avoiding writing
about suicide. I had made some references to suicide and I had
written briefly in earlier books about suicide, but there was
more that I knew I ought to say. So very many people kill
themselves, and such romantic nonsense and such cold scientific nonsense is written about these deaths. The nonsense
comes because the pain is so difficult to face and because we all
like to fantasize that if life became too difficult for us we could
choose the escape hatch of suicide. If I wrote what I know about
suicide I would have to give up the luxury of such fantasies and
resign myself to living out my life to its end, no matter how
bitter that end might be. I have the greatest scorn for those
people who preach one doctrine and practise another, and this
was what my dream was telling me. My dream showed me the
problem, prodded me to see what I should do, and then
showed me how to do it.

Dreams help us solve problems. Dreams help us *master* the events
we have encountered and the issues we have to resolve. The reason
we go on dreaming about the horrors and disasters of our lives is not
because we are crazy but because we are trying to master events and
issues which are very difficult to master. Do not be afraid of
nightmares. It is your self trying to help you.

Unfortunately, the drugs which doctors prescribe to help us sleep
stop us dreaming. When we stop taking such sedatives we dream all
the more, trying to catch up with the sorting out and the problem
solving.

So it is important to develop ways of helping yourself to sleep
without using sedatives except at times of crisis. If you have been
taking sedatives for some time you need to find out about them and

perhaps choose to discover other ways of aiding your sleep. You also need to reduce the amount you take very, very slowly, see the dreams you have as being good for you rather than bad, while at the same time improving your general health and well-being.

In your preparations for the journey you will need to think carefully about the antidepressant and other drugs you might at present be taking and to decide what you want to do about them. At this stage you might want to stay on them for a while, since you fear that if you come off them you might feel a great deal worse. Or you might want to come off the drugs but feel anxious about how to do this.

Whatever you wish to do, you need to feel that *you are in charge of your drugs*. You are not taking them like an ignorant, obedient child. You have found out just what these drugs are, how they are supposed to work, how they actually work for you, and you know how you want these drugs to work for you. There is some useful information in the chapter 'Drugs – Friend or Foe?' at the end of this book.

However, all these instructions about the journey can seem very burdensome, and my cheerfulness relentless. Under such a barrage it would not be surprising if you felt a return of your old, familiar hopelessness, and thought, 'Why bother? Why not take the easiest way out of the prison?'

Why not indeed? If only suicide were a solution. But it is not.

14

Suicide Is Not a Solution

Everybody contemplates suicide, and when we are depressed we contemplate it very seriously indeed, for it seems to offer a way out of the prison of depression without having to confront all the dangers and hurts that depression tries to shut out. We fantasize that in death we shall find solace and peace, but that is all we can do, fantasize. We cannot *know*.

The philosopher Wittgenstein once remarked that death is not a fact in life. What he meant was that our own death is not *fact* in our own life, but only a fantasy. We know that we shall die, but just what that experience will be for us we cannot know until we encounter it. We see other people die, but we do not know what they experienced as death. All we know is that they grow strangely still and silent.

All we know of our own suicide is our fantasies about it. We may tell ourselves that in killing ourselves we shall find peace and an end to all our woes, perhaps in the blackness of nothing or in another life, but, whatever we tell ourselves, it is a fantasy, a hope based on nothing but the fantasies that we and other people have created.

We may tell ourselves that we shall, in suicide, drift into a painless blackness where we know and feel nothing, or into an eternity of bliss, and so overlook the fact that suicide involves us in *choice* and *action*. We have to choose to die and we have to take certain powerful actions in order to kill ourselves. One part of us has to kill that part of us which is alive. That part of us which is alive wants to go on living.

The purpose of life is to live. Even when we are screaming to ourselves, 'I can't go on. I want to die', there is that other part of us keeping our body functioning and busily, as ever, doing everything to maintain our sense of self. This part of us which wants to go on living uses fantasies to maintain and defend the sense of self, so, in fantasy, we contemplate suicide as a way of preserving our self. Can I, by killing myself, go on being myself?

If we answer 'Yes' to this question we have, then, to find a way of killing off that part of us which is fulfilling the function of life, i.e. to live. So long as this part of ourselves is functioning, all of us, our total person, body and self, does not want to die, no matter how fiercely and passionately we tell ourselves that we do.

When every part of ourselves, our total person, body, self, soul, mind and spirit does want to die, we do not have to take any action. We do not have to swallow pills, or cut our throat, drown ourselves, fling ourselves in front of a train, throw ourselves off a high building, or put a noose around our neck. We simply die.

John came to see me to tell me that his mother had died. I had never met his mother, but I felt I knew her because John and I had talked about her and John's father so much. To people outside the family she was a quiet, polite, elderly widow, but to her family she was often difficult and cantankerous. In this mood she would complain about anything and everything. Nothing ever suited her. A sunny day was always too hot. A visit from a friend was always too tiring. The world had simply not been arranged to please her, and it ought to have been.

Her complaints irritated John, but he tried to do his duty by her. He and his wife provided a good home for her, and, when she became increasingly blind and frail, they agonized over whether she should go into a nursing home. Finally, after much time spent searching for a home which she might like, they found one nearby which they could visit frequently.

As they feared, no matter how comfortable the home and caring the staff, his mother was not satisfied. Not content with just complaining to John, she became very demanding, ordering the staff about and expecting not only that they should do her bidding but do it quickly. When John told me about this, and how ashamed he was of his mother's rudeness and lack of consideration, I commented that she had spent her life as the wife of a domineering man and as a shop assistant, being obsequious and compliant. Now she had a last chance to do to others what had been done to her. He could see my point, but doubted that the nurses would appreciate it.

Then his mother fell and cracked her ribs. She was taken to hospital for tests, and, as she could now see very little, these changes made her confused. She was never sure just where she was. All along she had denied that her sight was deteriorating and that·she could not do the things she wanted to do, but when the television screen had become nothing but a white blur she could deny no longer that she was virtually blind.

John told me how the first time he realized that his mother had changed was when he went to visit her, and instead of complaining that it was over a week since he had been to see her (it was only a day, but she had never been one to let the facts stand in the way of a good complaint) she just squeezed his hand in welcome. A nurse went by, and his mother did not call her over. She sipped her tea without saying that it was too hot, too cold, too sweet or not sweet enough, and when the nurse said, 'Did you enjoy your tea?' she said, 'Very nice.'

Over the next week she made no attempt to get out of bed, and when the nurses came to lift her into her chair she, like a rag doll, let them. By the following week she was no longer well enough to leave her bed.

John noticed that the nurses did not seem to find her behaviour strange. They looked after her tenderly, like she was a baby. When he asked what was happening, the senior nurse said, 'She's given up fighting.'

And so she had. She was no longer resentful that the world had treated her so badly. She had lived and fought, and now she had finished.

John sat at her bedside as she slipped into a coma and the cold, which started at her feet, crept slowly upward. 'I'd never felt cold like that,' he told me. 'Usually, when someone's feet are cold and you put your warm hands on them, the feet get warmer. Hers didn't. The cold was absolute.'

In the early hours of the morning, with barely a sound, she stopped breathing. Later John took her back to the village where she was born, and arranged the kind of funeral about which even she would not have complained.

The way John's mother died was not unusual. Indeed, it is very common, and not just among the old. All of us can die, and do die, when every part of us gives up struggling and accepts death. *If you have to harm yourself in order to die, you do not want to die. What you want is a painless way of being yourself without having to battle against a world which hurts and ignores you.*

Death does not give you that. All that death gives you is death.

Suicide is not painless. Because few of us nowadays actually see people dying, and because television and films are so censored, distanced and sanitized, we imagine that dying can be no more than slipping painlessly into a deep sleep. We do not realize just how much of dying is smelly, undignified and extremely painful.

Many depressed people have a fantasy of taking all their pills, lying down, and slipping painlessly away. The reality is something else.

The pills with which doctors will so readily supply you are designed as sedatives. They are not some kind of benign magic which creates calm and sleep. They are chemical substances which alter the functioning of the body. These alterations affect the efficient functioning of the heart, lungs and brain. The process of dying by taking a large enough amount of these drugs is a process not of going to sleep but of going into a coma where insufficient blood reaches the brain. This starvation of blood damages the brain. Many people, having taken an overdose, go into a coma and do not die. Instead, they spend the rest of their lives enduring the handicaps which this damage to the brain has created. These handicaps are usually far harder to endure than the problems which led such people to contemplate suicide.

Part of the fantasy we have about suicide deals with the effect our death will have on other people. In our fantasy we are deciding what this effect will be.

We might contemplate suicide as a way of having revenge on those who have hurt us. We imagine saying to them by our suicide, 'See what you made me do!', and we imagine them being overcome by life-long remorse, regret and guilt.

Such a fantasy contains the idea that, once dead, we shall still be able to *see* our erstwhile loved ones in their agony of remorse, regret and guilt. We forget that we do not know what being dead actually entails. Even if we do come back as ghosts to witness what happens after we die, will seeing those people suffer make us *enjoy* an eternity of being a ghost? As a ghost we cannot bring our revenge to an end by forgiving and being enfolded in the love that we always wanted. And what if our erstwhile loved ones aren't upset by our death? What if they are glad we are dead, or, worse, forget about us immediately? What would we, as a ghost, do then?

We might contemplate suicide as a way of making our loved ones feel happy. We say to ourselves, 'They'll be better off without me', and we imagine our loved ones loving us for being so unselfish as to remove our troubled person from their lives. We think, 'They'll soon forget me', as if by being forgotten by our loved ones all our errors and inadequacies are somehow expunged from the record, did not happen, had no effect. We tell ourselves that in killing ourselves everything will be put right. But it is not.

Suicide does have effects, but they are effects which we, in killing ourselves, can neither predict nor control. Whatever these effects are, they will be different from those we have created in our fantasy.

Fantasies are like films. We can run them backwards, reshoot the scene, edit out the bits we don't like, change the ending to suit ourselves. Real life is not a fantasy. When things happen, they happen, and we cannot change them. We can change how we feel about what happened, but we cannot change what has happened. When something does not work out the way we wanted, we cannot go back and do it again.

Fantasies tell a simple story, a chain of events where A leads to B, and B leads to C. 'I'll die, they'll be sorry, and I'll have my revenge.' 'I'll die, they'll be happy, and I'll have peace.' Real life is not a story. Real life is a continuous network of events in continuous motion, where one event creates ripples which spread in all directions, far and wide, forever and ever. We act, and we are responsible for setting in motion events which radiate out, creating their own ripples, on and on, forever and ever. As long as there are people who remember us, their memory of our action is another action which sends out ripples forever and ever. We cannot step out of real life simply by dying. Nor can we insist that, 'My death will have these effects and no other.'

Suicide has profound, long-lasting and widespread effects, which are very different from what we create in our fantasies. We should remember this whenever we indulge in such fantasies. We should remember, too, that the manner of our death stands as an example to those who come after us. Younger people always look to older people to show them how to live their lives. The courage of older people inspires us, their fear frightens us.

As parents we might have got everything wrong. We might have punished our children when we should have been patient. We might have been absent when they needed us, critical when they needed praise, cold when they needed warmth, unloving when they needed love. We might have destroyed our relationships and failed in enterprises where we might have succeeded. In total, we might have given our children nothing that they needed and everything that they did not want. We might feel that as persons and as parents we are utter failures. Nevertheless, we have something of inestimable value which we can give to our children. We can show them that we have the courage to go on living, and, when the coldness of death comes upon us, as it will in the fullness of time, we have the courage to accept death and let it take its course.

We can show that no matter what disasters befall us and what mistakes we make, we have the courage to keep on keeping on. Our courage inspires our children's courage.

If we kill ourselves we undermine the courage of those who knew us. Thus, when disasters befall them and they make mistakes, they find it so much harder to live their lives with courage. They, too, may lose their courage, falter and fail. Suicide 'runs in families', not because there is a 'suicide gene' any more than there is a 'depression gene', but because people learn from one another.

(D 33)

However, in learning we have a choice. We can choose to imitate others, or we can choose to observe others and resolve to do differently. We can choose to imitate ourselves and go on, year after year, doing what we have always done, or we can choose to change.

Suicide is not a realistic option.

Changing is.

So, on our journey, what do we need to find?

15

What You Need to Find
Along the Way

By saying to yourself, 'I accept and value myself', you give yourself permission to explore.

By saying to yourself, 'I accept and value myself,' you give yourself permission not to reject or feel guilty about what you may find.

Remember there are parts of you which you have been taught to believe are wicked or, at the very least, unsatisfactory. Now you need to undo that teaching, and see that such parts of you are just fine.

When we were children our parents and teachers were forever telling us that we must be unselfish and put other people's needs before our own. They told us this for two reasons. First, for their own selfish reason that if we acted unselfishly life was much easier for them. Second, for the very wise reason that people who are always selfish, who act in their own interests and no one else's, end up being alone and disliked. If our parents were wise, or lazy, they would let us discover that the wisest course to follow in life is to act selfishly on occasions and unselfishly on others, developing a flexible approach, realizing that it is in our own interests to be unselfish (or appear to be unselfish) while at the same time meeting our own essential needs. However, in families where sanctions come down thick and hard on children who act selfishly, such children grow up unable to be flexibly selfish and unselfish. They grow up believing that the only good action is an altruistic action. If you are one of these, then you may have difficulty in accepting that in the way we experience our sense of existence and see the threat of annihilation of our self there is no altruism. An introvert has to have a sense of personal achievement. An extravert has to have the presence of other people in order to survive.

Gareth was destined for the priesthood when he found himself doubting his vocation. 'Being in the priesthood runs in our family,' Gareth said.

I was momentarily sidetracked into wondering whether there is a priesthood gene which, if discovered, would mean that a sense of religious vocation is nothing more than the outcome of biochemical change. I put this thought aside and asked Gareth about his family. A tradition of service to others emerged. His father was a vicar, his grandfather an archdeacon. All the family members were doctors, lawyers, teachers and devoted husbands, wives and parents.

When Gareth spoke of himself he used the words and phrases of an introvert – 'sense of achievement', 'getting things under control', 'need to clarify', 'I'm falling apart'. But when I ventured a 'why is that important?' he hesitated, and then answered in terms of his relationship to others.

'Do you feel,' I ventured, 'that a life of selfless devotion to others would not give you a sense of achievement? That it would leave you feeling unsatisfied?'

'It's very wrong of me, I know, but that's how I feel. I'm trying to overcome it. I would not like to think of myself as being an introvert. They seem to me to be very selfish people.'

Many people whose experiences in childhood led them to con- clude that, at all costs, they must be good, and, by that meaning putting other people's needs before their own, find this recognition of their basic need to survive very threatening. It goes against everything they have been taught, and they react with fright, certain, even without consciously thinking about it, that their parents, their teachers and their God will punish them for daring even to think that underneath all their altruism is the need and wish to survive. Whenever I lecture about this, either in terms of ex- traverts and introverts or in terms of how aggression, which can range from mild determination to violence, is a vital attribute of every person, there are always people in the audience who become very distressed and often, because I have frightened them, get angry with me.

If you are having difficulty working out whether you experience your sense of existence as being a member of a group or as the development of individual achievement, clarity, and organization, ask yourself whether your beliefs about *what you ought to be* are preventing you from discovering *what you are*. Do you see the need for individual achievement as being selfish, and being selfish a wrong? Do you see needing other people to confirm your sense of existence as being weak or as using other people to your own advantage?

One skill we all need to develop is the ability to distinguish *what is* from *what ought to be*. Many people, not making this distinction, cause themselves great distress and waste much precious time in complaining that the universe is not what it ought to be, instead of determining what the universe, or their part of it, actually *is*, deciding how it ought to be, and then taking the necessary actions in order to turn what is into what ought to be. Saying, 'People ought not die of cancer' will never find a cure for cancer. That can only come from finding out what cancer is. Saying, 'I oughtn't to be selfish', or, 'I oughtn't to be weak' will not make you unselfish or strong. You have to begin by discovering what this 'selfishness' or 'weakness' actually is before you can make any changes. Usually when we set out to discover what something is, we discover that it is very different from what we thought it was.

How we experience our sense of existence, whether as a member of a group or in individual development, is selfish only in the sense that the purpose of life is to live. After all, if we do not keep ourselves alive we are of no use to anyone. If we do not look after ourselves we suffer physical and mental pain, and this pain turns us in on ourselves, so that we have less time and strength to give to other people. To be of use to other people we have to look after ourselves. To look after ourselves we need to know what our needs are and, of these needs, what is the most important. To know these things about ourselves we need to make quite clear to ourselves how we experience our sense of existence and how we see the threat of annihilation of our self.

We can live out our sense of existence in selfish or unselfish ways. As an introvert we can define our sense of achievement in terms of becoming powerful and wealthy, or we can define our sense of achievement in terms of achieving to benefit other people. As an extravert we can define our sense of being part of a group in terms of making other people depend on us or look after us, or we can define our sense of being part of a group in terms of creating a team to achieve a common purpose or giving to others an abundance of love and concern without demanding gratitude and loyalty in return.

Another problem that some people have in making quite clear to themselves how they experience their sense of existence is that they, like all of us, want to have everything. They want to insist that they can be both a member of a group and an individual achiever and that they never have to choose between them. I often find myself in the position of a parent explaining to a child, 'You can't have everything. If you want to go swimming early in the morning you can't stay up past midnight watching television. You can go swimming or you can watch television, but you can't do both.'

Life constantly presents us with situations where we have to make a choice. It is a waste of time and effort to complain. Better to know what your priorities are and so make your wisest choice. It is sad that we cannot have everything, but that is life.

The question of priorities is not just a matter of knowing what is most important to us but also what it is that we fear the most.

So, terrifying though it is, you must ask yourself, *which do I fear the most, being left utterly and completely alone, or having everything escape from my grasp and fall into utter chaos?*

Only by confronting our greatest fear can we discover that what we fear is an illusion. Alone, we do not disappear, and constant change is not chaos but freedom. Moreover, even though in fear we feel as if our self is dissolving or shattering, our self is not disappearing or shattering. *What is dissolving and shattering is the structure of meaning we have created.*

Whenever we discover that the set of conclusions which we have drawn about ourselves, our world and our future does not accord with what is actually happening, we feel as if our self is dissolving and shattering. But our self is not dissolving and shattering. What is dissolving and shattering is our set of conclusions.

It is very frightening to realize that we have got things wrong, and it takes time to sort out what is actually happening and to construct another set of conclusions. This is why change, any change, is so stressful. Even when your structure of conclusions was 'I shall die unknown and poor' and you discover that the actuality is 'I am becoming famous and rich' the dissolving and shattering of your first set of conclusions is very disturbing.

However, when your set of conclusions was along the lines of 'I am working hard at being good, and one day I shall be rewarded; my partner loves me; I am achieving my goals', and then you discover that the actuality is that no amount of goodness prevents disaster, that your partner does not return your love, and that you have failed to achieve your goals, the recognition of the actuality involves much disappointment, and to build another set of conclusions you have to recognize and accept certain things which you would prefer not to.

Nevertheless, by facing your greatest fear, and recognizing that it is just your set of conclusions which is dissolving and shattering, you can start building another set of conclusions with which you can lively easily, neither being afraid nor pretending to yourself that all is well when it is not.

Pat, whose story began this book, did just this. At first she was disgusted with herself for being so gullible as to believe that she would be rewarded for all her efforts to be good and for wasting so much of her life, but then she began to feel that she should not waste any more time. She retired from teaching, and, living on her pension and a small inheritance, she began painting for her own pleasure. She discovered that a talent unused does not disappear. All she needed was to learn a few skills and to practise. So she went to art college, and there she discovered that, now she was no longer doubting her own worth and living a life devoted to duty and obligation, she could actually get to know people. She realized, too, that her expectation that everyone she loved would leave her or not love her had stopped her from seeking love. Once she recognized that *the fact that certain people in the past have left or not loved us does not mean that all people are certain to leave or not love us*, a whole new world of joy opened up before her.

It is very important for us to know what we fear the most so that we can avoid putting ourselves in impossible situations or expecting more from ourselves than we can deliver.

For instance, many of you in the prison of depression have, by being depressed, put off facing up to the fact that your marriage is not happy. At some time on your journey out of your prison you will have to recognize that something is wrong with your marriage and to decide what action to take.

If you are an extravert and you have not consciously recognized your need for other people, you may have endured all kinds of humiliations and made all kinds of sacrifices because you cannot risk being alone. Once you see this clearly you can say to yourself, 'Surely I can find other people who will care for me and not humiliate me and expect me to sacrifice myself for them?' It is not wise to say to yourself, 'I shall manage on my own', because, even if you now know in your heart of hearts that when you are alone you don't disappear, having other people around you makes you feel alive and happy. So in planning, say, to end your marriage, make sure that whatever you do you have other people around you.

This is not to suggest that you should leap from one marriage to another. As we all know, such a leap usually means simply recreating the first unhappy situation. A necessary prerequisite to a happy second marriage is a considerable increase in self-understanding and the ability to communicate with one's partner. Rather you should discover the wealth of love and support that can come from friends.

If you are an introvert and you have not consciously recognized your need to achieve you may have stayed in an unhappy marriage rather than admit failure. Perhaps instead of trying to achieve anything for yourself, you have tried to get your sense of achievement through the achievements of your partner and your children, and they have failed to achieve what you expected. Perhaps they have let you down very badly, despite all the organization, careful control and direction you gave them. Once you see this clearly you can say to yourself, 'I cannot achieve through other people. I can only achieve through myself.' Then, whatever happens to your marriage, you will make sure that you have in your life something which gives you a sense of achievement. Do not let ideas like 'I'm too old', or 'No one in my family has ever done that' stand in your way.

By knowing how we experience our sense of existence and realizing that what we saw as the greatest threat is nothing but illusion we achieve the synthesis of how we experience our sense of existence and see the threat of the annihilation of our self. Out of this synthesis comes what I call the Successful Self, where we make the most of what we are, whether we are an extravert or an introvert. Where, as an introvert, we learn good social skills and to move confidently in our external reality, or, as an extravert, we learn how to be alone and to journey into our internal reality. Thus we become someone who develops their individuality and who has close, loving relationships. For much of the time we can enjoy both, and when we are forced to make a choice we know which to choose.

Thus, as an extravert, instead of always being afraid of being rejected and spending all your time and energy in trying not to be rejected, you elaborate more and better ways of establishing and enjoying relationships with other people. You discover that the more you understand yourself, that is, journey into your internal reality, the more you understand other people, and so your bonds with other people are strengthened.

As an introvert, instead of always being afraid that things will get out of control and thus spending all your time and energy organizing and controlling, you can put these skills to use in more and diverse achievements. Instead of obsessively cleaning your house, you paint pictures. Instead of organizing and controlling other people, or shutting yourself away from other people, you interact simply and openly with other people, and, instead of organizing everything into rigid categories, you enjoy the bliss of just going with the flow of life.

To achieve all this you need to discover what you really feel and label such feelings correctly.

Labelling Emotions Correctly

Here again we face the problem of distinguishing what *is* from what *ought to be*.

Of course we always have the problem of which emotion we fear the most – extraverts fear anger because anger threatens relationships and introverts fear fear because fear implies chaos and loss of control. Extraverts therefore tend to label their anger as fear (shaking with anger is very similar to shaking with fear), and introverts deny that they are afraid. In addition to the mislabelling and denying of certain emotions because they threaten our sense of self, we mislabel and deny other emotions because we believe that we ought not to have such feelings. Yet, if we do not know what *is* we cannot change what is into what we want it to be.

Since there is no way of knowing what other people feel, it is impossible to know exactly how other people experience each emotion. Yet the phrases we commonly use when we talk about different emotions do suggest that we feel certain emotions in similar ways.

Anyone who has suddenly become very, very angry knows what 'blinding rage' means, how in such anger our vision can become so narrow that we see nothing but what enrages us and what we feel towards the object of our rage is nothing but the urge to strike, render and kill. We become blind to what the consequences will be if we express this urge. The expression of this emotion is, and has been, the cause of much of the suffering of the human race.

The first step in changing what we feel and do is discovering what it is that we actually feel and do. If you have been taught that you ought not feel anger then you will need to discover that the jangle of feeling and bodily distress which comes on you from time to time is anger. Many people turn blinding rage into a blinding headache, with the useful consequence that they do not strike and kill their loved ones, the usual cause of our rages, but with the less than useful consequence that such people, in denying their anger, suffer great pain and so cannot get on with their daily living. Getting a blinding headache and retiring to your room is a great way of striking at your loved ones in a way which makes them suffer guilt but prevents them from retaliating, but it is not so great when your life becomes dominated by the fear of such headaches and the sorry round of drugs and doctors. What starts as a physical way of dealing with anger soon becomes a persistent physical illness. Better in the first place to acknowledge your anger.

I had been invited to speak at a conference on enemies organized by a branch of the Christian Campaign for Nuclear Disarmament. The night before the conference I stayed with Tim, one of the organizers of the conference, and so met his two small children, Jessica and Philip. Jessica was four and Philip two, and they were enchanting.

My task at the conference was to run a workshop about how we create enemies, and I planned first to read a short paper and then have a general discussion. The paper was one which I had written for such lectures and workshops where I have learned to my cost that many people reject totally and utterly the idea that they are aggressive. In this paper I spend considerable time in defining how I am using the word 'aggression', saying that we are aggressive when we seek to impose our construction of reality on the world and other people, and that we must be aggressive, otherwise other people's definition of reality will prevail and we shall become a nothing. Disagreements between people are arguments about whose construction of reality will prevail. Saying to your child, 'Clean your teeth before you go to bed', is an act of aggression just as is the child's, 'No, I won't'.

In this paper I argue that a family are almost constantly engaged in acts of aggression against one another, each trying to make his or her construction of reality prevail and each, when prevented from achieving this, getting to some degree angry. Parents and children who do not allow themselves to show their anger directly, with some shouting and plain speaking and, later, if they were wise, explanation, apologies, hugs and kisses, have to resort to acts of aggression involving guilt arousing tactics, and these in the long run are not wise.

Extravert children, threatened with 'Mummy won't love you if you do that' are likely to relinquish much of their own construction of reality, accept their parents' constructions, and so remain as children, tied to their parents for the rest of their lives. Introvert children are not so likely to be overwhelmed by this threat but can respond in kind. 'If you won't love me, then I won't love you.' In this battle the parent will win the first skirmishes, for the child finds it uncomfortable to share a home with a parent who refuses to speak to him, but in the long run the child wins. Withholding his love from his parent, he becomes indifferent to his parent, and, when the opportunity arises, he leaves home. If, in later life, the parents say to the now adult child, 'I didn't mean it when I said I didn't love you. I loved you all the time', the child is likely to respond, 'You lied to me in order to manipulate me. When I needed your love you withheld it. I learned to live without your love, and now I do not need it.'

I finished reading my paper and looked around the circle. One woman spoke out immediately. 'I cannot accept what you have said. It is not true that everybody is aggressive. I would never be aggressive to my children. It *is* possible to bring up children without being aggressive.'

She spoke with such a passionate assumption of superior virtue that other parents in the group were disinclined to reveal their own inability to bring up their children without anger ever being evoked.

When Tim drove me to the station we talked about the workshop and Tim said, 'I was remembering one evening when I was putting Philip to bed and he just wasn't co-operating. I've always had a quick temper, but usually it's over just as quickly. But this night I got so angry – I felt – I could have done anything to him. I really wanted to hurt him. I just had to leave him and let my wife take over. I can understand now how a parent could kill his child. I'd never understood that before, but I can now.'

Such understanding does not mean condoning. It means seeing
how, and, from that, knowing how best to help. It is our recognition
of our human weakness which joins us to others. Superior virtue
cuts us off.

The way to discover what your feelings are is to stop being busy
with your thoughts and actions and to turn your vision inwards,
listening to what you are saying to yourself and being aware what
you are feeling. Question whether the labels you have put on these
feelings are the right labels.

Our experience of our emotions can change over time. I remember, as a child, experiencing guilt as a fear of imminent punishment,
but as I got older guilt became a jangled, painful sense of things
being in disorder and that the disorder being my fault – an introvert's way of identifying chaos with fear. If I hurt someone I sense
that hurt as disorder. Good relationships and correct actions have
for me the all-important quality of smoothness and orderliness. We
use the label 'guilt' a great deal, but the feelings for which this label is
(D 34) used are different for different people.

Where loss and disappointment are concerned, there must be
some commonly felt feelings, for we speak of pain in the region of
our heart – 'heartbreak', 'heartache'. I had always thought that these
words were empty, tired clichés until I suffered a loss, and then I
found that anguish felt like a hand squeezing my heart; heartbreak
was like a knife entering my heart, and heartache a dull pain in the
centre of my chest which went on and on and on. This ache became
an aching emptiness, as if that which had been a heart had
(D 35) disappeared.

Depression is a response to and a protection from this aching
void. As you journey out of the prison of depression you will find
this void will grow smaller and the aching fade, and what you are
left with is a gentleness. If you try, as many people do, to prevent
future hurt by hardening your heart, you will simply exchange the
heartache that comes from broken relationships for the icy cold of
loneliness. Closeness to other people requires a gentleness of heart,
and a gentleness of heart means a vulnerability to pain and sadness.

It is our sadness which joins us to other people.

Yet we live in a society where we are expected to be cheerful.

It is very, very pleasant to be with people who are cheerful, who
are enjoying themselves and making light of their troubles. Laugh-

ter is good for us, body and soul. But it is insensitive, even cruel, to demand that a person be happy and cheerful.

Societies differ in how much cheerfulness is expected from people in public situations. In Britain, people are expected to look cheerful when they are talking to one another, but alone in public places they are allowed, indeed expected, to be serious. Whereas in the USA a cheerful face is expected in most situations. When I was talking about this with Alma, a therapist working in Florida, she said, 'I've been shopping in the supermarket and concentrating on what I had to get, and somebody, a complete stranger, has spoken to me, saying that I looked very serious and why didn't I look cheerful?'

When accosted in this way, Alma would have to smile, because in Western society women are supposed to smile. Indian and Muslim women do not smile at people they see as their inferiors, nor at strangers, but Western women are required to smile at everyone they encounter. Women smile at women to show that they are not dangerous, that they are grateful, taking their turn, not wanting to be a nuisance, wanting to support and be supported, and women smile at men because if they do not, they are punished. Sally Cline and Dale Spender, in their book *Reflecting Men at Twice Their Natural Size*, wrote:

> On the street men appreciate, indeed they *demand*, women's smiles. In bed they appreciate orgasms. Both in public and private women exist to please men. This means their emotions, like their bodies, are not truly their own. Women cannot afford valid or honest expressions of feeling.[48]

Sally Cline and Dale Spender in their interviews with women had found that if women wanted a quiet life with their menfolk, they had to remember always to please. Brenda who lived on large housing estate with her husband and child said:

> 'Some days I think my face will set like jelly into the fixed smile I put on when Jim leaves. It's still there for the milkman, who's a surly bugger and never smiles back, and the postman, who seems to expect a welcome before he hands over the letters. I even smile at the catalogue man who gives me the creeps. At work, the bloke in charge expects all five of us women to be jolly all the time, despite the fact that the work is boring, badly paid and most of us can't stand him. But we all do it.' Brenda says that at night she's sometimes so tired she feels like crying when

Jim comes home but she never shows it. 'All women on our estate know you have to perk up and smile when they get in. You know you have to perk up in bed, too, whatever you're feeling like.'

We asked Brenda whether smiling and simulating a sexual response when she didn't feel like it made her feel closer to Jim. 'Oh, no! No, not at all! The more I do, the more I feel kind of cut off from him, and from myself. I even feel cut off from the other women around here, who I know are doing it too. It's not like something we're proud of sharing. The more I smile and try to perk up in bed, the worse the cut off feelings get. It's funny really, because I thought acts like that were about caring for people. Well, they are in a way. But they don't connect me to the people I'm supposed to love. I'm not sure what's happening to me because I don't feel close to Jim any more, or to anyone.'

Families differ in how much cheerfulness they expect one another to show, but most parents want their children to be happy. Indeed, many parents find their own unhappiness easier to bear than their children's. But parents who say, 'I only want you to be happy', can be placing on their children an intolerable burden. Parents in saying this can be refusing to acknowledge their children's unhappiness, and so denying them the understanding, comfort and support that they need. The children, in turn, can find their parents' distress at their unhappiness more distressing than their own unhappiness, and so embark on a life of hiding their unhappiness from their parents. Thus a group of people can live together for several decades and never in that time ever actually talk to one another. They merely pass the time of day.

As parents we need to have the courage to recognize our children's unhappiness, not belittle it by telling them that they are immature or stupid or by offering them facile solutions, and we need to make the effort to see the unhappiness arousing situation from the child's point of view.

Cheerfulness can be used as a weapon in our battles with one another. We learn about this weapon quite early – when we discover that our first smiles produce quite amazing responses from the adults around us. We learn how our distress can produce greater distress in our parents, and we can use this knowledge to our advantage.

Tim is good company. He tells interesting stories and smiles and laughs a lot. When we were talking about his children he told me about a fight he had with four-year-old Jessica over how she should have had a pee before she got in the bath and how he had given her a small slap. Jessica, whose future undoubtedly lies in the theatre, made the most of this. Sobbing loudly she pulled away from him and said, 'I'll never smile again.' It was a dagger right to her father's heart.

We can use cheerfulness as a weapon against ourselves. We can see our sadness as weakness and punish ourselves with our forced cheerfulness.

We can use cheerfulness as a weapon against others by making our cheerfulness mean, 'I've got everything under control and I'm winning', thus trying to make others feel envious and inferior. This is a popular ploy, often used in competitive sports, in the business world, and between partners where the cheerful partner wants not only to ignore the sad or depressed partner's feelings but to scorn them as well.

We can use cheerfulness as a way of controlling people. 'Be what I want you to be and don't bother me with your troubles.' Doing this we can inflict great pain.

In the Californian sunshine Clara told me how, 'In the course of a year I became a mother, a widow and an orphan.' Three months after her baby was born her husband's cancer was diagnosed and he died soon after. Shortly afterwards her mother died. Clara said, 'If I could have died then I would have. It was like everything had been taken away from me. I have now gone through some profound depressions with strong feelings of abandonment.'

Clara explained, 'My husband's first wife was depressed all the time, and one of the things that attracted him to me was that I was generally a cheerful person, but on the other hand, like any other human being I had my low moments. It was as if he could not stand to have me depressed. It would plunge him into this feeling, "Oh my God, she's going to be there for the rest of her life." So in a sense I was prevented from adequately expressing those negative feelings, and now all the structure of my life had gone there was nothing to prevent from going as low as I could.'

The 'worst depression of my entire life' was when her baby insisted on being weaned. 'I felt completely irrelevant. There was no light at the end of the tunnel. There was just a tunnel at the end of the tunnel. I felt a great deal of resentment of

Californian sunshine. Everything seemed to be a tremendous burden. It was like swimming in Jello, black and purple Jello, that stained all my clothes.'

These were not the first losses which Clara had sustained. 'The sense of loss in my life has been long term. When I was eighteen my closest friend committed suicide and her parents blamed me for the death. Three years later my father, whom I just loved in a very straightforward wonderful way, dropped dead in his office.'

I asked, 'And that's the sadness you would have liked to have expressed during your marriage?'

'Yes. My husband never really understood the sense of loss that I had felt and the sense of guilt I had felt about the suicide of my friend.'

There was another profound loss which Clara had carried from her earliest childhood. 'This was the sense that I had had while I was growing up of being very much neglected. I didn't know whether my mother loved me or not. On her deathbed I took her hand and I said, "Mother I love you," and she said, not, "I love you too," but, "Yes, I know it." I've come to believe that she had her own problems. She was clinically depressed and she was physically ill. Her pregnancy with me was very difficult. My main memory of my mother was coming home from school and finding her asleep on the couch. I never had any new clothes, never had toys. I never had a sense that we kids had priority. Okay, she was a woman with her problems, she didn't give me everything, but I've done quite well in life.'

In this last profound depression Clara hit rock bottom. She contemplated killing herself, but her newly discovered Christian faith restrained her. She had always wanted to practise such a faith, but first her mother and then her husband had prevented her, since each had a strong antipathy to religion. Now with her faith and the support of dear friends she could say, 'The depression was a sense of a profound imbalance. I was falling over a cliff into a pit that I was never going to get out of. Now I feel like I have crawled out of the pit and back into the sunshine. I feel that life is worth living.'

On her journey out of the pit Clara did not take any drugs. She said, 'This I absolutely refused to do. After my worst moments I thought, "Should I do that, am I so out of control?" Then I thought, "I really don't want that." On top of everything else you then have a drug dependency and you don't know what's real and what's not. I have a number of friends who are on tranquillizers of various kinds. There are certain things you just have to go through, otherwise you're postponing feeling, and you're going to prolong the feeling for the rest of your life if you continue on these things.'

I said, 'You have to go through the mourning process.'

'Exactly. I think it's part of our idea that there's a cure for everything, take a pill for everything. But there are certain things you just have to get through and there's no getting around them. I'm very opposed to drugs. I try to avoid them as much as possible. Certainly I've had my anxiety attacks and depressions, but they're real, they're mine, I owned them, I faced them down, sometimes I felt faced down, but I came out of it. I believe that there's a certain toughness that comes from that. I try not to be judgmental towards those who are on tranquillizers, but I think it is an avoidance of the problem.'

Clara was left with one problem. 'I find myself having difficulty in dealing with a lot of Californian types here who do not seem to understand that life is real and that difficult things happen. The Californian 'Have a nice day' aspect of this place drives me nuts, so I try as much as possible to surround myself with people who understand that life is good and bad and who don't just see the sunshine and not look beneath the surface. Cheerfulness has its place, but you can't always be cheerful. I've discovered that it's okay not to be cheerful sometimes, that there are people who will accept you whether you are up or whether you are down, and that was a good thing to discover after many years of feeling that I could exhibit only one aspect of my personality.'

(D 36)

Had Clara been allowed to express the sadness she felt for the loss of her father, her friend and her mother's love and attention she would have been much better able to master the death of her husband and mother and, having learned to accept and express her sadness, these deaths would have been simply losses for her to mourn, not blows which shattered her world of meaning.

Part of the sadness which Clara had been forbidden to express was something she had taken in from her depressed mother. When, as small children, we are close to a parent, we know, at the level of our feelings, what our parent is feeling. We do not know what to call

these feelings, indeed, we are too young to apply language to them,
and so we express our knowledge of these feelings in images.
Because at that young age we still experience ourselves as part of our
parent and our parent as part of us, we can experience this image as
arising directly from our own feelings and not as a response to our
parent's feelings. As we get older and separate ourselves from our
parent this image remains with us, sombre, dangerous, inexplicable, but our own. It is a source of sadness, and can be mistaken for
an image of the our own depression. As I found:

> When, in my thirties, I was trying to sort out my feelings of
> sadness, loss and depression, I discovered an image which I
> called 'old death's head'. I realized that this related to my
> mother's depression, and that 'death' related to my mother's
> aggressively negative view of everybody and everything,
> which to me seemed to kill, or threaten to kill, everything
> around me, and to the threat she was to me directly. She
> threatened my developing self because she seemed to want to
> take me over and make me her thing, and she threatened me
> physically for, as well as hitting me, she would, in moments
> and anger and despair, threaten to kill me and then kill herself.
> Now I understand her sufferings I feel great pity for her, but
> then, as a helpless child, I was terrified. I cut myself off from
> her, and, as I got older, her threat made me angry. How dare
> she threaten to take my life away from *me*! Thus, when I
> discovered this image, I recognized the blackness of my
> mother's depression and my fear, and for the image I felt rage
> and contempt. The image now has faded and I can recall it only
> **(D 37)** by an act of memory.

Distinguishing what we took inside of our parent's depression
from our own depression is difficult. So is separating our longing for
the parent who so cruelly treated us from the fear and hatred of that
parent.

Anna Mitgutsch's novel *Punishment* is a tragedy, for it ends with
the heroine Vera saying of her mother (now dead some sixteen
years), who had so cruelly beaten her, but had tried to provide for
her so well:

> For sixteen years I buried her over and over, but she always rose
> up and followed me. She caught up with me long ago. She looks
> at me with the eyes of my child; she observes me from the

mirror when I think I'm unobserved; I meet her in my lovers, and I run her off with her own arguments. Then she punishes me with loneliness, and I try to win her back through achievement, brilliant achievement, the epitome of achievement. I never please her. I married her and then divorced her, but she transformed herself and lay in wait for me. Her embrace, granted so hesitantly and only in exchange for perfect behaviour, always turns into a grip in which I suffocate. I push her away and feel pushed away. I am her and say, *You are worth nothing*, and sink into grief for my loss, my loss of I, my loss of Thou, the loss of all the love in the world. Because there are only the two of us. She is everything that is outside, night and the sun, sleep and the rain, love and hate and every person who crosses and darkens my life, and most of all myself. She has transformed herself into me; she created me and slipped inside me; when I died sixteen years ago, when she beat me to death thirteen years ago, she took my body, appropriated my ideas, usurped my feelings.

She rules and I serve her, and when I gather all my courage and offer resistance she always wins, in the name of obedience, reason, and fear.[49]

Vera could not separate herself from her mother because she could not face the aloneness, which she felt as loneliness, of being an independent person in her own right. She could not find the courage to go through the process which we all, not just those of us who need to separate the images of our parent's depression from our own, or the love from the hate we have for a cruel parent, have to go through if we are to cease to be children and become adults in person as well as in body. We need first to judge our parents, and then to forgive them.

Finding Forgiveness

One of the immediate consequences of acting *as if* you accept and value yourself is that you cease criticizing and punishing yourself, and the blessing of forgiveness comes upon you.

You remember the child that you once were and you pity that child. Pity is painful, but it is better than the coldness and disgust that arise from the hatred you had for that child. You remember the adolescent you once were and see that the mistakes and foolishnesses of that adolescent were not deserving censure and rejection, but were the necessary struggle to sustain and develop your adolescent self. You remember the mistakes you made as an adult, and instead of berating yourself and feeling guilty, you see that you were acting as best you could given the knowledge and experience you had at the time.

As you act *as if* you accept and value yourself, the blessing of forgiveness extends to other people. You see that much of what was done to you was not done out of hatred and maliciousness but out of all too human foolishness. The foolishness was simply the result of the limitations of knowledge and understanding which the people concerned had at the time. You feel sadness, but that is better than hatred and fear, for sadness and pity draw us close to other people.

However, not all injuries can be seen as the understandable outcome of ordinary human foolishness. Some of you have suffered major injury at the hands of cruel, selfish people who treated you as an object of no importance. Finding forgiveness for a mother who was ill, depressed and over-worked is not impossible, but is it possible to forgive someone who abused and hurt you and did you great damage?

We are told so often that forgiveness is a virtue, something we ought to do. We can forget that forgiveness, like love, is spontaneous. It is a grace which follows understanding. It is not an act of will. However, many people, believing that they ought to forgive and that people will censure and reject them if they show their lack of forgiveness, pretend that they have forgiven. This pretence cuts them off from other people, and, if they pretend to themselves that they have forgiven, they are quite unable to deal with their own anger, resentment and hatred.

On the other hand, actively not forgiving the person who injured you, spending much of your time feeling and expressing your hatred, fantasizing and even carrying out acts of revenge, does not lead to a rich, fulfilling life. Indeed, you become a lesser person than you might have been and you waste your life.

A programme in the *Everyman* series looked at this question of how best to deal with people who have inflicted on us major injury and loss.

Catherine Hill is a very beautiful young woman. She was a passenger on a plane seized by hijackers. On the ground in Karachi, the hijackers deliberately bombed and shot the passengers trapped in the plane. Catherine was very seriously injured, and now has to live with her severely scarred and maimed body. She has neither forgiven the men who did this to her, nor does she spend time in hating them and wanting revenge. She explained:

'The first step is accepting what has happened to you. What happened to me has changed my body, changed my mind, changed my love life, changed my attitude to many things. I've accepted that now, and with that acceptance comes the will to rebuild my life, to extract from what has been the most terrifying and terrible experience positive aspects. I close the door on the question of the terrorists. I close that door right in their faces, I won't think about them. I don't want to have anything to do with them. I want to use all that possible anger, but I will use it in a positive way, because that's the cleverest thing to do. I want to respect my mind.'[50]

It is not just her mind that Catherine respects. She respects herself. She accepts and values herself, and so she knows how we can use our anger to defend ourselves and to carry our lives forward, overcoming the losses and injustices we have suffered.

Now that you are acting *as if* you accept and value yourself you are discovering that parts of you which you have been taught were bad and unacceptable are actually most valuable. You are now reassessing what it means to be good.

The Consequences of Striving to Be Good

You had already discovered that if you spend your life trying to overcome your sense of badness by trying to be good you spend your life being lonely. You never reveal yourself to people lest they despise and reject you, and so no one gets to know you. Moreover, when you become an expert on being good, reaching and maintaining standards of performance which other people find amazing, these same people find you intimidating. They dare not reveal to you how inadequate you make them feel, and so they shut themselves off from you.

Once you begin acting *as if* you are good and valuable, you discover the joy of doing good simply because it pleases you to do good. You have been brought up to believe that people will be good only if they live in fear of punishment, but now you discover that when you accept and value yourself you simply are good. Of course there are 'good' things which you no longer bother to do because you did them only because you thought you ought to do them, and now you see that they were unnecessary, but there are other 'good' things which you now see as truly good things to do, and you do them for their intrinsic goodness and the joy you get from doing them.

You had already discovered that if you spend your life trying to overcome your sense of badness by striving to be good, you spend your life expecting rewards which do not always come. Whenever some disaster befalls you, like Calvin, you admit your guilt and punish yourself.[51]

Now you are acting *as if* you are good and valuable you have given up a life dominated by the desire for rewards and the fear of punishments. Instead, when good things come your way you rejoice in your good fortune, and when bad things come your way you do not blame yourself or feel unjustly used, but simply deal with them in the best way, by looking after yourself and seeking help from other people.

Now you have discovered something important about the world you live in.

The World Is Neither Just Nor Unjust

The world simply *is*. Our ideas about justice are simply that, *ideas*.

Ideas, like actions, have consequences.

When we believe something, consequences follow. We may not like the consequences. We might refuse to accept them and deny that they exist, but no matter what we say and do, consequences follow and exist.

Beliefs, like everything else, have consequences which are beneficial to us and consequences which are harmful to us. We all try to get the beneficial consequences and not the harmful, but life will not let us. Do something, or believe something, and the consequences, good *and* bad, will follow as the night the day.

Take the belief that the universe, or everything that is, is governed by a Grand Design where goodness is rewarded and badness punished. The Grand Design might be thought of as God, or Allah, operating some kind of accounting system – an angel writing in a book of gold – where your good deeds are balanced by your bad, and if the balance tips to the bad, you are punished in Hell, or to the good, you are rewarded in Heaven or Paradise. Or the Grand Design might be thought of as the law of Karma, where the balance of your good and bad deeds determines your status in your next life. Such a belief is not exclusive to Hindus. I have met a number of depressed Christians who believe that their burdens, losses and the depression itself are punishments for their sins in a previous life. Or the Grand Design might be thought of in terms of the history of your race or nation. Yahweh will reward his Chosen People: the Party, as those Chinese students should have remembered as they sat in Tiananmen Square, will punish evil doers. Or the Grand Design might not be spelled out in any precise way, but just felt as something which must exist. 'There has to be an afterlife, otherwise life would be meaningless,' say those people whom life has disappointed, who can see no pattern other than that of rewards and punishments, and who have lost the ability to live in and enjoy the present.

In the way that houses can be built in many styles but still have one basic design, so the Grand Design can be expressed in many ways, but still have one basic design, which is that goodness is rewarded and badness punished.

What are the consequences of the belief in a Grand Design?

First, the beneficial consequences.

The Grand Design gives a pattern and explanation to an inhospitable planet and a vast universe which transforms our insignificance, placing us at the centre of the universe, and which turns a planet indifferent to our existence into a world which is there to serve us.

The pattern of the Grand Design transforms chaos and random chance into predictable stability.

The promise of the Grand Design is that we are not the victims of blind chance, but the creators and controllers of our own destiny.

There are rules to the game, and we can play to win. We do not have to pity the losers, for if they lost then this is evidence that they deserved to lose.

Thus a belief in the Grand Design gives us certainty, power and absolves us of the obligation of pity.

But along with these consequences come the others, the ones that are not so good for us.

One consequence is that to maintain our belief in the Grand Design we have to blind ourselves to much of what goes on around us and we have to corrupt our intelligence in explaining the functioning of the Grand Design which is not readily apparent in our lives.

For example, on Monday, June 5 1989, we could read these four news stories in *The Guardian*. In Beijing, China, the Chinese army machine-gunned and crushed beneath their tanks their fellow countrymen who wanted nothing but a better life for everyone in China. In the Urals in the USSR, two crowded trains carrying a thousand people, many of them children going on their summer holidays, were engulfed in a ball of fire as a gas pipeline exploded. In Stockholm, Sweden, the trial began of the man alleged to have murdered Olaf Palme, the Swedish prime minister who had devoted his life to improving the welfare of other people. In Iran, the Ayatollah Khomeini, a man who had sent millions of people to their death, died peacefully in his own bed. Shall we corrupt our own intelligence and sensitivity by claiming that the Chinese killed by their own army, the Russians burnt alive, and Olaf Palme, shot as he walked home from the cinema with his wife, were wicked people deserving of their fate? Shall we fantasize some heaven where those victims, wrenched from their home and loved ones, are now living happily, and some hell where the Ayatollah suffers eternal torture?

Of course we can indulge in such speculations when we ourselves are not the victim. Once we become a victim, we meet the most unwelcome consequence of a belief in the Grand Design.

Then, when bad things happen to us, we can only blame ourselves or feel angry and resentful for being treated unjustly.

If you want to have the security of a belief in the Grand Design of rewards and punishments, you cannot avoid the consequence that, if you are depressed, you will go on being depressed, and, if you are not depressed, you will become so when you encounter major disasters and disappointments in your life.

If you want to give up being depressed, give up your belief in a Grand Design of rewards and punishments.

This is not to say that you should give up your belief in God. You simply give up your beliefs of God as the Great Accountant and Judge in the sky, and see Him, instead, as the mystics of all religions have seen God – as a great Power beyond, above and inside us, a Power of which we are part and which we take on trust.

Such an understanding of God, or Allah, or Yahweh, or the One, or the Tao, or Nature, or whatever name seems best, frees us from being a cog in the faulty machine of rewards and punishments. In such freedom we can see things clearly, we can think clearly, we can assess what we do and, if we wish, decide to change.

In that freedom we can feel the pain of pity and sadness for the victims of the cruelty and ignorance of their fellows, and we can fear for the future of ourselves, our loved ones and our species, and, at the same time, we can lose ourselves in the present, savouring the taste of good food, the scent of a rose, the joy of companion-ship. **(D 38)**

In that freedom we discover that we do not have to fear our helplessness.

Our Helplessness Is the Source of Our Strength

When we believe in the Grand Design we are wedded to guilt. We feel guilty because we have erred: we feel guilty in case we might err: we feel guilty so as to be able to tell ourselves that we are always in control. We use our guilt to ward off the realization of our helpless-ness in a vast world where we can control very little, and so we prevent ourselves from discovering that helplessness has beneficial consequences as well as harmful ones.

To be weak and helpless and in the power of people who threaten to harm us is terrible, but it is even more terrible if we doubt our own worth and do not believe that we have the right to live our lives as we wish. The more we hate ourselves, the more we fear helplessness. If we value ourselves we know we have the right to live as we wish to live, and this knowledge gives us strength.

When we do not value and accept ourselves we experience ourselves as weak, and so try to bolster ourselves by taking pride in our competence and control. We dare not admit that there are huge areas of life where our competence and control are ineffective.

Thus we fail to discover how, by admitting our helplessness, we can enjoy the beneficial consequences of helplessness.

Admitting our helplessness, we can abandon our desperate attempts to control everybody and everything, and simply 'go with the flow', taking life as it comes. Many people, emerging from depression or from a major trauma, do this when they decide to 'take one day at a time'.

Admitting our helplessness, we can give up all the fabrications of our pride where we claim that we are special because we belong to some group or other and because we are so very good at being good. Instead, we can know that we are like everyone else, ordinary, and that to be ordinary is to be acceptable and valuable, and close to everyone else.

Admitting our helplessness and realizing our ordinariness, we can see that the disasters that befell us were not part of a Grand Design where we were, justly or unjustly, punished. We do not have to take the disasters which befall us personally.

Sheldon Kopp described how he discovered this after he had developed a brain tumour which threatened his life and his sanity. He wrote:

At the time I fell ill, I still believed that life had inherent meaning, and that I had an important part in what was to happen to me and to those around me. My tumour seemed an undeserved and tragic fate. How the hell did that fit into the grand scheme? Not only had I started out as the innocent victim of my parents' mistreatment, but nobly transcending that unfair disadvantage, I had gone on to transform my suffering into a continuing fight against injustice. Why should a good guy like me end up with a brain tumour?

It took me two more years of therapy to resolve this pseudoinnocent question. Knowing that my mother hated me was not enough. I remained excessively vulnerable to life's random mishaps. I could not keep myself safe from making too much of my occasional bad luck until I realized that though it is probably true that my own mother hated me, it was nothing personal.

Any kid living in that house at that time would have served as a suitable target. It was my misfortune to have been the one who wandered in. There was no special meaning to it all, no compensations for that less-than-perfect beginning. As an adult I was free to choose to do what I could to alleviate the suffering of others. I need only to understand that this compassionate activity would neither avenge my past nor assure my future.

The first time I entered into therapy my question had been, 'Why am I such an awful person?' The answer turned out to be, 'You are not an awful person. You only feel that way now because as a child you were treated as though you were bad.' This time my question was, 'Why me?' The answer turned out to be, 'Why not?'[52]

It is when we accept that 'Why not?' that we become free of our past. We are no longer trapped in a Grand Design of rewards and punishments. We are free to be good because it pleases us to be good and not because we feel compelled to be good. We are free to achieve because it pleases us to achieve, and to be close to people because it pleases us to be close to people. We are free of the expectation of reward and the fear of punishment. We are free to hope. We are free to turn pain from being a prison into a resource for strength and understanding. This is what Clara did.

When Clara was describing to me her blackest, worst depression she spoke of, 'The sense of constant pain and the real questioning of whether there was any redemptiveness to the pain', and said, 'Part of my religious belief is yes that's so, but even Christ on the cross questioned the redemptive nature of pain and suffering. It was at that point that I didn't want to live. I feel now as if a certain chapter in my life has closed. That was a period of great chaos, and order is being restored in my life. I feel that I am a stronger person because of what's happened, but I wouldn't wish this particular route to strength on anybody else. Something I've learned from this is that it's not a weakness to show that something significant has occurred in your life. Another thing I've learned is that you don't wait to tell people how much they mean to you. You do nice things all along the line.'

I asked her what she meant by 'the redemptive power of pain'.

She said, 'It's not so much goodness is rewarded, but there's a reason for pain and suffering. I think that it can be redemptive, I feel that it has been redemptive for me, but certainly I doubted it quite profoundly for quite a long time. I saw the

suffering of the people I cared about and it seemed so senseless.
But it's just life and just death, and I feel that what is important
is not so much what happens to you but how you react to it. For
whatever reason, I was able to become stronger, so in that sense
it was redemptive for me, but I don't think that pain and
suffering is of necessity redemptive for everyone. We can learn
something. I'm a great believer in education. There are times
where I think I can't teach anyone anything, that we're all
autodidacts, but perhaps that's the best way. I certainly have
learned from my own experiences. I wouldn't want to go
through them again, but I'm not sorry that I did. I don't feel that
because I've suffered I deserve some kind of reward. What I feel
is that, whatever it is I have learned and however, I have
become more attuned to other people's suffering because of my
own, and that I would like to give back some of that knowledge.
I feel not so much that I am owed something but that I need to
pay back. I find myself actually being able to give a tremendous
amount to other people in pain because I understand where
they've been and can at some level or other show them that just
by my being where I am now it doesn't always have to be that
bad.'

Thus can our pain and our helplessness bring us closer to other
people.

The journey out of the prison of depression is not just a matter of
changing yourself, for, in changing yourself, you change your
relationships with other people.

Changing Our Relationships with Other People

As soon as you decide to act *as if* you accept and value yourself, your
relationships with others change. No longer do you feel that you do
not have the right to exist and must work hard at being good, hoping
that others will then tolerate your existence. Instead, you will know
that we all have the right to exist for the simple reason that we do
exist.

As soon as you decide to act *as if* you accept and value yourself,
you know that you have the right to be treated with dignity and
respect. You will no longer accept the disgraceful behaviour of your
nearest and dearest. This will come as a terrible shock to them, for
you have never challenged them on this before, but have condoned

and acquiesced in their selfishness, cruelty and ignorance because that was what you thought you were supposed to do. Many people, I have found, do not realize how badly behaved their families are because disgraceful behaviour has always been the major part of family life, where tolerance, respect, dignity and kindness shown by *all* family members to *all* family members are extremely rare.

When you decide to act *as if* you accept and value yourself, you will realize that other people do not despise you as you once despised yourself. Instead, you will discover that other people can actually envy you. Because we are all brought up to believe that we are bad and have to work hard to be good, envy is very prevalent in our society. Now you will have to take account of other people's envy.

This is a troublesome consequence of deciding to act *as if* you are acceptable and valuable. When you believed that you were intrinsically bad you could shut yourself off from other people and avoid even noticing how complicated relationships are. Now you have to learn some skills in understanding the complexities of relationships and developing many flexible ways of dealing with these complexities.

Or you could choose to remain lonely.

16

Leaving Loneliness Behind

The woman caller to the radio phone-in said, 'How can I get to know people? I'm twenty-six and I'm a schoolteacher. Other people have interesting things to do at the weekend. I'm always on my own.'

I remembered the staff room of the school where, many years ago, I was a teacher. Twenty odd teachers in that room, and odd they were too. I was as well. I said to my caller, 'Some of us look at the people we know and say to ourselves, "I'm not going to have anything to do with that one, he's boring, nor that one, she's too old, and that one drives me up the wall the way she's always talking about her children, and that one, well, he's gay, and as for that one, it's not that I have anything against Asians but –" and so on. We're so picky we just cross everyone off our list. That way we never discover that every person is interesting, once you get to know them. Instead, we end up being lonely.'

My caller was surprised that I had described so accurately how she saw her teacher colleagues. I explained that I had once been a teacher, so I knew what staff rooms were like. I did not explain that in my first staff room I began a conversation with two colleagues, Nan Purnell and Alan Buckland, a conversation which has gone on for forty years, even though for half of that time we have been half a world apart. Nan and Alan made it very easy for me to get to know them, for, like my caller, I was both frightened of people and picky. Had I made more of an effort, I could have become friends with many more people in that staff room.

Still, if I had not lacked the skills of friendship when I was young, I would not now so readily pick up the signs of loneliness in the people I meet.

And I meet so many lonely people. The world is full of lonely people.

Why don't all the lonely people get together?

Why indeed!

All the lonely people do not get together because this loneliness is not *aloneness*, the state of being alone.

Loneliness is the state of being cut off from other people through fear of other people. Loneliness is felt as a barrier and an emptiness between yourself and other people. You reach out to other people, but the barrier intervenes. You take a step towards other people, and there is nowhere to put your foot. People come towards you, and your loneliness shuts them out.

It is your loneliness, rather than the absence of other people, which leads you to be alone.

Laura, writing to me, said:

'I don't see the threat of the annihilation of the self as falling into chaos, but as a fear of being invaded. My idea of being true to my "self" is stopping anyone else coming into contact with my "self" – I don't mean just in a physical sense, such as "invading my space", but mentally. It is a fear of allowing people to see into you, particularly a fear of letting anyone else understand what you're about, as though you will lose your identity if they do. The loneliness stems from the fact that the less you let others know you, the less you know of them, and the realization can be very depressing. The idea that you don't really know anyone and never will can be very disturbing. It really hit me recently when I had to go into hospital for a day, and the doctor stated at a talk session beforehand that I had to have someone come and collect me from the hospital, for medical reasons. It suddenly dawned on me that there wasn't anybody I could ask. It does little for your self-esteem to think that you are really on your own.'

How do we create for ourselves this state of loneliness?

We create it by our rules about our relationships with other people, our beliefs about our relationships, the skills we use in our relationships, and the emotions our relationships provoke in us.

Our Rules about Our Relationships

When we are children our parents, and then our teachers, lay down rules about whom we can be friends with, whom we can play with, whom we should avoid, whom we must ignore. Of course we can break these rules, but mostly we do not, because children police the rules themselves. We might be able to hide from our mother that we play with children of families she disapproves of, but we cannot hide this from the other children at school, and if they do not approve of our companions, they will make life very difficult for us.

As children we do not question why there are these rules. We take them as the immutable realities of the universe.

In the Australia I grew up in people were either Catholic or Protestant. Catholic children went to Catholic schools and Protestant children to state schools, called Public schools. The Protestant children called the Catholic children 'tykes' and the Catholic children called the Protestant children 'publics'. I never questioned that, as I went to a Public school and a Presbyterian church, I should have nothing to do with Catholic children. We were told all kinds of stories, which I later recognized as outrageous, about the Catholics, and the Catholics were told all kinds of outrageous stories about the Protestants.

In my second year as an undergraduate at Sydney University my friend Josie and I shared a room in the home of a Catholic family. One day, when I was talking to our landlady, Gladys, her six-year-old daughter, listening to our conversation, made a momentous discovery. 'Mummy,' she cried, 'is Dorothy a public?'

'Yes,' her mother said.

(D 39)   The little girl backed away from me, her eyes as round as saucers. 'Mummy, look at the devils dancing around her!'

I doubt if Catholic children are taught such things in Australia any more, for schooling there is no longer segregated, and Catholic and Protestant children have plenty of opportunity to discover that whatever undesirable characteristics each may have, dancing devils is not one of them.

However, similarly outrageous myths are taught as literal truths in all countries so as to divide people, one group from another.

Why do we divide one group from another, or, rather, why do we separate our own group from every other group?

We do so because we believe that our nationality is the best, our religion is the best, our race is the best, our class is the best, our political affiliation is the best, and all others are not merely mistaken and unfortunate, but actually wicked and dangerous.

Why do we do this? Why do we make other groups our enemies? We learn about our family's enemies from the instructions we get about which children we can play with, by listening to the conversations of the adults around us, from the patriotic songs we are taught and the ceremonies we take part in, from the sermons and prayers of our clergy, and from the comics we read, and the television and films we watch. We might be resisting our parents and teachers by refusing to learn to wash our hands before meals and to recite our multiplication tables, but we absorb this information about our group's enemies very readily. We have three reasons for doing this.

First, our group's enemies give an uncomplicated and definite structure to a world we often found complicated and amorphous. The world, we are told, is divided into Goodies and Baddies, and we are amongst the Goodies. Having enemies made us feel secure.

Second, our enemies were wicked, untrustworthy, cowardly, unreliable, faithless, dirty, greedy, selfish, uncaring and aggressive, whereas our group was virtuous, trustworthy, brave, reliable, faithful, clean, generous, unselfish, caring and unaggressive. As individuals we might not be valuable and acceptable, but at least we belonged to the best group in the world. Having enemies made us feel proud.

Third, as we learned the litany of vices which defined our enemies, we realized that we could compare ourselves to our enemies and so believe that, bad and unacceptable though we might be, our enemies were worse. Having enemies made us feel good.

In fact, our enemies were a tremendous help to us as we tried to deal with that feeling of unacceptability and badness. We could gather together much, or even most, of that horrible feeling and project it out on to our enemies. We could say, 'I am good. It is our enemies who are bad', and, as we said that, we felt closer to the members of our group. We might not get on with our family and might often feel victimized and betrayed by them, but, thinking of our enemies, we felt at one with our family. Remember how people in England came together once Argentina had been identified as the enemy! Those people who felt that war against Argentina over the Falkland Islands was wrong were made to feel very isolated. In earlier wars, anyone who refused to see their nation's enemies as their own enemies was jailed or killed.

We could hate our enemies for their wickedness, their faithlessness, their greed and filth, but, best of all, we could hate them for their aggression. Because they were aggressive we were in danger, and so we had to defend ourselves. Of course we were not aggressive, merely defending ourselves.

So our enemies, such wicked people that they are, allowed us to be virtuously aggressive. Whether we killed our enemies, in imagination as a child or in fact as an adult, or merely hated and criticized them, we could do so and still regard ourselves as good. As individuals we might not think of ourselves as being good, but as a member of our group we were.

Enemies hold a group together. Enemies provide a focus and an outlet for the aggression which otherwise could tear a group apart, whether the group be a family, a nation, a race, a class or a religion. Enemies help solve the problem of how to turn a wilful, demanding, aggressive infant into an obedient, conforming, compliant child.

To date, human beings have not been able to organize a society which does not need enemies. Yet, until we do, we shall not be able to end the arms race and solve the problems which threaten the future of the planet.[53]

So there are reasons more than simply ending your loneliness for understanding about enemies and finding ways of not being frightened by strangers.

The first step in understanding about your enemies is to work out who they are. Our political and religious leaders are always telling us who our enemies are, but sometimes one group of people **(D 40)** inspires our enmity more than another.

It is impossible to feel personal enmity towards a group of people who live far away and who have no connection with us at all. We need a *relationship* with our enemies. Our enemy has to conspire against us, infiltrate our ranks, and threaten us. If we see the Communists as our enemies, it is not the Russian people who threaten us, but their rulers who conspire against us, and their spies and supporters amongst us. If we see the West Indians or the Muslims as our enemies, it is not the people living in the West Indies or other Muslim countries who threaten us, but the West Indian and Muslim people who live near us.

Hence we can find our group's enemies living, not thousands of miles away but in our country, even in our very street.

Thus, as we go about our business, working, shopping, taking the dog for a walk, we can see, not an interesting variety of people with whom we could be friends, but enemies, people whom we must not just exclude from our lives but guard against as well.

And, worse, even though we have off-loaded our sense of badness and unacceptibility on to our enemies, saying, 'They are bad, not I', very few of us manage to do so completely. Most of us retain a sense of personal responsibility, and, as much as we say that our enemies are bad, our sense of our own badness and inadequacy remains. While we say that our enemies are bad, we know that our enemies are dangerous and that we are weak, and so we feel frightened.

Thus we build for ourselves a vicious circle where we try to assure ourselves that we are good by finding enemies and believing that they are bad, and then, because we see our enemies threatening us, we feel frightened.

The more that you feel that you are bad and unacceptable, the more you feel in need of enemies, the more wicked your enemies seem to you, and the more frightened you are of your enemies.

If you follow without question the rules you learned as a child about the relationships you as a member of your group were allowed to form, you have cut yourself off from other people through a fear of other people.

Our Beliefs about Relationships

Among the conclusions we drew as children were our conclusions about how we should treat other people. These conclusions became the beliefs about relationships which we carried into adult life.

Those of us who grew up in homes where there were lots of happy and accepting people being welcomed by our parents who clearly enjoyed their company, were presented with examples of people getting along well together and enjoying one another's company, and we drew the conclusion that relationships with other people were good, pleasant and desirable. Those of us who grew up in homes where visitors were only grudgingly made welcome, or not made welcome at all, and where we heard our parents privately criticizing and condemning relatives and acquaintances, drew the conclusion that relationships with other people were something to be undertaken with care, if at all. If, as well, we encountered situations where we, weak and helpless, were overwhelmed by powerful and dangerous adults, we drew the conclusion that we must put up a barrier and defend ourselves against other people.

Laura, as a child, concluded that she should put up such a barrier. In a letter to me she said, 'My family (my mother particularly) have always seen other people as "apart from us" or "other". This separation even includes my grandparents. If relatives or workmates visit, my mother wants them to give notice of their arrival, and, even then, watches them come through the front gate, saying, "Oh, they're here", with a tone of dread. As they're going, she waves them goodbye with her brightest smile – she's always very nice to them – then sits down wearily and says, "Thank God they've gone". As you might expect, we don't invite many people round to the house, and my conversational ability is nonexistent.

'When you've grown up amongst this separatist attitude, it becomes very difficult to believe that not everyone thinks like this. I've had school friends whose homes are more like bus stations – with friends, relatives and pets scattered liberally through every room – but no matter how welcome they tried to make me feel, I always saw every smile as false. I always felt uncomfortable. As I was leaving I always imagined them sitting down wearily, saying, "Thank God she's gone".

'I think that's why I've always been happy to "keep myself to myself". I got tired of constantly apologizing for my presence, for being sorry to disturb them. If you're on your own, you don't have to apologize to anyone. There's one unfortunate side-effect. I live in student halls, and when someone comes to my room to borrow a book or some notes, their whole attitude is apologetic. They feel as if they are disturbing me, interrupting my privacy, and they can't leave fast enough. No matter how nice I am, they never feel as though they know me well enough to feel welcome. Privacy has its disadvantages.'

If you have grown up with a barrier against other people, you are left with the powerful feeling that if you let down your barrier you will be swirled away and destroyed in a turbulent flood. You never risk letting down your barrier and discovering that an intimate relationship does feel like a flood, but it is a flood where you can discover the joy of being without barriers, a flood where you can float in bliss, not, as you fear, drown in helplessness and sorrow.

The ultimate irony of our lives is that, while we spend our lives seeking pleasure and satisfaction, we create and maintain the barriers which bar us from the greatest pleasure we can know, intimacy with other people.

However, you cannot be intimate with other people when you believe that you are bad and unacceptable, and, since you believe this, you have to bolster yourself up with pride, and pride takes many forms.

Like, *I keep myself to myself.*

You believe that there is virtue in limiting your relationships with other people.

So, you don't get to know your neighbours, you rarely invite people to your home and, when you do, you have rules about just who you invite and how and when this is done. No casual dropping in at your place. At work you maintain formality – no good, so you believe, ever comes of letting people be familiar. You say to the world, 'Thus far and no further.'

To the world you present a front, a role you have created to fool other people that this is you. You play this role very well, and many people are fooled by it, but behind it you are very lonely. Your role might have all the characteristics of a warm, wonderful person who gets on well with other people, but as soon as someone takes your role for real and makes a move to get close to you, you retreat and disappear from sight. **(D 41)**

Sometimes, the role you choose to hide behind includes being part of a couple.

In our society there is a very strong belief that every adult should be half of a couple, preferably a heterosexual couple, but a homosexual couple will do, provided it is a permanent relationship. This belief imposes great hardship on many people.

First, it implies that there is something wrong and inferior with people who are not half of a couple. There are a great many people who are not half of a couple – single parents, divorcees, widows and widowers, and people who decide that marriage, or a marriage-like relationship is not for them. If you believe that the only right way to live is as being half of a couple, your single state will make you feel inadequate and ashamed.

Second, this belief prevents many people from leaving an unhappy relationship. What they see as the shame and inferiority of the single state they regard as worse than the pain they suffer in their marriage.

An unhappy marriage is a lonely marriage. Loneliness in a marriage is far, far worse than loneliness in singleness, for the simple reason that when you are single there is a much wider range of things you can do to alleviate your loneliness than is available in marriage. You don't have to spend time being ashamed of or angry with your partner, you can choose your own friends, you can choose to pamper and indulge yourself in the privacy of your own home.

The other advantage of being lonely and not half of a couple is that you do not waste time longing for intimacy with a partner who refuses to be intimate.

My friend Anne Shotter, an experienced marital therapist, says that the major cause of unhappiness between couples is not just a lack of intimacy but a *fear of intimacy*.

When a couple first meet they are attracted by the roles which they present to the world, and through these roles they negotiate falling in love and making some sort of commitment. They might partake of all the intimacies of sex, but always they keep part of their self hidden. Then, as time goes by, this way of relating to one another in a guarded, fictionalized way becomes less and less bearable. Perhaps the birth of a child or a career opportunity demands a stronger commitment to one another. Perhaps one or both partners find the loneliness of their relationship less and less bearable. Sometimes, one of the partners recognizes this need for intimacy and overcomes his or her fear of intimacy to press the other person to stop playing a role and to come closer, but the other person, too terrified to do that, retreats even further. Sometimes both partners are too terrified of intimacy to recognize that for a relationship to endure two real people must actively engage in the relationship. A pair of puppets dancing while the real people pull the strings is not a relationship.

Thus, if you believe that there is virtue in keeping yourself to yourself, that not to be part of a couple is shameful and inferior, and that it is dangerous to reveal yourself to another person, no matter how much you love that person, you have cut yourself off from other people through a fear of other people.

Our Skills in Our Relationships

Being lonely requires some special skills, and you who are lonely have perfected these skills.

There is the 'sour grapes' skill. You remember Aesop's fable about the fox who saw a bunch of ripe grapes hanging high on a vine. He jumped again and again, trying to reach the grapes, and each time he missed. Finally, he went away, saying to himself, 'Those grapes are sour. I didn't want them anyhow.'

Like the fox, whenever you see something you might do which

could make you less lonely – such as joining a club, taking up a hobby, visiting friends – you can quickly and efficiently see that the grapes are sour – that the club is full of snobs, the hobby a waste of time, the friends are boring. Unlike the fox, you don't even make a few jumps. You can *know* that something is not worth doing, so you don't need to try.

One popular form of 'sour grapes' is the 'aren't those people ridiculous' skill.

My mother used to employ this skill in dealing with lady bowlers. This was the kind of bowls played where, in the open air, on a large, smooth rectangle of grass, shiny, heavy black balls were slowly bowled in the direction of a small white ball some twenty-five yards away. It was a very formal game, so the players dressed formally. The men bowlers wore white trousers and shirts. The lady bowlers wore white blouses and skirts and, since in Australia in the forties a lady wore a hat and stockings, the lady bowlers wore white hats and white stockings. In their tailored skirts, with corsets underneath restraining their middle-aged flesh, the lady bowlers moved with restraint and dignity.

However, to my mother, the lady bowlers were ridiculous. Often, as we drove by a bowling green, she would say to my father that she could not understand how a woman could be seen out in such 'a get-up'. My father loved a gentle tease, so if he thought she might have missed an opportunity to be contemptuous of lady bowlers as we drove by, he would call her attention to them so she could sniff her disdain.

My mother's 'lady bowlers are ridiculous' skill first came into operation when my father, finding that he was getting too old for playing cricket, joined the local bowling club. He had hoped that mother would not object to his playing bowls as much as she had objected to his sailing, football and cricket, and that, as the club was near home and was a social centre for its members, she would take up bowling too.

My mother's disdain for lady bowlers was one of the facts of the universe into which I was born, but once I was old enough to be interested in what my parents did and why, I pieced together from their comments what had gone on when, years before, my father had said to my mother, 'I'm going to join the local bowling club. Why don't you join too?'

There had been a row. She objected to his joining on the grounds of expense, sin (alcohol was sold in the bar), unsavoury people (his friends), and the fact that it was a waste of time. He countered by saying that he needed to play some sport so as to be healthy. Their rows had a pattern. Usually my father gave in immediately, but occasionally, when something was important to him, he did not, and sport and conviviality were important to him. Whenever my mother could not make my father give way she would retreat into an angry, hostile silence which, as I remember, could go on for weeks.

Such a silence distressed my father and he would offer a compromise. If my mother was weary of her silence she would, sometimes grudgingly and sometimes graciously, accept his offer. In the row about bowls the compromise was that he would join the bowling club and she would not.

However, my mother did not believe in forgiving and forgetting. Her oft-repeated refrain about the ridiculousness of lady bowlers was a constant reminder to my father that she merely tolerated and did not approve of his playing bowls. Her refrain was also a punishment of him for so frightening her by suggesting that she leave the safety of her home and meet *people*, the most dangerous and terrifying objects in her world.

My mother would never say that she was frightened of people. She simply created water-tight reasons as to why she could not meet people. These reasons always had to do with her health (she was prone to severe asthma attacks, so any situation could be defined as likely to provoke an attack and therefore should be avoided) and with the general iniquity and stupidity of people. Creating such reasons was her special skill.

So, on Saturday afternoons, my mother would be at home with me, a child, and later, when I escaped, alone, doing housework, sewing, reading a magazine, and, her most regular occupation, worrying. While on the bowling green, there was the clink of one ball against another, the gentle clapping of hands, and the soft murmur of voices.

If ever my mother felt that her usual skills for avoiding people were not enough, she would use another one, the popular skill called 'I don't have the time'. I grew up believing that my mother was always tremendously busy, and it was not until I was married with a small child and working full time as a teacher that it dawned on me that my mother, who never went back to her clerical work once she married and who trained her two daughters to do housework from the moment we could hold a duster, could not have had all that much to do. That realization led me to be more aware of how frequently and effectively many people use the 'I don't have the time' skill to avoid doing something that they don't want to do.

We can always have the time to do something which is important to us. We simply not do something less important. But every kind of work can be expanded to fill all the time available, so when we are asked to do something which we do not wish to do, we can say, very virtuously, 'I'd love to do that, but I haven't got the time'. This is a skill which lonely people polish to perfection.

Thus, if the skills which you use in relationships are aimed at scorning, limiting and avoiding relationships, you have cut yourself off from other people through a fear of other people.   (D 42)

Our Emotions in Our Relationships

Praise from my mother was a very rare commodity. The highest praise she could give to any of her few friends and acquaintances was, 'He's always the same'.

These friends and acquaintances who were 'always the same' never sprang surprises on her. They were *always* cheerful and calm, interested in what she said but did not ask prying questions, and respectful to her. They showed that they were pleased to see her and they never overstayed their welcome. They were *predictable*. They made her feel safe.

We enjoy a feeling of safety with another person where we feel:

1. that we can predict what that person will say and do,
2. that the person likes us,
3. that the person understands us.

We can find people who fulfil these criteria only when we accept and value ourselves. If you believe that you are unacceptable and worthless, then every person you meet can seem to be someone who is unpredictable, does not like you and does not understand you.

People often appear to be unpredictable to us, but this is only because we do not know what are the beliefs and conclusions that they use to make their decisions and to guide their behaviour. However, we can find out about a person's beliefs and conclusions by getting to know that person. If you spend time in conversation, asking someone how he sees himself and his world, and if you make that imaginative leap we call *empathy*, where we imagine ourselves being in another person's shoes and looking out of his eyes, you will gradually come to see the pattern of beliefs and conclusions which lead the person to do what he does. I have, over the years, had many such conversations with people who have done things which I would never dream of doing – often bizarre or criminal acts – and, in the end, while I might not have approved of or condoned what they had done, I understood why. I could then, as I was sometimes required to do by a psychiatrist or a judge, predict what the person was likely to do in the future. But to do this I needed not to be frightened of that person.

Not that my predictions were always correct. It is much easier to understand the past than to predict the future. However, the better you know a person, the better you can predict what that person will do and say, including whether that person will like you.

People, on the whole, take us at our own valuation.

If you like yourself, people will like you. If you accept yourself, people will accept you.

If you don't like and accept yourself you make it much harder for people to like and accept you. *Of course there are people who like and accept you no matter how much you dislike and reject yourself, but you make it hard for them to show their affection for you because you don't believe that they really care. You shut yourself off from them, push them away, and, fearing rejection, you reject them before they can reject you.*

The third criterion for feeling safe with another person is much harder to obtain. Generally speaking, people are very bad at understanding one another. *We can like, and, indeed, love, another person without understanding that person.* Many people cause themselves much grief by believing that proof that a person loves you is that that person understands you. Small children love their parents, yet could not possibly understand them. Parents love their children, and, very often, do not understand them.

Many of us, not understanding other people and being unskilled in ways of picking up information about other people, rely on good manners for getting along with other people. However, being treated politely is not quite enough. We all like the people we meet to take the effort to work out who we are and respond to us as we know ourselves to be. I always feel a flutter of irritation when a shop assistant, having carefully checked my Visa card on which is clearly stamped 'Dr D. Rowe', hands it and the stamped slip back to me and says, 'Thank you, Mrs Rowe'. I worked hard for my doctorate, and I take pride in my home, paid for by my years of hard work. I have tried saying to the shop assistant, 'A woman can be a doctor, you know', but that just causes the shop assistant pain and confusion. So I damp down my irritation by reminding myself that I do look like a doctor's wife.

I guess that on the third requirement we have to settle for the person making an effort to understand us. Perhaps if we were grateful for someone making the effort to understand us, we would find it easier to help that person to achieve an understanding of us by being prepared to reveal more of ourselves. However, *so long as you are convinced that inside you is something so disgusting and worthless that all people, seeing it, would reject you, you always put yourself in the impossible situation of wanting to be understood but without revealing any of your secrets.*

So, by fearing other people, you can neither understand others nor be understood.

Fearing other people and thus not understanding them, you find, whenever you venture any contact with other people, that you get involved in painful misunderstandings. You explain much of people's behaviour on the basis of your belief 'That person does not like me'. So when other people break appointments to see you, fail to phone, forget your birthday, and so on, you regard these events as proof, if proof were needed, that the person does not like you. The fact that people have jobs, families and inadequate diary keeping habits does not cross your mind, except to feel aggrieved that your erstwhile friend regarded his job or her sick child as being more important than you. You express your pride by abasing yourself in humility, 'Of course, I am of no importance at all', instead of understanding that we all, you included, have many commitments and it is not humanly possible to meet all of them all of the time.

Fearing other people, you fear other people's anger, for in your childhood experiences you saw anger tear relationships apart. You did not see, as more fortunate children did, that *it is possible to be angry with a person and go on liking and loving that person*.

Thus, when someone gets angry with you, or even when you suspect someone is angry with you, you see that anger as total rejection of you. If you are in the wrong, your pride will not allow you to say, 'I'm sorry. Please forgive me'. If the other person is in the wrong, your self-hatred will not allow you to defend yourself against injustice, but you will defend yourself by rejecting the person who you believe has rejected you. Indeed, you will often get your rejection in first, before the person has time to get angry, much less reject you.

Fearing other people and so not knowing them, you see them enjoying benefits which you have been denied, and you envy them. Envy, by itself, can be a useful emotion, spurring us on to get what we envy. But when we believe that we do not deserve to get what we envy, envy soon becomes mixed with hate, and that, indeed, is a horrible emotion, unpleasant to feel and damaging to ourselves and others if we express it. The mixture of hate and envy can make you fear people even more.

Your fear of other people makes you feel vulnerable and exposed and in danger.

Chris described to me how she hated leaving and entering her home, for it was set at the corner of a square where all the houses had adjoining lawns. She wanted to move to a house which she could enter and leave without being seen. Out in the open she felt not simply naked but without a skin to protect her, and every glance in her direction felt like the thrust of a sword.

She dressed as inconspicuously as possible, trying not to draw attention to herself in any way, but she knew that she could not prevent the neighbours seeing her and commenting on her. The comments, she was sure, would always be unfavourable.

Chris had grown up in a home where she had been noticed only to be criticized, so she well knew how everything she did, or failed to do, could be the object of criticism. She never entertained the possibility that other people might not criticize her, indeed, might envy her, for she had a beautiful home and an interesting job.

Chris was sure, too, that if people knew her and her history they would not be kind. Yet her story is one of the saddest I have ever heard and one which would lead anyone who knew it to feel immense sympathy for her. Her story, in the barest outline, was that her mother had committed suicide when Chris was a baby and her father soon married a woman who behaved like the traditional wicked stepmother. She gave Chris nothing but the bare necessities of life and showed her that she was not welcome in her house. Chris's father dared not protest, but, when his wife was absent, he would give Chris treats of sweets and ice cream and visits to the circus. Chris grew up believing that she had no right to the good things in life, so that when she was an adult and good things did come her way she could not enjoy them.

Her belief that people were always unkind and always untrustworthy extended from her neighbours to her doctor. She could not talk to him because he made notes, and these notes would be read by other people, and her private life would become public property to be gossiped over and criticized.

Chris and I had got together for just one discussion, and while she had been telling me her story I had been thinking that she might like to talk to a clinical psychologist who worked where she lived and whom I knew to be a very sensitive and caring person. Chris would find it easier to face the sadness of her childhood if she had a companion to help her along the way. But when she spoke so vehemently and with such certainty, saying that in the Health Service her privacy would not be respected, I refrained from suggesting that she contact my colleague.

This was one of those times when I wish I had a magic mirror which would let a person see how other people actually see her. If Chris had looked in such a mirror she would have seen, not the person she thought she was, but a charming, delightful, beautiful woman whom everybody would like very much.

The barrier of loneliness is something which we create out of our fear and our beliefs which serve to cut ourselves off from other people.   **(D 43)**

How can we dismantle this barrier?

Dismantling the Barrier

Over lunch in a workshop on psychotherapy a woman said to me, 'One of my clients was complaining to me about how lonely she was. She said that at Christmas time she received only six cards. I wanted to ask her, "How many did you send?"'

To maintain friendships and to end loneliness it is necessary to send out many cards and much more besides.

The problem is that when you do not value and accept yourself you have to spend all your time protecting yourself against hurt. You become very self-involved. All your trains of thought revolve around yourself. Some people get so bored with themselves that they give up thinking about themselves, get interested to something else, and are later surprised to discover that they no longer believe that they are valueless and unacceptable. But other people go on, year after year, absorbed in their own worries and fears, looking outside themselves only to find threats against which they must defend themselves.

The tragic paradox of the lives of most of us is that, convinced as we are that we are bad and unacceptable and have to work hard to be good, we strive to be kind, considerate and caring, and yet, because we are so absorbed in the conflicts which arise in us because we believe that we are bad and unacceptable, we do not notice what is going on around us and what is happening to other people.

Not noticing what is going on around you, you lose countless opportunities to enjoy your surroundings and to feel amazed, amused, delighted and at one with them.

Caroline had been coming to my house once a month for over three years. My semi-detached house has around it a small lawn, a garage and driveway at the back, a flower garden and path at the side and a large front garden. Each time she came Caroline parked her car in the driveway, walked around the side of the house to the front, climbed three steps and rang the front door bell. If, while approaching the front of the house or waiting for me to open the door, she had looked about her, she would have seen below the steps two white urns, between them an old path running some twenty-five yards to a gate overshadowed by a huge sycamore tree, and, on either side of the path, lawns, shrubs, flowers and trees, all enclosed by a high privet hedge on one side and on the other two sides a dry stone wall.

To talk, Caroline and I sat in my living room where a bay window overlooks the front garden. On one rare hot day I suggested to her that we sit in the garden.

'That would be nice,' said Caroline, and followed me out. She stood on the front lawn and looked about her with amazement. 'I didn't know there was a garden here,' she said.

At home Caroline did see her own garden, for she often told me about the pleasure she got from it, but when she came to visit me she was so anxious about herself that she became unaware of her surroundings.

Not noticing what goes on around you, you fail to notice what is happening to other people.

Derek usually talked to me about himself and mentioned his wife and sons only as bit players in his own great drama. If I asked how his wife felt about some issue he was expounding to me, he would say, 'She's worried about me.' Occasionally he would say, 'My depression is getting her down.' If I asked about his sons, he would say, 'You know what kids are, but I worry whether they'll be affected by my depression.' I listened for him to say something about his wife and children which did not include him, but he never did.

One day, our local newspaper carried a large story and photograph about his sons. They were champion swimmers and had just returned from an international competition where they had won several events. When I next met Derek I said, 'You must be very proud of your sons.'

He said, 'It was a complete surprise to me when a reporter and photographer turned up the other evening. I didn't know the boys were away competing. I thought they'd gone on a school trip.'

'Do you go and watch them swimming?'

'No. I can't stand the smell. It's the chlorine, isn't it? Always gives me a terrible headache.'

And we were back talking about Derek.

Derek did care about his children. No matter how depressed and ill he felt, he still went to work. Providing for his family was one of the standards he set himself, but such provisions did not include being interested in, or even noticing, what interested his family.

One of the great joys of accepting and valuing yourself is that you do not have to devote so much time to thinking about yourself. The same applies if you are simply acting *as if* you are acceptable and valuable. You have time for other things, and that means getting to know other people.

When you are lonely you long for someone to cross the barrier of your loneliness and take away your pain. You day-dream about someone rescuing you, like the prince who rescued Snow White, giving you love and admiration and carrying you off to live together happily ever after. Unfortunately, Prince Charmings – or the equivalent of whom you dream – are always in short supply. There are many, many people who would be willing to be your friend but they cannot take your loneliness from you.

The only person who is going to take your loneliness away is yourself.

And this is what you do. You make twelve decisions, and carry them out.

Twelve Decisions

1. Because I accept and value myself, I will end my loneliness.

It is necessary to make a conscious decision and a vow, because otherwise you will waver, going back to your old way of thinking that you are so bad and valueless that you do not deserve to have friends. If you keep forgetting this vow, write it down and pin it on your bathroom mirror or above the kitchen sink where you can see it every day.

2. I shall take the risk and approach other people.

Remember that people are not as dangerous as you fear. You were in danger from adults when you were a child, but *you are not in danger now*.

The majority of people mean well. There are very, very few people who actually and consistently want to destroy, damage and hurt other people. Of course we all, from time to time, get so frustrated and angry that we feel like destroying, damaging, and hurting the people who have frustrated us, but the majority of us try not to express these feelings destructively against the person we momentarily hate. Despite what the sensation-seeking media tell us about the crime rate, the vast majority of crimes of physical violence occur among people who know one another well. Murder, like incest, is a family affair. We are usually safe among strangers.

The majority of people mean well. Of course we often don't understand one another. We get irritated with one another, ignore one another, are impolite to one another, but, on the whole, we mean well. We all try to be helpful, we try to be generous. We don't always manage to give the right kind of help or the kind of supplies that people need, but at least we try.

Remember that when you insist on seeing a person as being frightening, you put that person in an awkward position from which there is no escape.

Over the years I have, in different situations, been told that I frighten certain other people. When I was a teenager attending a Methodist Fellowship, my friend Betty told me that I frightened the boys because I used long words and knew too much. Twenty years later I was told I was frightening the men psychiatrists for the same reason, and ten years after that I was told I was having the same effect on the men administrators. By then I knew how to deal with my clients' fear of me – we discuss it – but the men I was reported to be frightening would not enter into any discussion, because that would involve them in acknowledging that they sometimes felt inadequate.

So I was left being well aware that I was the victim of the 'she's a ferocious woman' ploy which men use to shut women up, and also feeling helpless, being cut off by their fear of me and unable to convey that, while I was critical of them, I wished them well. I thought they were stupid to be frightened of my expertise instead of making use of it, but, so long as they insisted on being frightened of me and not discussing this with me, there was no way I could bridge the gap between us.

So, when you decide to risk approaching other people, be it accepting your neighbour's invitation to a party, or joining a social club, or taking up a sport, or being involved in a charity, or joining a self-help group, don't make people helpless to welcome you by being frightened of them.

Don't pretend to be confident in social situations if you don't feel confident. It is much better to say to people things like, 'I feel nervous,' or, 'I haven't done this before'. People, knowing that you are frightened, will do whatever they can to make you feel less frightened. They usually do this by saying things like, 'There's nothing here to be frightened of', or 'I'm frightened too'.

Risking approaching people is always worth it.

However, there is something more you need to say to yourself.

3. I don't expect instant results, or results commensurate with the effort I have made.

One of the mistakes which friends and relatives of a depressed person, and people learning to be therapists and counsellors, often make is to feel that:

a) I have given this person my time and attention. Why isn't he better *now*?

and

b) I have given this person X amount of my time and attention. Why doesn't he show Y amount of improvement?

You can make two similar mistakes. You can think:

a) I have given this person my time and attention. Why isn't he close friends with me *now*?

and

b) I have given this person X amount of my time and attention. Why doesn't he show me Y amount of close friendship?

and you can think:

a) I have given this person my time and attention. Why haven't I stopped being lonely *now*?

and

b) I have given this person X amount of my time and attention. Why aren't I Y amount less lonely?

It takes people quite a long while to get to know one another, so you need to be patient with other people. It will take you quite a long time to give up the habits of loneliness.

In getting to know people you need to take into account how every society has its rules and practices about meeting and making friends.

Australians and Americans are always astounded at the reserve of the English. There are people in England whom I regard as close friends and whom I have known for nearly twenty years, yet I have never been invited to their homes. Whereas I am quite used to Americans whom I know only by letter inviting me to their homes, and I never hesitate, when I plan a trip to the States, just to write to friends there and announce that I am coming to stay. Similarly, when my American and Australian friends come to England, we take for granted that they will stay with me.

Australians and Americans, of course, take our friendliness and hospitality as proof of our superior virtue, but actually it is a result of our history. In the wilderness and emptiness of these two vast continents, the early settlers had to make every traveller welcome, whether stranger or friend, so that when they themselves travelled the same hospitality would be given to them. Travellers brought news and excitement to a monotonous and lonely existence. Such habits of friendliness and hospitality persisted over the years and became a national style. So Americans will greet you by your first name, and Australians feed you at any time of the day or night, as if you have been travelling without food for weeks through the empty bush. Never mind that you've just popped in from next door.

Although the customs of hospitality are different in different places, there is one thing which is the same everywhere. Close friendship takes time to grow. We need time to get to know one another. We need to listen to one another's stories and share experiences together.

Friendship is not just a matter of another person being interested in you. It is, most importantly, you being interested in the other person.

4. I will be interested in other people.

The best gift we can give to anyone is to be interested in that person.

Being interested means taking the other person seriously. The other person's concerns become your concerns. When you talk or think about the other person you don't say, 'Wouldn't you think she's . . . ?', in the way that we do when we want to criticize. You accept what the other person says and does, and if you don't understand why you try to find out.

Being interested means remembering things about that person, not just the obvious things, like names and addresses, but little things, like if they have milk and sugar in their coffee, or if they have a passion for old movies. You know how, when someone remembers those little things about you, you feel that that person has really noticed you and cares about you.

However, to learn about another person we have to listen, to notice, and to ask good questions. These are skills which we can learn.

5. I will improve my skills in listening and asking questions.

I am often asked by local mental health associations to give a short talk at their annual general meetings. These associations are not paternalistic charities which do good to poor unfortunates, but are co-operative enterprises between people who are concerned about mental health and people who have been at the receiving end of the psychiatric system and who call themselves 'users' and 'survivors'.

At one such AGM, I mentioned in my talk some of the short-comings of the local psychiatric hospital, and this caused a stir amongst some of my listeners who knew the place better than I did. I paused in my talk to discuss with one man some of the points which I had made, or, rather, for him to tell me, at some length, that I was right.

I was finding this talk rather difficult. The business meeting had gone on for much longer than had been programmed, so I had not only to say something interesting but to say it quickly and not go over time. It was a very hot evening and I had neglected to get myself a glass of water. By the time I had finished my talk and answered some questions, I was desperately in need of water. I actually felt quite ill.

I could see at the back of the hall a table set with cool drinks, but before I could move towards it, the man who had spoken to me blocked my path and began to elaborate on what he had previously said.

As soon as I realized that this was going to be a long conversation, I said, 'Look, I've just got to get myself some water. I'm gasping. Come with me.'

He followed me a little way, still talking. Then I found my path blocked by people standing in the aisle. The man went on talking, and I felt increasingly desperate. My desperation meant that I was not listening to anything he was saying.

Yet, had he noticed what was happening to me, he could have got me a glass of orange juice and assured himself of my undivided attention for the rest of the evening.

Being involved in our own concerns can become such a habit that we lose, or fail to acquire, the simplest of skills in communication.

The first skill is simply noticing what is happening to the person we are talking to. Even when we are not saying, 'I'm tired', or 'I'm worried', or whatever, we show what we are feeling by the expression on our face and the posture we adopt. We all know how to read the signs. It is just that some of us do not bother because we are not interested in the other person.

The next skill is *listening*.

Listening is more than hearing. In hearing another person we are simply waiting for that person to pause so we can talk, preferably about ourselves. In listening to another person we concentrate upon what the person is saying, we think about what the person is saying, and we speak only when what the person is saying suggests that it is appropriate that we say something. What we say then reflects what the other person has been saying.

In listening we ask questions so as to make sure that we are understanding the other person. We ask about the details of the story the person is telling us, and, most important, we find out what the story means to the person telling it. We ask, *'How do you feel about that?'*

In listening we do talk about ourselves, but not in the way we do when we are merely hearing.

In a conversation where we are merely hearing we talk about ourselves because we find ourselves more interesting than the person we are talking to, or because we want to be the centre of attention, or because we want to belittle the other person, or to make the other person feel envious of us. In a conversation where we are listening we talk about ourselves so as to draw closer to the other person. We want to show that we can share our experiences, but we *never* say, 'I know exactly how you feel'. Nobody can ever know *exactly* how another person feels. We share our experiences so that the other person will not be alone, so that the other person will feel braver, more hopeful and happier.

Sometimes, in listening and sharing, we feel sad together, and, more often, we laugh together.

In learning to listen we need to improve one important skill.

6. I will become skilled in seeing things from the other person's point of view.

Seeing things from the other person's point of view does not mean being in the other person's situation and seeing it in the way we see things, as we do when we say, 'If I were him, I would . . .'

Seeing things from the other person's point of view means thinking and imagining. It means asking ourselves questions and searching for an answer.

So, if we are trying to understand why a two-year-old has temper tantrums, we need to ask ourselves, 'What does it feel like to be only two feet high in a world of giants?' If we are trying to understand why a mother of three small children is always tired and dispirited, we need to ask ourselves, 'What does it feel like to be surrounded all day by people only two feet high?'

When we are trying to see things from another person's point of view we need to remember that, while we all draw conclusions from our experiences, very rarely do we all draw the same conclusions. Very often, when we tell ourselves we know what other people think, we are only confirming our own point of view.

On the afternoon when Caroline discovered my front garden, as we sat there she told me that for the past few weeks she had been feeling quite low and withdrawn. She had been doing some painting but she found it difficult to visit friends because when she was with people she did not want to talk and would find herself drifting off into her own thoughts. At home alone she wearied of her own company, but she was sure that her friends did not want to see her when she was such bad company.

I questioned whether she was actually seeing things from her friends' points of view. They had known her for a long time and cared about her. Surely they did not expect that she would be cheerful and talkative all the time? Wouldn't they want to do what they could do comfort her?

Caroline considered this and, while she knew it was true, she was reluctant to accept it. She had decided that she knew what her friends thought because then she could justify to herself what she was doing. When she wanted to withdraw into herself, thinking about her painting, exploring her own fantasies, not bothering to make the effort to get up and go out, she could justify doing this by saying to herself, 'My friends don't want to see me.'

The great attraction of telling ourselves that we know how other people see things without making the effort to check whether we are right is that we can claim that other people see things in ways which suit our purpose. If we tell ourselves that other people will reject us, we do not have to make the effort to meet people and get to know them. If we tell ourselves that other people will find us boring, we do not have to make the effort to talk to people.

Whereas if we make the effort to discover how other people see things, we find that they have drawn conclusions different from our own, and this can be very unsettling. But if we do not discover what these different conclusions are we shall be amazed and discomforted when we discover that people behave differently from what we expect. We are all the more amazed and discomforted because we so often forget that *all* actions have consequences.

7. I will try to improve my understanding of the consequences of my behaviour.

Nigel discovered that his eight-year-old son was stealing money from his mother's purse and spending it on sweets. Nigel said to me, 'I gave him a good hiding and told him I'd give him an even bigger one if ever I caught him stealing again.'

Three weeks later a policewoman called at Nigel's home. She said that Simon had been caught stealing sweets from the supermarket. She also said that she had had a quiet talk with Simon and he had told her that he was being bullied at school and had to buy the bullies off with sweets. When he could no longer use his mother's money to do this he had to steal sweets from the supermarket.

Nigel's thinking had been simple. 'Simon is doing something I don't like. I shall punish him. That will stop him stealing, and that will be the end of the matter.' He based this on the simple but erroneous notion that punishment stops people from committing crimes. If that were the case our jails would be empty.

Nigel had not tried to find out how Simon saw the situation. Instead he acted, and the consequences of his action were very different from what he expected. Simon not only stole again, but in much more serious circumstances. Moreover, he showed that, while there were people he feared more than he feared his father, he certainly did not trust his father. The conclusion that he had drawn about his father before he began to steal was that he could not expect his father to protect him and to be loyal to him.

All acts have consequences and they are usually different from what we expect.

Because we can so often grow up without acquiring or developing the skills in perceiving other people's points of view and without understanding that all acts have consequences, we fail to foresee the consequences of our actions.

Janet called to tell me that she and her boyfriend Gavin had split up. I wasn't sorry. I hadn't met Gavin, but from what she had told me about him I thought he didn't deserve such a fine woman as Janet. It sounded to me that he had manufactured the fight in order to end the relationship. I didn't say this to Janet because she was very upset and was now regretting that they had parted. She had been up all night, crying and pacing around, sick with anger and fear.

About midnight, she decided to phone Gavin to apologize. She would take all the blame and they could get together again. He did not answer the phone. She said to me, 'I knew he was there. So I just kept phoning every half hour or so and letting it ring. I thought, "If I'm here suffering, why shouldn't he?" After a while he disconnected the phone.'

I thought, but did not say, that she had given Gavin the justification he wanted for leaving her. Now he could say to their friends, 'Look at what that crazy woman has done to me,' and they might well sympathize with him rather than with her. Of course, like all of us, she wanted to have her cake and eat it too. She wanted to express her rage against Gavin and to have him love her, want her, and come back to her. She was expecting Gavin to accept her rage and herself, and this was something he was not likely to do.

In the situation where we want to have our cake and eat it too we can always try to get both, but we need to remember that in trying to get both we may lose both. It is always a good idea to know which is more important, having your cake or eating it, so that when we have to choose we can make the better choice.

Of course, in the heat of the moment, it is often hard to stop and think about the consequences of our actions. But, nevertheless, if you are to improve your skills in understanding and predicting people in order to end your loneliness, working out the consequences of what you and others do is tremendously important.

It is not enough just to work out the consequences. You need, too, to work out more flexible ways of dealing with the consequences, especially when the consequence is anger.

8. I will be more accepting of other people's anger and not always take it personally.

Anger is not the end of the world. Anger is just a storm which soon blows over.

Of course, when you were a child anger did seem to mean the end of the world, perhaps, the end of your life. Have you, as an adult, noticed how often even kind and loving parents will say to their children, 'If you do that again I'll murder you!' All children fear that their parents will kill them, because they know that if the parents are strong enough to protect them they are strong enough to harm them.

So we all, in adult life, have to improve our skills in expressing our own anger and in dealing with other people's anger.

Again it is a question of improving our skills in understanding other people's points of view and in predicting the consequences of our actions.

Very often, when we do understand the other person's point of view, we can see that the person's anger, though expressed against us, actually has very little to do with us. We just happen to be a convenient focus for anger which has been aroused by other people and situations. When we were small children we did not have the knowledge and experience to realize that when our mother was angry with us it was not because we were wicked but because she was anxious and sick. We knew nothing of the strains of marriage and the pain of the menstrual cycle. Once we acquire knowledge and experience we should be able to identify when we are not the cause of the anger being expressed against us. (If you operate on the principle 'Everybody hates me' you will not be able to distinguish when you are the cause of someone's wrath and when you are being unjustly attacked.)

Once we do identify this, we can then choose to express our fear by withdrawing from that person, or our pride by getting angry with the person who is angry with us, or we can choose to ignore that the person is angry and just behave normally, or we can choose to treat the person in the way we would treat him if he were sick, that is, we take what he is saying seriously but we remain calm.

Different situations call for different responses, and so you need to work out what the consequences of your choice will be.   (D 44)

Where you are both the focus and the cause of the person's anger you will need to find responses other than cutting yourself off from that person, for doing that simply reinforces your barrier of loneliness. It is best to try to find the courage to confront the person and to discuss the matter, but remember that most people are very unskilled in handling anger and the person who is angry with you may be too frightened of you to confront you and to enter into a discussion. In such cases writing a letter can be very helpful.

You need to examine your beliefs about making an apology. As children many of us were so humiliated whenever we apologized or were forced to apologize that we still see apologizing as a humiliating experience. We can believe that to apologize is to be diminished and demeaned. If this is what you feel you will need to think about this carefully.

When we see ourselves as being trapped, weak, worthless, and helpless, making an apology to our victors seems frightening and humiliating. When we see ourselves as being free, strong, valuable and confident, making an apology to those we have injured seems gracious and creative, allowing a relationship to be resumed and (D 45) **strengthened.**

Often in social situations we suspect that a person is angry with us and dislikes us, but he does not say so. He simply teases us.

Is all teasing malicious, or are there two kinds of teasing, malicious and friendly?

If anything shows how childhood experience stays with us, it is in our response to teasing.

Many of us grew up in families where everything was taken two thousand per cent seriously. People did not make jokes about one another. Criticism and anger were expressed directly or hidden behind dangerous silences. No one laughed at anyone, and if anyone seemed to be laughing at another person, that person got angry or withdrew in offended silence. There might be jokes about the dog, or people outside the family, but inside the family there were no jokes and certainly no teasing.

If you grew up in such a family you will remember how devastating it was when you went to school and the other children teased you. Because you were inexperienced in the techniques of teasing, you always rose to the bait and you never turned the tables on the children teasing you. So they teased you all the more. You grew up believing that all teasing was malicious and when, in adult relationships, someone teased you, you reacted with fear and anger.

Yet many people tease as a way of showing their love and increasing the sum of happiness.

My son needs spectacles for driving and had bought himself some very expensive prescription sunglasses made with those black, shiny lenses which hide the wearer's eyes completely and appear to the onlooker as a mirror. When I first saw him put them on I exclaimed, 'Tonton Macoute specs!' Edward laughed, greatly pleased. He knew that my comment was not a criticism but a tease, where the joke is the association of him, the gentlest and most open of people, with the sinister henchmen of Papa Doc in Haiti.

The purpose of friendly teasing is to give the person being teased the sense of being special. We each want to feel that we are an individual, different from everyone else, and different in ways in which we can take pleasure and pride. We can believe this about ourselves, but we need other people to confirm it. Friendly teasing is one excellent way of giving confirmation to one another.

We can laugh at one another in hate and bitter rejection. We can laugh at one another in love.

If you don't believe this, think of how we laugh at small children. Their quaintness and innocence arouse in us a sense of surprise, wonder and tenderness, and to express this we laugh at them in love.   (D 46)

Being able to distinguish friendly teasing from malicious teasing is an essential skill in getting along with other people. This is part of the skill of distinguishing real and imaginary enemies.

9. I will improve my skills in distinguishing real and imaginary enemies.

Never in the history of the human race has it been more necessary for us to make this distinction, because unless we create effective ways of co-operating we shall not be able to carry out the measures necessary to repair the damage to our planet caused by our greed and our violence to one another.

An enemy is a person who is engaged in, or wishes to engage in, harming us in some way. We all have enemies because we are all the victims of those people who are wasting and destroying the resources of the planet on which we all depend. We all have enemies because we are all members of some political, national, religious, racial, gender group which some other group hates and wishes to destroy. Here I am, as nice and friendly a person as you could ever wish to meet but, because I am white, non-religious and female, I have enemies. Many black people hate white people. To Muslims I am an infidel. There are many men who hate women. So I need to be careful.

However, if I meet a black Muslim man I would be quite wrong to assume that he, as an individual, is my enemy. The fact that we belong to a group does not mean that we share all the beliefs of that group. If I assume that all black Muslim men hate me, when I meet one such person I shall behave in such a defensive, hostile way that he will be discomfited, and, since we all dislike people who make us feel uncomfortable, he will dislike me and perhaps become my enemy. We can turn people into enemies simply by being frightened of them.

Sometimes the people we see as enemies are members of a group which we have created in our own mind.

> My mother was thirty-two when I was born, so by the time I was in my teens she was quite middle-aged. I attended a girls' high school where discipline was strict and the standards of scholarship extremely high. All the teachers seemed to me to be as old as my mother, and just as constantly critical as she was. I was frightened of my teachers, just as I was frightened of my mother.
>
> I generalized this fear to all middle-aged women. I assumed without thinking about it that every middle-aged women would disapprove of me. I could not conceive that a middle-aged woman could actually like me and want to be my friend. In my twenties, when I was teaching, this assumption caused me endless, unnecessary problems and hurt a number of innocent women who, had I the sense to realize it, were well disposed towards me.
>
> Had I carried this assumption into my own middle-age I would have become one of those woman who hates herself because she is so like her mother. Fortunately, in my thirties, I became involved in psychoanalysis and I saw that my enemy was a fiction of my own creating. Now I see middle-aged women as endlessly interesting and, with one or two exceptions, fellow conspirators against the wickedness and stupidity of the world.

(D 47)

To distinguish real from imaginary enemies it is necessary to look at individual people, not at a group, to discover that person's own point of view, and to take that point of view seriously, even though it may not accord with your own.

When you discover that someone you thought was an enemy is not an enemy, it is necessary to go through some process of reconciliation. Here you are likely to discover that you lack one essential skill. You know how to give. You do not know how to receive.

10. I will learn how to receive generously.

When you became an expert on being good, you learned how to give, and you do this very well. But when someone gave you something you were in trouble. You felt that you did not deserve the gift, and so the gift became a threat. To get rid of the threat you gave something back to the giver. Moreover, you feared that the gift put you under an obligation to the giver. Would what you gave back be sufficient to remove the obligation? This sense of obligation could make you angry with the giver.

Unfortunately, many of us have relatives and friends who never give a free gift. All their gifts come with the unstated message, 'Because I have given you this, you must do and be what I want'. In becoming an expert in being good you also became an expert in guilt, and so you respond to such an unstated message in just the way your relatives and friends want. In fact, you can hear that message even when it is not intended and react with guilt and obligation to every gift.

In learning to receive generously, again you must investigate the point of view of the person giving you the gift and determine whether the gift does come with the unstated message of obligation or whether it is a free gift given out of love and concern.

If you determine that the gift does come with the unstated message of obligation you then have three choices.

1. You can accept the gift as you always have, and feel guilt, anger and obligation.

2. You can state the unstated message to the giver and say that you cannot accept such a gift. To do this you must have completely abandoned your belief that you must never upset anyone ever and have developed some competence in dealing with upset people.

3. You can accept the gift as if it is a free gift, ignore the obligation, feel happy and enjoy the gift. To do this you must have given up being an expert in being good and have developed a competence in doing things which are not wholly admirable but are immensely enjoyable.

If you determine that the gift does come as a free gift, given out of love and concern, then you must receive it with the same generosity with which it was given. Let yourself feel joy, not guilt. Don't say,

'Oh, you shouldn't have.' Say, 'It's wonderful. I love it', and give the giver a hug and a kiss. All we want when we give a free gift is to see the other person's happiness.

(D 48)

Sometimes what gets in the way when we want to enjoy a gift is our envy.

11. I will let go of envy and allow myself to be sad.

As we sat in the garden Caroline apologized to me for still getting depressed. She always did this, no matter what I said, for she still believed that all gifts come with obligations, and, if I spend time with her, she should meet her obligation to me by becoming happy and hard working. Yet Caroline had many things in her life, including little money and indifferent health, which were not conducive to happiness, and even more things from her past which left a legacy of sadness.

Caroline spoke of how much her father had changed with the birth of his first grandchild. 'He thinks she's just wonderful,' Caroline said. 'He makes a tremendous fuss of her. Not like he was with me.' She sounded very pleased when she said this, pleased that gentleness and warmth had come where harshness and coldness had been.

'But it's difficult for you,' I said. 'If he was treating your niece the way he treated you, you'd be very upset. When you see him being loving to her, you can't but help ask yourself why he couldn't have been like this with you. And that must make you very sad.'

Caroline could have protected herself from this sadness by being envious of her niece. She could have said to herself, 'Why should she have what I was denied?' and used her envy, anger and resentment to hide her sadness from herself. But she loved her niece too much to feel such unpleasant emotions about her, and so she was left feeling sad.

Actually, envy is only possible when we distance ourselves from people. Once we get close to other people and discover their points of view, we discover also that *all* people have their own troubles. Every advantage in life has its own disadvantages. Envying people is a waste of time. And time runs out for all of us. Even if we never wasted time being frightened, angry, envious, lonely and depressed, we still could not fit into a lifetime all the marvellous things we could do.

However, once we set aside the defence of envy, we discover a well of sadness – all the lost opportunities, the failed hopes, the might-have-beens, the wasted time. We may be wise enough not to add to the sadness the anger, hate and resentment of pride ('How dare this happen to *me*!'), paranoia ('Somebody is always out to get me!') and guilt ('I deserve to suffer!'), but recognize that we should not take ill-fortune personally. Yet that still leaves the sadness.

The best way to live with sadness is to share it.

12. I will learn to share my sadness with others and to share their sadness.

Relentless cheerfulness is a bar to friendship. We hide behind it, fearing that if other people see our sadness they will reject us. Hiding behind relentless cheerfulness, we ignore the sadness which others feel.

Sharing our sadness means, sometimes, crying and letting ourselves be seen to cry, and accepting the other person's tears. Sometimes it just means a hug, or a hand held, a meal shared, a kindness exchanged. Sometimes it means uproarious laughter, as we see in our troubles and sadness the essential ridiculousness of human endeavour.

To do this, we need to give up the pride we took in our suffering and accept the universality of pain. In sharing sadness we recognize how unique we each are and yet how much the same and how splendidly ordinary we are.

One of the great paradoxes of human life is that, in the way that we are born and die and in between create our own unique world of meaning, we are always alone, yet the only way that we can live with this essential aloneness is to share our life with other people.

The way to leave loneliness behind is to learn to be alone and to share our lives with other people.

The next chapter is about some people who did just that.

17

Helping One Another

In 1987, Dartford Mental Health Association (MIND) invited me to give an evening lecture about depression. Denise Askham organized the lecture and, as she told me, it was the first time she had done such a thing and she felt nervous.

When I arrived I found that the lecture was being held in a college which was in a suburban part of Dartford. I thought the place was a little out of the way and the hall, a vast area with a stage, was far too large, but I was wrong. Nearly two hundred people came to that lecture.

As usual, I talked for about thirty minutes and then invited questions. This was not easy as there were so many people and the hall was so large. However, we managed somehow, and, in the course of the discussion, I said what I had so often said, that the best way depressed people can help themselves is to help one another. Form a group, get to know one another, support one another.

Just setting up the group and deciding how to organize it – where and when to meet, how to finance rent and refreshments – requires acting as if you can make decisions and get things done. Going along to the group means acting as if you have the courage to meet people and do something new. Mixing with other people means acting as if you are not frightened of other people and that there is no barrier of loneliness and depression between them and you.

And, of course, acting *as if* you can do and be all these things, you discover that you really can.

So, as usual, this is what I said.

Two years later Dartford MIND invited me to give another lecture. From the letter of invitation I learned that at the end of my lecture a group of people had decided to get together, and that the group had been very successful.

Denise had offered to help the group to find a place to meet, to contact other people who might like to join, and act as a (completely inexperienced) group leader. So I wrote to her to ask if she thought some of the people in the group would care to write to me about the group and say how, if at all, being in the group had helped them.

Denise wrote back to say:

'This was my first involvement with setting-up and running a group and I've found the experience deeply satisfying. People often told me how fascinating group work was but I never fully realized it until I was bang in the middle of it. Not only have I watched the members grow but I have too, and have learnt so much about myself.

'The group gelled together so much quicker than I had envisaged and only one person left, after a couple of weeks. The rest have been together since September, meeting weekly.

'We are at the stage now where most people are keenly trying out their newly found Assertiveness and we hope to spend time maintaining these new skills in the last couple of months of the group.

'I guess the letters speak for themselves and, for my part, I look forward to the next group with enthusiasm and a knowledge that for many they do "work".'

Cathy wrote:

'Belonging to a group has helped me gain confidence. Just knowing the other members of the group have similar problems binds us together, and I feel I am supported, which is something I need. People who don't suffer with depression fail to understand it, but fellow sufferers are sympathetic towards each other.'

Don said:

'Having suffered from depression since the mid 60s, and then, two years ago, being diagnosed as having cancer, of which I am now cured, I decided enough was enough. When Denise asked me to join her support group, I felt at last help was at hand. I find the group offers a form of psychotherapy whereby we can discuss our problems and receive helpful advice. You can also draw on one another's experiences. I find the chats on various topics, ie, assertion, very beneficial and have since found myself being more assertive in everyday life. It is, in fact, comforting to realize that you are not the only one suffering and I only wish there had been support groups years ago.'

Shirley said:

'After many years of anxiety and depression for various reasons and repeat prescription for Ativan for thirteen years, I have at last found my salvation – a group run by Denise of MIND.

'After several attempts to come off Ativan myself and failing, and several attempts to destroy myself, I was admitted to hospital. Once on the mend I again decided to make the effort to come off the Ativan. With the help of the hospital and the support of my family, I finally made it and took my last tablet four months ago.

'Although the hospital treatment and family help was absolutely marvellous, I know that if I had had to continue alone, I would not have made it. It was knowing that I had my weekly meeting with MIND to come to. To talk and express feelings and share experiences with people who have gone through, or who are still in, the same boat.

'We all have become great friends and know that we could turn to one another if help was needed, but, most of all, we know that Denise and MIND will always be there to talk to and help. I must emphasize the word "help", as to try and go alone or pull oneself together as was once suggested to me by a doctor is an impossibility.

'Thank you to the friends I have made at my group meeting, but most of all thank you MIND. Life is now once more worth living.'

Kath wrote:

'When the group took off everybody seemed to be able to chat and discuss things much more easily than me, I found this very hard to do, but as Denise explained to us, some people are better listeners than talkers. As time has gone by, I now feel more confident and comfortable, and the fact that I was not pressured at any time to talk was appreciated.

'As the weekly meetings have gone on, I feel, as I am sure other members of the group do, that we are good friends now, and not just members of a group. There is a great sense of trust, respect, understanding and, above all, caring, that we all seem to share. That alone, I think, proves the success of our group.

'Another important fact is that we give each other time at our meetings. If a member is feeling low or has had a problem, we take time to listen and talk. Even if that problem cannot be solved, it's just the sense of relief that one feels just knowing that others can relate to how you are feeling. I think the relationship that is shared now by us all would help us to help each other in any situation.

'Since joining the group, I've realized that it's the most positive and best thing I've done since giving up my job! I feel so much better these days, and what's so good is that we can all see an improvement in each other, and that's what it's all about.

'I'm sure many sufferers could find a lot of comfort and support by coming into a group as I've done, to help beat the terrible loneliness which is felt by many and find lasting friendship with lovely people.'

Jenny wrote:

'At first I didn't think group therapy would help me at all, as I am not used to showing my feelings. However, over the months, we have all got to know each other very well and what I have found most helpful is that everyone listens. We all have our own set of problems, but we share them with each other and, in doing so, I am sure we help ourselves.

'Some weeks ago, I did think I wasn't getting anywhere, but suddenly it's come to me that I have more confidence and actually find myself laughing a lot, whereas before everything looked so bad. I've still got the same problems but view them in a more optimistic light.

'I think that, as a group, it has worked very well and we have all become good friends. It's quite something to be able to talk to another person and actually know they are listening and not to see in their eyes that glazed look of disinterest.'

Sally told me more about herself:

'I was sexually abused by my neighbour from about the age of four, and learned from *Beyond Fear* that children often blame themselves for adults' behaviour and began to understand why I had allowed myself to be a victim all my life. I thought that I was very ugly and stupid, was bullied by the other children and had difficulty in making friends. Once I met my husband and started a sexual relationship with him I developed obsessional neurosis and became remarkably similar to 'George' in chapter

7 of *Beyond Fear*. I don't think that I hated anyone, but I think that I accepted the blame for my abuse and whenever I felt angry with anyone, I felt guilty about it and turned my anger in on myself, thus contributing to my obsessional behaviour and depression.

'When the group started, it was at first exciting and a wonderful relief to share with the others the experience of my illness with no need for pretence. Although our illnesses had different names, it appeared that my feelings and difficulties in my relationships with others were very similar to the others in the group. It became clear that some of us had allowed other people to take advantage of us and transfer their own problems, including emotional ones, on to us, and that we had dealt with this by turning our anger in on ourselves out of guilt, thus resulting in illness.

'Over the months we came to realize that unless we talk through our grievances with those who have aggrieved us, communication can break down, and we can spend years living a lie, often with the closest members of our families, and misunderstandings remain unresolved, sometimes on both sides.

'We have learned about assertiveness from Denise, and some group members have begun to put this into action; I have yet to do so. Most of the group members have improved by leaps and bounds, which has encouraged me. I have learned a lot just by watching the new approaches the others have had to themselves and other people. I think that the main benefit that I have gained from the group is the sheer relief of being able to talk more freely about myself, my anger and hurt and feeling less guilty about it, because I have learned that I can be angry with someone and still love them.

'The only difficulty I can see with a group situation is that there are sometimes items that I want to bring to the group but find that there is not the time. If we plan to bring the subject up next week, someone else then has something else that is more urgent and my problem is left. This is also the case with the others, which is one reason why the psychotherapy that I am also receiving is so invaluable.

'Once the group has officially ended, we hope to carry on meeting, as each other's support, friendship and honesty has been invaluable on our road to recovery.'

Lynne told me how she came to join the group. Some general practitioners, well aware of how useful talking to others is, can be quite ruthless in getting their patients to do so.

'It's ten years since I began taking antidepressants and tranquillizers for my depression; but when I think about it, I realize that it was a long time before then I experienced depression. For all those years I lived with the thought that I would never be released from my depressive state, and that prescribed medication was the only answer in trying to alleviate it.

'Last year, after seeing a new GP, it was suggested that I do more than take tablets for my unhappiness. He recommended that I seek therapy in order to discuss and assess my problems, and asked me to contact MIND. I had heard of the charity before, but never realized that they would be willing and able to help me. My GP insisted that I approach MIND myself, since if I really wanted to be well, I must initiate the action and genuinely want to get better. At this time I was hardly venturing from my room. I hated myself so greatly that I felt I wasn't worthy of living, and my thoughts continually led me to believe that to be released from my depression the answer was for me to die.

'Then one day, in the depths of despair, I summoned the courage to telephone MIND. Arrangements were made for me to attend an interview and consequently I was selected to join their Depression Support Group, starting in September.

'In the meantime, I was visited at home by the community psychiatric nurse, to talk with her about my problems, to find out their source and discover ways of coping with them, but I found these individual sessions so painful and traumatic that they opened the scar tissue of wounds I had forgotten I had. I didn't want anybody touching them, so I built a twenty-foot high wall around me so that the CPN could not reach me with only her ten-foot high ladder.

'My GP was dismayed that I refused for the CPN to attend any more and made me promise that I would begin the Depression Support Group meetings which were due to start shortly. Otherwise, he said, he would have no option but to hospitalize me and have ECT prescribed.

'His threat worked, in that I willingly attended the first group meeting, and to my surprise I saw the other members were just ordinary human beings like myself. They didn't have two heads nor had they labels across their foreheads proclaiming them as mentally ill. What they did have was what I had; a need to know that there are others like me, a need to feel that life is worth living, and an urge to see that eventually I will learn to cope with my problems. For the first time in a very long time, I knew that I wasn't going to be alone. It was as though someone had opened a window and I was letting myself free.

'As the meetings have continued, my twenty-foot high wall has been gradually reduced in height. Nobody needs a ladder to reach me any more. The group has accepted each member for what each of us is. We have a kind of respect for each other. We have come a long way on our journey, for the road to coping and recovery is winding and has its obstacles, but we have all fared well, we have braved the storms and found a hope that extends beyond tomorrow.

'We have shared our problems and experiences, our thoughts and feelings, our joys and sorrows, our hopes and fears, our laughter and tears. Being in a group has offered us security, it has given us a sense of belonging and the feeling of a new beginning. It is comforting to know that the journey will never have to be travelled alone, that there will always be someone there if ever you are set to fall, and to encourage and support you along the way.

'As to my medication; I no longer have antidepressants prescribed for my depression and my tranquillizers are being gradually reduced.'

The task which all of us in our adult life should carry out, if we are to regain and maintain our self-confidence and sense of self-worth, to cope with the crises and disappointments of adult life, and to face with equanimity our old age and death, is to come to terms with the fact that our parents were not perfect. For most of us this simply means relinquishing the prideful idea that we deserved Perfect Parents and looking at our parents with adult eyes, seeing them as ordinary, fallible human beings, and forgiving them for this. However, some of us had parents who were not merely fallible. They were wilful, selfish, careless and uncaring, and in no way could we describe them as 'foolish but well meaning'. With such parents, coming to terms with the fact that they were not perfect is very, very difficult.

How can you come to this kind of acceptance when you as a child have been the victim of sexual abuse and the adults who should have cared for you did not?

In a letter to me, Avril described what she had to contend with in her search to make sense of and end what was happening to her.

'New ideas about my life came to me . . . in particular a voice saying, "Is there any blood where there shouldn't be?", which seems to relate to early sexual abuse of which I became consciously aware five years ago, at the age of thirty-seven, and also, perhaps, to the distress I have felt as my periods have become heavier and heavier.

'Before my mother died she found some relief from pretence herself, and the gifts she gave me, although hard to bear, are not as hard as the unreality we tried to believe. She told me that she had wanted a boy, that I was "fat, red and overwhelming" and "like a little leech". And she told me about the abuse. It was awful. I felt corrupt and disgusting and betrayed. I have worked hard to come to terms with this and have sought, and found, much help. Through all my rage and grief, however, one thing is clear. I am not crazy. Crazy was when I remembered a man saying, "Go on, dear. Pretend it's a lollipop", and thought I had a morbid imagination. Crazy was when I dreamed of a man with broken glasses, grinning insanely behind a distorting window. (I learned that after the assault, he had fallen, perhaps pushed by my grandmother, from a first-floor window.) I am sure it will come as no surprise to you that I can now hear my nan saying, "Don't tell anyone, darling, or you'll get nanny into trouble." Or that I "remembered" nothing until she died. Or that she said, "Let's go and pick up the pieces", and that I now make stained glass windows. The fusion between my inner reality of fear and apparently unreasonable panics and the "actual reality" of true events which had been concealed even from my father came as a tremendous relief. Real-lief? Being given something of the truth was a gift of reality . . . very harsh, but preferable to comfortable lies.'

A child who has been sexually abused is left with a legacy not just of fear but of hate for the abuser. How can this hatred be exorcized? Talking about it is sometimes not enough.

Lisa Ball and Janice Costa work in a psychotherapy unit at Manchester. When they decided to set up a group for women who had, as children, been sexually abused, they incorporated into the programme of the group an ancient and popular custom for the disposal of hate – a ritual killing. This ritual killing would be of a large, lifesized doll representing the abuser.

It is important to remember that, while a group may be set up and run by one or two professional people, group leaders cannot make a group work. The success of the group depends not on the leaders, but on the way the people in the group come together as a group and support one another.

I asked Lisa and Janice if they would write me an account of the group and if they would ask other members of the group if they would write to me and tell me what they thought of the group.

Lisa and Janice wrote:

'The group is focal. A number of the women have had, or are still having, therapy for other problems (although these very likely stem from the abuse). We ask that they discontinue or suspend other forms of therapy while they attend the group, because we feel this would diffuse the issues.

'We use a variety of techniques, such as art therapy, psycho-drama, music, touch, talking and education. We focus on the wider abuse within the family and in society. Another issue is the removal of guilt from the victim on to the perpetrator. This inevitably leads us to anger, and from there to the view of self not as victims, but as survivors.

'There is also a lot of grief about the lack of childhood and the question: "Where was my mother?" As the women change, their perception of their family and others alters, which often leads to further loss and severance, but also to new and closer relationships, especially with their children.

'We introduce the doll when we feel the group is beginning to change from being a group of victims to a group of survivors, ie, from being passive to being active. This point comes at different times in the life of the different groups, so it is not predetermined by us when to bring the doll in.

'We also try to bring the doll in at a point when we feel the women have become less afraid of their own destructive power.

'The immediate effect of introducing the doll is that the women all recognize it as their abuser and this seems to render them just as powerless as they were when they were children.

'The doll is made of blankets, disposable sheets and Sellotape. It is very well made, so as to make it difficult to destroy. It is faceless and asexual, and larger than lifesize.

'Sometimes a woman will attack the doll on her own, but more often they have to encourage each other and be supported by one another and by the therapists.

'Inevitably, the death of the doll is painful, sadistic, prolonged and violent. This is followed by feelings of elation and satisfaction: "A Celebration", as some of the women said.

'Destruction is followed by sharing. In the first group we ran, the emasculated, maimed, shot, knived, burned and caged perpetrator was tried and condemned in court. He was condemned to live with pain, as the women have to. Afterwards, we all sat in a circle, holding hands, for a long time.

'In another group, the torture of the perpetrator was followed by ritual burning (eyes and genitalia last), while we all stood or danced in a circle around it.

'Typical feelings following on from this are the freeing of guilt and empowerment. It seems important that the therapists join in destruction of the doll. Perhaps it is permission to kill father, without losing mother.

'It may be significant that the majority of the women who have attended the groups we have run so far have chosen not to become or remain 'patients', but have decided to find a self-help group in Assertion Training or Self Defence. The third most popular option is the mixed analytic group, in the hope of learning to see men as people.

'We have to say that the women who come to the group and stay the course are survivors. We do not manage to reach the most damaged women, the ones who are abusing drugs or alcohol, or harming themselves in other ways. We find that, if we can get a woman to come and meet us, she usually decides she wants the group. But then quite a few drop out before the group begins.'

Lorraine wrote:

'Because of the affection and gratitude I feel for both Lisa and Janice, and because of the help I have myself received from reading, I will now try to recall some of my feelings, although this feels very difficult.

'When I was accepted for the group I was elated. The search had been a long hard one, taking some eighteen months from my initial realization that I needed some help. I was anxious and determined to make some changes in my life and vaguely understood that I had to learn and understand myself in order to do this. I had begun to read *Women Who Love Too Much*, *Father-Daughter Incest*, *A Woman in Your Own Right* and some novels, and was in a turmoil of change. Apart from one friend who lived in London, whom I was in telephone contact with, I had no one to share this turmoil with.

'When the group first met I was full of fear. I was sweating, feeling sick, slightly shaking. I felt that by being in the room with eight strangers, all there for presumably the same reason, that without saying a word, I had laid myself bare. It is difficult to describe that discomfort, but I was determined not to give up however bad I felt. I would have suffered anything in that room to make my life more healthy.

'The first few meetings were disturbing. People didn't turn up or were sometimes late, and some unable to speak at all, which made me feel unsafe, angry and sorrowful. But looking back, the trust and affection I felt grew quite rapidly and took me by surprise. These vulnerable, brave women; each time they spoke from the heart I felt as if they had given me a gift. There was a lot of fear about; particularly the fear of burdening other people with your problems, but it never felt like that. I so welcomed their honesty. I gained a tremendous respect for women. I didn't feel nearly so lonely, and I began to respect and listen to my feelings instead of hiding and denying them.

'Although I always felt anxious about the meetings, I noticed how I always drove to and from them like a "loony"; they were incredibly important to me. I somehow realized that the environment was safe and understood that I must work hard to make full use of the opportunity I had been given. If I hadn't been brave enough to say something I was determined not to allow fear to prevent me from speaking the following week.

'At some point, I began to look upon what was happening to me as a necessary journey. I was very aware of the time limit upon the group, which was twenty weeks. I knew what I wanted to achieve in that time. I also knew that when the group ended, I would need something else. That is, I didn't expect a miracle answer to all my problems within that time.

'Strangely, I feel as if I had been incredibly lucky. Logically, I don't believe in luck. I believe that people make their own lives what they are, but still I feel so lucky to have been involved in a group which gave me the opportunity, and incentive, to start to make changes in my life. To understand why I am sometimes so angry, why I have been so passive, why I have been so self-critical and self-destructive. Understanding why you feel as you do opens the gates for the even harder struggle of changing what you do.

'Attending the women's group allowed me to acknowledge the fear and pain I had inside me, to go on to express these feelings, not only to the group but to my abuser himself. With their help and support I was able to do this and soon afterwards was able to wake up in the morning feeling really happy to be alive. I didn't even realize that I hadn't felt that before. I would rate this as a gift, second only to the gift of the birth of my child.

'The strength that I found whilst attending that group made me feel brave and proud of myself. I came to understand that admitting you need help (far from being a weakness) takes courage. I respect that courage in myself and others.

'The group with all its different characters, at various ages and stages in their lives, represented the world to me. That world was loving and supportive. It changed my view of the wider world. It was almost as if I had had a loving family from the start while I didn't resent or fear the end of the twenty weeks, when it came. Once again, I feel lucky in that the next step in the necessary "journey" always seems apparent; whether it is a course or another group or another book.

'I had some very brief experience of one-to-one therapy, before attending the women's group. I honestly believe that were I still having individual therapy I would never have gained the self-knowledge and understanding of others that I gained so quickly from the group. I've still no idea why "the blind leading the blind" is so effective, but it is.

'I still have to deal with my situation as it is at present, but clearing away the past has somehow equipped me to attempt it with confidence.'

Christine expressed some reservations about the group:

'The group was, I found, geared much more to sexual problems themselves rather than to the effects of the depression on one's everyday life. I am personally not bothered about the male aspects of my life at the present time, but more in sorting out forty-odd years of mess caused by events early on in my life. The group therapy has helped me to distance myself up to a point from the events, but I still feel the same in a lot of ways and can't see myself being much different. I think it is something I shall have to deal with all of my life. This is where I found the depression coming back towards the end of the course. I felt no better in knowing how to deal with it, but it gave me more insight into the extent of all the damage done and the enormity of it all.

'One thing positive has come out of it, even though it is quite frightening really. It has enabled me to nudge my horizons and get my foot out of a rut that once again was threatening to engulf me.

'I have changed my job – so perhaps I will be able to change things eventually if I can gain personal confidence. I feel this is the key to the matter.

'As I say, the course was beneficial in some ways, but very off-putting in others. I think it all depends on how far on a person is in dealing with their own situation. I feel that a person has to be at a certain level of personal security to reap the benefits.'

Enid said:

'Going to the sexual abuse therapy group at Manchester Royal and meeting other women who had been abused was a new experience for me. It was talking about the abuse and it was understanding how they all felt and what they were going through. Also finding out that you all had the same feelings and thoughts about abuse, the abuser and sex.

'Being part of the group has made me understand what the group's aim is, which I think is a good thing, because you are able to meet women who have gone through the same experience. Knowing, also, that you are not alone, because when you read about abuse you feel such hatred for the abuser you go through all the emotions of the abused.

'The main thing for me was learning not to be ashamed of yourself inside, which isn't easy.'

Wendy wrote:

'I've decided to give you my personal feelings on therapy. The first few minutes of meeting each other, as we waited in the reception area of the day hospital, were nerve-racking but exciting. As we waited I felt very fearful inside because I just had no idea what would happen. I felt comforted by the fact that I already knew one of the therapists. We were all very different people and I think very brave. I imagined I might have to go through something even worse than the abuse I had suffered, like they might say, "take all your clothes off", but of course we didn't.

'We went into the room we would be using and there were chairs neatly and carefully set out in a circle – the exact number of seats for the women in the group. We weren't allowed to move these chairs in any way, which made me feel nervous. I also felt bare and unprotected because I didn't have a table in front of me to hide my lap. It was indeed a very tense first group. We played some games to try to help remember each other's names, which broke the ice a bit, and I think it broke the ice for the therapists as well.

'During the course of our time together, three people left the group, which out of eight left five, which was nice because I am able to cope better in smaller groups. I would say that I enjoyed creative groups the most because being creative myself I found it helped me express myself. I found that, unlike the two other younger girls, I didn't feel silly making things out of clay because I've used it in the past. I liked the feel of it, but found that I was a little inhibited by being watched by the therapists, who were pretending not to listen or watch, but I knew they were and I wished they had joined in.

'I enjoyed torturing a dummy, who I imagined to be my abuser, the best. God, he would have been killed a million times over from what I did to that dummy, which was him. Actually this was a special favourite time, because Lisa was with me (sitting close) and she was asking me what I was doing, and I was telling her and I enjoyed the closeness and it was a bit of a pretending and imaginative exercise.'

Patricia wrote:

'The group helped to give a feeling of support and understanding. We relied on one another a great deal. Lisa and Janice were very helpful in guiding us, but at first I felt that they were too gentle with us. I think they were afraid of pushing us too hard. But I do feel we would have achieved more in the allotted time if we had not been treated so gently. This is not a criticism of Lisa and Janice, it is just that I felt we needed more of a push.

'The feelings that came were very mixed. At times I was absolutely terrified of my reactions to things I realized I felt within myself. I was too afraid to let my feelings go in case I hurt someone. There was so much anger inside. It helped me to realize that other people (women) felt as I did. It gave you a feeling of togetherness, when before I felt I was alone.

'I can't say that I am cured and that I have given way to all my pent-up feelings, but I do show my anger more now. Sometimes I have felt that I haven't the same control over my anger as before, but maybe that is a good thing.

'One thing I found interesting is that none of us liked to have dirty hands. Did we feel soiled by past events? Also, when you enter one of these therapy groups you have to be totally committed to it or you are just wasting your own time and everyone else's. Also someone else could take your place.

'I do not feel guilty about hating my father now. Only sad that it should have come to that. Some fathers do things out of love for their children. Mine didn't. There was never any feeling of love in what he did, only threatening behaviour that gave him tremendous power over us. Maybe that was the thrill of it for him. Also the group makes you aware that it hasn't happened only to you and that other people have gone through much worse. You don't realize that that's possible. I feel I can live with my past now and not be ashamed in talking about it.'

Delia told me a good deal about her journey out of her prison. She shows how she found different therapists and different kinds of therapies useful at different times, and that not all therapies and therapists are useful.

'When I first set out on this road of self-discovery, I had all the naivety of a schoolgirl taking her first steps out into the big wide world.

'Looking back now, I can honestly say that, like most things, I discovered a mixture of both good and bad therapists. The more I talked and discovered about myself, the more determined I became to shed this victim skin. So from time to time, depending on how much courage I had, I would feel either positive determination or sheer terror.

'My career of therapy goes back some nine years, when

through bouts of extreme jealousy towards my partner and some alcohol abuse, I was referred to a clinical psychologist whose remedy lay in a short, sharp shock whenever I felt jealous. This took the form of an elastic band around my wrist with which I had to give myself a very hard and painful twang. Needless to say this method did not work.

'My next step was Gestalt therapy in 1982, where I was able to release some anger against my father. This was, in fact, the very first time I ever remember feeling good about myself (I was 34-years-old).

'Within this period I had remarried and had another son (I already had a nine-year-old boy from my first marriage), my relationships within the family were more strained and I was referred to Family Therapy by my doctor. Here I tried to work out the nuts and bolts of family life over a period of three years. This therapy was very helpful, as it was one-to-one and my husband accompanied me on several occasions.

'Looking back, I thought I was being realistic when, in fact, my reality was very negative (we actually taped one session and, when I listen to it now, I can hardly believe it's me talking). I feel saddened, as I recently heard that this particular therapy has ceased where I live, and I feel it is most helpful to women and men with young families.

'My next port of call was the Manchester Royal Infirmary in 1987, where I had individual therapy with a doctor. This did not work, as I felt a lack of the warmth and understanding I had previously experienced. After several weeks I managed to gain courage enough to express my feelings and I was referred to the Sexual Abuse Survivors Group which was starting in September. The most significant thing I got out of this group was the feeling of not being alone, and to actually hear other women echoing fears which I had felt for so long was very encouraging. So here I could acknowledge my own fears in a safe place. Although I can remember feeling very frightened and vulnerable a lot of the time, I also think I took on a slightly mothering role, as the rest of the group were a lot younger than I was.

'I also felt a great sense of loss when the group finished.

'I then requested some individual therapy to follow on from the group and was put on a waiting list. As time went on and I became more desperate, I went into private therapy with a women's group. Here I worked the hardest with a group of

women who supported each other and two therapists. One was
very gentle, the other more strict, so I tried to choose which one
to work with, depending on what I had in mind. In one session I
actually experienced sorrow, rage, anger and joy, all within the
space of three-quarters of an hour.

'That brings me up to date, as I am now doing some individual therapy at the psychotherapy unit where I am ex-
(D 49)   pressing a lot of my sorrow.

All the people whose words are reported here have one thing in
common. They all tried something new.

18

Trying Something New

We can think about our attitudes and beliefs and make all kinds of changes in our mind, but until we *act* we cannot be sure that what we are doing is nothing but day-dreaming, and that we are telling ourselves we have changed when we have not. This is why it is not enough to say over and over to yourself, 'I accept and value myself', and go on acting in all your usual ways which lead you to be lonely and depressed. Acting *as if* you are acceptable and valuable means doing something new.

Some of the new things you do on your journey out of the prison of depression will be pleasant and involve little risk. Some of the new things will be risky, for they will challenge your greatest fear.

Lynette, who had written to me about how the fear of death had haunted her all through her childhood, had experienced 'the feeling of total annihilation. It was like a giant wave coming to envelop me.' In her next letter to me Lynette said:

'The image of the great wave translated into a terrible fear of being engulfed by water – but I learned to swim and dive and after many panics I am learning to sail and the great wave has receded. Perhaps mental anguish can be overcome by translating a mental image into a physical one and attacking the latter.'

Sometimes the something new that needs to be done is to go back to the places where terrible events occurred. Many people in their journey out of depression go back to the scenes of their childhood. Then they can look with an adult's eye at the scenes which, in their memories, they see as a child. By putting these two perceptions side by side we can find a reconciling understanding.

Some people need to return to the places where, in their adult lives, their very self had been under the threat of annihilation. After the First and Second World Wars many service men and women returned to the battlefields, not just to pay their respects to their dead comrades, but to help themselves find peace and reconciliation.

Such healing journeys were not possible for the veterans of
Vietnam because Vietnam had not been accepted back into the
community of nations as Germany had been at the end of each
world war. So it was twenty years before veteran organizations
could arrange for some of their members to visit the scenes of the
fighting. By then, many people had recognized that such visits were
an important part of helping the veterans come to terms with their
experience of the war, and that such coming to terms was essential.
Since the war in Vietnam ended there has been a very high rate of
suicide among veterans and, while some 96,000 veterans have
sought treatment for what is now called Post Traumatic Stress
Disorder, it has been estimated that some eighty per cent of veterans
suffering in this way have not sought help.

One of the groups who went back to Vietnam was accompanied
by a BBC television team, and their work became the television film
Back to the Edge,[54] one of the *Everyman* series.

Joe La Fatch was one of the people in this group. He had gone as a
paratrooper to Vietnam in 1967, when he was eighteen, and was
wounded twice. He told why he had chosen to make the journey.

'I admitted to myself that I needed help. I actually did that a
while ago by talking to psychologists. I had a problem. I don't
know what life is supposed to be like, but I don't think it's what
it is for me. I was missing something and I wanted to straighten
that out. This is a continuation of that.'

Most of the soldiers who went to Vietnam had been conscripted
into the army. Joe had volunteered.

'There were two things very motivating to me. One was Presi-
dent Kennedy's speech when I was twelve or thirteen years old
– "Ask not what your country can do for you but what you can
do for your country". Also my personal feelings towards the
draft. I felt that it was very immoral, wrong, unfair. I didn't
want to excuse myself from having to come here, although
perhaps I could have gotten a student deferment. My parents
could have afforded to send me to school. It was putting
different values on human lives. Everybody wants to live. It's
like if your IQ's eighty we can afford to have you killed, and if
it's 130 you're more important and we want to preserve your
life. It was a class war in my opinion, the poor guys, the black
guys, the hillbillies, the gas station attendant's son fought in

Vietnam for the most part, I won't generalize, it's not true a hundred per cent, hardly anything is outside of mathematics. I guess I was going to select who my peers were going to be, and I'm glad it's those guys that I'm here with.'

At eighteen, Joe was a good man, kind, fair and just. In the film he told nothing of his childhood, but from what he had said we could guess that he had been taught as a child that the world is just and goodness is rewarded. In Vietnam, he discovered that this is not true. He said:

'There's no doubt about it, there's things that I see in my sleep, maybe about once a week. I don't have bad dreams every night, but I sure have one on a weekly basis. It was the death of a very close friend that I witnessed. He was point man. One day we were moving up a ridge line to the top of a hill. I was behind him in a position we call slack, and we were seeing a lot of signs of the NVA – trenches, cut down trees (they'd use the logs to make their bunkers) – you just knew they were there in their campsites, and I just sort of whispered to him, "Man, be careful. They're all over." He turned and gave me a little lopsided grin, and right at that time an NVA came out of a spider hole and shot him several times, right through the face. I saw the bullets going through and, yeah, well, I really thought a lot of the guy, and we helped each other through depression and exhaustion and we talked at night, and drank out of the same canteen and ate with the same plastic spoon, and shared your last little can of pork slices or whatever it took. What you needed I'd give to you, and what I needed you'd give to me. Brotherhood. And I was pretty devastated by that, and I got pretty nasty and mean after that, and I never wanted to feel that loss again. It put a barrier in, like, I'll work with you, and we'll help each other, but I don't want to be your friend. I don't want to know about your family or where you came from, or who you really are. We just help each other to survive and that's as close as it gets. I had never talked about it to anybody until now, and I guess, maybe, coming right out and saying it and admitting that it happened, ceasing to deny it may have been helpful in that regard.'

Now he knew what death is and what loss is, and he dealt with such loss in the way that most of us do, by resolving never to become attached again. Such protection cuts us off from other people, and this, for many of us, is our tragedy. But for Joe worse was to follow. His friend's death left him railing against the injustice of the world. Now he discovered that he himself was capable of such injustice.

The North Vietnamese army was able to carry out an ultimately successful guerrilla campaign because they constructed a maze of underground tunnels which went right under American lines. For the American troops finding and clearing these tunnels was their most hazardous operation. Joe described how he had to force himself to go down into these tunnels. On one such expedition he went into a bunker which was empty except for a bundle of rags cast aside in one corner. He moved on, heard a noise behind him, thought he was about to die, whirled around and emptied eight shots into the bundle of rags. Except it was not a bundle of rags, but a skinny old woman, 'just skin and bones. I shot the old lady and she died.'

Joe found, too, that he was not, as he had believed, a man of peace. One of his fellow soldiers was taken by the Vietcong, killed and hideously mutilated. He said, 'I'll never forgive or forget. I still sometimes get mad at the Vietnamese. I really liked that guy a lot.'

All this Joe had taken back home and kept to himself. Now, back in Vietnam, he could sit with his peers, as he called them, and talk.

'We've got an American expression when we're asked to go somewhere we don't really care for, the answer would be, "I don't want to go there, I didn't lose anything there." I did lose something here. I don't know what it was to put into words or how to explain it, but I guess that's why I'm here. I guess it was youth, innocence, or something like that. I didn't get to be like all the other boys and girls after this place. I was different. We all were, I think. Almost ostracized by our peers, although my peers are all here.'

Now he could let himself be held and hugged by two of his peers, as they assured him, 'No problem, man, no problem.'

At the end of the journey Joe could say:

'I don't have it constantly in my mind the way I used to. I'm not still hating enemy soldiers. They're not enemy soldiers any more. Maybe it was time to put that burden of hatred and resentment that lived way too long in my mind down. It looks like the old light at the end of the tunnel they used to talk about is starting to shine a little bit for me.'

One of the reasons I keep writing books is because people write to me and tell me that they find my books useful. This gives me great pleasure because it confirms my belief that I am better employed writing books than being a therapist. If you come and talk to me, you have to put up with me not always understanding you and some-times talking about matters which are completely irrelevant, where-as in reading my books you can concentrate on the parts that are relevant and ignore or argue with the rest. You can work at your own pace and by yourself or with other people as you choose.

Another pleasure I get from my readers' letters is that they contain the most wonderful stories, and being told stories while sitting in a garden is my idea of heaven.

Some readers write to me several times and tell me how the story of their life is developing. Alan did this, and he told me of the risk he had taken in confronting his greatest fear.

'You may remember that I wrote to you about being diagnosed as an alcoholic and then recognizing my depressive condition from your book *Depression: The Way Out of Your Prison*, after hearing you speak on a radio programme. What you said and wrote was immensely valuable to me and for a long while I tried to swap security for freedom.

'Looking back, I can see that I wasn't really prepared to reduce my demands for emotional security; I was still saying, "Look how I've given up drinking, look how good I'm being, now will you give me everything I want?" Yes – back in the same old prison, the "good" child demanding release from all pain and fear as the reward for being good, and when no such reward was forthcoming, I retaliated in the old childish way – tantrums and the bottle – "see what you're making me do".

'Inevitably, I lost my miraculous life-saver of a job and despite my subsequent return to sobriety, I lost my wife as well. I had always believed and feared that if she ever left me I would not survive. I would somehow fall apart, disintegrate into the useless mess that her leaving me implied. The night she left me, she told me how inadequate I was – final confirmation of my secret feelings about myself for as long as I can remember.

'For quite a while after she left, I lived in a whirling, see-saw emotional state, but I did survive. In my more sensible mo-ments I read *Beyond Fear* and then *The Successful Self*. Dorothy, I've been meaning to write to you for ages to tell you how I wish

I could meet you and talk to you and hug you and tell you what a *joy* you are. I realized I'd reached the stage you describe in *The Successful Self*. I had read Eric Berne and Fritz Perls, Alan Watts (and how!) and Dorothy Rowe, of course, and I knew the psychological and philosophical theories and, just as you say, the knowledge was in my head but not in my heart. I did need to actually do something to "unite the internal and external realities in a creative new act", as you put it.

'Well, I did something. I looked up a friend I had not seen for ten years and we spent a weekend in open, honest and productive jawing. My long-neglected linguistic ability has been exhumed and I'm working hard at my Spanish. I've taken a low-paid job with a local travel company (the joy of dawdling to work across the park), where there'll eventually be scope for my language skills (I didn't tell you that I learned basic Portuguese some years ago for a trip abroad and that's going to be brushed up next). The first bonus has already come to me – the people I work with are kind, friendly people who like me as I am, just as I like them. You're so right about that, Dorothy – the cure for the fear of other people is other people; just learning to accept and like ordinary, everyday people and finding that they respond in the same uncomplicated, accepting way.

'You're also right, of course, when you say that a new, creative act is risky but only such a risky act can change the core of meaning. And I am beginning to like myself at last, even the wobbly, grotty bits!

'Oh dear, I've been banging on for ages haven't I? I can only plead that you did say once that your idea of heaven was sitting in a garden listening to other people's stories (the garden will have to be taken as read!).

'I know it's early days yet, Dorothy, and there will be bad times as well as good, but as long as I can go on accepting this exciting, frightening new life, and the changes I can feel happening inside me, I am going to be all right.'

Sometimes the risk that a person takes is simply that of giving up what Jean called the bad habit of being depressed. The person simply recognizes what is the top priority in his life and goes after that. This is what Kathleen did.

Kathleen wrote to me and included with her letter her story.

'In December 1968, after a hysterectomy operation, and some rather odd treatment in hospital, I suffered a nervous breakdown and spent weeks in a mental hospital.

'Since then, any worrying circumstances, such as our sons' divorces, have left me emotionally upset, after which I suffered deep depressions almost annually for some years. My kind husband has suffered too. He has stood by me loyally, visiting me in mental hospitals and welcoming me home again.

'However, last Christmas, which we spent on our own, was too much. I've always loved Christmas, and tried to go through the motions of celebrating, but couldn't shake off my depression, or refrain from saying such things as, "If I were God, I wouldn't allow things like earthquakes."

'Finally, Bob said, "I'm sorry, but I shall have to go away for a while." I agreed and offered to make arrangements for him to stay with some good friends. Also, well in advance, I was trying to make plans for celebrating his eightieth birthday in March.

'Bob then left for church, but before he went he said wearily, "Don't make any arrangements for me to go away or for my birthday, I'm so utterly fed up that all I can do is pray."

'I was so shocked to think that I had hurt my husband so deeply that I was *on the instant* cured of my depression. It's hard to believe, but it's true.

'I met my husband out of church. He still looked worn and sad. I took his arm and smiled at him and said "Look, we're not going to think about me for a while. (I'm sick to death of psychoanalysis), we're going to think about you!" From that moment on we have become, once again, a happily married couple, loving each other, and at ease with our family and friends and our church.

'I'm telling this true story in the hope that it may help someone else who is suffering from depression.'

What Alexandra found was that she had to give up some very firmly held beliefs.

'Last year I wrote to you while I was passing through the deepest, darkest depression I have ever known. You were kind enough to write back to me and make one or two suggestions. I don't know whether you can recall this. However, I feel I have to write to you again because in that one year I have learnt and felt such a vast range of emotions and thoughts. I have gone through so much and experienced such a lot of mental anguish that for the first time in my life I seriously contemplated suicide.

'Throughout that depression, I would come across your books from time to time and I must tell you that *Depression: The Way Out of Your Prison* proved to be something of a turning-point for me, as I genuinely felt you were there, almost egging me on to confront this beast which had taken over my life.

'1988 was without doubt the worst year of my life (I'm still only twenty-five, but whereas last year I thought my life was finished now I'm starting to think that maybe I'll get to be reborn!) Everything I thought I was, or thought I would be, came crashing down around me. I had a "breakdown" in the true sense of the word because the lifestyle, beliefs, opinions, hopes and ambitions, and absolute truths I had built up for myself broke down one by one, until I was left with absolutely nothing and I felt like I had been completely wiped out – annihilated.

'I had always been brought up a staunch Catholic and while I may have questioned some of my beliefs, I never really rejected them. I lived my life very much upon the basis which my mother taught me; "If you are a good girl, you will be rewarded by God", and "If you pray hard enough, God will answer."

'So I was a very, very good girl. I believed all would come right and fit into place if I followed the rules (I realize now that I was a good girl through a sense of fear rather than a desire to be good for its own sake).

'I followed a rigid life plan. I created a philosophy which even went as far as thinking that if something bad happened, then God would feel sorry for me and next time it would be my turn to have good things happen. I demanded a fair world. I demanded justice.

'You can imagine that with such a definite outlook on life I thought I was safe, that I would escape much of the nastiness of life. So, when bad things happened, I wasn't just shocked, I was shattered and completely uprooted out of my cosy beliefs and philosophies.

'The demon of depression demanded that I turn in and look at the way I was living my life.

'In March of last year, I left a job I loved to embark on what I thought would be the start of a glorious career. It fitted into my Grand Design and as I saw myself as this glamorous independent career woman, I thought it would do my image good. It turned out to be a disaster. I was painfully lonely, I wasn't even sure I enjoyed the job, I craved security. The illusion of doing something which I thought would be very glamorous and the actual reality of being there were very, very different. So the absolute truths I held about career and profession were shattered. The first stage of my life plan lay in ruins. I left that job and took a lower-paid one, which left my confidence at a very low ebb.

'At the same time, the relationship which I hoped would develop into the love affair of my life, crumbled almost overnight. This man I thought I loved was really so unlike the image I had built up of him. I had looked at him purely on surface value, again I saw him slotting neatly into my life plan and when he didn't, I couldn't cope.

'So the absolute truths I'd held about love and relationships were, again, nothing like the reality. Because I'd been a "good girl", because I'd waited until meeting a nice man, I thought I would be rewarded with the perfect love affair. I was horrified when I found I didn't actually WANT that, I just wanted to want it. I quickly learnt I was dealing with real men with real flaws, not some comic book hero I had imagined would come along. I was grossly disillusioned. I wanted something which didn't seem to exist. I had set relationships on such a high pedestal that I thought they would be the answer to all my problems, but as I soon learnt that to be a myth I grew afraid, for if they wouldn't bring me happiness, what would?

'As more and more of my safety nets gave way beneath me, I grew more and more afraid. I was literally in a blind panic about life. Then, in July, the three friends I had more or less grown up with began to drift away. I must admit that one of my overriding fears had always been, "What will I do if they leave me?" I tried to devise a safety net to prevent this happening. But in July it did. My pleas to God went unanswered, as much as I struggled to get everything back on to an even keel, circumstances would not allow it.

'Firstly, my closest and dearest friend of the three told me she was gay and probably had been throughout our adolescence. Losing her in this way was like losing a limb. To suddenly realize that my "soulmate" wanted something so different from me left me feeling desolate. I was desperate to turn the clock back and for us to try to be as we were, but I was forced to wake up to the fact that things between us would never be the same again.

'I tried to compensate for the loss I felt by clinging to the other two friends. I turned to them in the hope that we could retain some of the security and familiarity of our childhood. But this wasn't to be either, for, in the summer of last year, one of the friends fell in love with a divorced man and he quickly took over where I had been once, and, finally, the third friend (probably the 'best' Catholic of the four of us) became pregnant the first time she ever made love with a man.

'You might think that these sorts of situations happen to thousands of girls each day, but when they happened to four good friends, whose priority had been their Catholicism and who spent a lot of time praying for good things to happen, you might begin to appreciate how it seemed as if the world I had spent most of life constructing suddenly blew apart in one year.

'I lost three good friends in one fell swoop and in the kind of circumstances I would never have even dreamed up for us.

'The loss made me very bitter (it still does at times) and with the bitterness came the inevitable questions; ''Why me?'', ''I've been good for you God, is this how you repay me?'', ''I stayed loyal, so why have you left me?''

'I began to think if there was a God then I hated him for picking on me, and gradually nothing made sense any more, and despite the fact I hung on literally with my life I felt my faith slipping away.

'The more I tried to hold on, the further from me it seemed to fall until, one day, there was nothing, only this terrible, terrible, black depression, like a huge gaping void where once my world had been.

'If ever I was to give a definition of depression I would say that it is the nearest you can be to dead while still maintaining all your body functions.

'I ''came out of my body'' on many occasions, by that I mean I stood apart from myself and saw someone else, someone unrecognizable, inhabiting my body and my life – not me! I had no part in it. I mean it literally when I say I felt physically detached from the world. It was not MY world any more. I could not identify with anything. Where were my friends, my hopes, my beliefs, my optimism, my love, my God? They had all, every single one of them, been snatched from me.

'The depression was truly the most disturbing experience that I have ever had. I felt as if there was an impenetrable barrier between myself and the rest of the world. I grasped at philosophies, beliefs, advice, guidance, anything to give me some sort of foundation and security, because everything I had constructed for myself had vanished. I felt as if I was running naked in a group of fully-clothed people.

'Of course, the hardest thing of all is that I had to reconstruct my meaning of life and death. If, as I now believed, the God I had always taken for granted was no longer there, then what about my DEATH. The prospect of my death became so terrifying that I could no longer enjoy life because I felt myself hurtling towards an awful END.

'And you are so right when you pin-point one of the common traits of true depression, the fact that life is terrible but death is worse. I was overwhelmed with a feeling of, if God isn't the point of my existence, what on earth is? I felt desolate and very helpless, the philosophy of despair and utter futility I had taken on board absolutely scrambled my mind, there was part of me battling to get through the day and another part which was dying a little bit at a time.

'So, in just one year, I ran the full extremes of emotion I was capable of. I never thought I could get so frightened or so low. I was surviving in all that time, not living.

'I still have a long, long way to go, I still don't trust or like myself that much. I still get bitter about everything that happened. Sometimes I feel desperately sorry for myself. I am still guilty of believing that someone or something has got it in for me and I am destined to have an unhappy life.

'I still don't have an alternative to the immense loss I suffered last year, but what I have learnt (thanks to you) is that the rigid absolute truths I held about life, love and the Universe just had to go, for they gave me no room for the joy and spontaneity which happens every day of our lives. In my book, safety came first.

'Maybe my mind had to "break down" because it could no longer function with such a rigid outlook any more. Maybe it craved flexibility when I forced rigidity upon it. Maybe it would have been impossible to get through the rest of my life with the notions I held previously.

'The disillusionment I felt at finding out that my absolute truths were absolute myths, nearly killed me. I'm still here, I've learnt more in a year than a whole lifetime and I am grateful that your words have always been there when the going got particularly tough. Your words have been there when there was been nothing else – not even my sense of SELF.

'Thank you so much for taking the time to wade through this letter, my apologies for the length of it but I feel I had so much to explain and I wanted you to know that the theories you hold about depression are not just theories, they are living facts, and, in my case especially, they have helped to clarify a little bit at a time just what was happening to me.

'I still get scared, I still don't know where I'm going or what I want any more, or what life will throw up at me next, but, for the first time in my life, there is no rigid life plan, and I have been forced to take, and enjoy, one day at a time.'

What Alexandra discovered is what many people have discovered, that it is not until we have lost everything that had cocooned us from the world (which is very different from what we want it to be) and when we have our backs to the wall at the bottom of the pit, that we can confront the stark truth of our life and our death.

Then we see that we cannot go on living like a child, expecting some parents, be it our own parents, or our lover, or our government, or our God, to save us and protect us, and crying in anguish and anger because this magical parent does not come. Instead, at the bottom of the pit, we take charge of our lives.

Now we can recognize the meaning of Sheldon Kopp's Laundry List of Eternal Truths.[55]

It is so very hard to be an on-your-own, take-care-of-yourself-'cause-there-is-no-one-else-to-do-it-for-you grown up.

We must live within the ambiguity of partial freedom, partial power, and partial knowledge.

All important decisions must be taken on the basis of insufficient data.

Yet we are responsible for everything we do.

You are free to do whatever you like. You need only face the consequences.

Learn to forgive yourself again, and again, and again.

We have only ourselves and one another. That may not be much, but that's all there is.

How strange, that so often, it all seems worth it.

The way out of the prison of depression can be quite amazingly simple. The ordinary life which you then have to face will not be simple, because it will be filled with events you cannot control and people you cannot predict. More crises and more losses can make you want to lock yourself in the prison of depression again. Old habits can be hard to break, but if you do find yourself in the prison of depression you need to remind yourself that this is just a temporary withdrawal.

Now you have the tools for working out, step by step, what it was that happened and made you feel so threatened that you needed to go back into that prison.

Did someone ignore your new closeness and friendliness and behave badly, even cruelly, so that you felt again the old stab to the heart, and, quickly, threw up the barriers against such pain?

Did someone make you angry and you, instead of dealing with this openly and confidently, turned it against yourself, blaming yourself and dragging yourself down?

Did you let that harsh, demanding part of your conscience get the upper hand and push you into working far too hard, so that you became tired, and with that tiredness the old, miserable, despairing thoughts came washing over you like a black tide?

Did your very best efforts at achieving something fail, or the people on whom you have lavished love desert you?

Now, too, you have the tools for getting yourself out of the prison of depression.

You know how to reassure yourself of your acceptability and worth.

You know how to contact someone who will help you talk things through and give you comfort and support.

You know how to be kind to yourself and to look after yourself.

You know how to be sad but not depressed. **(D 50)**

19

Journey's End

Journey's end is just a beginning. You have travelled far and come home to yourself.

You have discovered that what you thought was inadequacy, badness, even evil is actually something which is both good and bad, and yet neither good nor bad but the centre of our being, something which is intrinsically and essentially individual, and yet something which is joined to everybody and everything. When we deny the strength and truth of the centre of our self, when we believe that this centre is bad and unacceptable, we lose touch with ourselves and with the force of life which joins us to everything else. Denying or turning against the centre of our self is not an illness but a foolishness, and many of us are so foolish.

So, trust your own strength and truth, and beware of gurus, wizards and experts. I am, like the Wizard of Oz, a humbug, for I have told you nothing that you do not already know.

When you come to the end of your journey you will find, as you have always known, that you are you, and in yourself and in the world, you are at home.

IV

Discoveries

20

Discoveries

The Aims of these Discoveries are:

1. To help you make quite clear to yourself what your basic beliefs, values and attitudes, which give you your sense of who you are and which guide your every decision, actually are. All too often we use our basic beliefs, values and attitudes without ever bringing them clearly into our consciousness, and so we act without understanding why we do what we do.

2. To help you discover which of these beliefs, values and attitudes you regard as absolute and unchangeable.

3. To help you discover which of these beliefs, values and attitudes prevent you from changing.

4. To help you discover which of these beliefs, values and attitudes you will need to change if you are to give up being depressed.

5. To help you experiment with new ways of thinking, feeling and acting.

   Writing our thoughts down helps us to make them much clearer. Sometimes we don't realize that we know something until we see ourselves writing it down.

   These discoveries are not compulsory. They are only suggestions of possible paths to explore.

   The only right answers are the ones which are right for you.

   The discoveries can be done in any order and in any way that suits you. You can make notes, or write an essay, or a story, or a poem. Sometimes the best thing to do would be to draw a picture or sing a song.

   You can do them when and where you want.

   If you keep a diary (something useful to do when you're in the process of change) you might like to link your answers to these discoveries to what you are recording in your diary.

   You might like to keep your answers secret, or you might like to discuss them with others.

You might like to get your nearest and dearest to the discoveries too, and you might like to compare answers.

Discoveries

Discovery 1

If you could paint a picture of what you are feeling when you are depressed, what kind of picture would you paint?

As you think about this picture, what memories and associations come to mind?

What connections do you see between these memories and associations and your picture?

Discovery 2

Are you an extravert or an introvert?

If you have not already worked this out, choose something that you do which is important. It might be skiing, or cleaning your car, or being in a choir, or reading newspapers, visiting friends – anything.

Now ask yourself, 'Why is this important?', and write down the reason.

Now look at the reason and ask yourself, 'Why is this important?'

Go on asking this question and examining the reasons until you come to the answer which shows what you see as the purpose of your life and what you see as the greatest threat to you.

If, in answering these questions, you say, 'It makes me feel good', or, 'It's pleasant', or, 'It's stimulating', or 'I enjoy it', work out just what you mean by 'feeling good', or 'pleasant', or 'stimulating', or 'enjoyable'. For instance, by 'feeling good' do you mean a feeling in relationship to other people, or a feeling of achieving something?

With achieving, some people (extraverts) achieve as part of their relationships – being accepted into the group, not being rejected, being the centre of attention, being admired and loved by many people – while at the same time trying not to be so successful as to attract enmity and rejection from the members of their group. Other people (introverts) achieve for themselves. They are pleased when the people they approve of approve of them, but the person they want most to approve of their achievement is themselves. Being rejected by others because they are so successful might hurt them, but it is not a major concern which would prevent them from achieving. High achieving, or would be achieving, introverts believe that anyone who does not agree with them and does not approve of what they do is a fool.

Remember that what you are examining is not what you do but *why you do it.*

Discovery 3

Write a list of all the people in your life who are important to you (remembering that people who give us a really bad time are as important to us as those who give us a good time because they interfere in our life).

Beside each name put which you think they each are, an introvert or an extravert.

Then, when you have the opportunity, get them to tell you what they see as the purpose of their life and what they fear most. You might be able to ask some of them this directly, although with others you will have to slide in that revealing question, 'Why is that important?'

How many did you get right?

Discovery 4

What words do you use to refer to your sense of badness and unacceptability?

Turn your thought inwards and focus on how you experience yourself as bad and unacceptable using your own words.

Let the image you have of this come clearly to mind.

Describe this image.

Discovery 5

Write down the experiences you have had which made you feel that you were, in your own words, bad and unacceptable.

This exercise is one that you will need to come back to as you remember different things.

(Your answers to this exercise could be the essence of a bestselling novel, or an autobiography which your nearest and dearest will pay you a large sum of money not to publish.)

Choose one of these experiences from childhood and tell the story twice, once from the point of view of you as a child and once from the point of view of you as an adult.

Discovery 6

Which of these ways of preserving yourself did you choose?

Defining yourself as bad usually goes along with any of the other three.

Discovery 7

As you were growing up you were constructing what the story of your life would be. Write this story down.

John Lennon once said, 'Life is what happens to you while you're making other plans.'

Now that you've written down your plans, write the story of your life.

Now look at the places where those two stories diverge and make a list of these.

Which of these divergences make you feel pleased?

Which of these divergences make you feel disappointed?

Which of these divergences make you feel angry and resentful?

Which of these divergences make you feel frightened?

Discovery 8

Below are thirteen pairs of statements with a 1 to 9 rating scale between each pair.

Rate yourself twice on each statement – first *as you feel now*, and, second, *as you would like to feel*.

For instance, on the first of the statements you might rate yourself now as 2 and as you would like to be as 9.

I am totally bad and unacceptable	1 2 3 4 5 6 7 8 9	I am totally good and acceptable
I am afraid of everybody all the time	1 2 3 4 5 6 7 8 9	I never fear anyone ever

I hate everybody all the time	1	2	3	4	5	6	7	8	9	I like everybody all the time
I envy everybody all the time	1	2	3	4	5	6	7	8	9	I never envy anybody ever
Life is totally horrible	1	2	3	4	5	6	7	8	9	Life is totally wonderful
Death is totally terrifying	1	2	3	4	5	6	7	8	9	Death is totally acceptable
My past was totally unhappy	1	2	3	4	5	6	7	8	9	My past was totally happy
My future will be totally unhappy	1	2	3	4	5	6	7	8	9	My future will be totally happy
I am always a pessimist	1	2	3	4	5	6	7	8	9	I am always an optimist
Anger is always wicked	1	2	3	4	5	6	7	8	9	Anger is always good
I never forgive anybody anything	1	2	3	4	5	6	7	8	9	I always forgive everybody everything
I never forgive myself anything	1	2	3	4	5	6	7	8	9	I always forgive myself everything

I never										I always
feel	1	2	3	4	5	6	7	8	9	feel
forgiven										forgiven
for										for
anything										everything

If you like doing sums, you could subtract the first set of ratings from the second set, square the differences to get rid of any minus signs, and total. For instance:

	As I am now	As I would like to be	Differences	Differences squared
1.	1	8	7	49
2.	2	7	5	25
3.	5	5	0	0
4.	4	6	2	4
5.	2	8	6	36
6.	1	6	5	25
7.	3	7	4	16
8.	1	9	8	64
9.	2	6	4	16
10.	4	6	2	4
11.	7	6	−1	1
12.	1	4	3	9
13.	3	9	6	36
			Total	285

Here you see an enormous difference between how you feel now and how you would like to feel. The biggest total you could get would be 832; the smallest is 0, where you see no difference.

You could, if you wished, repeat this exercise from time to time to see if you have changed.

Discovery 9

What meaning do you give to death – the end of your identity or a doorway to another life?

If you see death as the end of your identity, what do you need in this life to make it satisfactory?

If you see death as a doorway to another life, describe this life. What standards do you have to reach in order to go on to a better life?

Discovery 10

What advantages do you get out of being depressed?

By being depressed, what are you managing to exclude from your life?

Whom are you protecting?

Whom are you afraid to upset?

What is it that you need to control?

Discovery 11

Wanting total
security   1   2   3   4   5   6   7   8   9   Wanting total freedom

Where do you rate yourself on this scale?

Where would you like to rate yourself on this scale?

Discovery 12

How would you describe the way you usually relate to other people – controlling them, being dependent on them, or varying between the two? Or some other way?

What changes do you need to make in yourself in order to get closer to other people?

Discovery 13

Complete the following list about yourself:

I take pride in –

1.
2.
3.
4.
5.
6.

7.

8.

and so on.

Discovery 14

(a) Your boss has just told you that you are incompetent and don't deserve your salary. List as many different reasons as you can for why he might have said this, *other than* that you are incompetent and don't deserve your salary.

(b) Your mother has just told you that she regrets the day you were born. List as many different reasons as you can for why she might have said this, *other than* that you're so bad and useless that no one would want you for their child.

(c) Your father has helped your brother out when your brother was short of money but he has never done this for you. List as many different reasons as you can for why he might have done this, *other than* 'My father does not love me'.

(d) Your best friend did not send you a Christmas card and has not telephoned you. List as many different reasons as you can for why he/she might have done this, *other than* that he/she doesn't like you any more.

(e) Your spouse/lover has forgotten your birthday. List as many different reasons as you can for why he/she might have done this, *other than* that he/she doesn't love you any more.

(f) Your son refuses to keep his room tidy, no matter how much you complain. List as many different reasons as you can for why he might do this, *other than* 'He does this just to annoy me because he hates me'.

(g) Your daughter won't bring her friends home, she hides her letters and her diary, and she won't let anyone overhear her telephone calls. List as many reasons as you can for why she might do this, *other than* 'She is ashamed of me'.

(h) Your three-year-old refuses to eat the meals you have so carefully prepared. List as many reasons as you can for why he might do this, *other than* 'I'm a rotten cook'.

(i) A shop assistant is rude to you. List as many reasons as you can for why she might have done this, *other than* 'She doesn't like me'.

HOW TO SCORE

Reasons where you say or imply something negative about yourself, eg concerning the shop assistant, 'I must have made her angry'. *Score:* 0.

Reasons which include you, though not in a negative way, eg 'She wanted to go to lunch and I walked in'. *Score:* 1.

Reasons which have nothing to do with you, eg 'She looks tired'. *Score:* 5.

The bigger the score the better.

Discovery 15

Suppose that your mother was able to say to you what you want her to say. If so, what exactly would you like to hear?

Rate the chances that *she will one day actually say this* from 0 in a 100 to 100 in a 100.

How did you arrive at this figure?

Will you *a)* Try to change the odds in your favour? If so, how?

b) Go on feeling disappointed and hurt that the odds are lower than you want?

c) Accept the situation and stop fretting about it?

Repeat the exercise with regard to your father, and any other person in your life who has not shown you the amount of love and appreciation you would like.

Discovery 16

WHO DOES WHAT?

	you	your partner	child/children	someone else	nobody
tidies things away					
the vacuuming					
scrubs the floors					
the dusting					
cleans kitchen					
cleans stove					
cleans bathroom					
cleans toilet					

cleans windows

collects and sorts the dirty clothes

does the washing

does the ironing

puts the clothes away

collects and sorts clothes for drycleaning

delivers drycleaning

collects drycleaning

shops for food

puts groceries away

cooks meals

stacks dishwasher

empties dishwasher

washes up

empties waste-paper baskets

puts rubbish in bin

organizes rubbish for collection

Does the above arrangement make you feel:

a)   guilty
b)   that you are doing your duty
c)   a martyr
d)   tired
e)   resentful
f)   pleased
g)   it should be changed
h)   it can be changed

WHO SAYS

	you	your partner	nobody
'Let me do that. You're not doing it properly.'			

'I help her with her shopping.'

'If a job's worth doing, it's worth doing well.'

'I don't mind cooking but I hate washing up.'

'I try to stay out of her kitchen' (or any other reference to 'her kitchen').

'I don't mind washing but I hate ironing.'

'I don't mind ironing but I hate washing.'

'When you tidy the place I can't find anything.'

'Why do you make such a fuss about visitors coming?'

'Can't you put anything away?'

'A woman's work is never done.'

'This place is really squalid' (or words to that effect).

Write down any other often used sayings.

You and your partner might like to do these two discoveries separately and then compare answers. Refrain if this will lead to murder!

Discovery 17

> The rich man in his castle,
> The poor man at his gate,
> God made them high and lowly
> And ordered their estate.

Do you believe this?

To answer the following questions you might want to use categories other than working-, middle- and upper-class.

What class were you born into?

Have you changed your class?

If so, how did that come about?

How would you define your present class?

What rules must you follow or standards must you maintain to be in this class?

What are the advantages of belonging to this class?

What are the disadvantages of belonging to this class?

Discovery 18

What books, films, music influenced you when, as a child, you were working out what sort of person you ought to be?

Describe this ideal person.

How successful have you been in becoming this ideal person?

Discovery 19

Draw your family tree, going back to all your ancestors that you know about, even though you might not have met them.

Pick out the ones who you feel in some way influenced you – perhaps a great uncle your parents warned you about, or a cousin your parents praised.

Write down what you know of each of these people and describe how what you know influenced you.

As an example, here is part of my family tree and an account of how my father's father influenced me.

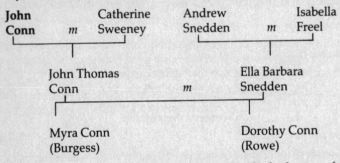

| **John Conn** | *m* | Catherine Sweeney | Andrew Snedden | *m* | Isabella Freel |

| John Thomas Conn | *m* | Ella Barbara Snedden |

| Myra Conn (Burgess) | Dorothy Conn (Rowe) |

I never met my grandfather, John Conn. He died when my father was sixteen. He was killed in an accident in the sulphide mine where he worked to support a wife and six children. My father often spoke to me about his father.

Dad had a photograph of his father's funeral, which showed a horse-drawn hearse and a line of carriages and men on foot in the emptiness of the road from the little town in the bush to the cemetery. He would say, 'The mining company didn't even send a wreath.' In those days there was no pension, no compensation. It was through this story that I, as a small child, was made aware how rich and powerful people can use and abuse people who have no money or power. My grandfather taught me my politics.

Dad was a great story-teller, and when I was small he told me many stories, but the ones I liked best were those about when he was a soldier and when he was a boy. I would say to him, 'Tell me about when you were a soldier', or, 'Tell me about when you were a boy', and he would always have something fascinating to relate. His stories about when he was a boy often included his father. He would tell me how his father taught him to swim and run and play football, how his father would take him fishing, or camping in the bush. Since I spent most of my time in the company of adults who noticed me only to criticize me (that is, my mother, my sister and my teachers) it was very reassuring to find that there was, or had been, another person as caring and non-frightening as my father. Years later, when I was studying clinical psychology and thinking about how parents influence children, I could see how, just as it is possible to trace legacies of pain from one generation to another, so it is possible to trace legacies of love and hope from one generation to another. My grandfather gave my father unconditional love, and that my father could give me.

Discovery 20

Write a description of your mother, not from your point of view but from that of someone *who was the same age as she was and who knew her very well*.

Write a description of your father, not from your point of view but from that of someone *who was the same age as he was and who knew him very well*.

Discovery 21

What were your mother's favourite warnings?

How did/do they make you feel?

Discovery 22

When you are with a person who is depressed, if you could paint a picture of what you feel, what kind of picture would you paint?

Discovery 23

What advantages does your partner get from you being depressed?

Discovery 24

What does your partner say to you which makes you withdraw and become silent? Write down the exact words.

What is the meaning that lies behind these words?

Why do you withdraw and become silent?

Discovery 25

Margaret said, 'I have become the kind of person I like.' Write a description of you as the kind of person you like.

From this description, list the attributes you are now going to act *as if you own*.

Take one of these attributes and think of a situation where you are likely to find yourself and where you could act as if you possessed this attribute.

Write down how you usually behave in this situation.

Write down how you will behave differently now you are acting as if you have this attribute.

Now go and do it.

Write down what you did and how it all turned out.

Discovery 26

What quotations have you come across that you find wise and worth meditating upon?

If you pray, what prayers have brought you peace?

What music speaks to you directly?

What changes can you make in your routine so you can have more time to read poetry, or meditate, or pray, or listen to music?

Discovery 27

What kind of meaning do you need to find which would enable you to master your experience and so allow you to get on with your life?

Discovery 28

What have you learned from your experience of depression which you feel would be helpful to other people?

Discovery 29

Make a list of all the obligations, duties and responsibilities in your life which you find to be a burden.

Now score each one according to the following criteria. Each can have several scores:

A. My conscience tells me that I must do this.

B. Other people expect me to do this and I feel I can't say no.

C. This task is very demanding because I have my high standards to maintain.

D. I would enjoy doing this if I didn't have so much else to do.

E. If I felt better about myself I wouldn't put so much into doing this task.

F. If I had more self-confidence I would refuse to do this task.

Now look at the items scored E or F and, bearing in mind that you are now acting as if you are acceptable and valuable, work out how you will deal with these tasks differently and so reduce your level of stress.

Discovery 30

In what ways do your loved ones fail to treat you with respect and dignity?

In what ways do you fail to treat your loved ones with respect and dignity?

Using the principle 'You only get back what you give away' (ie, if you're rude to people, they will be rude to you) how could you change how you treat them so they might (I only say 'might' – some people are incorrigibly badly behaved) treat you with respect and dignity?

Discovery 31

If you feel that you eat too much, make a list of all the food you usually eat, and then make a list of all the words and phrases you would use to describe them. As well as words like 'sweet' and 'salty' put in words like 'comforting' and 'makes me feel satisfied'.

Now rate each food on each description from 7 as the most and 1 the least.

You could draw up a table like this one.

	I really enjoy	sweet	comforting	friendly	good for me
steak	7	1	5	5	6
ice cream	7	7	6	7	2
apples	6	4	4	5	7
chocolate	7	7	7	7	1
chips	5	1	6	5	2

I have filled in this table for myself. It explains why there is more of me than there need be.

What does your table tell you about the dieting which did not work for you?

Can you remember when you learned to see certain foods as friendly and comforting?

Discovery 32

Make a list of all the pleasant things you like to do and which are there in your life to do if you so choose – like going for a walk, patting a dog, visiting an art gallery, and so on.

Now you are acting as if you are good and valuable, you are doing more things and so discovering more pleasant things to do. Add these to your list as you find them.

If you put this list in some place where you can see it before you go to bed, you can check just how many pleasant things you have done each day.

Discovery 33

Write down the fantasy you have about how you would commit suicide.

What would you hope to gain from committing suicide?

How realistic is this? (Remember that you will not *know* that you are enjoying eternal rest.)

What effects will your suicide have on other people immediately and in the long term?

Discovery 34

How does guilt feel to you?

Discovery 35

How do loss and disappointment feel to you?

Discovery 36

How do you use cheerfulness?

Discovery 37

If you had a depressed parent, can you identify in the images of your depression and your sense of intrinsic badness an image which, as you bring it clearly into consciousness, seems to relate to your parent's depression. What does this image mean?

Discovery 38

Describe the Grand Design in which you believe and which causes you to feel guilty, or persecuted, angry and resentful.

How could you change this belief so that you could still have a religious or philosophical belief which is meaningful but does not mean that you have to live in terms of rewards and punishments?

Discovery 39

When you were a child did your parents and teachers tell you that you should not mix with certain people?

Who were these people?

What were you told about them?

From your adult viewpoint, what do you think of what you were told? Was it accurate? Does it apply today?

Discovery 40

List the political, national, racial, religious, class and gender groups to which you belong.

List all the enemies which each of your groups considers themselves to have.

Which of these group's enemies do you regard as your enemy?

Discovery 41

Describe the role which you present to other people.

How does this differ from the person you know yourself to be?

Discovery 42

List the excuses you use to avoid having to meet people.

Discovery 43

Make a list of all your beliefs which have the effect of building the barrier of your loneliness.

Which of these beliefs do you intend to change?

Discovery 44

Think of a situation in which you received the full blast of someone's anger which had been aroused by something that had nothing to do with you.

Did you respond by:

1. Withdrawing from that person
2. Getting angry with that person
3. Ignoring the fact that the person was angry and just behaving as if nothing was wrong
4. Treating what the person was saying seriously but not getting upset.

What would have been the consequences if you had responded in each of the other ways?

Discovery 45

What are your feelings and beliefs about making an apology?

Which of these do you intend to change and why?

Discovery 46

What are your beliefs about teasing?

Which do you intend to change and why?

Discovery 47

What enemies of groups of people you dislike did you create by generalizing your feelings about one person to a group of people?

What were the consequences of doing this?

Have you changed, or do you intend to change, and, if so, what are/will be your new beliefs and actions?

Discovery 48

How do you feel when someone gives you something? It may be an actual present, or it may be a gift of time, or love, or interest, or concern.

Do you need to improve your skill in receiving generously and, if so, how?

Discovery 49

As you were reading the letters in Chapter 17, which of the fears and misconceptions mentioned do you recognize that you hold or have held?

How could, or did you change them?

Discovery 50

What are the new things that you intend to do? Or are doing?

What tools do you now have for working out what happened to you and for getting yourself out of the prison of depression?

How is being sad different from being depressed?

*　　*　　*

When you have finished working on these discoveries you might like to make a summary of what you have found – as an essay, a story, a picture, a poem, or a song. That way you will see your discoveries clearly and make them yours for ever.

V

Technical Footnotes

21

Is Depression a Physical Illness?

This chapter deals with the following issues:

1. Speaking publicly, most psychiatrists say that it is certain that depression is a genetic illness. They say that biological tests are now available which reveal the existence and the progress of the disease. They say that while some depression has psychological and social causes, most depressive illness has a biological cause and is best treated by the biological methods of drugs and electroconvulsive therapy.

2. However, psychiatrists' own research does not support these public declarations. The research shows:

a) There is no agreement among psychiatrists about how many kinds of depression there are and what names they should be given.

b) No gene causing depression or mania has been discovered; studies which suggest a genetic basis have yet to be replicated; and the adoption and twin studies to date take no account of the personal experience of the subjects in these studies, thus rendering the results most suspect.

c) The biological tests for depression are unreliable.

d) Despite treatment with drugs and electroconvulsive therapy, episodes of depression continue to recur and the long-term prognosis for most depressed people thus treated is very poor.

3. Psychiatrists, other doctors, many psychologists and other health professionals, private health care organizations, health insurance companies and drug manufacturers all support the view that depression is a physical illness because such a view maintains practices which confer prestige, power and wealth on such professional and business people.

4. The belief that depression can be explained and treated

biologically runs counter to current research and practice in the treatment of undoubtedly physical diseases like cancer and heart disease, where the attitudes held by the patients are seen to play a vital part in the causation and outcome of the disease.

5. The belief that a gene can cause depression or any of the other mental illnesses or disorders is based on a misunderstanding of how people feel, think and act, and contains within it a logical error which makes the belief a nonsense.

6. The belief that a gene can cause depression or any of the other mental illnesses or disorders harms the people thus affected and their children.

7. Depression often appears to start without warning, like a black cloud descending out of the blue, but once the person having this experience considers in clear detail the circumstances in which this occurred, the suddenness of the depression is no longer a mystery to be explained only by, 'It's a physical illness'.

To understand anything we need to put it in historical context.

The History of Depression

Descriptions of depression have been found all through written history, but it is only in the last one hundred years that it has been regarded as a physical illness. In the Middle Ages, the Christian Church called it *accidie*, the sin of despair. To sin is to live unwisely, so, as the name accidie slipped out of use and was replaced by *melancholia*, the advice given to the depressed was to live wisely.

The American psychologist Vicky Rippere reviewed the cures for depression as advocated in the sixteenth, seventeenth and eighteenth centuries and summarized them as:

> The basic notion of circumspect, temperate living, based on knowledge of one's own individual and constitutional susceptibilities, the focus on enhancing efficient biological functioning through attention to diet, sleep and exercise, the strategy of deliberately avoiding known physiological and psychological precipitants, the notion of the individual as a member of a supportive social network, the practice of systematically preparing to face adversity, and, finally, the concept of personal responsibility and initiative in choosing to live with care.[56]

What happened to such wisdom?

Traditionally, the Church offered asylum for the troubled and the insane, but in the eighteenth century many institutions for the insane were established by lay people. Some of these, like The Retreat in York, England, run by Quakers, had good conditions and produced excellent results. However, there was money to be made out of the care of the insane, and so disreputable institutions flourished.

Andrew Scull in his *Museums of Madness* wrote:

> Prior to the segregation of the mad into specialized institutions, medical interest in and concern with the mad was for the most part quite slight. In historical terms, of course, the idea that insanity was a disease was not without precedent. For many centuries, though, the medical approach to lunacy had either been ignored or forced to compete with theological and demon- ological perspectives. An occasional medical treatise revived the ancient Greek view that insanity was an illness, but few medical men took any active *practical* interest in the treatment of madmen. Physicians had been placed in charge of the Bethlem Hospital only from the end of the sixteenth century onwards, and since none of those appointed to this position published any books on insanity or made any claims to provide effective therapy, their impact on promoting the medical cause was minimal. As late as the first half of the eighteenth century, James Munro (1680–1752), the physician at Bethlem, was almost the only doctor in and around London who specialized in 'treating' the mentally ill. Thereafter, however, the increas- ing reliance on private madhouses and charity asylums as a means of coping with insanity prompted a quickening of medical interest and involvement in the area.
>
> Most early madhouses were private speculations run for profit. Given the difficulties others experienced in managing the insane and the lack of legal restrictions on entry into the business or upon the actual conduct of the business, they were generally a very profitable investment. Initially, the traffic in human misery was a trade monopolized by no single occu- pational group. Speculators from a wide variety of backgrounds looking for easy profits, as well as more 'respectable' groups such as the clergy, all sought to gain a share of the lucrative market. It was precisely at this stage that the medical profession

(or rather, diverse individuals laying claim to possess some sort of medical training and knowledge) first began to assert an interest in lunacy. A number of doctors trying to gain a share of the lucrative new business, and possibly also trying to improve the treatment of the insane, began opening madhouses of their own or became involved in efforts to set up charity hospitals for the care of lunatics . . .

From about 1815 onwards, a veritable spate of books and articles purporting to be medical treatises on the treatment of insanity began to appear. Similarly, the claim that instruction in its treatment formed part of the normal curriculum of medical training . . . was . . . reinforced . . . All of this activity probably stimulated at least in part the increased attention all members of the educated élite were giving to insanity, in the wake of two major parliamentary inquiries into the subject within the short space of eight years, and in consequence of the revelations of the second of these about conditions in madhouses. But more importantly than that, it represented an effort to reassert the validity of the medical model of mental disturbance, and to ensure a maximum of professional autonomy in the treatment of lunatics . . .

By the [Parliamentary] Acts of 1828 and 1845, the medical profession had acquired a virtually exclusive right to direct the treatment of the insane, and, thereafter, its concern became one of maintaining, rather than obtaining, a monopolistic position. The profession's control of asylums, the only legitimate institutions for the treatment of insanity, effectively shut out all potential competitors, for the latter would have to oppose unsubstantiated claims to demonstrated performance. Furthermore, the asylum doctors' institutional base gave them a powerful leverage for getting the community to utilize their services (thereby indirectly supporting their professional authority), quite apart from whether those doing so were convinced of their competence. For while the employment of the asylum by the relatives of 'crazy' people or by local Poor Law authorities did not necessarily reflect acceptance of the superintendent's claims of his esoteric definition of what was 'really' wrong with the troublesome people they sent him, their ready use of his services unavoidably added to the aura of legitimacy surrounding his activities. So long as his services were so much in demand, it was difficult to avoid concluding that he was performing a useful and valuable task for the community.[57]

Asylums under their medical superintendents grew, housing in their cells and wards many thousands of people, crowded together in appalling conditions. The architects who designed those inhuman buildings and the people who were responsible for the care of the patients were blind to the sufferings of the inhabitants. Scull wrote:

> Though use was made of therapeutic rhetoric, early medical approaches to the treatment of the insane remained in many ways firmly wedded to the past, and were legitimated more by reference to classical authority than by rational demonstration. While more overtly coercive means of controlling the lunatic (for example, whipping and the use of chains) were given a medical gloss, in practice even the standard medical techniques of the time (such as bleeding and the administration of cathartics) were primarily employed as useful ways of disciplining and restraining 'patients'.

In the 1880s, Emil Kraepelin was the physician in charge of a large asylum in Munich. He observed that his patients tended to behave in one of two ways, and these he called the mental illnesses of *manic-depressive psychosis* and *dementia praecox* (later called schizophrenia). In making these distinctions, in speculating about the causes, and in following the outcome, Kraepelin took no account of the degrading conditions in which his patients lived. He took little account of the personal history of each patient, except to note whether mental illness appeared in other members of the patient's family. Thus he established the basic assumptions and practices on which psychiatry has operated ever since.

The Classification of Depression

Psychiatrists did not for long remain satisfied with the classification system which Kraepelin had devised. Since no two people who are depressed behave in exactly the same way psychiatrists set about trying to classify different kinds of depressive illness, and these categories proliferated – endogenous and reactive depression, manic-depression, involutional melancholia, masked depression, affective psychosis, metabolic depression, senile depression, unipolar and bipolar depression and so on. Professor Kendall in a paper called 'The classification of depression: a review of contemporary confusion' wrote:

> The complexity, and absurdity, of the present situation are vividly illustrated by the fact that almost every classificatory format that is logically possible has been advocated by someone within the last twenty years and some more or less plausible evidence offered in support. There are classifications of depression embracing one, two, three, four, five, six, seven, eight, nine categories . . . The ninth revision (of the International Classification of Diseases) contains between nine and thirteen different categories to which a depressive illness may now be allocated.[58]

In the United States, the classificatory system used is not the International Classification of Diseases but the *Diagnostic and Statistical Manual of Mental Disorders* (DSM-III-R).

While psychiatrists use terms like 'mood disorder', 'major depression', 'endogenous depression', 'biological depression', 'unipolar depression', 'clinical depression' and 'psychotic depression' to refer to what they believe is an inheritable illness, there is no unanimity as to what this illness actually is.

In the *Review of Psychiatry*, 1988, Martin B. Keller, in his chapter 'Diagnostic issues and clinical course of unipolar illness', concluded that:

> Whether depression is a single disease that varies from mild to severe along a continuum or whether it represents subtypes that differ in phenomenology, pathophysiology, and etiology has been a long standing topic of debate among clinicians and researchers. However, there is now strong agreement that major depression is a very heterogeneous condition or group of conditions. Subtyping depression in order to reduce this heterogeneity would be of assistance in making more accurate predictions about prognosis and the likely response to treatment.
>
> Clinical experience and research has led to a variety of systems for subclassifying major depression. However, efforts to validate subtypes of major depressive disorders have made only minimal contributions to our power to predict familial background, the presence of precipitating factors, course and outcome, laboratory findings, or response to treatment.

Despite this lack of 'scientific' success in validating these subtypes, many of them remain in widespread clinical use and
researchers continue to make vigorous efforts at validation . . .
the 'endogenous' concept still retains enormous popularity,
and in all likelihood will remain in widespread usage, with
continued efforts as validation.[59]

What Psychiatrists Say Publicly

Dr Donald F. Klein, Professor of Psychiatry at Columbia University
College of Physicians and Surgeons and Director of Research at New
York State Psychiatric Institute, and Dr Paul H. Wender, Professor
of Psychiatry and Director of Psychiatric Research at the University
of Utah College of Medicine, are both winners of the American
Psychiatric Association's Prize for Psychiatric Research. They have
written a book for the public called *Do You Have a Depressive
Illness?*[60], which they describe as 'in essence a written version of the
"course" we give to the depressed patients we treat'. They begin by
saying that:

> Most serious depression requires medical treatment and there-
> fore is a medical problem, even though it may be precipitated or
> worsened by psychological factors.

They conclude their book with:

> During the past twenty years – unbeknownst to the average
> and even the psychologically sophisticated layperson – a com-
> pelling body of information has accumulated indicating that
> many mood disorders (both severe and mild forms of depres-
> sion, and manic-depression) are biological illnesses whose
> most effective treatment is medical. At present only psychi-
> atrists trained in biological methods are adequately equipped
> to diagnose and treat these depressive illnesses. Other profes-
> sionals can contribute to the treatment, but the patient with
> depressive illness should have the initial advantage of skilled
> diagnosis and advanced biological treatment.

Dr Mark S. Gold, Director of Research at Fair Oaks Hospital in
Summit, New Jersey, and Delray Beach, Florida, has written a book
called *The Good News About Depression*.[61] He begins:

> You couldn't have picked a better time in human history to feel
> miserable.

At long last there are effective treatments and cures for depression. These have been developed and implemented by a handful of psychiatrists and neuroscientists who have worked tirelessly, and often without recognition, throughout the past two decades to bring a new *science* to the practice of psychiatry and the relief of mental suffering.

We who work in this new field call it *biopsychiatry*, the new medicine of the mind. If you have ever sought help from a psychiatrist, your doctor, a psychologist, a social worker, a nurse, or a minister because you're depressed and you can't seem to shake it, you will see as you read this book just how different, how straightforward, is the biopsychiatric approach to your pain. Biopsychiatry *works*, and because it works, it is sweeping through top academic and research centers in the United States and abroad, ushering in a new age optimism in psychiatry and psychotherapy after years of treatments – from talking to taking pills – that don't work, or don't last.

What is biopsychiatry? In two words it is *medical psychiatry*. It returns psychiatry to the medical model, incorporating all the latest advances in scientific research, and, for the first time in history, providing a systematic method of diagnosis, treatment, cure, and even prevention of mental suffering . . .

Biopsychiatry is closing the conceptual gap between body and mind. Our understanding has penetrated the very cells of key brain areas, to the submicroscopic spaces between nerve cells and structures on the cells, the chemicals that are synthesized in tiny amounts, the cell walls, the ions that penetrate them.

We now have a working conception of the brain's mood anatomy, including which of the brain's chemical 'messengers' are important in good and bad moods. Embracing the most advanced laboratory technology, we've developed tests to diagnose, to monitor, and to predict the course of depression. We now have tests to identify subtypes of depression in order to choose the appropriate treatment or blend of treatments. When medication is required, other tests can identify the correct dosage for each individual and still others can tell when it's working.

Incredibly, we are on the verge of identifying chemical and genetic traits in children and relatives of depressed people to let them know who will be at risk of severe depressive illness during their lifetimes. This means that someday soon, as we develop appropriate precautions for the at-risk population, we will be able to prevent depression from taking its deadly toll. By identifying certain chemicals in the blood, we may even be able to predict who is at risk of suicide.

Klein and Wender have no doubt that:

The majority of cases of depressive illness appear to be *genetically transmitted* and *chemically produced*. Stated differently, the disorder seems to be hereditary, and what is inherited is a tendency to chemical imbalance in the *brain*. Antidepressant medications apparently have a compensatory effect on the imbalance that is believed to cause the depressive illness . . .

In early 1987 the National Institute of Mental Health announced that researchers had located a gene that triggers a variety of manic-depression, dramatically confirming the hypothesis that had emerged from the adoption studies and other evidence. As science writer Philip J. Hilts wrote in the *Washington Post*, the discovery established 'biological proof of the theory that (manic-depression) is an inheritable, genetically based disease.'

However:

Although depressive illness does occur at a higher rate in particular families, it does not always 'breed true' and sometimes can skip generations. A grandparent may have the disorder, but his or her children may escape, or may have related problems with alcohol; subsequently the grandchildren may show symptoms of the illness. The type of depressive illness can also vary from one generation from another. It is not uncommon for a parent to be manic-depressive and for the child to have a depressive illness without the manic aspect. Finally, heredity does not seem to be an all-or-none matter. Close relatives may inherit either severe forms of mild forms of depressive illness or manic-depression.

Gold agrees. He says:

Depression runs in families . . . Children who receive the affected gene or genes become vulnerable, or predisposed, to affective disorder. In other words, *depression is an inherited illness.*

However, he is not too sure about the gene being discovered. In his concluding paragraph he says:

Steadily we will improve our ability to diagnose state and trait markers and develop pharmacological agents that will target precise receptors without adversely affecting others. Identification of genetic markers will follow; manipulation of affected genes possibly awaits us in the next century.

Klein and Wender explain:

The information that supports the view that depressive illness results from a chemical imbalance comes from studies of both people and animals. Human studies have shown that seriously depressed persons may differ from normal persons (1) in brain electrical activity, both awake and sleeping; (2) in brain chemicals thought to play a major role in the regulation of emotion; and (3) in the chemistry of certain types of blood cells. A few studies that have been made of the brains of depressed people who have committed suicide indicate that there are some chemical differences between these brains and those of non-depressed persons. Investigators are also beginning to learn a great deal from new technical instruments such as the PET scan, both from brain activity in persons with illnesses of this kind and about brain changes induced by medication . . .

During the past thirty years there has been an explosion in knowledge about the structure and functioning of the brain. One major discovery has been that nerve impulses are transmitted chemically in the brain. In brain activity, neurones (cells) release minute amounts of specific chemicals – neurotransmitters – that reach other cells and cause them to react in various ways. There are many kinds of brain chemicals, and the different portions of the brain use different ones. Drugs that affect depressive illness and manic-depression – antidepressants and lithium – either increase or decrease the effect of brain chemicals, thus elevating or depressing mood. The drugs seem to act in several ways, and people with depressive illness apparently differ from one another in terms of their particular response to medication. For example, the drugs can prevent important neurotransmitters from being absorbed or broken down by other brain action, or they can make neurones more sensitive to smaller amounts of such neurotransmitters.

Klein and Wender are reassuring about the effects of such drugs. They say:

All drugs produce side-effects – rarely, severe ones. The risk of the major psychiatric drugs, used in therapeutic amounts with the recommended precautions, is low, probably much lower than the risk of taking penicillin or of having anaesthesia in routine surgery . . . Antidepressants have been studied carefully for almost thirty years in the treatment of large numbers of patients. Bad effects from long-term treatment have never been described (*cf* 'Drugs – Friend or Foe'). Further, these medications do not produce severe withdrawal problems on discontinuation. It is always advisable to discontinue any drug slowly. However, if these drugs are discontinued too abruptly, the worst that happens is that patients temporarily have flu-like symptoms.

Gold warns of over-enthusiasm in prescribing:

The huge doses of antipsychotics which [psychiatrists] were prescribing turned out to have a ghastly and often irreversible side-effect called Tardive Dyskinesia, which causes involuntary movements of the face and tongue. Tranquillizers were prescribed for every little twinge of anxiety, and they turned out to be addictive. Antidepressants caused such unpleasant, and occasionally dangerous, side-effects that many patients quit taking them.

Nevertheless, Gold is in favour of vigorous prescribing. He writes:

There is 'an international undertreatment of depression', claimed a commentator in the *British Journal of Psychiatry* . . . All too many practitioners prescribe the same dosage level for all adult patients, regardless of differing blood plasma levels. Clinicians continue to underdose many patients with medication after medication, until the patient is termed refractory or nonrespondent or treatment-resistant. Another study of this group of patients showed that almost two-thirds had not received an adequate antidepressant trial.

For Klein and Wender antidepressants are not a cure. They write:

Antidepressant medications do not affect the natural history – the lifespan – of the depressive illness. They control the symptoms while nature is taking its healing course. In this respect they are similar to aspirin, which, for example, controls the fever of flu or the pain of headache but does not shorten any illness that may be present. If antidepressants are stopped too soon, the patient may relapse. In order to prevent this, most psychiatrists wait six months after a depression has responded before they gradually reduce the dose. If depressive illness is still present, symptoms recur, but an increase in dosage will bring them under control rapidly. If symptoms do not reappear when the drug dosage is reduced, the episode has probably run its course and the medication can be discontinued . . .

Patients frequently ask this important question, 'If I have had one attack of depression, can I expect to have more?' The answer is 'Yes'. A person who has had an attack of biological depression is much more likely to have another attack than a person who has never had one. Unfortunately, we do not know the odds of recurrence for any one person, and we do not know when recurrence is likely. Sometimes attacks occur regularly every spring and fall, sometimes they appear years apart, and sometimes a person suffers a depressive episode and then never has another one. Manic-depression is much more likely than other forms of depression to recur frequently.

Gold agrees that depression is likely to recur:

The ongoing NIMH Collaborative Study of the Psychobiology of Depression, conducted at America's premier academic hospitals, reports that only 60 per cent of depressed patients have recovered six months after treatment, and only 34 per cent are completely free of symptoms. Of those who fully 'recover' during treatment, 19 per cent relapse within six months and 24 per cent develop new symptoms.

However, Gold is convinced that vigorous medicating accompanied by the use of monitoring tests does cure depression. He denies that antidepressants are simply painkillers:

A painkiller will remove the pain but not the conditions which causes it; the pain will return when the medication wears off. Cough medication may tame the hacking, but you're in for it again later while your flu hangs on. Antidepressants operate at a more fundamental level, restoring the brain to normal functioning. Should your symptoms return when antidepressant therapy stops, probably the treatment did not last long enough. Or possibly the symptoms indicate a withdrawal reaction from stopping abruptly rather than tapering off . . . [Antidepressants] *can* cure [depression]. After antidepressant therapy many persons lead a life free of this debilitating disease. The outlook is especially hopeful if we catch it early. For those with a chronic condition, however, a treatment 'package' of medication and psychotherapy can substantially reduce the number of future episodes. We believe that medication may actually 'teach' the brain's neurones to respond differently. Possibly, too, the medication returns the neurones to a level of functioning at which the brain's restorative mechanisms can take over.

So, the public message is perhaps cheering; that is, if you do not suffer from depression. If you do, you may still be worried. The three psychiatrists quoted here agree that depression is a genetic illness, though two of them say that the gene has been discovered and one of them says it is only a matter of time before it will be found. Two of them say that depression cannot be cured but only ameliorated, while one of them says it can be cured, provided you consult a psychiatrist who, like him, is a biopsychiatrist.

To sort this out we need to see what psychiatrists say when they talk to one another, that is, what is reported in their learned journals.

What Psychiatrists Say Privately

In the 1988 *Review of Psychiatry*, published by the American Psychiatric Press, the chapter by Lynn R. Goldin and Elliot S. Gershom on 'The genetic epidemiology of major depressive illness'[62] begins with:

Major depressive illness, or unipolar depression, is a common psychiatric disorder in most populations. The disorder is more common in relatives of patients who have had an episode of major depression than it is in the general population. Monozygotic (MZ) twins are more often concordant for depressive illness than are dizygotic (ZD) twins. These observations are consistent with a genetic etiology. However, there are several factors that complicate genetic interpretations. The risk of depression is not only affected by the diagnostic criteria used, but also by factors such as age, sex, birth cohort, and possibly other cultural variables such as urban residence and socio-economic status. There have been a substantial number of genetic studies of depression, but many issues are still unresolved. The most important of these are: (1) the genetic relationship between unipolar and bipolar illness; (2) evidence for heterogeneity of depression based on clinical characteristics of patients or pattern of illness in their families; (3) mode of inheritance; that is, single gene or polygenic trait; (4) association or linkage with known genetic marker traits; and (5) underlying biological risk factors.

In this chapter we will review epidemiological family, twin and adoption studies that have addressed these various issues. In addition, we will review studies that have examined the mode of transmission of depression and the relationship of depression to genetic market traits. Finally, we will consider which genetic strategies currently hold the most promise for our ability to answer these questions.

Goldin and Gershom conclude that:

Major depression, when defined stringently, is a heritable disease. Family members are at significantly increased risk for developing various affective disorders compared to the general population. However, the risk of major depression in both the population and in the relatives of patients varies with diagnostic criteria, age, sex, cohort, and possibly other factors. Milder disorders such as DSM-III dysthymia or RCD (Research Diagnostic Criteria) minor depression may not be heritable. Biological and genetic studies should focus on patients and family members who have more severe diagnoses . . .

Some analyses of family data have indicated that unipolar and bipolar illness share some common genetic liability factors. Other studies do not confirm this unitary hypothesis in general, but indicate that certain subgroups of unipolar may share liability with bipolar. Single major genes that cause susceptibility to depression have not been found by analysing the segregation pattern of the illness in families. Linkage studies have not found any genetic marker trait chromosomally linked to a susceptibility gene for depression.

Studies of traits such as MAO and CFF metabolites have not found them to be predictive of some genetic susceptibility for depression. Abnormality on the DST also does not appear to indicate some homogeneous form of illness. However, vulnerability to increased sensitivity to cholinergic REM induction may be a marker of affective disorder.

Future studies need to continue to focus on ways of resolving the heterogeneity of major depression using clinical and biological traits. Linkage studies are now a very powerful strategy for detecting disease susceptibility genes because of the almost unlimited number of markers available. However, linkage and other biological studies need to be applied carefully. Families for analysis should be selected to have a severe form of the illness. Stringent criteria should be used to classify family members as affected or unaffected because broad criteria increase the likelihood that many individuals will have a nongenetic illness. *Defining a highly inheritable subtype of depression using clinical, biological, or genetic marker traits remains a critical challenge to this field* [my italics].

In the same volume, James C. Ballenger examined 'Biological aspects of depression: implications for clinical practice'.[63] He looked at the research on abnormalities of sleep, biological rhythms, neuroendocrine studies of cortisol, the dexmethasone suppression test (DST) and thyroid abnormalities, at neurotransmitter abnormalities, and concluded with:

This chapter provides a selective review of various biological investigations in depression with particular emphasis on those findings which might have a current or future clinical relevance. *There is no coherent 'biology' of depression, nor is it likely that there will be in the near future* [my italics]. Research has tended to focus on one area to the exclusion of others, and this, coupled with the inherent complexity of the work, has prevented definitive elucidation of even single mechanisms; certainly coherent relationships among areas of research have been impossible to date . . . While such hints of convergence and basic explanations of biological mechanisms in depression are exciting, more definitive understanding of these mechanisms probably awaits decades of further research. The practical and widespread use of biological factors clinically is probably also relegated to the future. Despite increasing confidence in certain findings, particularly sleep changes, HPA axis abnormalities, and certain of the urinary and CFS measures, none is ready for routine use by the clinician. The early and uncritical use of DST reflected both the great need for external and easily obtained measures, as well as the difficulties of moving these biological measures into routine practice.

Again Martin B. Keller in his chapter 'Diagnostic issues and clinical course of unipolar illness'[64] concluded that:

> Although 80 to 90 per cent of patients with major depression do recover, a substantial proportion of them will have at least one subsequent episode, and many will have an average of five to six subsequent episodes. The complete recovery rates for patients with dysthymia are considerably lower than those for patients with major depression.

Traditionally, this inheritable depressive illness, whatever name it was given and however it was defined, has been diagnosed retrospectively. If a patient responded to drugs or to electroconvulsive therapy he had an inheritable depressive illness. This was very cheering for the psychiatrists, for quite simply and directly the disease was diagnosed and cured, or at least was under control.

It was not so cheering for the patients whose illness kept recurring. As anyone with any kind of chronic illness or disability knows, doctors tend to lose interest in patients with chronic complaints.

In Britain in 1988, Dr A. S. Lee of University Hospital, Nottingham, conducted an eighteen-year follow-up on eighty-nine inpatients with 'primary depressive illness' and reported his results in a paper entitled 'Foretelling the future of depressives' to the Royal College of Psychiatrists Winter Quarterly Meeting. He found that:

> Less than one-fifth of the survivors had remained well, and over one-third of the series suffered unnatural death or severe chronic distress and handicap. Psychotic/endogenous patients were much more likely to be readmitted and to have very poor outcomes. Over half of the severely disabled survivors had no contact with mental health professionals in the year before the follow-up . . .
>
> Conventional wisdom is that psychotic/endogenous depressives respond better to biological treatments and that their short-term prognosis is correspondingly good. This study suggests that, like the hare in Aesop's fable, they may race ahead of the tortoise-like immediate progress of their neurotic counterparts, but in the long term they tend to relapse more frequently, to fare much worse and to be forgotten by psychiatry.

Dr R. Ramana and Dr M. W. Battersby, commenting on the studies by Dr Lee and Dr Murray and on a similar outcome to a study in Australia by Professor L. G. Kiloh and his team,[65] wrote:

> Both studies clearly show us that a significant proportion of depressed patients do poorly in the long term. The findings of two major studies in the pre-treatment era (Lundquist, 1945; Rennie, 1942) are broadly similar to those of the present studies. We wonder why it is that, almost fifty years later, with innumerable treatment methods at our disposal, we are still faced with such a dismal outcome for depression. Are we not using these therapeutic tools appropriately, or are they of no use in ameliorating the poor long-term outcome? It is unfortunate that neither of the current studies have attempted to correlate outcome with treatment. There is clearly a need for further long-term prospective studies into the outcome of depression and the effect of different treatment methods, both short- and long-term, on prognosis.

So it seems that there is a considerable discrepancy between what psychiatrists say publicly and what the research shows. One psychiatrist well known for his research into the genetic basis of depression is Professor Peter McGuffin of the University of Wales. He concluded his review paper entitled, 'Major genes for major affective disorder?'[66] with:

> It will be a fascinating prospect to see whether Kraepelin's manic-depressive insanity described at the end of the nineteenth century will, by the end of the twentieth century, have that constitutional basis discovered and understood at a molecular level.

All the evidence that depression and manic-depression are inherited illnesses rests on the adoption and twin studies. These studies have been carried out by doctors interested in genetics, not in how we each create our own world of meaning. So in adoption studies heads are counted, not opinions sought.

Adoption studies show that there tends to be a higher correlation between depression in the adoptees and their biological family than between the adoptees and their adopted family. This is taken to point to a genetic inheritance. Unfortunately in these studies no attempt is made to distinguish between those subjects who were adopted at birth and those who had formed their primary bond with their mother, only to have it broken by death or separation, and who then were adopted. There is now ample evidence, notably from the work of George Brown and Tirril Harris,[67] that the loss of the mother in early childhood is a vulnerability factor in the development of depression in adult life. This is not a genetic factor, but just the conclusions which the child draws about the loss – perhaps, 'If I had been really good my mother would not have died', or 'My mother rejected me so I must be bad'.

In the adoption studies no attempt is made to distinguish those adoptees who do not know that they are adopted from those who do know, and, in the second case, what it is that they know. What adoptees know of their biological family depends very largely on what their adopted family tell them. How many adoptees are told that their biological family were wicked, or mad, or defective and inadequate in some way? How often was this information conveyed with the instruction, 'Don't be like your biological family', or the prediction, 'I expect you'll end up like your family'? How often did the adoptees hearing the instruction determine to disobey it in order to have their revenge on their adoptive parents for their failure to be the perfect parent? How often did the adoptees hear the prediction as an instruction, and so made it a self-fulfilling prophecy?

It would seem that the only way to determine a genetic component by adoption studies would be to find those adoptees who were adopted at birth, did not know that they were adopted, and had an adopted family who did not project negative expectations on to them. It is not likely that there would be many such people.

The question of expectations is likewise ignored in all the twin studies. These studies show that if one monozygotic (MZ, identical) twin becomes depressed there is a fair chance that his twin will also experience some depressive reaction at some time, while if one dizygotic (DZ, fraternal) twin becomes depressed there is less chance that his twin will also become depressed. Such studies do not examine just how similar identical twins see themselves to be, and how much they and their family expect that they will behave in identical ways. In the very few cases where identical twins have been raised separately, the questions about what adoptees and their adopted families know and expect apply.

In case I had misunderstood the significance of the twin studies, I wrote to Professor McGuffin and put these points to him. He replied:

I am afraid that none of the published adoption work that I know of provides adequate answers to your perceptive questions. Our recent Maudsley twin study did try to address the issue of MZ 'micro-environment' but we are still analysing the results.[68]

In his review article 'The genetics of depression and manic-depressive disorder'[69] Professor McGuffin wrote:

> It is now well established that certain forms of adversity, such as life events which carry a severe or a moderately severe threat, have a strong association with the onset of depression.[70,71] Unfortunately there have been few attempts to study environmental stress and familial/genetic factors in the same population . . . The interplay between genes and environment is complex[72] . . . It was found that both depression and threatening life events tend to cluster in families, and so it is possible that a liability to develop depressive illness and propensity to experience (or to report) unpleasant life events are different manifestations of the same familial diathesis.

That is, certain families seem to have a predisposition to depression and to experience, or to report, many setbacks and tragedies. Some psychiatrists are so wedded to the notion of a depression gene that they are ready to claim the presence of a 'bad luck gene', without considering how such a gene would require us to rewrite history (prevalence of the gene in Hiroshima?), our literature (Job's answer to God?) and to reorganize our travel security (airlines not checking travellers' baggage but their DNA?).
Professor McGuffin and his colleagues are not so foolish. As he wrote:

> It is tempting to speculate that the most salient personality factor involved in the familial association between life events and depression is related to cognitive style. It may be that a certain cognitive set is associated with the perception of events as threatening, the retention of such events in the memory, and the tendency to develop depressive responses.[73]

So it seems that the only evidence that depression is an inheritable disease is that in succeeding generations of some families certain individuals get depressed. The same observation could be made that in succeeding generations of some families certain individuals vote Tory. Does this mean that there is a gene for voting Tory? In the USA, is there a Republican gene? Will those of us who don't carry these genes become the objects of genetic engineering?

A hundred years of research has not established that depression is a physical illness. Yet psychiatrists, even those who use or advocate psychotherapy, insist that depression, though perhaps affected by environmental and personality factors, is, in essence, a physical illness.

Why Psychiatrists Insist that Depression Is a Physical Illness

First of all, because psychiatrists are kindly people. They see so much human suffering, and they wish to alleviate it. If ever you have sat with a depressed person and seen the agony on that person's face, you would long for a pill that would take that suffering away.

Pity is one of the most painful emotions, and helplessness one of the most uncomfortable. When we pride ourselves on our competence, as most health professionals do, we find being unable to help those we ought to help quite frightening, and so we rush to do something to help the clients that we pity.

Over the last eighteen years I have conducted numerous workshops for health professionals on depression. I get them to talk about how they feel when they are with someone who is depressed. The predominant feeling they talk about is fear – fear of their own helplessness and fear that the person's depression will awaken their own. At one of these workshops, a general practitioner, one of the kindest people I have ever known, said, 'When I see a depressed patient coming through my office door, I reach for the quickest acting antidepressant. That makes me feel much better.'

Warm, wonderful and truly human people though we health professionals are, we do fight amongst ourselves. Psychiatrists, psychologists, social workers, psychiatric nurses, psychotherapists, all struggle for position, power and money.

If depression is not a physical illness, then no one profession can claim it as its own. But if it is a physical illness, then it is the province of the psychiatrists. As someone who has worked in psychiatric hospitals and sat in case conferences and management committees for over twenty years, I know only too well that the arguments over whether or not depression is a physical illness are not conducted with the courtesy and objectivity of scientific discourse. They are conducted angrily, bitterly, vindictively, in the way that a family battles over the legacy of a will. It is not scientific results that are at stake, but money.

Ever since the first psychoanalysts went to the United States a number of psychiatrists have been interested in psychological explanations of depression and the other mental illnesses. Many, on completing their training as psychiatrists, have gone on to train in one of the psychotherapies. In Britain, the belief that all mental illnesses were physical illnesses was the basis of the theory and practice of psychiatry until the early 70s when the antidepressant drugs were clearly not living up to their promise, and psychologists, who were becoming increasingly numerous in the National Health Service, were demonstrating the effectiveness of their therapies. Many British psychiatrists then saw the writing on the wall. They discovered psychotherapy. The Royal College of Psychiatrists formed a Division of Psychotherapy and created, for consultant psychiatrists only, the post of consultant psychotherapist.

However, in the United States and Britain there were many psychiatrists who were, and are, steadfast in their view that depression is a physical illness. In the United States they refer to themselves as biological psychiatrists or biopsychiatrists, and in Britain they think of themselves as Right, Objective, Scientific, Sensible and Giving Proper Leadership, unlike their psychotherapeutic colleagues. The disagreements between the psychiatrists who believe in psychotherapy and the biological psychiatrists can be very bitter. Gold is very scathing about psychiatrists who do not practise medicine. Klein and Wender stake their claims very clearly.

The psychiatrists who are best qualified to make this diagnosis [of biological depression] have been well trained in modern biological psychiatry. Many nonpsychiatrist physicians, such as internists and family practitioners, diagnose and treat depression, but unfortunately many have not had the training necessary to distinguish between biological and psychological depressions. Indeed, this is true of some psychiatrists. Similarly, many well-trained psychologists and social workers are skilled in the treatment of psychologically produced depressions but have not been taught to distinguish between biological and psychological depressions. One's best chance of getting an accurate diagnosis, therefore, will be from a psychiatrist well trained in the new biological psychiatry.

To the outsider this may seem to be just an argument about
scientific results. However, Gold gives the game away when he
says:

> Why would people put themselves through the four years of
> torture at medical school if they didn't want to become doctors?
> Why not simply become a psychologist and not bother with all
> that dreadful stuff like biochemistry and patients leaking blood
> and oozing pus, not to mention internship and residency years,
> in which you work yourself to death with little sleep and less
> financial reward?

The answer is *prestige*. Psychiatrists may be the butt of jokes,
but an MD is an MD. A few decades ago medicine had a
hammerlock on psychoanalysis, and medical school was thus
the best route to a psychoanalytic institute. Psychologists and
other professionals established their own institutes, and only
during the psychiatrist shortage have some of the MD-only
institutes opened their doors to psychologists. None the less,
doctors are esteemed in our society far more than PhDs. This
esteem is bankable . . .

Psychiatrists would probably charge more, if psychologists
and other nonmedical therapists weren't competing for the
dwindling psychotherapeutic dollar. In 1980 (when only 2 per
cent of graduating medical students decided to become
psychiatrists) the worst year so far in the psychiatrist shortage,
US universities awarded 22 per cent more PhDs in clinical
psychology and counselling than they had the year before.

Psychiatrists have sunk bottomward on the earnings totem-
pole in medicine. They can expect to make 30 per cent less than
the average physician.

Over the last decade, insurers have consistently reduced their
coverage of outpatient psychiatric expenses. These days, a major
medical policy that covers 80 per cent of all outpatient doctors'
fees and a maximum $500 dollars a year for outpatient psychi-
atric care is considered 'generous'. How many people can
afford a long-term course in psychotherapy any more? Ten years
of analysis could easily run to $100,000 – minus $5000 reimbursable (that is, if the insurance carrier doesn't impose a lower limit).
Patients – from those who just want to figure themselves
out to those who are ill and in pain but not sick enough to be hos-
pitalized – will have to hand over their life savings to get help.

In 1984, at the order of the Federal Office of Personnel Management, Blue Cross/Blue Shield substantially reduced mental health benefits for federal workers. Psychiatrists in the Washington, DC area experienced an immediate 10 to 15 per cent reduction in billable hours.

Some medical students, as well as psychiatrists, inaccurately blame the insurance pullback on psychologists and, in some states, social workers, who have successfully fought for the right to equal reimbursement for their services. It isn't their fault, however, that they provide the same *nonmedical* services – psychotherapy – for their patients as do psychiatrists.

A Blue Cross spokesperson explained, 'With psychotherapy, the problem is that the psychiatrists can't specify the problem or the likely outcome, and can't give a good description of the method in between either.'

Health insurance pays for the treatment of medical illness. Are psychiatric patients medically ill?

Much of the remainder of this book will be devoted to this question, to which the answer is very often yes. Some patients with the symptoms of depression may not know that they are suffering from serious bodily illnesses (expenses currently reimbursable). Some are suffering the effects of drug and alcohol abuse, although they may not appreciate the relationship of their abuse to their symptoms (treatment reimbursable). Many are suffering from the brain disease of depression, often genetic in origin, for which a number of treatments are available, including medication and special types of psychotherapy (partially reimbursable). Others are suffering from life problems that lead to depression and for which psychotherapy is often helpful (rarely reimbursable, at a very low rate).

If tomorrow psychiatrists suddenly decided to act like doctors, they'd probably save their patients a lot of money, not to mention torment. They would uncover the predicted high rate of medical illness among their patients with depressive symptoms, and these individuals would find their psychiatric expenses reimbursable at the *medical* rate. This in itself would cheer them up!

Similarly, there is no reason why a psychiatrist cannot provide an accurate diagnosis and prognosis of biological depression, which is, after all, a brain disease. In other words, in approaching psychiatry as a medical specialty, we could easily provide the insurance companies with the information they require (and the patients with the treatment they need) in order to cover psychiatric expenses.

To reverse the trend of reduced benefits – and the shortage of psychiatrists – all psychiatric practitioners, old-time and new, will have to change their ways.

So, psychiatrists will make more money if they insist that depression is a physical illness. But what about the competition for that money?

Roy Amara, writing on 'Health care tomorrow' in *The Futurist* pointed out that:

> The number of physicians will continue to rise until the end of the century. The doubling in the annual number of new physicians that took place in the 1960s has left a legacy of excess capacity for the balance of this century and into the next.[74]

Where are all these doctors going to find patients? John C. Nemiah gave the answer in his Adolf Meyer lecture at the 1988 Annual General Meeting of the American Psychiatric Association. He called his lecture 'The varieties of human experience'.

> Those who are familiar with the history of American psychiatry during the past forty years know that the first *Diagnostic and Statistical Manual of Mental Disorders* (DSM-I) referred to psychiatric syndromes not as *disorders*, but as *reactions*. DSM-I was infused with the concepts of Adolf Meyer, which viewed psychiatric illness as the *reaction* of a human being to a troublesome life event. With the inevitable swing of scientific dialectic, such notions no longer predominate, and have yielded place to different basic assumptions and approaches. In the evolution of psychiatric nosology over the last four decades, in the transition from DSM-I to DSM-III, the focus of attention has shifted from the living person to his illness as a thing in itself, from dynamic process to static phenomenology, and, to a large extent, from psychology to biology. To oversimplify, one might say that we have given up the motion picture for a photographic still.[75]

The DSM-III-R turns every difficult aspect of human life into a medical disorder, and thus psychiatrists lay claim to being the only profession which has the expertise to deal with such disorders. The 'medicalization' of human life has not progressed so far in Britain because most psychiatrists work within the National Health Service and so do not need to compete for patients. However, the changes coming into the Health Service in accordance with government policy could mean that psychiatrists will be competing for patients, and therefore will be tempted to increase the number of possible patients in the way that their American colleagues have done.

However, it is not just the psychiatrists who make money out of depression being defined as a physical illness. Insurance companies do. Hospitals do. Psychiatric nurses, administrators, porters, cooks, domestics, all make money out of depression being treated as a physical illness. Most of all, drug companies make money out of depression being called a physical illness.

Lucy Johnstone in her book *Users and Abusers of Psychiatry*[76] wrote:

Pharmaceutical companies are among the most powerful and profitable on earth. In fact they have been ranked first or second most profitable industries in the world since 1955.[77] 'The multi-nationals have financial strength that in many cases exceeds that of many governments . . . Each of the ten largest multi-nationals earns annual revenues greater than the gross national products of two-thirds of the countries in the world.'[78] It has been estimated that the market for one company is about 100 million dollars from these drugs in America alone,[79] while the Britain, where minor tranquillizers are by far the most common-ly prescribed drugs, enough of them were distributed in 1981 to allow for thirty tablets for every man, woman and child in the country.[80] Diazepam is reported to be the most widely pre-scribed drug in the world.[81] The major tranquillizers are a similar success story for the drug industry; an estimated 150 million people take them worldwide.[82] Drug companies spend around £5000 a year on every GP in Britain or £150 million a year in total[83] to promote their products and the annual NHS drugs bill is around £2,000 million.

The idea that depression is an inherited illness supports a multi-billion dollar industry. Many people have a vested interest in maintaining the belief that depression is a physical illness.

But if the scientific evidence does not support the idea that depression is a physical illness, and if the drugs used do not prevent recurrences of depression, why do psychologists not make this knowledge public? Would they not gain from revealing this?

Why Psychologists Insist that Depression Is a Physical Illness

Psychologists have to live.

The organizations which provide mental health care in the United States are such that *this chapter can be written only by someone who is independent of the system*. Most clinical psychologists in the United States are not. Financially and conceptually they are dependent upon psychiatrists.

To qualify as a clinical psychologist and to be licensed to practise a person must obtain a doctorate in psychology and then pass the State and National Licensing Examinations. The National Examinations include an extremely thorough knowledge of the volumes of the *Academic Review*.[84] The only way to acquire this knowledge, as I have seen many of my friends and colleagues doing, is to memorize them, page by page.

This process always reminds me of the Thirty-Nine Articles of the Church of England. In England in the seventeenth century the only men who were allowed to attend university, and so enter the professions, were those who had memorized and professed belief in these Thirty-Nine Articles. The *Academic Review* is to clinical psychologists what the Thirty-Nine Articles were to seventeenth-century professionals – a declaration of faith and a declared intent to work in a particular way. Of course it was possible to learn these Articles and lie in professing belief in them, just as it is possible to learn the contents of the *Academic Review* without believing them, but to learn, remember and use something in which you do not believe is very difficult. It is much easier to learn and to believe.

The volumes of the *Academic Review* follow the traditional view that depression is a physical illness. They do not question it in any way.

Even before clinical psychologists launch themselves into memorizing the *Academic Review* they have been learning to use the DSM-III-R. Though their education in psychology has taught them about the weaknesses of all classificatory systems, they have to use the DSM-III-R in order to fit in with the requirements of the insurance companies, who want a diagnosis for each patient, and the psychiatrists with whom they work.

Most clinical psychologists in the United States are dependent upon psychiatrists for work. They may need psychiatrists to refer patients to them, or they may be part of a management structure which makes them responsible to a psychiatrist. Thus many psychologists would think it not in their best interests to express publicly ideas contrary to those held by psychiatrists. They prefer, with the agreement of the psychiatrists, to carve out an area of work for themselves while leaving the 'genetic mental illnesses' (actually the most difficult people to help) for the psychiatrists.

Hence many clinical psychologists in the United States support the view that depression is a physical illness.

Even in Britain, where most clinical psychologists work for the National Health Service and are neither financially nor managerially dependent on psychiatrists, many clinical psychologists hold fast to the belief that depression is a physical illness. They would support the findings of the research which Jesse H. Wright summarized in the chapter on the cognitive therapy of depression in the *Psychiatric Review*.

> Unipolar major depression is the major indication for cognitive therapy. Substantial evidence has been collected that cognitive therapy is effective for unipolar major depression . . . There has been no controlled research to support the use of cognitive therapy with patients who have major depression with psychotic features. Electroconvulsive therapy or pharmacotherapy with combined tricyclic antidepressants and antipsychotic drugs remain the treatment of choice for such patients . . . [There is] some support that cognitive therapy can be used successfully in depressed inpatients. However, it is recommended that cognitive therapy usually not be used without medication in the treatment of hospitalized patients until further outcome research is completed . . . Cognitive therapy has been used adjunctively for patients with bipolar depression, but it is not considered a primary treatment for this disorder.[85]

Psychologists simply do not want to admit that their therapies do not always work. It makes them feel competent and secure when they can say, 'The reason that this patient did not get better is because he had a biological depression'. It is even better to identify those patients who are really difficult to get along with and to give a 'medical' reason for not trying to, rather than to admit to inadequacy.

This dismissal of their unsatisfactory patients saves psychologists from having to face up to the fact that they do not have methods to help those people who have brought from their tragic childhoods a profound sense of intrinsic badness, inadequacy and worthlessness.

The techniques of behavioural and cognitive therapies for depression, when used by an empathetic, enthusiastic therapist can be extremely helpful for the person who has brought from childhood a modicum of a sense of intrinsic goodness, adequacy and worth and who has encountered difficulties which have shaken and diminished his self-confidence. Under his depression such a person still believes that he is worth saving, and so he can work with his therapist to come to terms with the unwelcome changes in his life and to re-establish his self-confidence and optimism.

Such an alliance between patient and therapist can be effective within a few weeks or months. However, with those people who have no memory of a time when they did not feel intrinsically bad, inadequate and worthless, the therapeutic alliance needs to exist for much longer and to demand from the therapist not explicit, summarizable techniques, but the indefinable profundities of concern, empathy, hope, sharing, attention, strength, patience and love.

Over the years many therapists, practising in different ways, have built up a large body of knowledge about this way of working with depressed people. However, to discover this knowledge and use it effectively, you have, as a person and as a therapist, to apply it to yourself. My observations of the psychologists and psychiatrists who hold to the belief that depression is a physical illness lead me to the conclusion that self-knowledge is not something that they value and pursue. They prefer to see themselves as experts and their patients, by being ill and incompetent, as their inferiors.

The intellectual dishonesty of those psychologists who explain away their therapeutic failures by claiming the presence of a biological depression is clearly seen when we consider what is happening in the research into the undoubtedly physical illnesses of cancer and heart disease.

The Cause and Outcome of Cancer and Heart Disease

It is common knowledge now that over the last ten years the most fruitful research into cancer and heart disease has been in discovering the ways in which the people who get these diseases see themselves and their world, that is, the kind of meanings these people create about themselves and their world, which is, of course, the way they think and feel.

Seeing yourself as needing to compete and to achieve in a fairly relentless way, while at the same time interpreting your world in untrusting and cynical ways, can be an important part of the recipe for a heart attack. Believing that you have to keep your feelings to yourself, that you must not protest and show your anger, and feeling helpless and hopeless are an important part of the recipe for cancer. 'According to Professor Hans Eysenck of the Institute of Psychiatry, the characteristics of our personality may be six times more important in determining whether cancer develops than all known medical factors put together.'[86]

In these major diseases and in other diseases, including AIDS, it seems that the outcome of the disease is not basically determined by the physical process of the disease but by the attitude of the person who has the disease. Believing that you are valuable, caring for yourself and living with hope enable the people with these illnesses to go on living. I have a friend, Lorna, who is in her forties but who, according to the medical textbooks, should have died over twenty years ago. She has cystic fibrosis, an inherited disease of the lungs caused by a recessive gene, and the life expectancy of someone with this disease is supposed to be no more than ten to twenty years. However, Lorna values herself and her life. She loves her family and she has a strong Christian faith. So she meticulously carries out the daily routines which keep her lungs functioning, and, despite bouts of illness, she makes sure that she, her husband and her daughter, lead ordinary but fulfilling lives.

How strange it is that illnesses which are so clearly physical are so directly affected in cause and outcome by what the person thinks and feels, yet what the person with biological depression thinks and feels is considered to be no more than a symptom of the illness – 'irrational guilt', 'depressed mood', 'loss of interest'.

A striking characteristic of the psychiatrists who believe in biological depression is their lack of interest in how we think.

How Important Is Thinking?

Mark's father had died suddenly and soon after Mark became depressed. He and his father had never been close, but now he remembered with anguish his father's hard work and sacrifices so that Mark could have a good education. However, when Mark said to his psychiatrist, 'I can never forgive myself for not doing more for my father', the psychiatrist said, 'That's just your illness speaking', and recorded in Mark's case notes the presence of the symptom 'irrational guilt'.

To have your profound concerns dismissed in this way is extremely painful, and it is confusing to be told that what you think and feel is nothing but the outcome of some biochemical change. In such a situation it is impossible to get the person telling you this to accept your point of view.

This is a popular ploy in the power struggle over whose definition of reality will prevail. Power, in the last analysis, is not about weapons or money or brute strength or feminine wiles, but about having the right to make your definition of reality prevail over all others. As children we might say, 'Mummy, I'm hungry,' but our powerful mother says, 'No you're not. You're tired and you're going to bed.' As adults we might say, 'The most important thing in life is to care for other people,' but Mrs Thatcher, our powerful Prime Minister, said, 'The most important thing in life is to get value for money.'

We can, of course, continue with our own beliefs no matter what the people who would be powerful tell us, but to do this we must have confidence in ourselves. If we lose confidence in ourselves we feel that what we think could be wrong. Then we are more likely to be defeated by the power ploy, 'That's your illness speaking'.

However, this power ploy contains a major logical problem.

In explaining the thoughts and feeling of a depressed person as being nothing but the outcome of biochemical changes in the brain, psychiatrists use a deterministic, reductionist model of the brain which says that thought is nothing more than the outcome of biochemical action in the brain. A brain produces thought in the way that a car engine produces exhaust smoke. The sign that a brain is not functioning properly is that it produces 'irrational' thoughts in the way that a malfunctioning car engine produces black, oily exhaust smoke.

The problem with this model of the brain and thought is that it allows no way of distinguishing a rational thought from an irrational thought. 'That's your illness speaking' is as much an outcome of biochemical causes as is 'I can never forgive myself'.

If 'I can never forgive myself' is nothing but the outcome of the biological action of the brain, then so is:

Be ye kind to one another, even as God for Christ's sake hath forgiven you.

I was angry with my friend:
I told my wrath, my wrath did end.
I was angry with my foe:
I told it not, my wrath did grow.

Man is born to trouble as the sparks fly upward.

That is the land of lost content,
    I see it shining plain,
The happy highways where I went
    And cannot come again.

Depend upon it, Sir, when a man knows he is to be
hanged in a fortnight, it concentrates his mind
wonderfully.

I have measured out my life in coffee spoons.

What life is this if, full of care,
We have no time to stand and stare.

As long as war is regarded as wicked, it will always
have its fascination. When it is looked upon as vulgar,
it will cease to be popular.

There is no greater illusion than fear,
no greater wrong than preparing to defend yourself,
no greater misfortune than having an enemy.
Whoever can see through all fear
will always be safe.

The grace of our Lord Jesus Christ, and the love of
God, and the fellowship of the Holy Spirit, be with us
evermore. Amen.

Yea, all which it inherit, shall dissolve
And, like this insubstantial pageant faded,
Leave not a rack behind. We are such stuff
As dreams are made on, and our little life
Is rounded with a sleep.[87]

If thought is nothing more than the outcome of biochemical
changes in the brain, then *all* thoughts are equally trivial and
valueless.

Psychiatrists try to resolve the logical problem which they have
created by leaving their 'thought is the result of biochemical change'
model and using the élitist argument of, 'My thought is rational and
your thought is irrational'. Thus when Dr Eliot Slater and Professor

Martin Roth wrote their textbook *Clinical Psychiatry*, which became
the bible for British psychiatrists, they said:

> It is the objective world in which we live and to which the
> subjective world must pay deference. It is more important to
> know what the facts are than what the patient makes of them.[88]

But who decides what is a fact? Why, the élitist psychiatrists of
course.

However, when psychiatrists use the élitist argument they have
actually abandoned the 'thought is a result of brain activity' model
and are using the model of thought which says that we are continuously engaged in perceiving, thinking, feeling and imaging in
the process of drawing conclusions and constructing values, attitudes, opinions and beliefs in order to give meaning to our circumstances and to guide our decisions. If we use this model of thought
we then have grounds for arguing that one thought can be better
than another.

Using this model of thought the psychiatrist, instead of dis-
missing Mark's feeling of guilt about his father, could draw on his
own experience to offer Mark another meaning which he could give
to his father's death, perhaps by saying, 'I felt like that when my
father died, but then I decided that the best way I could repay my
father was to be a good father to my children.'

In this model of thought the person is not portrayed as the passive
recipient of biochemical blows. Instead, the person is portrayed
as an active agent whose actions can be understood in terms of
that person's own thoughts, feelings and values; that is, the interpretations which that person makes of what happens to him.

It then becomes clear that neither biochemical changes nor genes
can cause behaviour. It is our *interpretation* of the changes in our
body which determine our behaviour.

If, for instance, there is a biochemical change which leads us to
perceive ourselves as being energetic and excited, those of us who
value ourselves and who see life as full of opportunities will use this
energy and excitement to be joyously active and creative, while
those of us who hate ourselves and who see life as nothing but a
source of fear and resentment will use this energy and excitement to
flee into that frantic activity which is called mania. Similarly, if there
is a biochemical change which leads us to perceive ourselves as
being tired and ill, those of us who value ourselves will rest and look
after ourselves, while those of us who hate ourselves will berate

ourselves, not look after ourselves, and despair at failing to meet our obligations.

However we interpret the biochemical changes in our body, our interpretations are linked to matters outside our body – our relationships to other people, the obligations and restrictions of the society in which we live, the limitations, opportunities and uncertainties in the economic and political forces which impinge on us, the advantages and disadvantages which ecology confers on us and, last but not least, the interpretations which other people seek to impose on us.

Thus Mark was faced with a dilemma. He could submit to the psychiatrist's power and define himself as having a genetic illness which cannot be cured but only managed with drugs and electroconvulsive therapy. Or he could decide that there was something important he had to understand about himself and his life, and that by thinking about this, perhaps talking it over with someone, he could arrive at an understanding which allowed him to accept himself and thus to get on with his life.

Psychiatrists too face a dilemma. In explaining that painful isolation we call depression, should they continue to use a model of the brain and thought which is logically unsound and which negates human experience, but which confers on them power and prestige? Or should they use a model which requires them to seek to understand how each of us makes sense of our experience? With this second model comes no power or prestige, for in the business of living no one is an expert.

If psychiatrists recognized that they had no more expertise in living than anyone else, they might then be able to see what harm their insistence on a genetic cause for depression is doing to so many people.

What it Means to Be Told That You Have a Genetic Illness

The simple-mindedness and lack of awareness of biological psychiatrists is seen at their clearest in their self-satisfaction at 'proving' that depression is a genetic illness. Now, they say, parents do not have to feel guilty if their children become depressed.

This shows an amazing unawareness of how ordinary, loving parents feel. My friend Lorna's greatest anxiety is not about herself but about her daughter, who has a one-in-four chance of carrying the cystic fibrosis gene. Lorna cannot hide from her daughter her own sufferings and the fact that the disease is fatal. Moreover, Lorna has to be very careful in her dealings with her own mother, for this old lady was most affronted when she was told that Lorna had inherited this disease. 'There's nothing wrong with my family,' she said, 'Lorna brought it on herself by working too hard.'

Of course we parents can feel very guilty about the things we did to our children when we were young, inexperienced and harassed parents, but such guilt can be assuaged by showing our children that we love them unconditionally. Children will forgive their parents anything, provided they are *sure* that their parents love them and accept them as they are.

Not understanding this, biological psychiatrists believe that it is very wrong to blame parents for how their children turn out. However, *if parents cannot be blamed when their children turn out badly, they cannot be praised when their children turn out well. Since most of our children turn out well, we parents are being deprived of the credit which our years of hard work deserve.*

Biological psychiatrists deny that there is a connection between childhood experience and later depression. Klein and Wender[89] advise that medication must come before psychotherapy since:

> The patient who has been receiving psychotherapy usually has to go through a process of unlearning about his depression. The psychotherapist may have been emphasizing factors that are less relevant or even inaccurate. For example, the psychotherapist may have been focusing on lengthy exploration of the patient's childhood, which in most instances – contrary to popular notions – has nothing to do with severe depressions.

Instead, Klein and Wender believe that it is very important that parents who are depressed should determine which of their children are at risk. They wrote:

> At the same time that medical researchers have learned more about the genetic origin of depressive illnesses, they have recognized that the evidence points to an increased likelihood of the appearance of depression in particular families. The chances that any one child will develop depression cannot be estimated exactly, but it has been predicted, for example, that 30 per cent of the daughters of mothers with depressive illness will develop depressive illness themselves. This is obviously distressing, but an awareness of genetic tendency helps a concerned parent or the vulnerable individual to detect the illness when it is beginning to develop. Early detection can

mean proper treatment. The depressed child, adolescent, or young adult may be spared unnecessary pain and the sometimes cumulative and far-reaching difficulties that stem from depressive illness.

The BBC television series *The Mind Machine*, produced in association with WNET, New York, includes one programme called 'Portrait in Blue'.[90] The actual portrait shown at the beginning of the film is one of a young girl painted by Van Gogh shortly before he killed himself after a life marked by severe depressions. The presenter and author of the series, Colin Blakemore, Professor of Physiology at Oxford University, is shown visiting the village in France where Van Gogh died. With him is his wife, Andrée, of whom Colin Blakemore says, 'Her moods vary too, and sometimes she gets very depressed.'

Colin Blakemore explains, 'By the latest estimates more than 20 per cent of us will experience some serious mood disturbance during our lives. Andrée is the only one in my household to suffer so far. But this is a worldwide problem and it hits some families very much harder than others.'

With these words we are shown a young boy and we hear a woman's voice saying, 'Clinton is our twelve year old. He is our third son and one that I think has the beginnings of what we call the family curse. Matthew' (and now the camera goes to a young man who smiles nervously and looks away) 'is our oldest son. He's twenty-one and I know Matthew has it. Dr Wender is treating Matthew. Matthew's very like his father was at his age. That's when Doug and I were courting. Joshua' (now the camera goes to a teenager who is smiling shyly and looking down) 'is fourteen. Joshua is a normal, good boy, happy, everyone likes him and he doesn't seem to have any problems, thank goodness. Rebecca' (the camera moves around the circle to a young woman who looks at her mother and then shuts her eyes) 'is nineteen, our only daughter. I think Rebecca has some definite depression problems. She has low times that are hard for her to deal with. Joseph' (the camera moves to a young boy who tries to smile but then looks very anxious) 'is eleven and he has some of the problems that Doug had at that age when we check back in family history and undoubtedly has the beginnings of it. Lastly Douglas' (a grey-haired man sits without response or expression) 'is our primary patient, the one that is being treated, that we have hope for.'

Douglas Barton says, 'I remember when I was seven years old, getting to go to my aunt and uncle's house. I should have been excited when I got there. The animals were there, the barns and the granaries were there, just joyous things to do. There was no joy in it at all. It was absolutely bleak. I felt hopeless. I couldn't understand what was going on. At the time there were only two kinds of sickness, the stomach flu, and you could identify that, and a broken limb, and you could identify that. I'd had both. I didn't identify this as a disease. It was something I didn't understand.'

A photograph is shown of Douglas Barton as a small boy looking very sad. Nowhere in the film is there any attempt to enquire into any personal reasons for his sadness. Nor does the film enquire into how our parents can teach us to be optimistic or fearful, courageous or frightened, to see ourselves as valuable or as inadequate and worthless.

Instead the film goes to Professor Wender (of Klein and Wender) who explains, 'What Doug shows is an example of someone who has had a depression ever since childhood. He's suffered thirty-seven years of pain. Sometimes it got better and sometimes it got worse. It never went away. And it was the kind of pain he was embarrassed to have and about which he was reluctant to complain. He, like many people, believed that it was a manifestation of some kind of personal weakness or spiritual difficulty rather than a disease.'

Later in the film, after we have been shown that the change in Douglas Barton came about by his taking the drugs which Professor Wender prescribed, Professor Wender says, 'I'm delighted that Doug Barton responded the way he has and I'm delighted that he's been able to discuss his illness with his kids, some of whom seem to be developing the same disease, and I'm delighted that this articulate man has been so open about this so that the kids' unhappiness is going to be mitigated somewhat by the fact that their father takes this as an unfortunate disease but not as a sign of psychological weakness of some sort.'

The Barton children who are interviewed are not all that delighted at being told that they have inherited a biological depression. They have seen their father's sufferings, and they have been told that this is their fate.

Matthew Barton says, 'The fact is there's a profound difference between being depressed because you got a bad grade in school or your girlfriend dropped you, or any of the normal reasons that human beings gets depressed, and the way we get depressed. It's a physical depression. It is without cause.'

Of course, knowing that you are doomed to a life of misery, dependent like your father on pills, is a great deal worse than getting bad grades or losing a girlfriend. And who would want to marry a man with such an illness? Even if some girl did, would he want his children to suffer as he is suffering?

Clinton Barton says, 'Things happen without any reason. I can get depressed one day, just after I get an A on a test and right after that I can get depressed. It can happen any time.'

Of course, what is the point in doing well at school, or of looking forward to anything if you know that you are never going to be happy and successful? And what do the other children at school think of you when they know you have this illness?

What none of the Barton family appear to have questioned, perhaps because they have not been taught by Professor Wender just how genes function, is that it is odd that as many as four out of the five splendid Barton children have inherited this disease. Even with a dominant gene inherited in the Mendelian manner, like the colour of our eyes, there is only one chance in two of inheriting that gene. With a recessive gene like cystic fibrosis, the chances of a child inheriting it is only one-in-four. If the Barton children knew this they might wonder whether there was not something else going on in their family.

As these Barton children see it, they are members of a family caught up in a tragedy which they can neither understand nor question. A professor of psychiatry has told them that they have biological depression and that their fate is sealed.

Andrée Blakemore describes how she feels when she is depressed. 'At its worst, I can't do anything. I just want to lie down, hands clasped, and just try not to think. My mind is absolutely confused, thought rushing around all over the place, things I've got to do, the manuscript I've got to read and I can't possibly read it for another ten years. This is how I feel it's going to last for ever. I'm totally incapable of doing things. Perhaps in the middle of this somebody telephones. I lift it up and put on an act and I can answer it quite sanely. But in general I feel very wretched and I have ambivalent feelings. One hour, say, I will feel that I am dying and I begin to panic and get very agitated about that. The next hour I feel that I have to die, I have to find a way out, to escape.'

The only drugs she has found which ease this suffering are

imipramine, a tricyclic antidepressant, and benzodiazepine, a tranquillizer about whose addictive properties much has been written.

Returning to Van Gogh, Colin Blakemore explains, 'Van Gogh
carried an inherited curse. Andrée, too, seems to have inherited her
susceptibility.'

Over a photograph of herself and her father on her wedding day,
Andrée says, 'I had highs and lows and I accepted it as being part of
me. My father also had it. Again it was in the 50s, and he was
ashamed of it, didn't know what it was. I remember days when he
would take me to school, in January or February, we'd both be very,
very low. We didn't discuss it. We knew that our moods were the
same. We didn't think to talk about it. We just accepted it.'

Later in the film this fine, brave woman says, 'Some days I think
about the fact that I've had three children. I really fear that one of
them will be like me. But at least, if one of them is like me, then we
can prepare her for that. We know how to approach the problem,
although it's going to be no less wretched for her. I think she would
have even more support than perhaps I've had.'

Back in the cornfields where Van Gogh painted his last pictures,
Colin Blakemore says, 'For Vincent there were no antidepressant
drugs, no ECT.'

Colin Blakemore then describes in considerable detail the horrific
circumstances of Van Gogh's death. The final scenes are of Colin
and Andrée Blakemore visiting the grave of Van Gogh, and the final
words are hers.

'Van Gogh died at the age of thirty-seven, and one just felt what a
waste, and one feels, well, perhaps, that's the way I'm going to go.'

This is an immensely tragic film, tragic not just because of the
suffering of Andrée Blakemore and the Barton family, but of the
millions of depressed people who have seen this film and been told
that they are doomed to a life of suffering and depression, reliant
not on themselves but on pills, electroconvulsive therapy and
psychiatrists.

What is tragic, too, is the selfish and petulant blindness of those
men who do not see the subtle differences there are between people,
the way we are, at one and the same time, all human beings and our
own individual selves. This blindness refuses to see that all of us,
depressed or happy, are always engaged in making sense of what
goes on around us, drawing conclusions and using these conclusions to make decisions and to predict our future. Such blindness
treats us, not as people, but as objects. As objects we are

diminished, demeaned, our truth is ignored, and we can be used and abused most cruelly.

The reason for this blindness is the ambition of those men who wish to impose on others their belief that the mind is no more than a machine and that our sufferings are no more than the malfunction of a machine. In doing so, these men acquire power, prestige and money, and they deny their awareness of their own experience of living and their own responsibility for the lives that they lead. To this end they will present themselves as scientists while denying the actual results of scientific research.

In doing this they not only increase the sufferings of those people who are depressed, they denigrate all of us. The biological psychiatrists are saying that whenever we fall into despair, doubt our own worth, regret our actions, rage against out fate, what we are saying and feeling are of no more importance than red spots in measles.

And in doing this they actively prevent people from coming to understand why the prison of depression comes upon them.

Understanding Why

Someone who is depressed will often say, 'The depression came over me suddenly. There was no reason for me to get depressed. It must be a physical illness.'

There is a very good reason for saying this. The events which led up to the construction of the prison were very painful and very frightening, and we all try to deal with painful and frightening events by blotting them out of our memory. In saving ourselves from danger we can act with a speed and strength that we could never call upon at ordinary times. We dash out of the path of a speeding car; we carry our children out of a burning house; in a moment we can put a wall around our self and save it from annihilation.

However, if you say to a psychiatrist, 'The depression came over me suddenly. There was no reason for me to get depressed,' and this is what he wants to hear, he will ask no further questions. He will not accompany you back through the painful events and support you while you look at and name the horrors which threaten you so.

I have met many people who have had psychiatric treatment for ten or twenty years and who have never told their story. They have had dozens of interviews with consultants, junior doctors and psychiatric nurses, but never have they been given the opportunity to tell their story as they would tell it. Never have they been able to say what parts of their story and their present circumstances are important to them and why, or, if they did, the psychiatrist took no notice. The psychiatrist decided for himself what were 'the facts' of the person's life, and what the person thought of these 'facts' and other matters was ignored or discounted.

Yet, had the psychiatrist given the person time to talk in his own way, and if he asked questions aimed at increasing his understanding and not simply at gathering 'the facts', the suddenness and the apparent inexplicability of the depression would cease to be a mystery explicable only by saying, 'It's an illness'.

When Alice first came to see me she said, 'My depression must be physical. I was gardening, and I enjoy gardening, and then suddenly there it was. Another time I went to a concert by the Moscow State Orchestra. It was wonderful, deeper, better than anything I'd ever heard. But after about ten minutes I wanted to be at home. It wasn't that I was lonely and wanted someone with me – it was – depression.'

We went on talking. Alice asked, 'In your books you talk a lot about a person's childhood. Is it necessary to remember your childhood? I can't remember mine, not until I was twelve or thereabouts.'

She did remember some things from her childhood – how her mother was a businesswoman who had little time for Alice. She expected Alice to stay out of her way, to be responsible for her younger sister, to be always well behaved and to work hard. Alice grew up being obedient, hard working, always trying to please other people and to be loyal to them. She received few rewards for her goodness, but she doubted if, for all her striving to be good, she deserved any. As she said, 'If I am not feeling guilty then there is something wrong with me.'

These were the attitudes she carried into her marriage, and her husband readily accepted them, for then he could manipulate her through her guilt and be sure that she would blame herself when he behaved badly. Which he did. He embarked on a series of affairs and finally left her for a younger woman.

Throughout their marriage her husband had refused to accept her anger, just in the way that her mother had done. So she kept her anger buried, but sometimes it burst out, whereupon her husband said that she was mad.

Her husband always refused to enter into any discussion with her and responded to her entreaties with silence. However, when she became so depressed that she could not carry out her household duties, her husband, who by then was a consultant at a major hospital, arranged for his psychiatrist colleague to visit her. When she told this man that her husband would not discuss their relationship with her, he advised her to adapt herself to her husband's ways and to feel grateful for being a consultant's wife. This angered and disgusted her, but she did not reveal this, any more than she would reveal that her husband had affairs with other women. She felt that she should be loyal to him. She did not realize the full extent of her husband's perfidy until some months later when she discovered from a friend that this psychiatrist himself had a mistress.

Her loyalty to her husband prevented her from telling her friends about what was happening to her, and so she isolated herself and was without anyone to support and comfort her.

After her husband had departed to set up a home for himself, his mistress and their baby, Alice was left with a large house and garden, two teenage children and a very limited income. Her husband, as unfaithful husbands are wont to do, ceased to give her any assistance in maintaining the house and garden, lost interest in their children, and became mean. This is the process whereby men sever their ties with their wives. They manufacture a hate for their wives and the women, well trained in guilt, blame themselves.

So Alice blamed herself, and she felt even more guilty. 'I try to work out what I did wrong in my marriage, so if I ever get married again I won't make the same mistakes again.'

Sometimes she got angry, but the strength of her murderous rage frightened her. She felt, too, anger that her rage against him could not be expressed. She feared that her rage would tear her apart.

To talk about all this to me took time, so it was over an hour before we returned to the topic of the sudden appearance of her depression. I had remarked that it is a good idea to identify the circumstances where we feel vulnerable, and getting tired is usually one of these.

'That's what happened when I was gardening that Saturday,' said Alice. 'I had been pushing myself to get one big job done. I should have stopped at six and had a hot bath – I always find a hot bath makes me feel better – but I was still in the garden at nine and it was just about dark. It was a job my husband always used to do – cutting back a huge privet hedge.'

Alone in the garden, darkness coming on, struggling to finish a near impossible task, she felt rage against her faithless, cruel husband, and thought, 'I tried so hard to be good. Where is my reward? Why am I abandoned by everyone I love? Why am I alone? What have I done that I am punished like this? Why? What will become of me?'

Alice in that garden was not reacting to a fantasy, something she imagined, something she exaggerated and misperceived. She was seeing reality plain, and it was terrible.

We cannot bear too much reality. We have to turn away, throw up a shield, hide behind a wall. In the prison of depression we can contemplate the past and the future. We can ignore the reality of the present.

The reality of the present was what the music of the Moscow State Orchestra had brought to Alice. When we listen to music – really listen and not just hear – we are living in the present. Not thinking of the past and future, we feel no guilt. We are at one with the music. We are happy. But we can continue in this state only if we can allow ourselves to be happy. If we, like Alice, cannot allow ourselves to be happy, if we have been brought up to believe that we were not put on this earth to enjoy ourselves and that to breathe is to be guilty, then listening to music is dangerous. Our conscience, like Alice's, will punish us. Moreover, great music speaks of that universal sadness which we all share. If we have learned to accept our sadness, then music, in touching our sadness, takes us out of time and into contentment. If we, like Alice, still feel the sadness as a mortal wound, then music, in touching our sadness, creates agony and returns us to the past and future where guilt is waiting to pounce. Against such pain, Alice had to protect herself with her old familiar depression.

The belief that depression arises out of biochemical changes in the brain and these changes from a gene is based on an illogical fantasy which has little relationship to real life. This fantasy was created by men who lacked the courage and wisdom to face reality and to accept their own insignificance and ignorance. Facing the reality of life does require courage, but unless we can face reality we cannot change it.

22

Drugs – Friend or Foe?

Drugs give you a sort of start, so if you want you can.
Caroline

To make drugs your friends who give you a start, you need to know all that you can about them. If you don't know anything about the drugs your doctor prescribes and just take them more or less the way he tells you to take them, the drugs become your foe.

Not knowing, you can make mistakes in taking them, and that can cost you dear. You can become quite ill, or even die. Not knowing, you can fail to realize that the unpleasant symptoms you experience are the result of the drugs and instead blame yourself for being stupid enough to be even more ill and depressed. Not knowing, you feel that the doctor has power over you and that you are helpless. Not knowing, you feel that having to take drugs just proves how inadequate and worthless you are.

To find out about drugs is not difficult. Whenever a doctor prescribes any drug you should ask him what it is and what its effects will be. Nowadays, most doctors are more willing to give explanations than they used to be. My mother always said that the reason that doctors would not explain what they were doing was that if they did you would eventually know just as much as they did. Or just as little. Experts need their secrets so they can be experts.

However, no matter how willing and able a doctor is to inform his patients, not all the information can be imparted at a consultation, and few of us, as the research shows, remember accurately and completely what the doctor tells us.

You can find the information you need in books which are easily available in bookshops and libraries.

Here I have listed the drugs commonly prescribed in the treatment of depression and outlined some of the problems associated with them. The interactions between different drugs taken simultaneously are not well understood, and many people become the victims of 'polypharmacy', where drugs are prescribed in dangerous combinations.[91] Whenever you are prescribed more than one drug for any or different conditions, you must ask your doctor about possible interactions.

The books I have used in this chapter are:

Handbook of Psychiatric Drug Therapy, by Steven E. Hyman, MD, Fellow in Genetics at Harvard Medical School, and George W. Arana, Associate Professor of Psychiatry at Tufts University School of Medicine, published by Little, Brown and Company, Boston and Toronto, in 1987.

British National Formulary, a Joint Publication of the British Medical Association and the Royal Pharmaceutical Society of Great Britain, Number 18, September, 1989.

Medicines, A Guide for Everybody, by Peter Parish, published by Penguin, Harmondsworth, in 1989. 'Professor Parish is a distinguished physician, university teacher and researcher. He has dedicated himself to encouraging the appropriate and safe use of medicines and his influence is worldwide. He is a Doctor of Medicine, Member of the Royal College of Surgeons, Fellow of the Royal College of General Practitioners and a Member of the Faculty of Community Medicine of the Royal College of Physicians.'[92]

At the beginning of his book Peter Parish points out:

The action of a drug is a complex chemical and physical process which may take place locally in certain cells, organs or special tissues; or more generally upon most cells in the body. Some drugs act outside the cell, some on its surface and others within the cells. In most cases we still know very little about how drugs actually act within the body; but we know a good deal about the effects of that action . . .

It must always be remembered that a drug's effects are like shot-gun pellets – some land on target and others do not. We must therefore try to think of a drug in terms of its full spectrum of benefits and risks . . .

Unfortunately there are many disorders for which there is no cure. In the absence of a real cure and in the presence of patients who react favourably to *anything* which is done to help them, 'treatments' tend to proliferate. *It is a good rule of thumb that if many treatments are in use for the same disease it is because there is no real treatment known for that disease.*

There are three things which you should know about any drug you might take:

1. Its name.
2. The beneficial effects it could have.
3. The unpleasant or harmful effects it could have.

It is not enough, indeed, it is certainly dangerous, to identify your drugs only by their colour – 'the pink one', 'the black and green one'. However, the actual names can be a problem, for every drug has at least two names.

There is the *pharmacopoeial* or *generic* name, which relates to the chemical composition of the drug.

And there is the *brand* or *trade* name, which is the title the manufacturer has given to the drug. Since different manufacturers give different names to the same drug, or the same manufacturer markets the one drug under different names in different places, a popular drug may have many trade names.

Thus a chemical compound with the pharmacopoeial of diazepam has a long list of trade names – Valium, Alupram, Atensine, Diazemuls, Evacalm, Solis, Stesolid, Tensium.

You need to be quite clear as to what benefits the drugs could bring you, how long these benefits will take to arrive, and how long they will last. You need to be aware that, while doctors call the unpleasant or harmful effects of drugs 'side-effects', thus implying that these effects are not important, such effects are very important indeed for the person who has to endure them. You need to weigh up the benefits and the deficits in the light of your own circumstances. For instance, an antidepressant drug like amitriptyline has a sedative effect. This could be fine for you if you are taking things easy and getting plenty of rest, but if you still have your living to earn, having to push against this sedative effect could be an additional burden.

The main problem in learning about the drugs used in the treatment of depression is that there are just so many of them. By contrast, otitis media, infection of the middle ear, a painful condition which can have serious complications, is treated with only three or four antibiotics. As I have suffered from this often I know which of these drugs is the most effective for me.

Each psychiatrist develops his own method for finding his way around the maze of the drugs used by his profession. Psychiatrists' prescribing techniques are rather like the techniques for sailing a boat singlehandedly. There is a general pattern which all such sailors follow, but each sailor develops his own idiosyncratic technique. What I am describing here is the general technique which most psychiatrists follow more or less. It is the outcome of a mixture of equivocal research results, broad generalizations from small samples, habit, and professional dogma. If you consult a psychiatrist who prides himself on his individualism you could well find him following a different pattern.

So, suppose you make your first visit to a psychiatrist and he diagnoses you as suffering from depression.

The first drug he is likely to offer you is a *tricyclic antidepressant*. He can choose from:

GENERIC NAME	TRADE NAMES
amitriptyline	Domical, Elavil, Lentizol, Tryptizol, Amitril, Endep, Elavil
amoxapine	Asendin
butriptyline	Evadyne
clomipramine	Anafranil, Anafranil SR
desipramine	Pertofran, Norpramin
dothiepin	Prothiaden
doxepin	Sinequan, Adapin, Curetin
imipramine	Praminil, Tofranil, Imavate, Janimine, SK Pramine, Presamine
iprindole	Prondol
lofepramine	Gamanil
maprotiline	Ludiomil
mianserin	Bolvidon, Norval
nortriptyline	Allegron, Aventyl, Pamelor
protriptyline	Concordin, Vivactyl
trazodone	Molipazin, Desyrel
trimipramine	Surmontil
viloxazine	Vivalan

The first of these drugs was discovered in 1958. Those of you who are old enough to remember the 40s will recall the excitement and relief that penicillin and then the other antibiotic drugs brought. Diseases which had for centuries killed people now virtually disappeared. So when these first antidepressant drugs went into use many doctors predicted that depression would become just as rare as typhoid and pneumonia had become. Unfortunately, this did not happen. The incidence of depression has actually increased, and along with this increase an increase in the number of antidepressant drugs.

According to the *British National Formulary* (4.3.1. Tricyclic and related antidepressant drugs):

> The term 'tricyclic' is misleading as there are now 1-, 2-, and 4-ring structured drugs with broadly similar properties.
>
> These drugs are most effective for treating moderate to severe endogenous depression associated with psychomotor and physiological changes such as loss of appetite and sleep disturbances; improvement in sleep is usually the first benefit of therapy. Since there may be an interval of 2 to 4 weeks before the antidepressant action takes place, electroconvulsive treatment may be required in severe depression where delay is hazardous or intolerable . . .
>
> DOSAGE. About 10 to 20% of patients fail to respond to tricyclic and related antidepressant drugs and inadequate plasma concentrations may account for some of these failures. It is important to achieve plasma concentrations which are sufficiently high for effective treatment but not high enough to cause toxic effects . . .
>
> MANAGEMENT. The patient's condition must be checked frequently, especially in the early weeks of treatment, to detect any suicidal tendencies. Limited quantities of antidepressant drugs should be prescribed at any one time as they are dangerous in overdosage. Some of the newer drugs, for example mianserin and trazodone, seem less dangerous in overdose than the older tricyclics.
>
> Treatment should be continued for 2 to 4 weeks before suppression of symptoms can be expected and thereafter should be maintained at the optimum level for at least another month before any attempt is made at dose reduction. Treatment should not be withdrawn prematurely, otherwise symptoms are likely to recur. The natural history of depression suggests that remission usually occurs after 3 months to a year or more and some patients appear to benefit from maintenance therapy with about half the therapeutic dosage for several months to prevent relapse. It may be appropriate during the early stages

of treatment to add an hypnotic to correct the sleeping pattern or an anxiolytic to allay anxiety and agitation.

CHOICE. Antidepressant drugs can be roughly divided into those with additional sedative properties, for example amitriptyline, and those with less, for example imipramine . . .

SIDE-EFFECTS. Arrhythmias and heart block occasionally follow the use of tricyclic antidepressants, particularly amitriptyline, and may be a factor in the sudden death of patients with cardiac disease. Although the use of the older tricyclic antidepressants has been associated with reports of convulsions and of hepatic and haematological reactions, the frequency of these side-effects appears to be much higher, and deaths have been reported, with the newer non-tricyclic antidepressants. In particular, mianserin has been associated with haematological and hepatic reactions and maprotiline has been associated with convulsions. Patients being treated with these drugs therefore require careful supervision. In the case of mianserin a full blood count is recommended every four weeks during the first 3 months of treatment; subsequent clinical monitoring should continue and treatment should be stopped and a full blood count obtained if fever, sore throat, stomatitis, or other signs of infection develop.

Other side-effects of tricyclic and related antidepressants include drowsiness, dry mouth, blurred vision, constipation, urinary retention, and sweating . . . The patient should be encouraged to persist with treatment as some tolerance to these side-effects seems to develop. They are further reduced if low doses are given initially and then gradually increased.

This gradual introduction of treatment is particularly important in the elderly, who, because of the hypotensive effects of these drugs, are prone to attacks of dizziness or even syncope. The tricyclic and related antidepressants should be prescribed with caution in epilepsy as they lower the convulsive threshold . . .

LACK OF RESPONSE. In patients who do not respond to antidepressants, the diagnosis, dosage, compliance, and possible continuation of psychosocial or physical aggravating causes should be carefully reviewed; other drug treatment may be successful. The patient may respond to low-dose *flupenthixol* (Fluanxol) or MAIOs. MAOIs should preferably not be started until at least a week after tricyclics have been stopped: they should not be started until 5 weeks after fluoxetine has been stopped. *Tryptophan* appears to benefit some patients when given alone or as adjunctive therapy.

Next your psychiatrist will consider whether you are anxious. The received wisdom of psychiatry is that there is depression with anxiety and depression without anxiety, though how anyone could go around thinking, 'I am bad. I am guilty. I am without hope,' and not be anxious is beyond my imagining. Still, how is a psychiatrist to know that a person is anxious if that person does not tell him?

You tell your psychiatrist that you are anxious. So now he will consider giving you an *anxiolytic*, more commonly known as a tranquillizer, made from a chemical composition known as *benzodiazepines*.

GENERIC NAME	TRADE NAMES
alprazolam	Xanax
bromazepam	Lexotan
chlordiazepoxide	Librium, Tropium
chlormezanone	Trancopal
clobazam	Frisium
clorazepate dipotassium	Tranzene
diazepam	Valium, Alupram, Atensine, Diazemuls, Evacalm, Solis, Stesolid, Tensium
ketazolam	Anxon
lorazepam	Almazine, Ativan
medazepam	Nobrium
oxazepam	Oxanid, Serax
prazepam	Centrax

Peter Parish said of these drugs,

[The benzodiazepines] were discovered in 1933 but it was not until 1960 that chlordiazepoxide was shown to produce 'taming' in wild animals. The taming effect was then shown to work on monkeys and, because of this, clinical trials were carried out on man which demonstrated its anti-anxiety effects. They are referred to as anti-anxiety drugs, anxiolytics, anxiolytic-sedatives, minor tranquillizers, tranquillizers or 'tranks'.

Depending on the dose benzodiazepines will calm you down but they *impair* brain function and in larger doses they send you to sleep – they are 'downers'. Common adverse effects produced by the benzodiazepines include drowsiness, light-headedness, sedation, lack of coordination and difficulty in walking (ataxia). These effects may occur after a single dose as well as after repeated doses and they may persist the following day. They may particularly affect the elderly, who may become confused and their memory may be affected. Elderly patients may also develop incontinence or they may develop difficulties in passing urine . . .

They can reduce ability to carry out skilled tasks so that they can affect ability to drive motor vehicles and operate moving vehicles. They can increase the effects of alcohol.

These drugs can produce opposite effects (paradoxical effects) in some people. Instead of acting as 'downers', they act as 'uppers' and the patients become excited, aggressive and confused . . .

Because of their effects on the brain they produce addiction in some people if taken regularly every day for four to six weeks. Addiction means that you cannot manage without them because if you stop you get *withdrawal symptoms* . . .

If you stop taking benzodiazepines suddenly you may develop severe anxiety, tension and panic attacks, poor concentration, difficulty in sleeping, nausea, trembling, palpitations, sweating, and pains and stiffness in your face, head and neck. You may become very aware of sensations in your body, very aware of light and you may experience strange feelings of movement. You may feel depersonalized (outside of yourself) and unreal (as if you are in a dream). In severe cases of physical addiction withdrawal may cause you to have fits, become confused and have a mental breakdown with delusions and hallucinations. You can even get the dt's (delirium tremens).

Withdrawal symptoms occur two to three days after stopping short-acting benzodiazepines, eg, oxazepam (Oxanid) and lorazepam (Almarazine, Ativan). With the others, which are longer acting, withdrawal symptoms occur about seven days after stopping them. Withdrawal symptoms usually last from one to three weeks but can go on for months.

In mild cases, symptoms of withdrawal can be like the original anxiety symptoms and lead the doctor to continue the treatment or even increase the dose! However, do not forget that your anxiety symptoms can return, which means you need help but certainly not by regular daily use of 'downers' over months and years.

Note: You can become 'addicted' to benzodiazepines if you take them regularly every day for as short a period of time as four to six weeks.

These drugs can affect your ability to perform skilled tasks (psychomotor function) and may produce effects on your brain like chronic alcoholism.

Benzodiazepines should be taken in as low a dose as possible, as infrequently as possible and for the shortest time possible. Intermittent use (eg, for one or two weeks during a severe attack of anxiety and then several weeks without them) is better than continued use and may prevent you from becoming addicted. But do not forget that you should try to do *without* them as soon as is possible.

Suppose you tell your psychiatrist that you are not sleeping. Now he will consider whether to give you an *hypnotic*.

GENERIC NAME	TRADE NAMES
benzodiazepines	
chlormezanone	Trancopal
flunitrazepam	Rohynol
flurazepam	Dalmane, Paxene
lormetazepam	–
nitrazepam	Mogadon, Nitrados, Noctesed, Remnos, Semnite, Surem, Unisomnia
temazepam	Normison
triazolam	Halcion
other hypnotics	
chlorate hydrate	Noctec
chlormethiazole	Heminevrin
dichloralphenazone	Welldorm
methyprylone	Nodular
triclofos sodium	–

The *British National Formulary* (4.1.1. Hypnotics) warns:

Benzodiazepines should be used to treat insomnia only when it is severe, disabling, or subjecting the individual to extreme distress.

DRIVING. Hypnotics and anxiolytics may impair judgement and increase reaction time, and so affect ability to drive or operate machinery; they increase the effects of alcohol. Moreover, the hangover effects of a night dose may impair driving the next day.

Before an hypnotic is prescribed the cause of the insomnia should be established and, where possible, underlying factors should be treated. However, it should be noted that some patients have unrealistic sleep expectations, and others understate their alcohol consumption which is often the cause of insomnia.

Transient insomnia may occur in those who normally sleep well and may be due to extraneous factors such as noise, shift work and jet lag. If an hypnotic is indicated one that is rapidly eliminated should be chosen, and only one or two doses should be given.

Short-term insomnia is usually related to an emotional problem or serious medical illness. It may last for a few weeks, and may recur; an hypnotic can be useful but should not be given for more than three weeks (preferably one week). Intermittent use is desirable with omission of some doses. A rapidly eliminated drug is generally appropriate.

Chronic insomnia is rarely benefited by hypnotics and is more often due to mild dependence caused by injudicious prescribing . . .

Hypnotics should **not** be prescribed indiscriminately and routine prescribing, especially in hospitals, is undesirable though commonplace. Ideally, they should be reserved for short courses in the acutely distressed. Tolerance to their effects develops within 3 to 14 days of continuous use and long-term efficacy cannot be assured. A major drawback of long-term use is that withdrawal causes rebound insomnia and precipitates a withdrawal syndrome.

Where prolonged administration is unavoidable hypnotics should be discontinued as soon as feasible and the patient warned that sleep may be disturbed for a few days before normal rhythm is re-established; broken sleep with vivid dreams and increased REM [rapid eye movement] may persist for several weeks.

So you collect your drugs from the pharmacy and take them as prescribed. Time goes by and you might find yourself feeling much happier. Or you might not. On your next visit to your psychiatrist he decides to change your prescription. He might increase the dose of the tricyclic, or change from one tricyclic to another. If neither of these makes any improvement he then decides to try something different, a *monoamine oxidase inhibitor* (MAOI).

GENERIC NAME	TRADE NAMES
isocarboxazid	Marplan
phenelzine	Nardil
tranylcypromine	Parnate

Steven Hyman and George Arana wrote:

Iproniazid, the first of the MAOIs, was synthesized as an antituberculous drug in the 1950s. It was noted clinically to have striking stimulant and antidepressant properties and was subsequently shown to be an inhibitor of the enzyme monoamine oxidase (MAO). Although its hepatoxicity precluded its continued clinical use, other MAOIs were developed. It is not proved that the therapeutic action of these drugs is related to their ability to inhibit MAO . . .

The precise mechanism by which the tricyclic antidepressants and the MAOIs are effective for depression is unknown, although there is pharmacologic evidence that they affect monoamine neurotransmitter systems in the brain . . . As yet, no fully convincing theories have emerged.

Phenelzine and isocarboxazid are hydrazine derivatives and are irreversible blockers of MAO, whereas tranylcypromine reversibly inhibits MAO. Tranylcypromine is the only available nonhydrazine MAOI; it has structural characteristics similar to amphetamine and does have some stimulant properties. ·

The stimulant properties of tranylcypromine (Parnate) mean that if you stop taking the drug abruptly you will have quite severe withdrawal symptoms, comparable to those experienced when coming off amphetamine (speed). Not realizing this, many people have thought that they were still dangerously depressed and have gone back on the drug. While Steven Hyman and George Arana link stimulant properties only to one MAOI, many people have found similar withdrawal difficulties when they have been taking one of the other MAOIs for an extended period. It is necessary to reduce the dose very, very slowly, making sure that your body has adapted to each level before making a further reduction.

MAOIs have other problems. Peter Parish wrote:

> The adverse effects of MAO inhibitors may occasionally be greater and more serious than those of any other drug used in the treatment of psychological disorders. The risk of liver damage with currently used MAO inhibitors is low. But these drugs may cause excessive stimulation of the brain, causing trembling, insomnia, sweating, agitation, and rarely hallucinations, confusion and convulsions. A fall in blood pressure is usual and dizziness, headaches, delayed or inhibited ejaculation, difficulty in passing urine, weakness, fatigue, dry mouth, water retention (oedema) and skin rashes may occasionally occur.
>
> Interactions with other drugs may produce serious effects. What is called hypertensive crisis may occur when certain drugs or foods are taken with MAO inhibitors. This is caused by a sudden increase in blood pressure which may cause severe headache, bleeding into the brain, heart failure and death. The foods which may produce this interaction all contain amines such as tyramine which may affect the blood pressure. The MAO inhibitors prevent the breakdown of tyramine in the liver and allow it to work at the nerve endings, releasing a chemical (noradrenaline) which sends up blood pressure. Tyramine is present in cheese and various other foods. Patients taking MAO inhibitors should always carry with them a warning card which lists the prohibited foods and drugs.

If you are prescribed an MAOI, read the Treatment Card very carefully and make sure you understand it fully.

The Treatment Card prepared by the Pharmaceutical Society and the British Medical Association on behalf of the Health Department of the United Kingdom recommends that you carry the card with you at all times and show it to any doctor or dentist who may be about to give you treatment. It also asks you to read the following instructions carefully.

> While taking this medicine, and for 14 days after your treatment finishes you must observe the following simple instructions:
>
> 1. Do not eat CHEESE, PICKLED HERRING or BROAD BEAN PODS.
> 2. Do not eat or drink BOVRIL, OXO, MARMITE or ANY SIMILAR MEAT or YEAST EXTRACT.
> 3. Eat only FRESH foods and avoid food that you suspect could

be stale or 'going off'. This is especially important with meat, fish, poultry or offal. Avoid game.

4. Do not take any other MEDICINES (including tablets, capsules, nose drops, inhalations or suppositories) whether purchased by you or previously prescribed by your doctor, without first consulting your doctor or your pharmacist.

NB *Treatment for coughs and colds, pain relievers, tonics and laxatives are medicines.*

5. Avoid alcoholic drinks.

Keep a careful note of any food or drink that disagrees with you, avoid it and tell your doctor.

Report any unusual or severe symptoms to your doctor and follow any other advice given by him.

If neither the tricyclics nor the MAOIs make any difference to your state, or if you have described to your psychiatrist how, from time to time, as well as being depressed, you feel elated and active, he might decide to prescribe *lithium*.

GENERIC NAME	TRADE NAMES
lithium carbonate	Camcolit 250, Camcolit 400, Liskonum, Pharsal, Priadel, Lithobid, Eskalith, Eskalith CR, Lithonate, Lithotabs
lithium citrate	Litarex, Cibalith

The *British National Formulary* (4.2.3. Antimanic Drugs) states:

Lithium salts are used for their mood regulating action in the prophylaxis and treatment of mania and in the prophylaxis of manic-depressive illness (bipolar illness or bipolar depression) and in the prophylaxis of recurrent depression (unipolar illness or unipolar depression) . . .

Lithium salts have a narrow therapeutic/toxic ratio and should therefore not be prescribed unless facilities for monitoring plasma concentrations are available. Patients should be carefully selected . . .

Lithium toxicity is made worse by sodium depletion . . .

In long-term use therapeutic concentrations of lithium have been thought to cause histological and functional changes in the kidney. The significance of such changes is not clear but is of sufficient concern to discourage long-term use of lithium unless it is definitely indicated. Patients should therefore be maintained on lithium treatment after 3–5 years only if, on assessment, benefit persists.

If you are taking lithium you may feel sure that there is something very wrong with you because you feel so unreal, and even when you are not depressed everything seems so flat. All the joy and colour of life have disappeared and you feel uninspired and uncreative. Steven Hyman and George Arana say:

> Patients on lithium may also complain of dulling of their affects [emotions], a sense of depersonalization, or a general 'greying' of their mental life. Although such subjective complaints may easily be mistaken for depression, they may be caused by lithium. They are bothersome to patients and may lead to lithium refusal unless a serum level can be found at which the patient has adequate prophylaxis without excessive mental side-effects.

Suppose many months go by and you are no better, or, having got better, you suddenly become very depressed again. Or, perhaps, you have not responded to these drugs in the way that the psychiatric textbooks say that you should respond, and your psychiatrist feels himself to be at at the end of his tether. He may now be calling you a 'therapy resistant patient'. Or he gives you another diagnosis, perhaps 'schizo-affective psychosis', or decides that you are really a depressed schizophrenic. (The longer you go on being depressed the more different diagnoses you will be given.) So he decides to give you an *antipsychotic* drug.

GENERIC NAME	TRADE NAMES
phenothiazines	
chlorpromazine	Chloractil, Largactil, Thorazine
fluphenazine	Moditen, Prolixin, Permitil
methotrimeprazine	Noziman, Veracil
pericyazine	Neulactil
perphenazine	Fentazin, Trilafon
prochlorperazine	Buccastem, Stemetil, Vertigon
promazine	Dolmatil
thioridazine	Melleril
trifluoperazine	Stelazine

butrophenones

benperidol	Anquil
droperidol	Droleptan
haloperidol	Dozic, Fortunan, Haldol, Serenace
trifluperidol	Triperidol

diphenybutylpiperidines

fluspirilene	Redeptin
pimozide	Orap

thioxanthenes

chlorprothixene	Taractan
flupenthixol	Depixol
zuclopenthixol	Clopixol

others

oxypertine	Integrin

depot injections

flupenthixol decanoate	Depixol, Depixol Concentrate
fluphenazine decanoate	Modecate, Modecate Concentrate
fluphenazine enanthate	Moditen Enanthate
fluspirilene	Redeptin
haloperidol decanoate	Haldol Decanoate
pipothiazine palmitate	Piportil Depot
zuclopenthixol decanoate	Clopixol, Clopixol Concentrate

Steven Hyman and George Arana comment:

The antipsychotic drugs have been in clinical use since the 1950s when chlorpromazine, a phenothiazine derivative, was synthesized in France . . .

Although usually referred to as 'antipsychotic drugs' the agents in this group have other therapeutic usages (eg, as antiemetics, preanaesthetics, and in the treatment of some movement disorders). The term *neuroleptic* (meaning causing a neurological disorder) has also been applied to these compounds because of the profound motor effects they produce. These neuroleptic effects make the antipsychotic drugs among the most problematic in psychiatry.

While antipsychotic drugs are the cornerstone of treatment for a wide variety of psychotic disorders, their side-effects may be severe, and some (eg, akathisia or akinesia) can even mimic or exacerbate the symptoms for which the drugs were originally prescribed. Long-term use of these agents can result in the syndrome of tardive dyskesia, producing long-standing or permanent abnormal involuntary movements . . . Antipsychotics have little place in the treatment of depressed patients who do not have overt psychotic symptoms because they increase the risk of anticholinergic toxicity, produce akathisia, which may result in worsening agitation, and may result in masked facies, bradykinsia, and blunted affect [emotions]. The development of these side-effects in the course of antidepressant treatment can make it difficult to judge improvement in the depression. In addition, they create a risk of tardive dyskinesia.

Many psychiatrists, in treating someone who is overtly very anxious, or who has not improved on other antidepressants, will prescribe *compound antidepressant preparations*.

GENERIC NAMES	TRADE NAMES
amitriptyline and chlordiazepoxide (a tricyclic and a benzodiazepine)	Limbitrol 5 Limbritrol 10
fluphenazine hydrochloride and nortriptyline (a phenothyazine and a tricyclic)	Motipress Motival
tranylcypromine and trifluoperazine (an MAOI and a phenothyazine)	Parstelin
amitriptyline hydrochloride and perphenazine (a tricyclic and a phenothyazine)	Triptafen Triptafen-M

The *British National Formulary* (4.1. Hypnotics and anxiolytics) states:

The use of preparations listed above is **not** recommended because the dosage of the individual components should be adjusted separately to be appropriate for the individual patient. Whereas antidepressants are given continuously over several months, anxiolytics are prescribed on a short-term basis.

Other drugs which are used in the treatment of depression are:

GENERIC NAMES	TRADE NAMES
tryptophan (**banned, April 1990**)	Optimax, Optimax WV, Pacitron
fluvoxamine maleate	Faverin
flupenthixol	Fluanxol
fluoxetine hydrochloride	Prozac

Tryptophan is sometimes prescribed along with an MAOI. The *British National Formulary* advises that in this case the dose should be reduced and discontinued if the patient develops blurred vision or a headache. In the USA the drug company Eli Lilly markets fluoxetine hydrochloride under the name of Prozac, and calls it a new wonder drug for depression. In the UK where the drug has been available for much longer the *British National Formulary* lists 20 unpleasant side-effects, including a rash necessitating that treatment be discontinued, anorexia with weight loss, headache, fever, and sexual dysfunction, and gives the serious warning that the drug 'may impair performance of skilled tasks, e.g. driving'. In addition, the Committee on the Safety of Medicines issued a special warning.

> Combination therapy with other antidepressants including MAOIs, lithium, or tryptophan, may enhance the serotonin-related effects of **fluvoxamine** or **fluoxetine**. While potentially beneficial in some selected cases, these combinations can increase severity of serotonin-related side-effects; in the most severe cases a life-threatening serotonin syndrome of hyperthermia, tremor, and convulsions may develop. Such combination therapy should be used with care.

So you might have done a tour of all the drugs psychiatrists use in the treatment of depression and still be depressed. You would not be alone in this, though you may feel that you are, for it has been estimated that some 12 to 15 per cent of depressed people, having had drug treatment, are still depressed after two years.[93] Or you might have found a drug which is particularly helpful, so if your depression recurs you will take that one again. You might have worked out how to use the occasional tranquillizer to help you with one or two high-anxiety, unavoidable situations, and the occasional sedative so as to get some sleep while weathering a crisis. Or perhaps you used the drugs as an aid in getting what you want, and now the life you lead is very different from before.

When Peter Parish described the symptoms of depression he said:

Patients may experience a few or many of these symptoms.
Some symptoms may be mild and some intense, and according
to all sorts of factors in his upbringing, his culture, his personality and his environment, the patient will react in different ways.
Certainly in Western society the puritan ethic of 'being firm and
standing on one's own feet' may produce awful feelings of guilt
and unworthiness in which suicide appears to be the only way
out. The whole problem is far too complex to be simply labelled
'depression'. Some patients may need individual or group
therapy, others may respond to counselling or to drugs, some
just want a new house and a cheque for £50,000, others want a
new husband or wife, all need to be taught how to relax . . .

Some of us can tolerate physical pain better than others and
some of us can tolerate mental pain better than others – but at
some stage we all may need help. Some of us may respond
better to one drug and not to another or to one doctor and not to
another. Some will respond to individual therapy and others to
group therapy. We all vary and it is, therefore, wrong to say
that all depressed patients should receive drug therapy and it is
equally wrong to say they should all have psychotherapy. What
is certain, however, is that doctors within the limits of their
present knowledge must aim at giving the maximum benefit
with minimum risks to the maximum number of patients. At
present, the responsible and rational use of drugs appears to
offer the most hope in this direction.

The responsible and rational use of drugs is not the responsibility
of the doctor alone. It is equally the responsibility of the patient.

23

Choosing a Therapist

Talking to a therapist is not compulsory on the journey out of the prison of depression. However, not all of us are blessed with friends who will listen, not criticize and give us time to talk. So it is sometimes necessary to find someone who does this for a living.

Just how to find a therapist who will actually help you on your journey is quite a journey of discovery in itself. Apart from finding someone conveniently near you who either works for the National Health Service or whose services you can afford to buy, you have to discover what kind of therapy the particular therapist practises and whether the therapist has those personal qualities which inspire your trust. The first of these you can find out by asking, though the names which the therapist uses to refer to kinds of therapy may be bafflingly unfamiliar to you. The second only time will reveal. What follows here is some information which you might find helpful.

Different Kinds of Therapy

Therapies divide into two kinds: **exploratory** and **prescriptive**.

In **exploratory** therapy you and the therapist enter into a conversation, the aim of which is for you to discover more about yourself. The conversation is structured in the sense that it occurs at an arranged time, at a certain place, goes on for a period of time determined by the therapist, and is exclusively about you. Some therapists say absolutely nothing about themselves, and some may say something about themselves but only in relation to you. The therapist's own concerns should never be the focus of the conversation. You hold the stage. Progress is marked by a sense of discovery.

All of the therapist's questions and comments are directed at revealing and clarifying your feelings, opinions and beliefs. The emphasis is not so much on what happened to you but how you feel about what happened to you. The therapist uses three basic questions which can be framed in many different ways,

'How do you feel about that?'

'Why is that important to you?'

'Would I be right in thinking that what you mean is – ?'

Some therapists encourage you to talk freely simply by offering you a comfortable chair, couch or cushion and a listening look. Others use games, or play acting, or drawing, painting, modelling clay or music.

The therapist's task is to make sense of what you say and do. This necessarily requires the therapist to have developed a framework, a theory of meaning, in which to categorize and explain what you are saying and doing. The therapist's theory of meaning will comprise what he has developed from his own personal experience and what he has made of the theories of meaning he has encountered in his professional training. It is this second part which explains why there are so many different kinds of exploratory therapies.

The theories which underlie the exploratory therapies are all theories about how we each create our own individual world of meaning. The theories differ in the words or jargon that they use, the parts of human experience which they emphasize and the parts that they ignore. Broadly speaking there are four main theories:

Psychoanalytic – based on the work of Freud and Jung.

Rogerian – based on the work of Carl Rogers.

Group or Gestalt – developed from the work of Kurt Lewin, Fritz Perls and the 'growth centre' leaders at places like Esalen in California, and Jacob Moreno and psychodrama.

Personal Construct and Transactional Analysis – based on the work of George Kelly and Eric Berne.

In actual practice only the Freudian and Jungian psychoanalysts would claim that they work solely within the purity of their own theory. Other therapists would say that they use or have been influenced by all of the theories in one way or another.

Psychoanalytic therapy, more usually called *psychoanalysis*, will involve you in a considerable outlay of time and money, because meeting with your therapist will take place several times a week for several years. The basic idea of psychoanalysis is that all we can bring to a new situation is our past experience and we have to make sense of every new situation by projecting on to this new situation the constructions of meaning which we have created earlier in our life. The psychoanalyst, by not talking and perhaps even sitting out of sight of the client, is supposed to create a 'blank screen' on which the client can project all his feelings, beliefs, wishes and conclusions. This process is called 'transference', and the psychoanalyst's job is to make some sort of sense of these projections. Thus you might find yourself getting angry with your psychoanalyst, and he interprets your anger as being the anger you felt against your father who had failed to meet your needs. This may be quite right, or partially right, or simply because the psychoanalyst is very aggravating. Psychoanalysts always discount this third possibility.

The history of psychoanalysis is a history of major fights between analysts. Freud demanded total loyalty from his followers, and when one of his disciples failed to obey, he was cast into outer darkness. Thus Jung departed and set up his own kind of psychoanalysis where what was to be uncovered in the course of the analysis was not sexual conflicts, as Freud and the Freudians did, but spiritual needs. Even those disciples who remained true to Freud fought most bitterly amongst themselves. One of the bitterest fights concerned Melanie Klein who insisted on the importance of the fantasy lives of babies, how to a baby a cold wet nappy was not just that but a whole universe of longing, pain and betrayal.

If you seek psychoanalysis, you could be offered Freudian, or Jungian or Kleinian psychoanalysis.

To become a psychoanalyst means making a total commitment to a long training, a theory and a practice – a commitment not dissimilar to that necessary to become a priest. Many people, realizing the importance of psychoanalysis but not wanting to make such a commitment, undergo less extensive training, perhaps during or after they qualify in another profession like psychiatry or psychology, and become *psychotherapists*.

Some psychotherapists say that they practise *dynamic psychotherapy*, which follows the rules of psychoanalysis, where the therapist does not engage in any social conversation with the client and says very little except to interpret what the client has said. Dynamic psychotherapy has been taken up by many psychiatrists interested in therapy in the National Health Service, so you may well be referred to one such psychiatrist, usually called a Consultant Psychotherapist. This might be a good experience, or it might not, since it is the practice of consultant psychotherapists to select the people they want to take on for therapy. If the consultant psychotherapist decides that he does not have the skills necessary to help you, he will not say to you, 'I am sorry. I cannot help you because I don't know how'. He will say, 'You are not suitable for psychotherapy', using the old psychiatric trick of blaming the patient when the patient fails to respond to the psychiatrist's ministrations. If this is said to you, recognize it for the ignorant cruelty that it is and do not take it to heart, feeling that there you have failed yet again.[94]

Carl Rogers was a very kindly man who recognized the importance of paying attention and actually listening to another person. He developed a method of *reflecting back* what a person said and thus showing that what had been said had been heard and understood. This way of doing therapy was taken up by those therapists who preferred to call themselves counsellors. The British Association of Counselling defines *counselling* as giving 'the client an opportunity to explore, discover and clarify ways of living more resourcefully and towards a greater well-being'.[95] There are large counselling organizations like Relate (formerly the Marriage Guidance Council), which offers counselling to couples, and the Samaritans, who offer counselling to anyone who feels troubled. A Samaritan will listen to you even if you don't feel like committing suicide. There are many individuals not members of any organization who call themselves counsellors. Some work privately, some as volunteers.

The practice of both psychotherapy and counselling incorporate ideas from the four main theories of how we create meaning. All psychotherapists and counsellors are concerned with understanding the client's own individual language, just in the way that personal construct psychologists like myself try to elucidate the client's meaning using his own words. In this book you can find examples of where I am trying to do this. (*See* George and Ruth in Chapter 3.) When psychotherapists and counsellors conduct *group therapy* they use the theories that have been developed by different group therapists over the years. In group therapy you might sit in a circle with others and talk, or you might intersperse the talk with play acting or games.

Some psychotherapists and counsellors use both exploratory and prescriptive therapy. For instance, you might find yourself too frightened to leave the safety of your home because you have had a panic attack in some public place and you are terrified that it might happen again. Or you might have developed a fear of dogs, or of going in a lift, and this fear is preventing you from living a normal life. Such fears are some of the forms that our most terrible fear, the fear of the annihilation of the self, can take, and need to be recognized and dealt with as such. This would be the focus of the exploratory psychotherapy or counselling. At the same time, you could use some practical help coping with the specific fear which is interrupting your life. This would be the focus of the prescriptive therapy.[96]

Prescriptive therapy follows the old formula 'You're doing it wrong. This is how you do it.' You have had people saying that to you all your life, so you know that sometimes being told you're doing it wrong and being taught how to do it better is extremely useful, and sometimes it is a disaster. The same applies to prescriptive therapy.

If, in seeking a therapist, you are offered the chance to consult a *psychologist*, find out beforehand what kind of therapy this person practises. Whatever kind of therapy psychologists practise, they always feel that it is *the right one*, and so they will not hide from you what they propose to do. Whereas psychiatrists will often say that they are psychotherapists but in fact practise in the traditional way of drugs and ECT. If the psychologist practises exploratory therapy he (it could be a she – there are many women psychologists) will murmur something vague about psychotherapy, or talking, or exploring. If he says, 'I'm eclectic', he means that he hasn't made up his mind yet but does whatever seems to be the best thing at the time. Or he will tell you he practises *behaviour therapy*, or *rational emotive therapy*, or *behavioural psychotherapy* (this is behaviour therapy with the name changed to convince the ignorant that it is better than behaviour therapy) or *cognitive therapy*, which is a mixture of behaviour therapy and a very shallow understanding of Personal Construct Psychology.

One of the prescriptive therapies in the hands of an aware and sensitive therapist can be extremely effective in helping you to gain needed skills, like being able to go to places and to talk to people. However, a prescriptive therapy is not going to be of much use to you when you are starting your journey from the bottom of the pit. It is only when you are quite sure that you deserve a decent life that you can then identify the skills that you lack and seek to gain them. If you decide to consult a prescriptive therapist, do not accept that you *as a person* are deficient in any way. Accept no insults.

Behavioural psychologists will tell you that you are stupid because you have 'poor coping strategies'. Rational emotive therapists will tell you that you are stupid because you have 'irrational thoughts'. Cognitive therapists will tell you that you are stupid because you have 'dysfunctional cognitions'. Indeed, Aaron Beck, in his *Cognitive Therapy of Depression*, wrote, 'Depressed people are prone to structure their experiences in relatively primitive ways'.[97] How's that for a put down!

None of these kinds of therapists understands that what they describe in such perjorative terms are the conclusions which you *correctly* drew from your experience.

If you are a young, inexperienced child and you are being severely punished by parents who are declaring that you are bad and that because they love you they are punishing you, then surely the only correct conclusion to draw is that you are bad and that your parent is right to punish you. You would have had to be much older, wiser and stronger, to have drawn any other conclusion. Moreover, it was a conclusion which helped you to keep out of trouble, because from then on you tried to obey your parent.

If your life has been filled with difficulties and tragedies – suppose you were born to parents who drank and quarrelled, and if your father disappeared and your mother put you in an orphanage where you were neglected and abused – then surely the correct conclusion to draw is that people are not to be trusted and that the world is an unhappy place?

To call such conclusions 'poor coping strategies', or 'irrational thoughts', or 'dysfunctional cognitions' is to denigrate and ignore the sufferings of courageous people.

The only place where you got into difficulties is where you did not go back and check whether the conclusions you drew still applied totally or even partially. But we all fail to go back and check. There is not enough time to go back and check all our conclusions. If our conclusions seem to be working as good predictors, we don't go back and check. If that is stupid, then we are all stupid.

Therapists of all persuasions say that their therapies work, and of course they do. *All therapies work, but no therapy works perfectly*. There are two reasons for this. The first is because we all resist change. The second is that, when someone offers us another way of living, we accept the offer only when we trust and value that person.

A therapy is only as good as the therapist who practises it.

Kinds of Therapists

All therapists should carry a health warning:

BEWARE: THERAPY CAN DAMAGE YOUR HEALTH.

When you go looking for therapy you feel vulnerable and weak.

You long for someone to save you, to wave a magic wand and make everything better. You go to a therapist hoping that that person has the power to make you better. You see the therapist as being especially wise and powerful, and so you invest the therapist with power.

The therapist can do three things with the power you give him:

1. He can use that power for his own ends.
2. He can use that power to benefit you.
3. He can refuse to accept the power you offer him.

When a therapist uses this power for his own ends he treats you as an object of no importance, which is the same destructive treatment which led you to go into therapy. Many therapists allow themselves to be corrupted by the power they have assumed. In his book *Against Therapy*, Jeffrey Masson shows how many of the great names in therapy have used their power against their clients. Freud regarded his theories as being more important than his patients. Jung contributed to the anti-Semitism of Nazi Germany. Fritz Perls seduced his female clients.[98]

This last activity is common, with the male therapist lying to his woman client, claiming that his sexual power is even more potent than his conversational power. The belief that all a woman needs to cure her is 'a good fuck' is as prevalent amongst male psychiatrists and therapists as it is among men generally. Jeffrey Masson has gathered evidence from women who were sexually abused as children and has found that when a woman reveals this to a male therapist she is then very likely to be approached sexually by that therapist. I actually heard one male therapist defend himself and his colleagues by saying that a woman who has been sexually abused will often behave seductively to the male therapist who would naturally be aroused. This therapist showed no recognition that the behaviour which men call 'seductive' is behaviour which the women, as abused children, had to develop as a way of defending themselves against the powerful, abusing male. Sylvia Fraser describes this.[99]

The therapist's job is not to respond personally to the client's behaviour but to interpret it and understand it. Unfortunately, women, whether in or out of therapy, are always in danger from those men who take as a law of the universe and an excuse for whatever they do that old saying, 'A standing cock has no conscience'.

Another area where a therapist may have no conscience about how he uses his power is that of money. Where a therapist makes his living from doing therapy, it is not in his financial interests for clients to finish therapy. Unscrupulous therapists will use their power and the knowledge they acquire about their clients to keep their clients feeling weak and fearful. They let their clients get to the stage of seeing that their misery arose out of their childhood experiences, but they will not let their clients move from the resentment and anger aroused by this discovery and on to the freedom of realizing that while bad things have happened to you, you should not take this personally. They want to keep their clients as children and charge them for the privilege.

Some therapists are corrupted by power not for reasons of sex or money but because of the prestige they feel will accrue to them when they prove their theory. They are interested in their clients only as research subjects. Woe betide you if you fail to behave as the precious theory predicts you will behave! Many thousands of psychiatric patients have been used as subjects in the research trials on drugs. I remember one irascible psychiatrist writing in a patient's notes, 'This woman refuses to admit that she is better on Surmontil!' Nowadays there are quite a few therapists who want to give their therapy the veneer of scientific respectability and so conduct research in psychotherapy. The ethical guide-lines of such research state that the client should be fully informed about the procedures before the therapy starts. If you are offered therapy in these circumstances, make sure that you know exactly how many sessions you will have and what kind of therapy it is. If you feel that your therapist regards the research as being more important than you, complain, and, if your complaints are not heeded, leave. Your welfare is more important than the research.

Where a therapist uses the power you give him to benefit you, the outcome will be a mixture of good and bad, as are always the results of a benevolent dictatorship. You will learn a few useful skills and feel the comfort of being loved by a powerful parent, but you will not grow up to be an independent adult.

Often the therapist who behaves like a benevolent dictator is someone who holds the view that human beings are inherently flawed. Sometimes such a therapist sees the flaw as something from which they are exempt. Psychiatrists who believe that every form of human woe is caused by a gene regard themselves as free of all such genes. Prescriptive therapists see people as being inherently stupid, but they themselves, of course, are intelligent. Sometimes the therapist holds the Christian view of human nature, which is that we are born in sin and our life is a struggle against our inheritance of Original Sin. Many Freudian and Jungian analysts, while not using the term 'Original Sin', see people as having at the centre of their being something bad and potentially dangerous. Therapists who believe in some version of Original Sin would claim to have recognized this inherent flaw in themselves but through their own therapy have learned to keep it under control. Such therapists see life as an inevitable tragedy. Many people like to believe that their life is tragic. Their pride will not let them see just how ordinary they are.

Whether the inherent flaw is pictured as a gene, or stupidity, or Original Sin, any course of therapy based on this idea has to be in terms of keeping this basic flaw under control. If you enter into such you will simply be doing what you have always done – trying hard to be good in order to overcome your sense of intrinsic badness.

A therapist who believes in the intrinsic badness of human beings is concerned, not with freedom, but with control and power.

So, what you need to find is a therapist who will disappoint you. You need a therapist who refuses to accept the power that you offer him.

Such a therapist, in your first meeting, both tells and shows you that 'I have no special power. I have no magic wand, no magic word, no magic pill. I am an ordinary person who is prepared to accompany you on your journey.'

One such therapist is my friend and colleague David Smail. In his book, *Taking Care: An Alternative to Therapy*, [100] David wrote:

As I tried to show in *Psychotherapy: A Personal Approach*, [101] what most often psychotherapists *actually* (as opposed to professedly) do, is to *negotiate* a view of what the patient's predicament is about which both the patient and therapist can agree (which is to establish, as closely as one ever can, what is the truth of the matter), and then to *encourage* the patient to do what he or she can to confront those elements of the predicament which admit of some possibility of alteration. This almost inevitably means that patients begin to criticize aspects of a social 'reality' which before they had always taken for granted, and, with courage or grace, to learn actively to dissent from and oppose the constraints it had placed upon them: to overcome the tyranny of objectivity. I would now lay more emphasis than I did in that book on the value of *comfort*: for many people, psychotherapy provides the only source of comfort they are likely to find in what has been, for them at least, a predominantly cruel world . . . My experience both personally and professionally is that the greatest comfort derives from having one's view, however despairing it may be, confirmed by someone else who is not afraid to share it.

The search for such a therapist is a matter of trial and error. In Florida I talked with a therapist who herself had been through this search.

Susan said, 'I know what it is to be depressed – two major times – in my early twenties and just recently in my forties. What it felt like to me was complete exhaustion. I'd totally run out of steam. It engulfs. It's like a fog that rolls in and envelops. I think that in some way it becomes protective. I understand these two depressions now. The first happened about nine months after my son was born. As a student I had been very active in many kinds of things. Suddenly I was a mother, something I knew very little about. I was disconnected from myself and I feel in a way that's what happened in a later move to Florida.'

Susan told me how, as a child, 'There was no way of getting a response from my parents. My mother was preoccupied with my dad and my dad lived in a world of his own, influenced alternatively by episodes of mania and depression. They were not uncaring, there were just limits to what could be expressed. I'm a very reserved person. As a child I spent a good deal of my life – seventh through twelfth grade – in the library. I left the house at eight o'clock in the morning to go to school. I would get out of school and go to whatever extra-curricular activity there might be. I would eat supper in a restaurant and I would go back to the library until nine o'clock at night. It upsets me to talk about it. I lived at the public library. They talk about bag ladies. I was a bag girl with a book bag. I had these stack of things I carried in and out.' Here Susan cried.

Later she went on, 'When parents are unable to offer some validation about who you are as a child, uncertainty evolves. You never know how you are or who you are, and you have to tread carefully. After moving to Florida I did go to see someone to talk about all this. I had two disastrous beginnings in trying to work on it. I knew that my world had fallen apart. This psychiatrist had some questions which he was going to ask come hell or high water, all set out on a printed sheet. I was sitting there crying, and I could have cried and cried. Within the first ten minutes one of his questions to me was, "How often do you have sex with your husband?" It took five sessions for me to tell him where to go. He said, "Why didn't you tell me you were angry?", and talked about my anger with my father. At this point it was not my anger with my father but the psychiatrist's obsessive style which interfered with my ability to experience him as paying attention to me. Questions should be asked in the context of something. There was no context. I was crying my eyes out. I felt that he was a technical disaster.'

She went on, 'The second experience was with a woman. I cried again, and as I was walking out the door of her session she said something to me like, "I have strength, would you like a hug?" and I patted her on the shoulder and I said, "That's okay." You know what it was, I really feel like, with all that goes on with me, I still consider myself as strong. I felt as though she was somehow saying, "You poor little thing, vulnerable little creature". I suppose that's how I presented myself, I'd cried for an hour. I did want the comfort, but I wanted it to be subtle. We met only once.'

I commented, 'You don't want to be pitied.'

'Exactly. I want someone to engage me, to challenge me to figure it out. But I wanted it done gently. I am still sorting out my third attempt to find a therapist. It was very powerful, something that I never anticipated. The transference was such that I seemed to exist in one world for an hour a week and then going about existing in another. It was like leading two lives. And also, ultimately, I felt that I had walked into transferential quicksand. I felt as if I held my own. It was a struggle to do that, but I felt as though I did. I came out of there with a much clearer sense of myself, even though coming to that was so terribly painful. The focus was not on the depression as such. We ended up focusing on my relationship with my father. I came out with a much more integrated sense of myself at many levels. I feel stronger having survived that experience because of the intensity. When you experience your own regression you need to hold things together. It required everything I could muster. My therapist was a person I would describe as responsive. Certainly not a blank slate. I knew very little about him, and I began to know a lot about him. I learned just from the experience of him in the room. I wonder about a therapy that re-creates – you re-experience the losses so intensely, and then you feel for a period of time that it's there, you're loved, and then you have to say goodbye and have to re-experience that same painful sort of thing.'

I said, 'Perhaps sometimes in that second goodbye you realize that you don't have to be destroyed by it, that that is just part of the continuous change.'

'And that is why what happened is still reverberating. When I talk about feeling stronger, now I feel I can go on, whereas with other losses and goodbyes I've not been certain. I've felt threatened by the thought of going on. Before when I have made major changes I've cut off my previous experiences. There's been no on-going sort of corridor to connect the early experience with the later experience and with the present, so I haven't had the benefit of reaching back to my own experience, and these experiences seem sometimes that it must be someone else who did this, who wrote that or worked in this way, and so you don't have the benefit of the fullness of yourself. I've lived here, and I've lived there, and there, we've lived in many places. I feel as though there's a corridor through which I can go back now. Instead of having a door at the end of each experience that closes, these doors are now open to me and I can reach back and pull the whole of myself together.'

'So you've made your story continuous, a proper story.'

'Yes, exactly, that's the difference. You go looking for a therapist at the worst possible time, and that's not the time to go shopping when you're at your most vulnerable. Then you feel more alone.'

'What you said about being the bag lady – you've got sympathy for the child you once were. You feel very sorry for that little girl. It's sadness, it's mourning, but it's going on.'

'That's what that crying was about. Months of crying, even though I talked. I was like a faucet. I had an image of glass canisters filled with water, and at a certain point it came to an end. The tears had emptied out, and it was at that point that I was somehow going on and could think about going on. What it also meant for me in therapy was being able to be vulnerable, to feel, to actually feel that child again. That's why it was so intense and so helpful. I remember at one point saying to my therapist, "You know what I would ask you if I could ask you anything at all, if I had one wish?" I would have asked him to tell me a story and I pictured how I would have sat. I would have sat with my knees up like a little child. It was really a re-experiencing of myself. I've never allowed myself to experience that degree of vulnerability. I told him once that he created a luxurious emotional environment. We would laugh because he had a tiny office, it was just a mess, but the atmosphere was one of acceptance and warmth. I sensed his belief that I had the strength to survive the process. It's been helpful to me in terms of my work, particularly with people who are really struggling. I have a sense that I understand much more fundamentally what people talk about, that feeling of coming apart at the seams, that level of anxiety and that level of vulnerability. It's something I have some real gut sense of. I think that people have a sense of that in me too.'

So, in your search for a therapist, may you be as lucky as Susan.

For some people one good experience with a therapist is sufficient. For others, like Delia (in Chapter 17), a different kind of therapy is helpful at different times.

No therapy should go on for ever. All therapists, like all teachers, all gurus, should be outgrown. Therapists are no more than ordinary people.

24

Technical Terms – Keys to the Jargon

acupuncture is an essential part of the ancient traditional medical practices of China but is becoming increasingly popular in the West, although Western medicine cannot account for how acupuncture works. However, its effectiveness in the control of pain is so clear that many general practitioners and physiotherapists have now added acupuncture to their treatment skills. In Chinese medicine the body is considered to be governed by two essences or energies called Yin and Yang, which are at once opposed and complementary, and which travel through the body along twelve meridians. Health is a perfect balance of Yin and Yang and disease is a disturbance of the balance by influences such as emotion and the weather. Acupuncture is the insertion of needles at precisely determined points in the meridians in order to remove blockages along the meridians and to restore the balance of the two energies.

assertiveness is a popular term because it carries the connotation 'good' where the equivalent word 'aggressive' carries the connotation 'bad'. To be assertive is to expect that other people will accept that we hold a point of view different from them, that we have the right to hold this point of view and even to impose our view on to other people. *Assertiveness training* is learning how to speak up for ourselves and how to behave aggressively, that is, to try to make our definition of reality prevail, while not being rejected or attacked by those who are the object of our assertiveness.

behaviourism, behaviourist, behaviour therapy, behavioural psychotherapy Behaviourism is a theory about behaviour which recognizes the importance of rewards and punishments in our lives. Behaviourism calls rewards and punishments 'reinforcements' and shows how 'positive reinforcements' increase the incidence of behaviours thus reinforced and 'negative reinforcements' decrease the

incidence of behaviours thus reinforced. *Behaviourists*, the practitioners of this theory, originally insisted that all they needed to
study was behaviour, which they could see, and that it was not
necessary for them to study what people thought and felt. They did
not realize that behaviourism is actually a theory of meaning, for a
reward is a reward only if the person receiving it thinks that it is so.
Initially, *behaviour therapy* followed a simple plan where desirable
behaviour was rewarded and undesirable behaviour punished, and
ignored what the person thought and felt. As the limitations of this
kind of therapy became apparent (*see* Delia's comments, p. 287)
behaviour therapists started to take some account, while trying
to appear not to, of what their patients thought. The type of person
who espouses behaviourism is similar to the type of person who
wants to explain all human thought and action in terms of
biochemical change, that is, a person who finds it difficult to
understand the complexities of human thought and who has little
tolerance for doubt and ambiguity. Since we are always capable of
holding two opposite thought simultaneously, eg, we hate the
people we love, our thoughts and feelings are always complex,
changeable and full of contradictions and uncertainties. When
therapists who called themselves *rational emotive therapists* or *cognitive therapists* began to emerge and showed themselves to be likewise
unable to tolerate the complexities and contradictions of human
thought, behaviour therapists borrowed their techniques and, as
ever, devised their own jargon. Thus cognitive therapists call their
patients' thoughts 'dysfunctional' and behaviour therapists call
them 'irrational', when what they mean is that the patient is stupid,
being unable to think as the therapist does, logically and rationally.
While it might appear that *behavioural psychotherapy* might have some
understanding of and tolerance for the complexities of human
thought and feeling, it is simply a combination of behaviour and
cognitive therapy. The simple and straightforward techniques of
behaviour and cognitive therapy can be useful where what is at
issue can be structured as a problem which can then be solved.
Where what is at issue relates to life's insoluble dilemmas, like, How
much should I be an individual and how much should I submerge
myself in my group? How shall I balance my needs for freedom and
for security? How shall I face my death?, then behaviour therapy
and cognitive therapy have nothing to offer. Deciding whether to
consult a behaviour therapist or a cognitive therapist is like deciding
whether to consult a plumber. If your problem is faulty drains, then

a plumber is what you need. But if you want a beautiful picture to hang on your walls, or some music to celebrate an event, you don't need a plumber. You need an artist who understands uncertainty and creativity.

Buddhism, like all religions, covers a wide range of belief and practice. For millions of Buddhists, Buddhism is a Grand Design of rewards and punishments where the placing of a piece of gold leaf on a statue of the Buddha will, it is hoped, bring rewards. Other Buddhists follow the teachings of Buddha which describe how what we take to be reality is nothing but the fictions or structures we create. Suffering comes from not recognizing that reality is continuous and continually in the process of change. 'Suffering,' said one wise Buddhist, 'is the attempt to make reality repeatable.' Liberation comes from the recognition that structures are simply structures and that we are part of everything and everything is part of us.

cerebrospinal fluid (CFS) is a watery fluid surrounding the brain and the spinal cord. It is reabsorbed into the veins of the skull and backbone. The formation and absorption of CSF are balanced to maintain a constant pressure. It serves the brain and the spinal cord as a shock absorber.

client is the term used by therapists who do not like using the term *patient* for those people who come to consult the therapist.

chromosome is a collection of *genes*, and each gene determines one element in what is inherited in a body.

cognitive therapy has been defined by Arthur Freeman as 'a relatively short-term form of psychotherapy that is active, directive, and collaborative between patient and therapist. The goal of therapy is to help patients uncover their dysfunctional and irrational thinking, reality test their thinking and behaviour, and build more adaptive and functional techniques for responding both inter- and intrapersonally. Specifically, cognitive therapists work directly with their patients, proposing hypotheses and strategies for testing them, developing specific skills, and teaching a model for coping/adaptation. The focus is collaborative – that is, the therapist and patient working together as a team, rather than the patient being "in therapy". Collaboration is not always 50–50. With the severely depressed individual, the therapist's activity must be high enough to supply the initial energy to complete the therapy work so that the collaboration might be 80–20, or even 90–10. The CBT [Cognitive-Behavioural Therapist] therapist would rely not only on restatement but on restructuring, active intervention and direction rather than a vague and aimless therapeutic wandering, and on collaboration rather than confrontation. Cognitive therapy is a coping model of psychotherapy as opposed to a mastery model. The goal of cognitive therapy is not to "cure" but rather to help the patient to develop better strategies to deal with his life and work. By helping the patient to uncover his dysfunctional thoughts and irrational belief systems, the cognitive therapist begins to teach a model for patients to utilize on their own . . . All human beings have the capacity to distort reality in a number of significant ways. If the distortion is severe enough, the individual may lose touch with reality and be labelled psychotic. However, the neurotic distorts reality in particular significant and dysfunctional ways . . . These distortions are fuelled by the basic life schema, or underlying assumptions (similar to Ellis's rational and irrational beliefs). These irrational belief systems or rules for living become a substrate or wellspring from which these cognitive distortions emerge. These schema are often established early in childhood. When an external event stimulates a particular schema, certain specific distortions or more general styles of distortion are seen. Schema may be family schema, religious schema, cultural or personal schema.'[102]

The inventor of *cognitive therapy* is Aaron Beck, Professor of Psychiatry at the University of Pennsylvania. Beck has taken good care not to distress his fellow psychiatrists in the way that Thomas Szasz (*The Myth of Mental Illness*[103]) does by attacking the biological model of mental illness. Beck and his disciples always say that there is such a thing as biological depression and that drugs are an essential part of treatment, but that cognitive therapy is effective in the treatment of unipolar depression and when used in combination with drugs in the treatment of bipolar depression and other conditions. Indeed, cognitive therapy can be used to get patients to take their drugs. Jesse H. Wright showed how patients could be helped to change their 'negative distortions' about drugs. He lists 'Common Negative Distortions about Drugs' as:

'Drugs are just a crutch.'
'Drugs are really dangerous.'
'I am the one who will get the severe side-effects.'

'People who take drugs are weak.'
'You should be able to do it by yourself.'
'I'll get addicted.'
'I won't be able to work if I'm taking medication.'
'A drug couldn't really work. I'm having an existential crisis.'
'How could a drug help when the problem is really my wife.'
'Drugs are overused; my doctor is just a pill pusher.'[104]

As it has always been in psychiatric hospitals, a patient's rejection of any form of treatment is seen as nothing more than a symptom of the patient's madness. Cognitive therapy is not a therapy aimed at the liberation of the individual. It is a treatment aimed at control.

cohort (birth) is a number of people who possess a common characteristic, such as being born in the same year.

correlation is a statistical term referring to the likelihood of two events or two series of events occurring together. Thus biological psychiatrists will point to the correlation of the presence of depression and certain biochemical changes in the brain. They deduce that the biochemical changes must cause the depression. This is an incorrect deduction, for *a correlation is not a cause*. The fact that two events occur at the same time does not mean that one caused the other. A correlation simply shows how likely it is that if one event occurs the other event also occurs. The reason why the two events occur together may have very little to do with the events themselves. For instance, in the 30s, a statistician discovered a significant correlation between the increase in the number of telegraph poles in the world and the number of communists. Did this mean that communists were caused by telegraph poles? Could we abolish communism by cutting down all the telegraph poles?

counsellor is someone who tries to listen in an accepting, positive, empathetic way, giving information when required but little advice. Most counsellors have completed a training course in counselling, but many have chosen to seek further training in one or more of the psychotherapies. Some counsellors see their listening as being concerned with a specific problem or situation, and so limit their range of inquiry and the time they spend with a client, while other counsellors work in ways indistinguishable from those of a psychotherapist. In the pecking order of therapists, they are at the bottom. Psychotherapists believe that they are superior to counsellors and psychoanalysts believe that they are superior to psychotherapists. However, in practice, it is often better to consult a counsellor, for counsellors have little power and prestige to guard and misuse, and their heads are not so cluttered with the theories and prejudices which psychoanalysts, psychotherapists, psychiatrists and psychologists acquire in their professional training.

cystic fibrosis is 'an uncommon hereditary defect of numerous glands, including the mucous glands of the bronchi, the sweat glands and the digestive glands. It is a recessive character – both parents carry the abnormal gene without showing signs of the disease, and there is a one-in-four chance that a child of the marriage will inherit the gene from both parents and develop cystic fibrosis.'[105]

depression, anaclitic, is the term used by Rene Spitz in his studies of small children who were deprived of any kind of ordinary mothering during the Second World War. A baby who is adequately fed and kept warm but who is not held and talked to will grow grey and still and eventually die. A toddler who is likewise adequately fed and housed but who has no one to pay attention to him will become severely withdrawn and be retarded in his development. Such children show very clearly that we need other people to notice us and treat us as fellow human beings, not as objects, and that this need is as important as our need for food, air and water.

depression as defined by behaviour therapists is seen as the outcome of many negative reinforcements without a balance of positive reinforcements, leading to maladaptive habits and irrational beliefs.

depression as defined by cognitive therapists is seen to result from cognitive dysfunctions concerning how the person regards himself, his future and his experiences. Beck *et al*. wrote, 'A way of understanding the thinking disorder in depression is to conceptualize it in terms of "primitive" vs "mature" modes of organizing reality. As is apparent, depressed persons are prone to structure their experiences in relatively primitive ways. They tend to make broad global judgements regarding events that impinge on their lives. The meanings that flood their consciousness are likely to be extreme, negative, categorical, absolute, and judgmental. The emotional response, thus, tends to be negative and extreme. In contrast to this primitive kind of thinking, more mature thinking automatically integrates life situations into many dimensions or qualities (instead of a single category), in quantitative rather than qualitative terms, and according to relative rather than absolutistic standards. In primitive thinking the complexity, variability, and diversity of human experiences are reduced into a few crude categories.'[106]

depression as defined by *The Depression Handbook* is a state where we experience ourselves as being cut off from other people and our environment, and being in some sort of prison. This state is a defence which we can use whenever we discover that there is a major discrepancy between what we thought our world and our life were and what our world and life actually are, and this discovery threatens to destroy our sense of identity. Depression, as a defence, is extremely useful as it holds a person together when the threat of the discrepancy seems overwhelming, but, since it is based on self-disgust and involves isolation, depriving the person of essential contact with other people, it is expensive of health and strength and is extremely painful. While depression is experienced as a state within the person and is constructed from the conclusions the person had drawn from his experience, such conclusions are responses to the actions of other people, and so a person's depression can be understood only in the context of the person's history, his relationships, and his religious, racial, political and economic conditions.

depression as defined by psychiatrists involves many different kinds of depression:

agitated depression where the depressed person is anxious, restless, irritable, distracted and excitable.

bipolar depression where the person is sometimes depressed and sometimes so active as to be described as manic.

bipolar disorder, as defined by the DSM-III-R, consists of periods of *mania*, which is characterized by abnormally and persistently elevated, expansive or irritable mood, inflated self-esteem or grandiosity, decreased need for sleep, pressure to keep talking, flight of ideas, distractability, increase in goal-directed activity, and excessive involvement in pleasurable activity, which have a high potential for painful consequences, and *depression*, which is characterized by depressed mood, diminished interest in activities, significant weight loss or gain, insomnia or hypersomnia, psychomotor agitation or retardation, fatigue, feelings of worthlessness and inappropriate guilt, inability to concentrate or make decisions, recurrent thoughts of death. Bipolar disorder is divided into the following disorders:

bipolar disorder, manic, unspecified
bipolar disorder, manic, mild
bipolar disorder, manic, moderate
bipolar disorder, manic, severe, without psychotic features
bipolar disorder, manic, with psychotic features
bipolar disorder, manic, in partial remission
bipolar disorder, manic, in full remission
bipolar disorder, depressed, unspecified
bipolar disorder, depressed, mild
bipolar disorder, depressed, moderate
bipolar disorder, depressed, severe, without psychotic features
bipolar disorder, depressed, with psychotic features
bipolar disorder, depressed, in partial remission
bipolar disorder, depressed, in full remission
bipolar disorder, mixed, unspecified
bipolar disorder, mixed, mild
bipolar disorder, mixed, moderate
bipolar disorder, mixed, severe, without psychotic features
bipolar disorder, mixed, severe, with psychotic features
bipolar disorder, mixed, in partial remission
bipolar disorder, mixed, in full remission
bipolar disorder Not Otherwise Specified (NOS)
cyclothymia

(Note that the diagnosis which includes 'in full remission' means that no matter how well and happy you may be, according to the DSM-III-R, you are still ill.)

clinical depression is used by psychiatrists in two ways. First, as a term meaning, 'You cannot go on struggling with ordinary daily life. You must stop trying to work and you must rest.' Second, 'What you are feeling is not just ordinary blues or depression but something which only I, as an expert, can diagnose and treat.' The first use is meant to be kind and helpful: the second is a power ploy.

dysthymia is the DSM-III-R term for *depressive neurosis*, whose symptoms include depressed mood, eating and sleep disturbances, tiredness, poor concentration and decision making, low self-esteem and feelings of hopelessness. It can occur as a *primary type*, where it occurs on its own, or as a *secondary type* imposed on some other deleterious condition.

endogenous depression relates to a severe depression where the diagnosing psychiatrist sees nothing in the patient's life which the psychiatrist thinks would cause a person to be depressed. For instance, many psychiatrists, not being women, believe that all a woman needs to be happy is a home, a husband and children, and so when a woman who possesses these necessary and sufficient conditions for her happiness presents him with depression the psychiatrist diagnoses endogenous depression. Although the research findings do not support this practice, the preferred treatment for endogenous depression is electroconvulsive therapy (ECT), and so a great many women who have failed to find their happiness in a home, a husband and children, also find that a burst of electricity through their brain does not instil this happiness either.

involutional melancholia refers to a severe depression occurring at and after the menopause. The word 'involutional' is used in medicine to refer to the shrinkage of an organ, as the uterus will shrink after pregnancy and in the menopause. There used to be a lot of involutional melancholia about, but now it has apparently disappeared and been replaced by *depression in the elderly*.

major depressive disorder, as defined by the DSM-III-R, consists of the depressive symptoms listed above under *bipolar disorder* and is divided into the following disorders:

    major depression, single episode, unspecified
    major depression, single episode, mild
    major depression, single episode, moderate
    major depression, single episode, severe, without psychotic
      features
    major depression, single episode, with psychotic features
    major depression, single episode, in partial remission
    major depression, single episode, in full remission
    major depression, recurrent, unspecified
    major depression, recurrent, mild
    major depression, recurrent, moderate
    major depression, recurrent, severe, without psychotic
      features
    major depression, recurrent, with psychotic features
    major depression, recurrent, in partial remission
    major depression, recurrent, in full remission
      depressive disorder NOS

(Thus the DSM-III-R lists some thirty-nine types of depression.

Does this one gene produce thirty-nine varieties, or are there thirty-eight inheritable genes?)

manic-depressive psychosis is where the person is periodically depressed and then active enough to be called manic and be considered by the diagnosing psychiatrist to be out of touch with reality and lacking insight. *Lacking insight* means not accepting the psychiatrist's definition of reality.

neurotic depression is where the person is somewhat depressed but is not out of touch with reality and apparently agrees with the psychiatrist's definition of reality.

psychotic depression is where the person is severely depressed and does not accept the psychiatrist's definition of reality. For instance, a person who has a strong belief in a God who judges us and who believes that he is intrinsically bad will, in the depths of his despair, have a sense of being damned. A psychiatrist who does not have such a belief in God and so does not understand a sense of damnation will call his patient's belief that he is damned 'irrational guilt', or 'delusional guilt', or 'delusion'. If the patient will not accept that his belief in damnation is irrational, he shows 'lack of insight'. 'Irrational guilt' and 'lack of insight' are, in the psychiatrist's understanding, two symptoms of psychosis.

reactive depression is a depression where the psychiatrist believes that the patient has a rational reason for being depressed. For instance, if the patient says he is depressed because his dog died and the psychiatrist is a dog lover, then the psychiatrist will diagnose reactive depression, whereas if the psychiatrist has no interest in dogs, the depression must be endogenous.

retarded depression is where the depressed person finds it hard to move or carry out everyday activities like getting out of bed.

schizoaffective disorder is another term for psychotic depression, but where the person is considered to have got out of touch with reality before becoming depressed.

seasonal affective disorder is where the person gets depressed in autumn or winter.

unipolar depression is where the person is depressed and shows no sign of being active enough to be called manic.

deterministic refers to the theory of cause which is linear (in a straight line) and comes from the past. A leads to B and B leads to C, and so on. Such causes are spoken of as being 'necessary and sufficient' to bring a certain event into being. Thus a lack of vitamin

C is a necessary and sufficient cause to bring the disease scurvy into being. However, a deterministic explanation like this cannot account for why a certain person or group developed scurvy. To do this, it is necessary to discover the situational causes (the ill person is on a long sea voyage), economic causes (the person is too poor to buy citrus fruits), and political causes (his government is at war and food is in short supply). Nowadays, many scientists have abandoned the linear deterministic model of cause and use a network model of cause where many events are linked like a net and affect one another in complex ways, often called *feedback*, which can lead to a *final common pathway* which leads to the event. Such a network model is used by scientists studying cancer and heart disease. These scientists recognize that thinking of cause as coming entirely from the past is inadequate in understanding people, and so incorporate in their network model concepts of how, while the past pushes us, the future, or, at least, our beliefs about the future, pulls us forward. People's beliefs about themselves and their future are an important part of the causal network which determine the incidence and outcome of cancer and heart disease. Curiously, biological psychiatrists still adhere to a linear, deterministic causal model of depression and other 'mental illnesses'.

DSM-III-R is the Diagnostic and Statistical Manual of Mental Disorders. It is the official system for classification of psychological and psychiatric disorders drawn up and published by the American Psychiatric Association. Along with the *International Classification of Diseases* (ICD), the DSM is the major guide for the classification, treatment and prognosis of mental illness. It can cure such diseases at one stroke, as happened when homosexuality was removed from its list of disorders. It can also create diseases at a stroke, such as 'Uncomplicated bereavement' (Classification number V62.82), 'Marital problem' (V61.10), and 'Academic problem' (V62.30).

dizygotic refers to twins resulting from the simultaneous fertilization of two eggs (zygote) by two sperm cells.

deoxyribonucleic acid (DNA) is the nucleic acid enclosed in the central nucleus of a cell. It can make an exact copy of itself when a cell divides. It is organized into paired structures called *chromosomes*, and each chromosome is an assembly of hundreds of *genes*.

dexamethasone suppression test (DST) 'has been the most widely utilized and studied biological test in psychiatry. The initial enthusiasm associated with the DST was based on the hope that it would be the first genuine diagnostic test in psychiatry. This initial enthusiasm has given way to more cautious utilization and study of the DST . . . It appears that the DST does not substantially improve the clinician's ability to determine who should receive antidepressant treatment . . . The DST has limited specificity and therefore limited diagnostic utility when patients with major depression are compared to those with non-major affective disorders or other severe acute psychiatric illnesses . . . However, the "confirmation" provided by a positive DST is useful to some depressed patients, making it easier for them to accept antidepressant treatment. The clinician must realize that a positive DST does not predict an improved response rate to antidepressants, nor should a negative DST discourage a trial of treatment if clinical symptoms support such a decision.'[107]

electroconvulsive therapy (ECT) is 'given in a special room where the patient lies on a bed and is given a general anaesthetic and a muscle relaxant. Padded electrodes are placed on her head and an electric current of about eighty volts is passed through her brain. She will probably wake up confused and with a headache, and will need to rest for about an hour afterwards. Standard length courses of ECT consist of four to twelve individual shocks given a few days apart.' Lucy Johnstone uses the pronoun 'she' in this description because many more women than men receive ECT (a ratio of 2.27 to 1).[108]

In a review article entitled 'Which depressed patients will respond to electroconvulsive therapy?' Allan I. F. Scott[109] wrote, 'There are important theoretical and practical difficulties in the measurement of clinical outcome. There is no agreed definition of recovery after ECT. There is debate about the quantitative improvement that is required, and about the timing of this assessment. When follow-up is extended beyond the period of hospital stay, the method of assessment may be unsatisfactory; for example, some recent outcome studies have relied on follow-up by telephone. The majority of patients with endogenous depression do well in the short term after ECT, but there is a greater variability of outcome as the length of follow-up is extended. Recent outcome studies have found that less than one-third of patients remain well six months after ECT[110] . . . There are no physiological measures or tests which are superior to clinical criteria in the selection of depressed patients for whom ECT would be an effective treatment . . . Crow *et al* have argued that the only consistent clinical predictor of a specific response to ECT is the presence of delusions.' [111]

Perhaps what ECT teaches a patient is to keep to herself any ideas of which her psychiatrist disapproves. The problem for her is remembering this, for, as Lucy Johnstone wrote, 'The commonest effects are loss of memory for events that took place before ECT was given (retrograde amnesia), and/or loss of memory for events that occur after the ECT (anterograde amnesia). Memory loss may span all areas of life experience. Thus, patients may be unable to recall educational and professional experiences; films, books, and plays; important social events such as birthdays and family gatherings; names and faces of friends and acquaintances; household details such as how to do the chores and where things are kept; familiar locations such as the layout of the local shops or town; what happened to them in hospital; inner thoughts and feelings; and public events such as elections and news stories . . . Some degree of retrograde and anterograde amnesia is an effect widely acknowledged by ECT's advocates, although they usually describe it as mild and short-lived.'[112]

encounter group is 'a small group which focuses on intensive interpersonal interactions (or "encounters"). The group usually has as its goals the removal of psychological barriers and defences, achieving openness, honesty and the willingness to deal with the difficulties of emotional expression. Group members are encouraged to deal with the "here-and-now" and to eschew intellectualization and personal history. Encounter groups and their use in psychotherapy began with the human potential movement.'[113] Encounter groups can be a power trip for a power-mad therapist; they can also be great fun.

epidemiologist is a scientist who studies the occurrence and distribution of disease in a population of people.

exploratory therapy is that form of therapy where the therapist and client are concerned with uncovering and clarifying the issues in the client's life without the therapist telling the client how he should deal with these issues.

Freudian refers to anything to do with the work of Sigmund Freud, the founder of psychoanalysis.

gene is a unit of deoxyribonucleic acid (DNA). A *chromosome* is an assembly of hundreds of genes. Many people assume that each of certain characteristics which we identify and label has a matching gene. Thus there is a gene for the colour of your eyes, a gene for a disease like cystic fibrosis, a gene for different kinds of personality, a gene for depression, and so on. However, it should not be assumed that there is a direct relationship between the different categories we use to describe what we do and feel and the selection of genes we inherit. While geneticists can work out the likelihood of certain characteristics following from a *dominant gene* (eg, brown eyes) or from a *recessive gene* (eg, cystic fibrosis) there is not an isomorphic (having the same structure or form) relationship between most of the genes and the categories into which we divide our appearance and activity. The action of most genes is dependent on the action of other genes and many other conditions.

genetic fingerprinting is the technique which identifies an individual's unique DNA code.

genetic markers or **genetic marker loci** 'are normal variants of genes or proteins that are due to a single locus, some of which are mapped to human chromosomes. Some of the most commonly studied markers are ABO blood types, which are detected on the red cells, and HLA antigens, which are detected on leukocytes . . . The development of a set of powerful methods of molecular genetics has revolutionized the study of human genetic diseases . . . Variations in DNA sequences (called restriction fragment length polymorphisms, or RFLPs) can thus be identified. This technique has produced hundreds of new marker loci and it is expected that before long there will be markers covering the entire human genome (the complete array of genes]. Thus, if a susceptibility to a disease exists, it will be detectable by linkage if enough markers are tested . . . *Association of genetic markers* to diseases are detected by comparing the frequency of a given marker in samples of unrelated patients and unrelated controls. If the frequency is significantly different, then there may be some etiologic association between the marker and the disease. For example, specific HLA antigens are associated with diseases such as juvenile diabetes and multiple sclerosis. These associations have been consistently found in different populations and suggest some etiologic determinants in the HLA region. However, it is possible to find spurious associations due to unknown differences between the control and patient populations. In addition, significant results can be found by chance, especially in small samples. It is therefore very important to be able to replicate a potential association in a new study. Several studies have looked for ABO and HLA associations to affective disorders but no consistent results have been found . . . [In *linkage studies*] if a disease gene is chromosomally linked to a marker locus, then in families the marker type will be transmitted along with the disease in a predictable manner that can be analysed statistically . . . There have been many linkage studies in affective disorders, but, for the most part, studies have been done in bipolar families or in samples containing both bipolar and unipolar families. A few studies have focused on linkage in unipolar families . . . In general, association and linkage studies have not demonstrated evidence for a single gene susceptibility for unipolar illness. However, the disorder is likely to be heterogeneous and different investigators have used different diagnostic criteria. With the large number of available RFLP markers, it may be useful to do linkage studies in families with a well defined depressive illness. This strategy has begun to be followed in bipolar illness.'[114]

Gestalt therapy is 'a form of psychotherapy associated with the work of Frederick (Fritz) Perls (1893–1970). It is based loosely on the Gestalt concepts of unity and wholeness. Treatment, which is usually conducted in groups, focuses on attempts to broaden a person's awareness of self by using past experiences, memories, emotional states, bodily sensations, etc. In short, anything that could contribute to the person forming a meaningful configuration of awareness is an acceptable part of the therapy process.'[115]

Grand Design is a system of beliefs about the nature of Life, the Universe and Everything which states that there is some system of universal justice in which the good are rewarded and the bad punished.

heterogenicity means dissimilarity. *Homogenicity* means similarity.

homeopathy is a method invented by Samuel Hahnemann at the end of the eighteenth century based on the principle that like cures like. Homeopathic medicine consists of an infinitely small portion of a substance which, in larger doses, would produce similar symptoms to those of which the patient is complaining. A *homeopath* is a person trained in homeopathy and may or may not be also trained in medicine. A homeopath treats the person, not the disease. Since homeopathy does not lend itself to the kind of research methods used in medicine, doctors are usually sceptical of its claims to cure, but many people find that they are helped greatly by homeopathic remedies. The great benefit of homeopathic remedies is that, unlike the drugs used in medicine, they can cause no harm.

HPA axis is the hypothalamic – pituitary – adrenal axis.

humanistic is 'often referred to as "the third force" in psychology after psychoanalysis and behaviorism, [and] it is largely the creation of Abraham Maslow, who projected an important set of values into modern psychology. He viewed psychology as too concerned with that which was neurotic and disturbed (psychoanalysis) or that which was explainable with a mechanistic theory (behaviourism). A humanistic view in Maslow's sense would involve a science concerned with higher human motives, understanding and esthetics. Other major theorists associated with this general approach are Carl Rogers, Alfred Adler and Rollo May.'[116]

Jungian is anything associated with the work of Carl Gustav Jung.

linkage is used in genetics where 'two or more genes are said to be linked if they tend to be passed from generation to generation as a unit. The mechanism of linkage is chromosomal and the closer the genes are to each other on the chromosome the more closely they will be linked. Thus, all the genes on a chromosome are said to form a *linkage group*.'[117]

mania, manic are used to refer to a person who is behaving in an excitable way, with much activity and talking, often without much reference to other people present. Sometimes the person being described as manic is simply very happy, but more often the apparently happy activity is a cover for the intense fear from which the person is trying to escape.

Mendelian refers to the principles of heredity formulated by Gregor Mendel, the founder of genetics, which hold that certain characteristics, such as eye colour or height, are inherited in definite, predictable combinations.

metabolic, metabolism refer to 'the chemical changes by which foods are converted into components of the body or consumed as fuel, the chemical structure of the tissues is modified, and waste products broken down into substances that can be eliminated.'[118]

monozygotic twins are formed when a single fertilized egg divides in two.

patient is the word used for a person consulting a doctor or certain therapists. The word itself describes what such a person should be – patient. A good patient is one who is obedient, uncomplaining, uncritical and grateful.

penetrance is the frequency that a particular characteristic is found in a group of people, all of whom possess the genetic configuration for that characteristic. This concept is necessary because we can inherit a tendency to something without that something ever revealing itself. An inherited tendency which rarely reveals itself is said to have low penetrance, while one that usually reveals itself is said to have high penetrance.

personal construct psychology derives from the work of George Kelly but is not an entirely new theory. The ancient Greek philosopher Epictatus said, 'It is not things in themselves which trouble us but our opinion of things.' In the Talmud it is written, 'We see things not as they are but as we are.'

phenomenology is a philosophical doctrine which advocates that the scientific study of immediate experience be the basis of psychology.

polygenetic refers to a characteristic which is derived from a number of genes.

prescriptive therapy is any therapy where the therapist tells the client what to do.

principle of partial reinforcement refers to the way in which animals and humans will persist in a behaviour which is sometimes rewarded and sometimes punished, the rewards and punishments following a pattern which the recipient cannot comprehend.

psychiatrist, psychologist, psychoanalyst, psychotherapist A *psychiatrist* is a medical doctor. He (most psychiatrists are men: most patients are women) has qualified as a medical doctor, worked in various psychiatric institutions, and qualified by examination for entry to the Royal College of Psychiatrists (in Britain), the American Psychiatric Association, or similar institutions in other countries. Some psychiatrists (relatively few in Britain, slightly more in the USA) also undertake training in psychoanalysis and psychotherapy, and may work as *psychoanalysts* or *consultant psychotherapists*. Some psychiatrists reject all psychoanalytic, psychotherapeutic and psychological explanations of human behaviour and believe that all behaviour, including thought, can be explained in terms of biochemical changes in the body. Such psychiatrists call themselves *biochemical psychiatrists* or *biopsychiatrists*.

Most psychiatrists use both biochemical and psychological explanations of human behaviour. All psychiatrists can prescribe drugs, order and administer electroconvulsive therapy, and, within certain legal restrictions, confine a person without his permission in a psychiatric institution. The qualifications for entry into one of the professional institutions for psychiatrists include some psychology but do not qualify the psychiatrist to call himself a psychologist.

Lucy Johnstone, a clinical psychologist observing the behaviour of psychiatrists, wrote, 'The whole practice of psychiatry is based on traditionally masculine values. Psychiatrists strive very hard to present psychiatry as a legitimate and respectable branch of medical science, so that they can maintain their claim that the psychiatric service must be headed by doctors rather than, say, nurses or social workers or a team of professionals working as equals. This means that there is an overriding emphasis on diagnosing, labelling and categorizing patients and prescribing medical-type solutions to their problems. The prime example of this is the Diagnostic and Statistical Manual of Mental Disorders (known as the DSM-III), the psychiatrist's guide to diagnosis, which, in 472 pages, labels and divides psychiatric problems into literally hundreds of sections and sub-sections in a manner which in a patient would be seen as a sign of obsessive-compulsive-disorder (DSM definition: "repetitive and seemingly purposeful behaviours that are performed according to certain rules or in a stereotyped fashion"). The same attitude is evident in many psychiatric textbooks, which devote pages to the discussion of "undifferentiated neuroses", "relative frequency of common symptoms", "differential diagnosis", "biochemical and endocrine investigations", "genetic factors and prognosis", while psychiatric journals carry articles with daunting titles like "Information processing and attentional functioning in the developmental course of schizophrenic disorders", or, "A controlled comparison of flupenthixol and amitriptyline in depressed outpatients", or, "Affective disorder: Is reactive depression an entity?", or, "Biochemical and pharmacological studies: the dopamine hypothesis", and so on . . . While all this may have its relevant aspects, what is so striking is the absence of the real person to whom all these diagnoses and hypotheses are attached; the disregard of relationship factors, so that all psychiatric problems are assumed to be rooted in one person only; and the lack of any socioeconomic context to put it all in. Amidst all this important and scientific-sounding literature, the human reality of the lives of distressed men and women is in danger of getting lost altogether. Prestige in psychiatric circles is not generally gained by having an interest in psychotherapy and wide experience in helping people with relationship problems; indeed this may be a positive handicap. Psychiatrists rise to the top of their profession by research and publication in respectable, scientific, objective fields, and may be able to carve out a distinguished position for themselves while having no aptitude whatsoever for forming therapeutic relationships with their patients. The only other approach to have gained a firm foothold in psychiatry, (cognitive) behaviour therapy, is of a goal-oriented, symptom removing nature.'[119]

A *psychologist* studies behaviour. He or she (there are about equal numbers of men and women in the profession, though, as in all professions, there are more men than women in senior positions) holds a first degree in psychology and other degrees and diplomas in some branches of psychology. Many psychologists hold a doctorate (PhD) and therefore use the title doctor. All psychologists are members of a professional institution. In Britain, psychologists qualify for entry to the British Psychological Society and are called 'chartered psychologists'. In the USA, psychologists must pass a licensing exam administered by the State in which the psychologist expects to practise. Other countries have their own professional institutions for psychologists.

Some psychologists specialize in occupational psychology and work in industry and management. Some specialize in educational psychology and work in educational institutions. Some psychologists specialize in clinical psychology and work in psychiatric institutions, in health centres, and in private practice. Clinical psychologists divide into *behaviourists, cognitive therapists,* and *psychotherapists.* Behaviourists and cognitive therapists practise *prescriptive therapies* such as *behaviour therapy, behavioural psychotherapy, rational emotive therapy,* and *cognitive therapy,* while psychotherapists practise *exploratory therapies* such as *Gestalt, encounter, transactional analysis, psychodrama, personal construct therapy,* and *psychoanalysis.*

A *psychoanalyst* may or may not be a medical doctor. He or she undergoes a training which includes an analysis with a qualified psychoanalyst lasting some five years and working as a psychoanalyst under the supervision of a qualified psychoanalyst. In the USA there are two main schools of psychoanalysis, Freudian, derived from the work of Sigmund Freud, and Jungian, derived from the work of Carl Jung. In Britain there is a third school called Kleinian, derived from the work of Melanie Klein, a pupil of Sigmund Freud.

A *psychotherapist* is anyone who has trained in any of the many different schools of psychotherapy and who may or may not have professional qualifications. A psychotherapist is more likely to practise one of the exploratory therapies rather than a prescriptive therapy, but some psychotherapists practise both.

psychodrama is 'a psychotherapeutic technique developed by J. L. Moreno in which the individual acts out certain roles or incidents in the presence of the therapist and, often, other people who are part of the therapy group. The procedures are based on the assumption that the role-taking allows the person to express troublesome emotions and face deep conflicts in the relatively protected environment of the therapeutic stage.'[120]

rapid eye movements (REM) are the rapid, jerky eye movements which occur during sleep when the person is dreaming.

rational emotive therapy is 'a form of psychotherapy developed by Albert Ellis which focuses on the rational, problem-solving aspects of emotional and behavioural disorders. Ellis's approach is highly directive, consisting in large measure of telling the client what he or she must do in order to be happy and then "encouraging" him or her, often through confrontation and encounter, to act and think accordingly,'[121] that is, like Albert Ellis.

reductionist theory is a theory which seeks to explain an event by reducing it to its smallest constituent parts. Thus a reductionist explanation of an event like a cake would be that a cake is nothing but the outcome of the chemical changes which occur when a mixture of flour, sugar, butter, milk, sodium bicarbonate and water is heated to a specific temperature for a certain amount of time. Such an explanation is not completely reductionist, since the chemical changes themselves can be reduced to molecules, molecules to atoms, atoms to electrons, and electrons to particles. However, no adequate explanation can be reached at the sub-atomic particle level since these particles behave in ways very different from the constituents of higher levels, being largely random in their movements and very much affected by the presence of an observer. (Sub-atomic particles are in this like human beings who behave differently when they think they are observed from when they think they are unobserved. Many psychiatrists and psychologists are unaware of this and believe that, when they are making scientific observations of their patients and experimental subjects, these patients and subjects behave no differently from how they would behave if they were not being observed. It is not known whether sub-atomic particles observe the observer, draw conclusions about the observer, and use these conclusions to guide their behaviour, but human beings certainly do.) Thus a completely reductionist explanation of any event is not possible until physicists discover the ultimate constituent stuff of the universe and understand how it behaves. Another problem for reductionist theories is that at each level in the process of reduction some constituent of the event is discarded and therefore is not accounted for by the theory. Thus an event like a cake being explained in terms of sub-atomic particles or even in terms of chemical changes requires that aspects of the cake – taste, smell, hunger satisfaction, celebratory meaning – be discounted and thus not accounted for by the theory. Similarly, a reductionist explanation of depression or any other aspect of human experience cannot account for most of that experience. A reductionist theory of genetic inheritance and biochemical changes cannot account for how we think, feel and behave.

tardive dyskinesia is a 'side-effect' of the major tranquillizers and lithium.[122] It is 'characterized by uncontrollable movements of the lip, tongue, and face, fidgeting hands, tapping feet, rocking backwards and forwards, grunting, and other bizarre involuntary mannerisms. If the major tranquillizers are stopped as soon as the first signs are detected these movements generally disappear. Often, though, the symptoms of tardive dyskinesia only emerge when a patient cuts down or stops his or her medication – sometimes weeks or months later. Again, the movements may gradually fade, but some people are left with a permanent, irreversible disability for which the only "treatment" is to go back on the major tranquillizers again. The trap in doing so is that, although the symptoms of tardive dyskinesia will once more be masked, in the long term the drugs will increase the neurological damage that led to the problem in the first place.'[123]

therapist can be applied to anyone practising any kind of therapy.

transactional analysis is 'a form of psychotherapy originally developed by Eric Berne. It is practised in a straightforward group setting in which the primary goal is to have the client achieve an adaptive, mature and realistic attitude to life, to have, in Berne's words, "the adult ego maintain hegemony over the impulsive child".'[124]

X-linked gene is a gene on the X-chromosome.

yoga means union of the self, soul, essence with the oneness of everything. '*Hatha yoga* is the physical route to the achievement of this happy state, as distinct from the yogas of work (karma), devotion (bhakti) and so on. In hatha yoga we focus, with the aid of breath, on befriending the body, on coaxing it into action, on bringing it to a state of physical balance. When perfect lightness comes in a physical posture, and perfect freedom, it means that we have succeeded, and that we are so balanced – standing, sitting or lying flat – that there is no imbalance in the way gravity works on any part of us. Perfect balance means that we have concentrated perfectly – if only for a second – and the work towards, as well as the achievement, brings balance to the mind.'[125]

Footnote

The American Association for the Advancement of Science Conference in February, 1990, was told that

> Mental illnesses are proving more stubborn to molecular analysis than the first results over recent years suggested.
> Dr Kenneth Kidd of Yale University told the meeting that the discovery three years ago of a genetic marker on chromosome 11 linked to the development of manic depression in a large extended family has failed to stand up.
> 'The possibility of a single marker for manic depression has turned out to be too optimistic,' he said. . . . 'If there are two or three major genes involved we should be able to identify them, but if there are many minor ones we may never find them.' . . .
> And even if reliable linkages are found in mental illnesses, Dr Kidd said that researchers were only just at the borderline of knowing what to do with such controversial findings.
> 'Genes are clearly involved in predisposing people to develop mental illnesses, but there are other important factors. One of a pair of identical twins can develop mental illness and the other not.'[126]

References

1 Ballenger, J. C., 'Biological aspects of depression: implications for clinical practice', in Frances, A. J., and Hales, R. E., (eds) *Review of Psychiatry*, American Psychiatric Press, Washington DC, 1988.
McGuffin, P., 'Major genes for major affective disorder?', in *British Journal of Psychiatry*, 153, 1988.

2 Keller, M. B., 'Diagnostic issues and clinical course of unipolar illness', in Frances, A. J. and Hales, R. E. (eds) *Review of Psychiatry*, American Psychiatric Press, Washington DC, 1988.
Kendall, R. E., 'The classification of depression: a review of contemporary confusion', in *British Journal of Psychiatry*, 127, 15–28, 1976.

3 Kiloh, L. G., Andrews, G., and Neilson, M., 'The long-term outcome of depressive illness', in *British Journal of Psychiatry*, 153, 1988.
Lee, A. S., and Murray, R. M., 'The long-term outcome of Maudsley depressives', in *British Journal of Psychiatry*, 153, 1988.

4 Beck, A. T., Rush, A. J., Shaw, B. F., and Emery, G., *Cognitive Therapy of Depression*, Wiley, Chichester and New York, 1979.
Emery, G., *Getting Un-Depressed*, Simon and Schuster, New York, 1988.
Burns, D. B., *Feeling Good*, New American Library, New York, 1980.

5 Rowe, D., *The Experience of Depression*, Wiley, Chichester and New York, 1978; reissued as *Choosing Not Losing*, Fontana, London, 1989.

6 Rowe, D., *The Construction of Life and Death*, Wiley, Chichester and New York, 1982, Fontana, London, 1989.

7 Rowe, D., *Depression: The Way Out of Your Prison*, Routledge, London, 1983.

8 Rowe, D., *Beyond Fear*, Fontana, London, 1987.

9 Rowe, D., *The Successful Self*, Fontana, London, 1989.

10 Rowe, D., *Choosing Not Losing*, op. cit.

11 West, Julia, 'Comparison of depressive symptomatology between Saudi and American psychiatric outpatients in an Eastern Province medical centre, Saudi Arabia', in *International Journal of Social Psychiatry*, 31(3): 230–234, 1985.

12 Tweedie, J., 'The vision of life seen in depression has a truth in it', *The Guardian*, April 17, 1982.

13 Wakeling, Pat, in *Choosing Not Losing*, op. cit.

14 Peanuts cartoon, *Daily Mail*, September 30, 1985.

15 Fraser, Sylvia, *My Father's House*, Virago, London, 1989.

16 Grade, Michael, 'Me and My Psyche', *The Guardian*, March 25, 1989.

17 Boesky, Ivan, quoted in *People*, March 6, 1989.

18 Mitgutsch, Anna, *Punishment*, trans. Lisel Mueller, Virago, London, 1988.

422

19 Jules Feiffer cartoon, *Observer*, February 20, 1977.
20 Fraser, *op. cit.*
21 *Depression: The Way Out of Your Prison*, *op. cit.*
22 *The Construction of Life and Death*, *op. cit.*
23 *The Successful Self*, *op. cit.*
24 Bloom County cartoon, *The Guardian*, March 13, 1989.
25 'As We Forgive Them', BBC TV *Everyman* Series, 1989.
26 Fraser, *op. cit.*
27 Watterson, Bill, *Something Under the Bed Is Drooling*, Andrews and McMeel, Kansas City, 1988.
28 Greenwell, Jane, 'House Call', *The Guardian*, April 19, 1989.
29 Kington, Miles, 'Some People Do, and Some People Don't', *The Independent*, March 18, 1989.
30 Rowe, D., *Living with the Bomb: Can We Live Without Enemies*, Routledge, London, 1985.
31 Harrington, Mona, '"Working Girl" in Reagan Country', *The New York Times*, January 15, 1989.
32 Humphries, S., Mack, J., Perks, R., *A Century of Childhood*, Sidgwick and Jackson, London, 1988.
33 *The Successful Self*, *op. cit.*
34 *A Century of Childhood*, *op. cit.*
35 Fraser, *op. cit.*
36 Watterson, Bill, *Calvin and Hobbes*, Sphere Books, Penguin, Harmondsworth, 1987.
37 Bebbington, P., 'Social epidemiology of depression and the neuroses', in *Current Opinion in Psychiatry*, Vol. 2, No. 2, 1989.
38 Puttnam, David, quoted in *Time*, May, 1989.
39 Eliot, T. S., 'Little Gidding', *Four Quartets*, Faber, London, 1974.
40 Kopp, Sheldon, *If You Meet the Buddha on the Road, Kill Him*, Sheldon Press, London, 1972.
41 *Beyond Fear*, *op. cit.*
42 Henley, W. E., 'Unconquerable', *The Albatross Book of Living Verse*, Collins, London, 1984.
43 Julian of Norwich, *Revelations of Divine Love*, Penguin, Harmondsworth, 1970.
44 Tzu, Lao, *Tao Te Ching*, trans. Gia-Fu Feng and Jane English, Wildwood Press, London, 1973.
45 Baum, Frank, *The Wizard of Oz*, Puffin, Harmondsworth, 1980.
46 *Beyond Fear*, *op. cit.*
47 Shaun O'Brien, P. M., *Premenstrual Syndrome*, Blackwell, Oxford, 1987.
48 Cline, Sally, and Spender, Dale, *Reflecting Men at Twice Their Natural Size*, Fontana, London, 1988.
49 Mitgutsch, *op. cit.*
50 'As We Forgive Them', BBC TV *Everyman* Series, 1989.
51 Watterson, Bill, *Calvin and Hobbes*, *op. cit.*

52 Sheldon Kopp, *Who Am I Really?*, Science and Behavior Books, Inc., Palo Alto, California, 1986.

53 *Living with the Bomb*, op. cit.

54 *Back to the Edge*, BBC TV *Everyman* Series, 1989.

55 Kopp, Sheldon, *No Hidden Meanings*, Science and Behavior Books, Inc., Palo Alto, California, 1975.

56 Vicky Rippere, 'Behavioural treatment of depression in historical perspective', in S. Rachman (ed) *Contributions to Medical Psychology*, Vol. 2, Pergamon Press, Oxford, 1980.

57 Scull, Andrew, *Museum of Madness*, Penguin, Harmondsworth, 1979.

58 Kendall, op. cit.

59 Keller, op. cit.

60 Klein, Donald F., and Wender, Paul H., *Do You Have a Depressive Illness?*, New American Library, New York, 1988.

61 Gold, Mark S., *The Good News About Depression*, Bantam Books, New York, 1986.

62 Goldin, Lynn R., and Gershom, Elliot S., 'The genetic epidemiology of major depressive illness', in *Review of Psychiatry*, American Psychiatric Press, Washington DC, 1988.

63 Ballenger, op. cit.

64 Keller, op. cit.

65 Lee, A. S., 'Foretelling the future for depressives', in *Abstracts of the Winter Quarterly Meeting*, Royal College of Psychiatrists, 1988.
Lee and Murray, op. cit.
Kiloh *et al.*, op. cit.
Ramana, R., and Battersby, M. W., letter to *The British Journal of Psychiatry*, 155, 125, 1989.
Lundquist, G., 'Prognosis and course in manic-depressive psychosis', in *Acta Psychiatrica et Neurologica Scandinavia*, Suppl. 35, 1945.
Rennie, T. A. C., 'Prognosis in manic-depressive psychosis', in *American Journal of Psychiatry*, 98, 1942.

66 McGuffin, op. cit.

67 Brown, G. W., and Harris, T., *The Social Origins of Depression*, Tavistock, London, 1978.

68 Personal communication, October 12, 1989.

69 McGuffin, P., and Katz, R., 'The genetics of depression and manic-depressive disorder', in *British Journal of Psychiatry*, 155, 294–304, 1989.

70 Brown and Harris, op. cit.

71 Bebbington, P., 'Psychosocial etiology of schizophrenia and affective disorders', in (ed R. Michels) *Psychiatry*, Lippincott, Philadelphia, Pa., 1985.

72 McGuffin, P., Katz, R., and Bebbington, P., 'The Camberwell Collaborative Depression Study, III. Depression and adversity in the relatives of depressed probands', in *British Journal of Psychiatry*, 152, 775–782, 1986.

73 McGuffin, P., and Katz, R., 'The genetics of depression: current

approaches', in *British Journal of Psychiatry*, 155 (suppl. 6), 18–26, 1989.

74 R. Amara, 'Health care tomorrow', in *The Futurist*, Nov/Dec, 1988.

75 Nemiah, J. C., 'The varieties of human experience', in *British Journal of Psychiatry*, 154, 459–466.

76 Johnstone, Lucy, *Users and Abusers of Psychiatry*, Routledge, London, 1989.

77 Braithwaite, J., *Corporate Crime in the Pharmaceutical Industry*, Routledge, London, 1984.

78 Klass, A., *There's Gold in Them Thar Pills*, Penguin, Harmondsworth, 1975.

79 Hughes, R., and Brewin, R., *The Tranquillizing of America*, Harcourt Brace Jovanovich, New York, 1980.

80 Lacey, R., and Woodward, S., *That's Life! Survey on Tranquillizers*, BBC in association with MIND, 1985.

81 Blackwell, B., *The Sociopharmacology of Minor Tranquillizers*, Presentation to the World Congress on Mental Health, Vancouver, 1986.

82 Hill, D., 'Tardive dyskinesia: a worldwide epidemic of irreversible brain damage', in N. Eisenberg and D. Glasgow (eds) *Current Issues in Clinical Psychology*, Gower, Aldershot, 1986.

83 Lacey and Woodward, *op. cit.*

84 *Academic Review*, vol. 3, Licensing Exam Review, New York, 1987.

85 Wright, Jesse H., 'The cognitive therapy of depression', in *Review of Psychiatry*, American Psychiatric Press, Washington DC, 1988.

86 Jacob, P., 'Cancer: something to shout about', *The Guardian*, February 27, 1990.

87 *Ephesians*, 4:32.
Blake, W., 'A Poison Tree', in *Songs of Innocence*.
Book of Job, 5:7.
Housman, A. E., *A Shropshire Lad*.
Dr Johnson, in Boswell's *Life of Johnson*.
Eliot, T. S., *Love Song of J. Alfred Prufrock*.
Davies, W. H., *Leisure*.
Wilde, Oscar, *The Critic as an Artist*.
Tzu Lao, *The Tao te Ching*, trans. Stephen Mitchell.
Corinthians 13:14.
Shakespeare, William, *The Tempest*.

88 Slater, E., and Roth, M., *Clinical Psychiatry*, Baillière, Tindall and Cassell, London, 1970.

89 Klein and Wender, *op. cit.*

90 'Portrait in Blue', in *The Mind Machine* series, a BBC TV production in association with WNET, New York, 1988.

91 Johnstone, *op. cit.*

92 Hyman, Steven E., and Arana, George W., *Handbook of Psychiatric Drug Therapy*, Little, Brown and Company, Boston and Toronto, 1987.
British National Formulary, a Joint Publication of the British Medical Association and the Royal Pharmaceutical Society of Great Britain, Number 18, September, 1989.

Parish, Peter, *Medicines, A Guide for Everybody*, Penguin, Harmondsworth, 1989.

93 Scott, J., 'Chronic depression', in *British Journal of Psychiatry*, 53, 287–297, 1988.

94 Rowe, D., 'Introduction' to, *Against Therapy*, by J. Masson, Fontana, London, 1989.

95 Knight, Lindsay, *Talking to a Stranger*, Fontana, London, 1987.

96 *Beyond Fear*, op. cit.

97 Beck *et al.*, op. cit.

98 Masson, op. cit.

99 Fraser, op. cit.

100 Smail, D., *Taking Care*, Dent, London, 1987.

101 Smail, D., *Psychotherapy: A Personal View*, Dent, London, 1978.

102 Freeman, A., 'Cognitive therapy: an overview', in Freeman, A., and Greenwood, V. B., (eds) *Cognitive Therapy: Applications in Psychiatric and Medical Settings*, Human Sciences Press, Inc., New York, 1987.

103 Szasz, Thomas, *The Myth of Mental Illness*, Oxford University Press, Oxford, 1975.

104 Wright, Jesse H., 'Cognitive therapy and medication as combined treatment', in Freeman, A., and Greenwood, V. B. (eds) *Cognitive Therapy: Applications in Psychiatric and Medical Settings*, Human Sciences Press, Inc., New York, 1987.

105 Wingate, Peter, *The Penguin Medical Encyclopaedia*, Penguin, Harmondsworth, 1988.

106 Beck *et al.*, op. cit.

107 Ballenger, op. cit.

108 Johnstone, op. cit.

109 Scott, Allen I. F., 'Which depressed patients will respond to electroconvulsive therapy?', in *British Journal of Psychiatry*, 154, 8–17, 1989.

110 Coryell, W., and Zimmerman, M., 'The dexamethasone suppression test and ECT outcome: a six-month follow-up', in *Biological Psychiatry*, 18, 21–27, 1983.
Lipman, R. S., *et al.*, 'Dexamethasone suppression test as a predictor of response to electroconvulsive therapy – six-month follow-up', in *Convulsive Therapy*, 2, 161–167, 1986.
Katona, C. L., *et al.*, 'The dexamethasone suppression test and prediction of outcome in patients receiving ECT', in *British Journal of Psychiatry*, 150, 315–318, 1987.

111 Crow, T. J., *et al.*, 'The Northwick Park ECT trial: predictors of response to real and simulated ECT', in *British Journal of Psychiatry*, 144, 227–237, 1984.

112 Johnstone, op. cit.

113 Reber, Arthur S., *Dictionary of Psychology*, Penguin, Harmondsworth, 1988.

114 Goldin and Gershom, op. cit.

115 Reber, op. cit.

116 *ibid.*
117 *ibid.*
118 Wingate, *op. cit.*
119 Johnstone, *op. cit.*
120 Reber, *op. cit.*
121 *ibid.*
122 Dinan, T. G., and Kohen, D., 'Tardive dyskinesia in bipolar affective disorder: relationship to lithium therapy', in *British Journal of Psychiatry*, 115, 55–57, 1989.
123 Johnstone, *op. cit.*
124 Reber, *op. cit.*
125 Stephanie Alexander, personal communication.
126 Williams, Nigel, 'Setback to genetic depression theory', in *The Guardian*, February 19, 1990.

Index